W9-BKV-359

ARAM PUBLIC LIBRARY
Delavan, Wisconsin 53115

# Hot Gimmick

If you think being a teenager is hard, be glad your name isn't Hatsumi Narita

With scandals that woul[d] make any gossip girl blus[h] and more triangles than yo[u] can throw a geometry boo[k] at, this girl may never figu[re] out the game of love!

# Tell us what you think about Shojo Beat Manga!

Our survey is now available online. Go to:

**shojobeat.com/mangasurvey**

Help us make our product offerings better!

FULL MOON WO SAGASHITE © 2001 by Arina Tanemura/SHUEISHA Inc.
Fushigi Yûgi: Genbu Kaiden © 2004 Yuu WATASE/Shogakukan Inc.
Ouran Koko Host Club © Bisco Hatori 2002/HAKUSENSHA, Inc.

ARAM PUBLIC
Delavan, Wisconsin 53115

Story and Art by Miki Aihara | Creator of *Honey Hunt* and *Tokyo Boys & Girls*

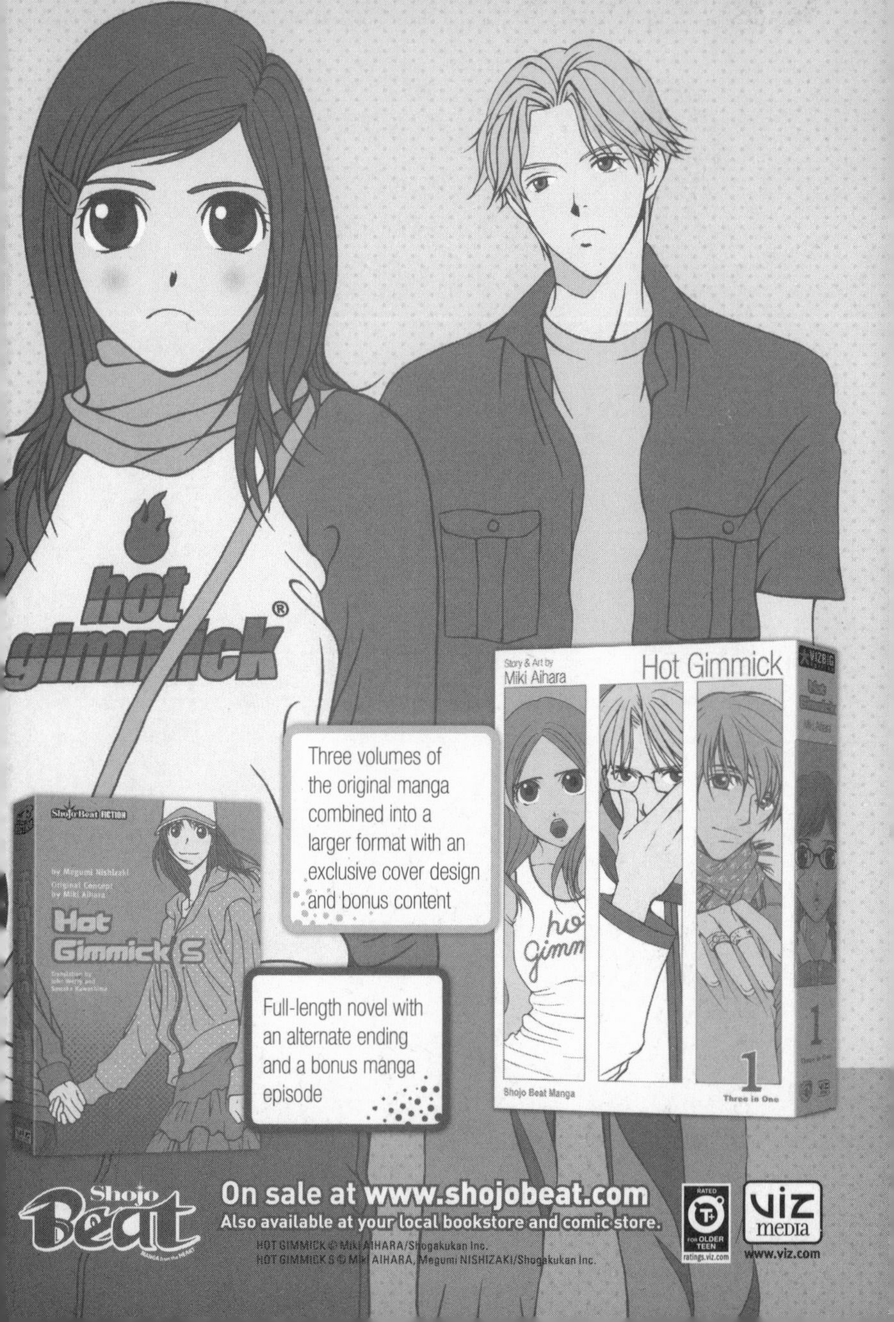

hot gimmick®
Story & Art by Miki Aihara
Hot Gimmick
Shojo Beat Manga
1
Three in One
Three volumes of the original manga combined into a larger format with an exclusive cover design and bonus content
Shojo Beat FICTION
by Megumi Nishizaki
Original Concept by Miki Aihara
Hot Gimmick S
Full-length novel with an alternate ending and a bonus manga episode
Shojo Beat
On sale at www.shojobeat.com
Also available at your local bookstore and comic store.
HOT GIMMICK © Miki AIHARA/Shogakukan Inc.
HOT GIMMICK S © Miki AIHARA, Megumi NISHIZAKI/Shogakukan Inc.
RATED T+ FOR OLDER TEEN
ratings.viz.com
VIZ media
www.viz.com

# Be With You

## Is it possible to experience first love for a second time?

The answer, as *Be With You* proves, is yes—a million times yes

Be With You

Takuji Ichikawa
TRANSLATED BY TERRY GALLAGHER

The **hit novel** that inspired the manga series

SB FICTION

Shojo Beat
MANGA from the HEART

On sale at:
**www.shojobeat.com**
Also available at your local bookstore and comic store.

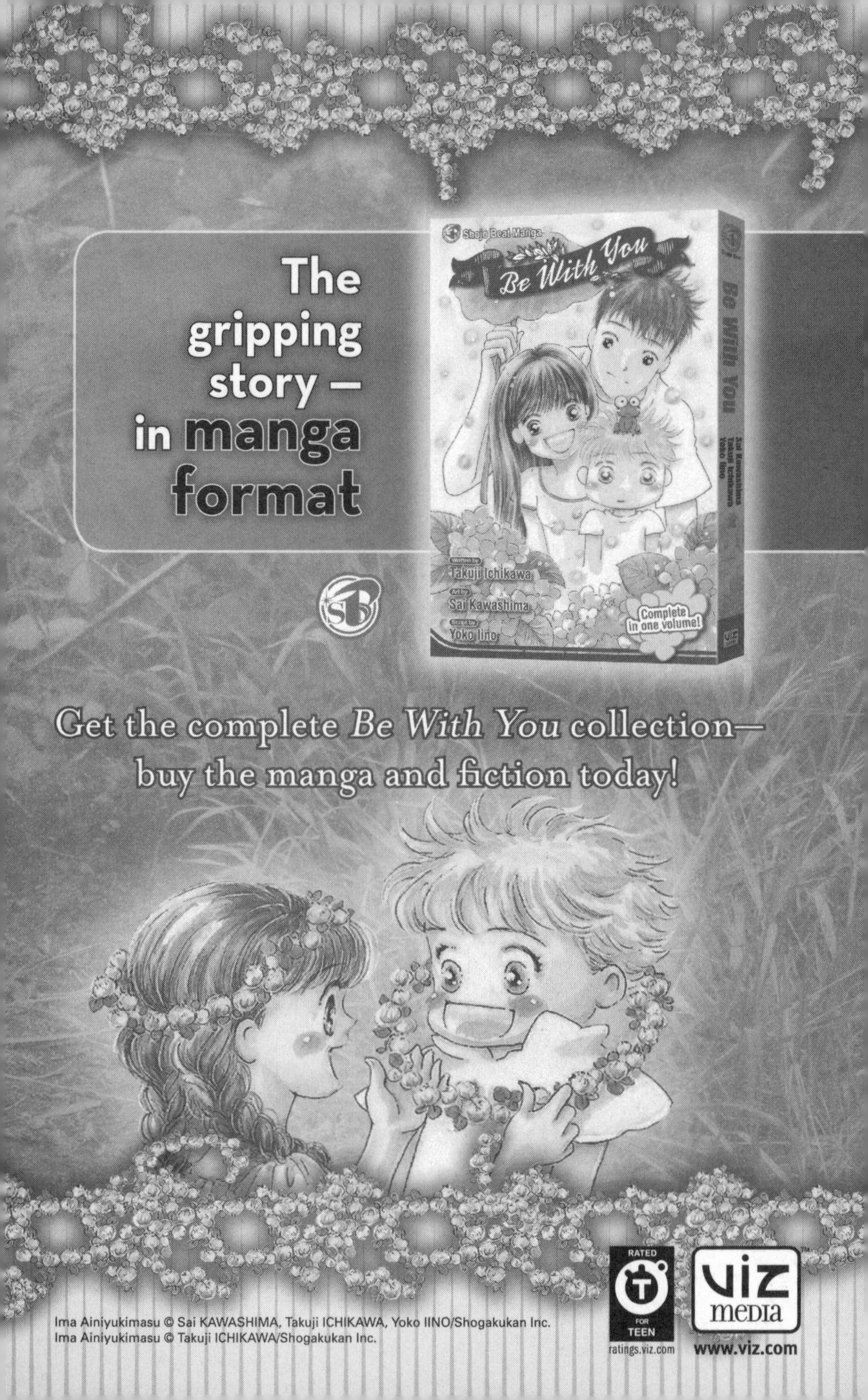
The gripping story — in manga format
Shojo Beat Manga
Be With You
Written by Takuji Ichikawa
Art by Sai Kawashima
Script by Yoko Iino
Complete in one volume!
Be With You
Sai Kawashima
Takuji Ichikawa
Yoko Iino
Get the complete *Be With You* collection—
buy the manga and fiction today!
Ima Ainiyukimasu © Sai KAWASHIMA, Takuji ICHIKAWA, Yoko IINO/Shogakukan Inc.
Ima Ainiyukimasu © Takuji ICHIKAWA/Shogakukan Inc.
RATED T FOR TEEN
ratings.viz.com
VIZ media
www.viz.com

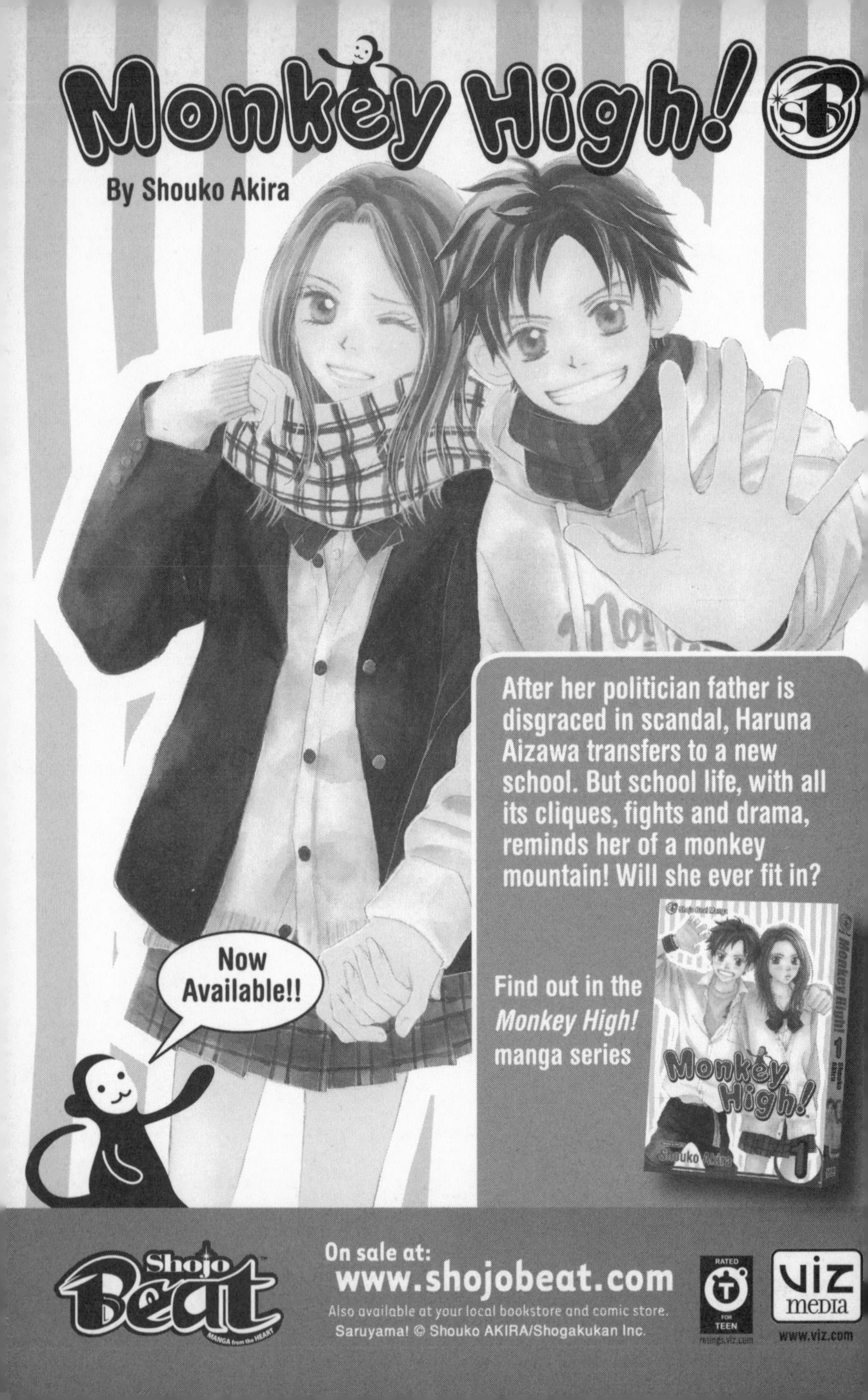
Monkey High!
By Shouko Akira
After her politician father is disgraced in scandal, Haruna Aizawa transfers to a new school. But school life, with all its cliques, fights and drama, reminds her of a monkey mountain! Will she ever fit in?
Now Available!!
Find out in the *Monkey High!* manga series
Shojo Beat
On sale at:
www.shojobeat.com
Also available at your local bookstore and comic store.
Saruyama! © Shouko AKIRA/Shogakukan Inc.
RATED T FOR TEEN
ratings.viz.com
VIZ media
www.viz.com

# We Were There
## Vol. 6
### The Shojo Beat Manga Edition

STORY & ART BY
## YUKI OBATA

Adaptation/Nancy Thistlethwaite
Translation/Tetsuichiro Miyaki
Touch-up Art & Lettering/Inori Fukuda Trant
Design/Courtney Utt
Editor/Nancy Thistlethwaite

VP, Production/Alvin Lu
VP, Publishing Licensing/Rika Inouye
VP, Sales & Product Marketing/Gonzalo Ferreyra
VP, Creative/Linda Espinosa
Publisher/Hyoe Narita

BOKURA GA ITA 6 by Yuuki OBATA © 2004 Yuuki OBATA
All rights reserved. Original Japanese edition
published in 2004 by Shogakukan Inc., Tokyo.
The stories, characters and incidents mentioned
in this publication are entirely fictional.

No portion of this book may be reproduced or transmitted in any form
or by any means without written permission from the copyright holders.

Printed in Canada

Published by VIZ Media, LLC
P.O. Box 77010
San Francisco, CA 94107

Shojo Beat Manga Edition
10 9 8 7 6 5 4 3 2 1
First printing, September 2009

www.viz.com

store.viz.com

RATED
T+
FOR OLDER TEEN

PARENTAL ADVISORY
WE WERE THERE is rated T+ for Older
Teen and is recommended for ages 16 and
up. This volume contains sexual themes.
ratings.viz.com

Around volume 5, I stopped trying to synchronize
the season in the manga to the season when
the Japanese magazine is published. It became
a lot easier for me, but it also lost that fresh,
in-the-moment feeling. So I've decided to
match the seasons again, even though the
characters in the story will age very quickly...

Yuki Obata's birthday is January 9. Her debut manga, *Raindrops*, won
the Shogakukan Shinjin Comics Taisho Kasaku Award in 1998. Her
current series, *We Were There (Bokura ga Ita)*, won the 50th Shogakukan
Manga Award and was adapted into an animated television series. She
likes sweets, coffee, drinking with friends, and scary stories. Her hobby
is browsing in bookshops.

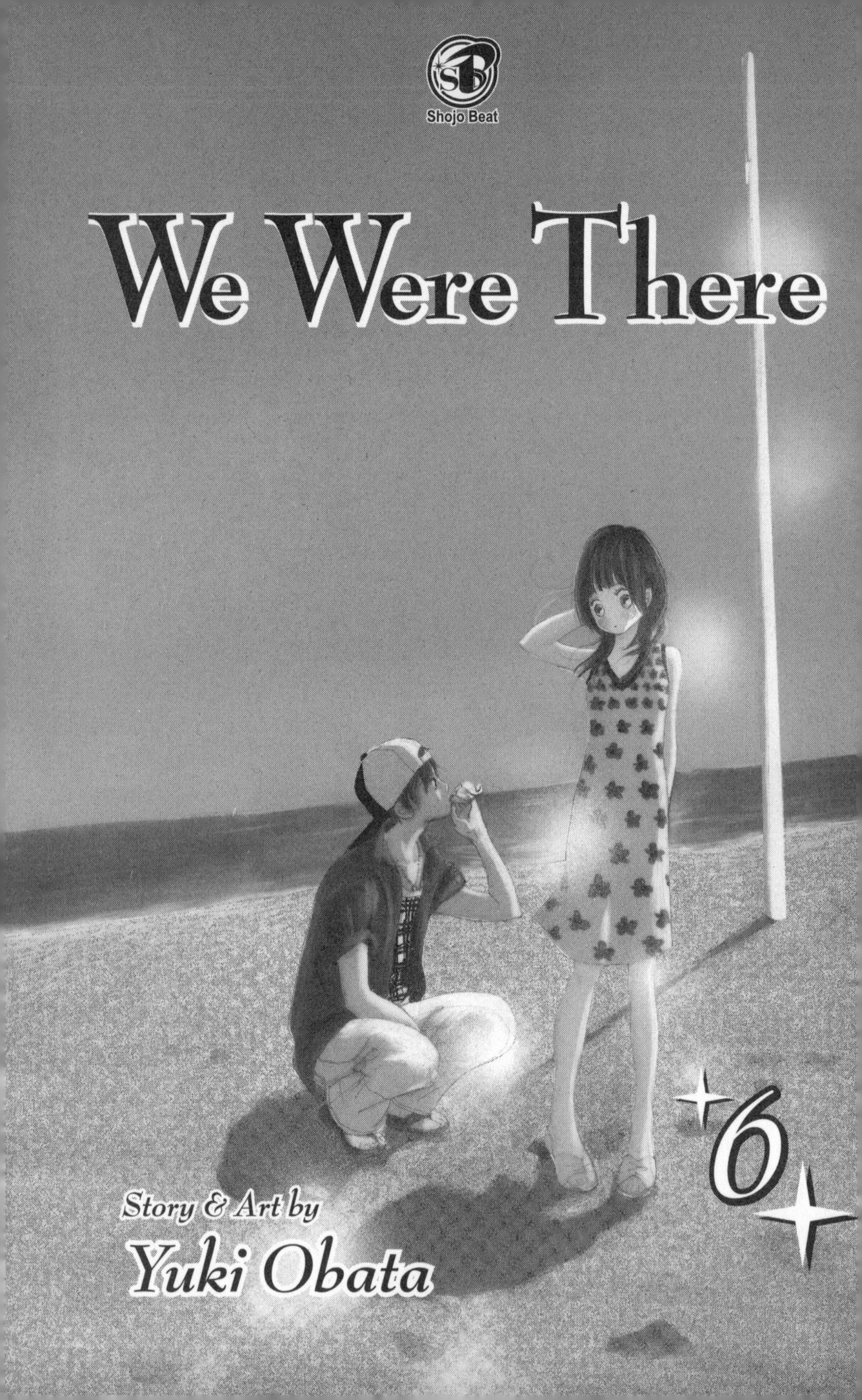
Shojo Beat
We Were There
6
Story & Art by
Yuki Obata

# Contents

# Characters

**Masafumi Takeuchi**
*Yano's childhood friend. He's kinder and more modest than Yano.*

**Nanami Takahashi**
*She's earnest but a bit forgetful at times.*

**Motoharu Yano**
*Nanami's popular classmate. His girlfriend Nana-san died.*

# Story

Having fallen in love with Yano, Nanami gradually begins to get the hang of being his girlfriend. But realizing that Yano still can't forget his ex-girlfriend, she breaks up with him. Meanwhile, Takeuchi, who had hidden his feelings for Nanami, starts to make his move—even though he's been Yano's best friend until now...

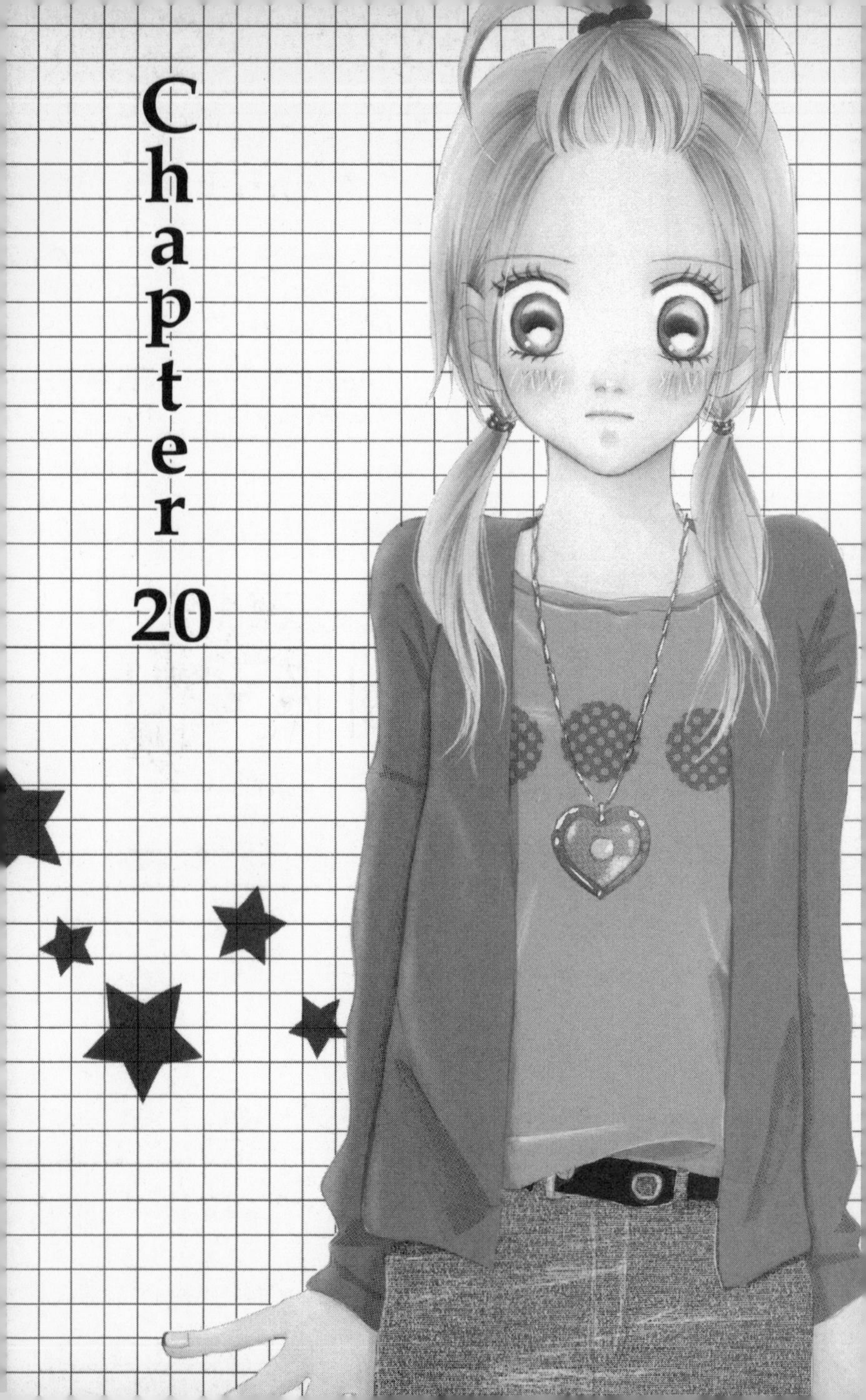
Chapter 20

Nanami's School Life

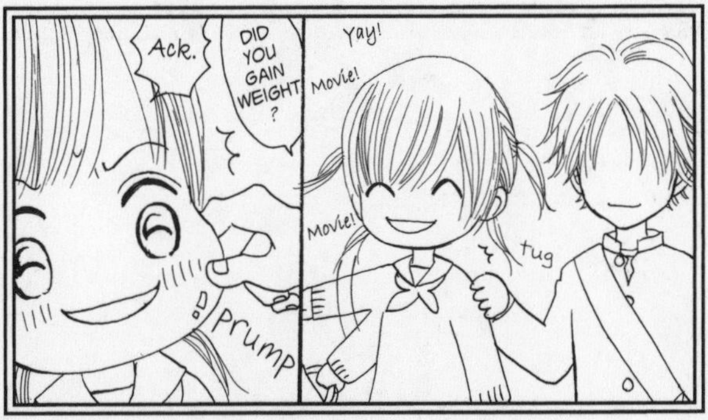
Yay!
Movie!
tug
Movie!
DID YOU GAIN WEIGHT?
Ack.
Prump

Continued on page 108...

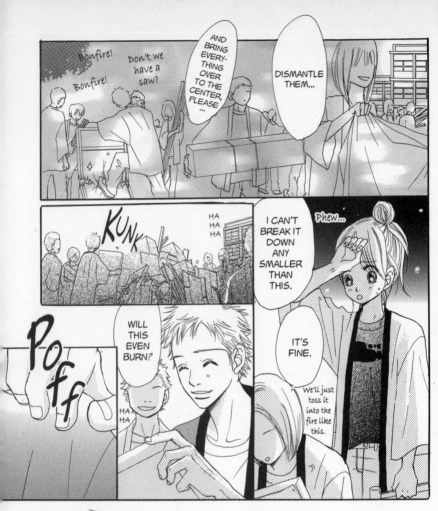

DISMANTLE THEM...
AND BRING EVERY-THING OVER TO THE CENTER, PLEASE...
Don't we have a saw?
Bonfire!
Bonfire!
Phew...
I CAN'T BREAK IT DOWN ANY SMALLER THAN THIS.
IT'S FINE.
We'll just toss it into the fire like this.
HA HA HA
KUNK
WILL THIS EVEN BURN?
HA HA
Poff

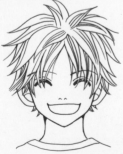

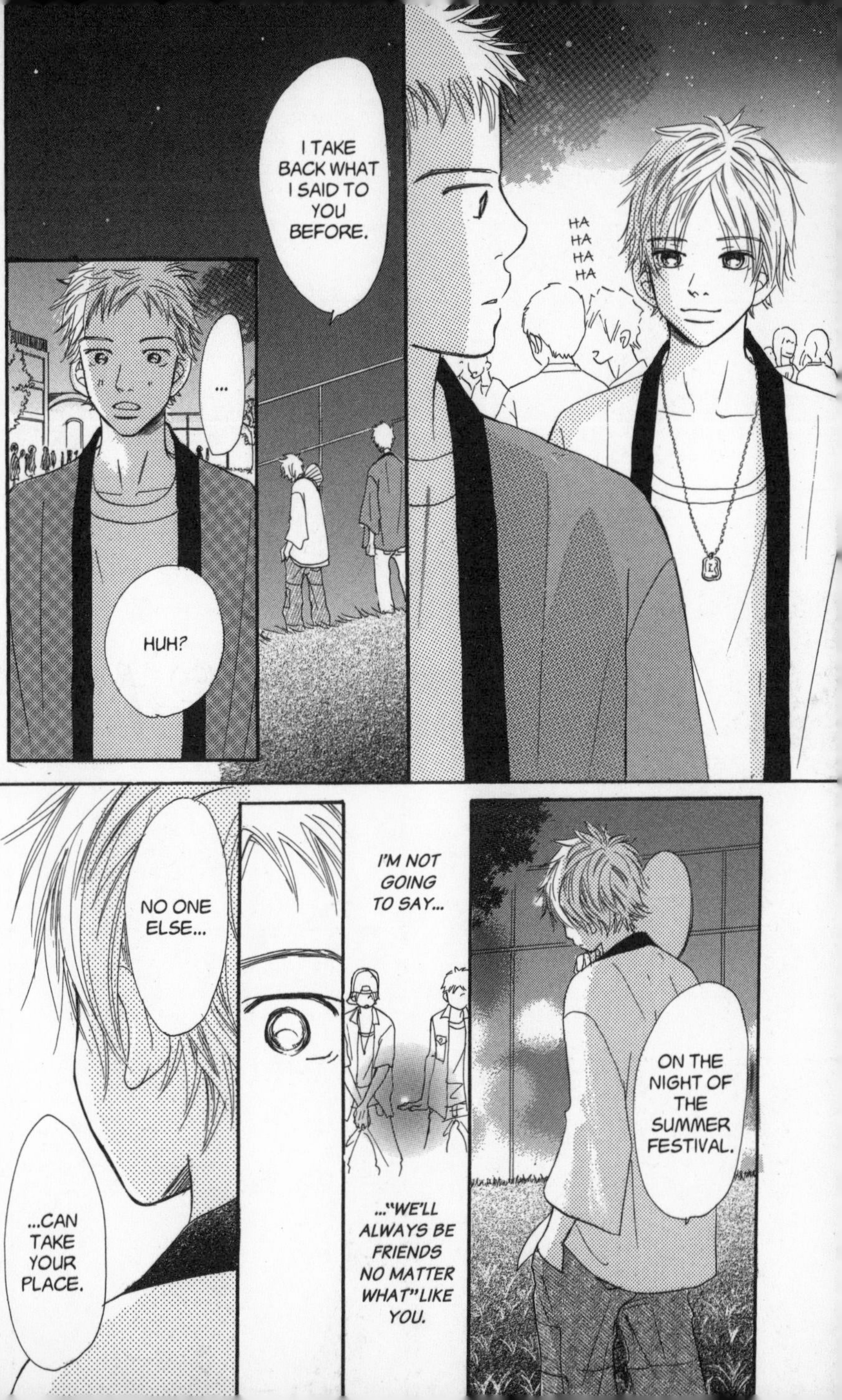
HA HA HA HA
I TAKE BACK WHAT I SAID TO YOU BEFORE.
...
HUH?
ON THE NIGHT OF THE SUMMER FESTIVAL.
I'M NOT GOING TO SAY...
..."WE'LL ALWAYS BE FRIENDS NO MATTER WHAT" LIKE YOU.
NO ONE ELSE...
...CAN TAKE YOUR PLACE.

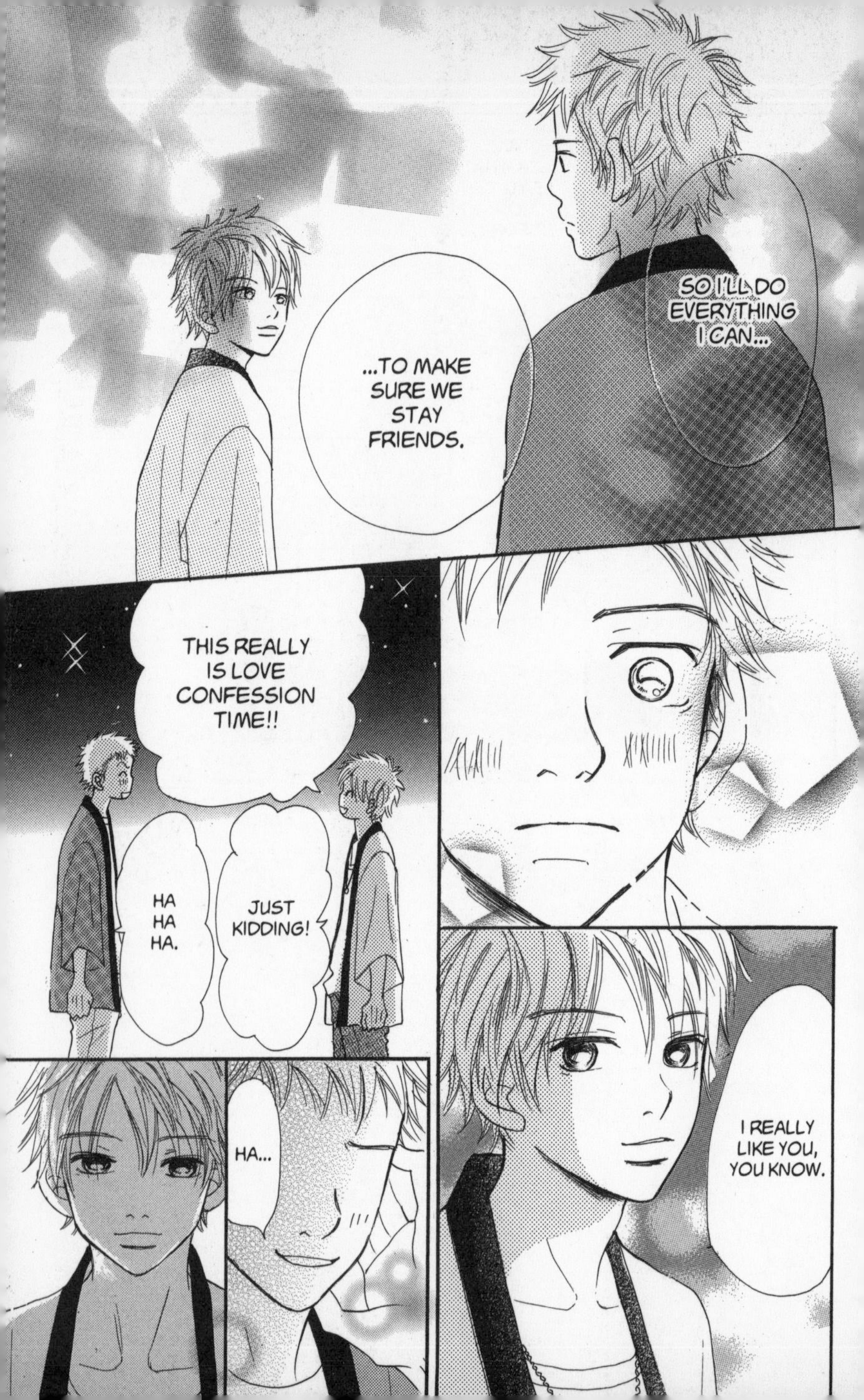
SO I'LL DO EVERYTHING I CAN...
...TO MAKE SURE WE STAY FRIENDS.
THIS REALLY IS LOVE CONFESSION TIME!!
JUST KIDDING!
HA HA HA.
I REALLY LIKE YOU, YOU KNOW.
HA...

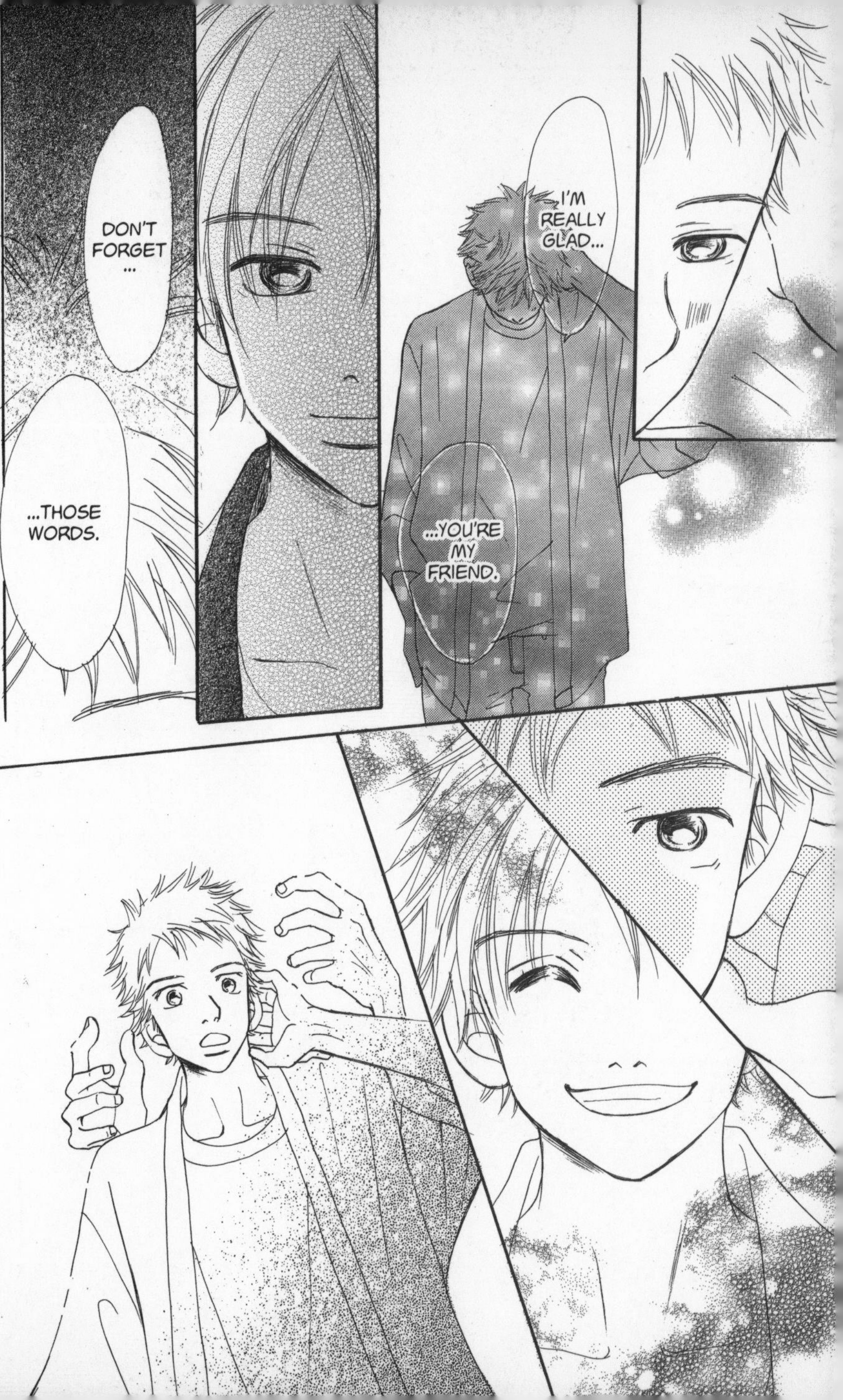
I'M REALLY GLAD...
...YOU'RE MY FRIEND.
DON'T FORGET ...
...THOSE WORDS.

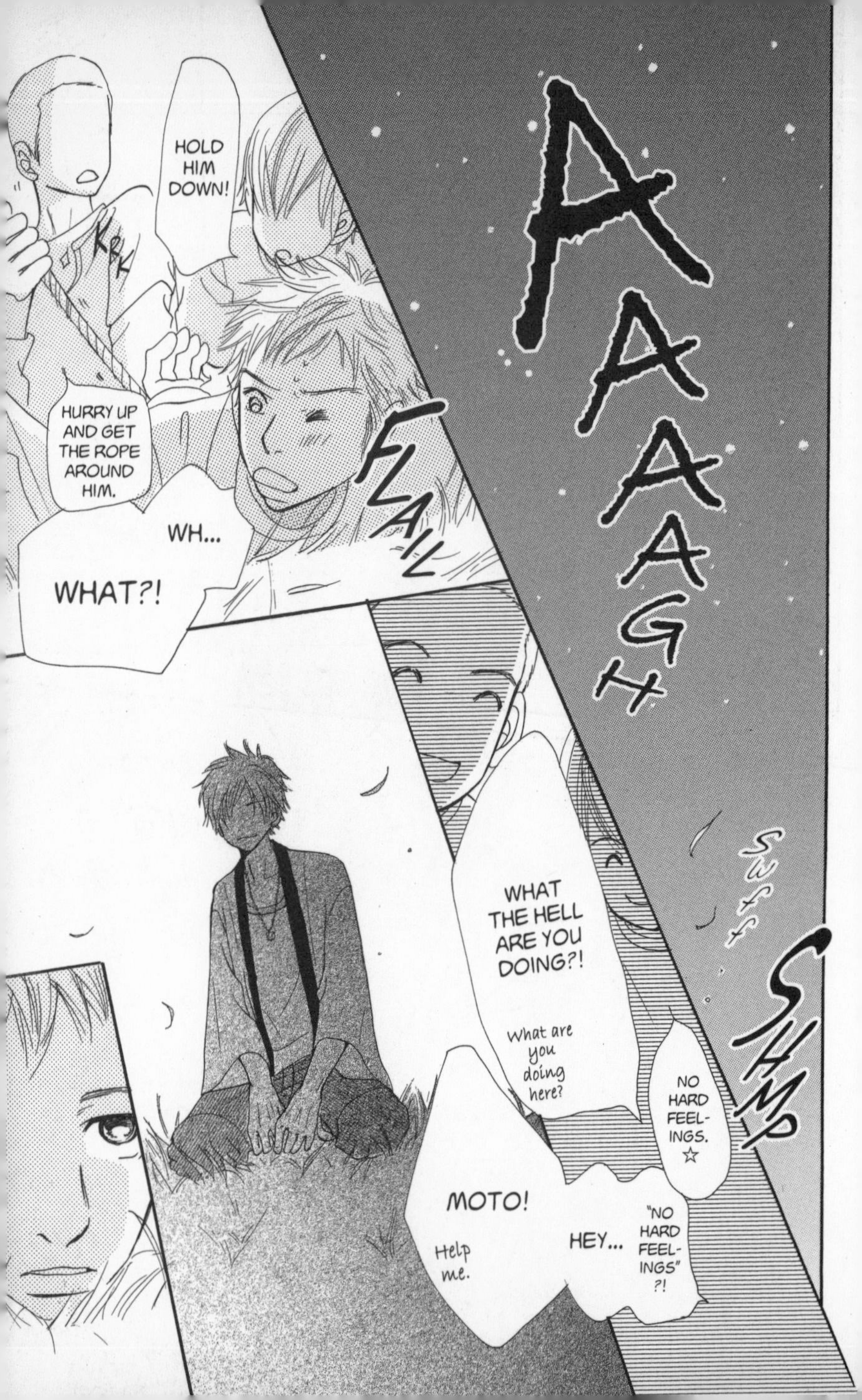
AAAAGH
HOLD HIM DOWN!
KRK
HURRY UP AND GET THE ROPE AROUND HIM.
FLAIL
WH...
WHAT?!
SWFF
SHMP
WHAT THE HELL ARE YOU DOING?!
What are you doing here?
NO HARD FEELINGS. ☆
"NO HARD FEELINGS"?!
HEY...
MOTO!
Help me.

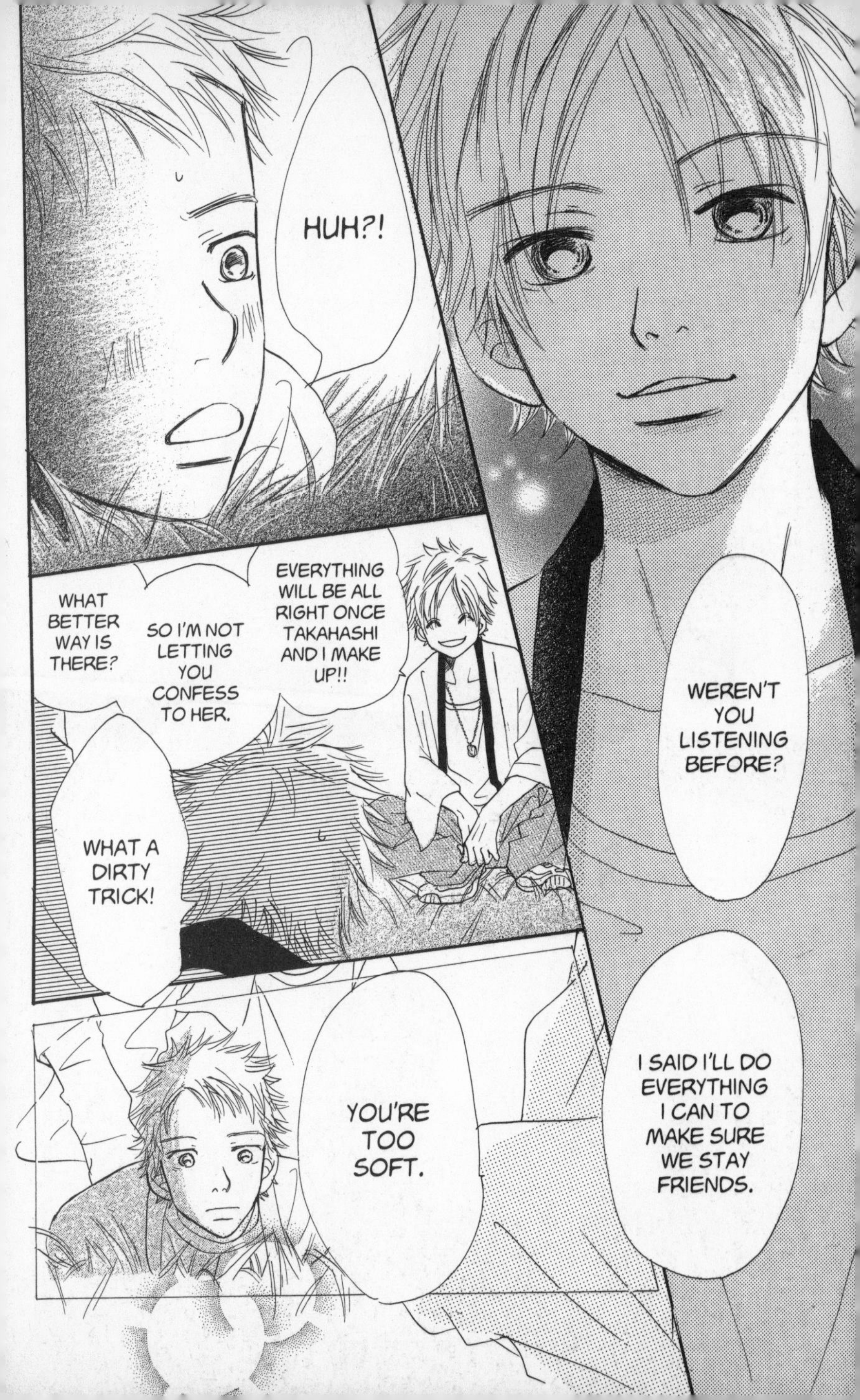
WEREN'T YOU LISTENING BEFORE?
I SAID I'LL DO EVERYTHING I CAN TO MAKE SURE WE STAY FRIENDS.
HUH?!
EVERYTHING WILL BE ALL RIGHT ONCE TAKAHASHI AND I MAKE UP!!
SO I'M NOT LETTING YOU CONFESS TO HER.
WHAT BETTER WAY IS THERE?
WHAT A DIRTY TRICK!
YOU'RE TOO SOFT.

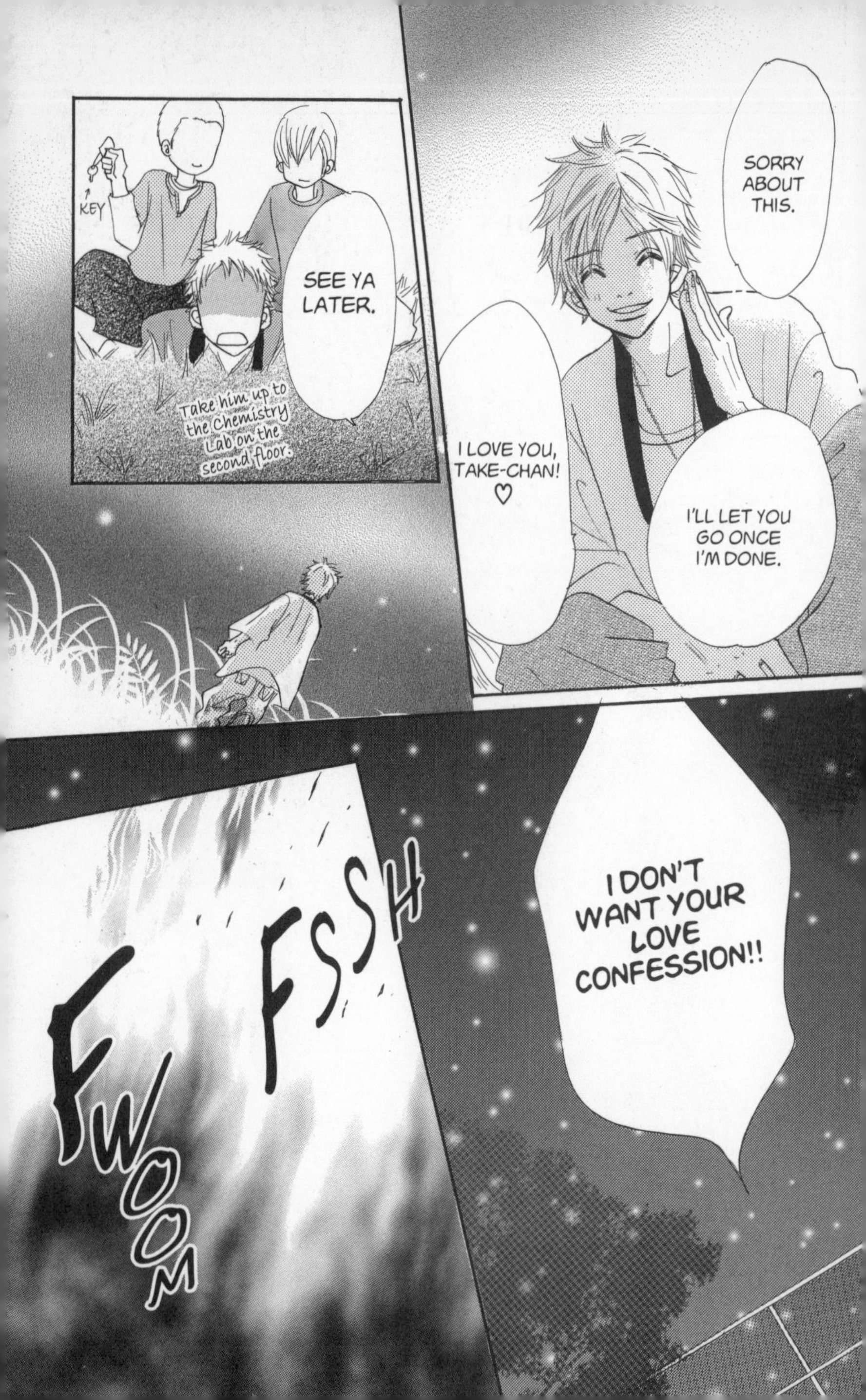
SORRY ABOUT THIS.
I LOVE YOU, TAKE-CHAN! ♡
I'LL LET YOU GO ONCE I'M DONE.
KEY
SEE YA LATER.
Take him up to the Chemistry Lab on the second floor.
I DON'T WANT YOUR LOVE CONFESSION!!
FSSH
FWOOM

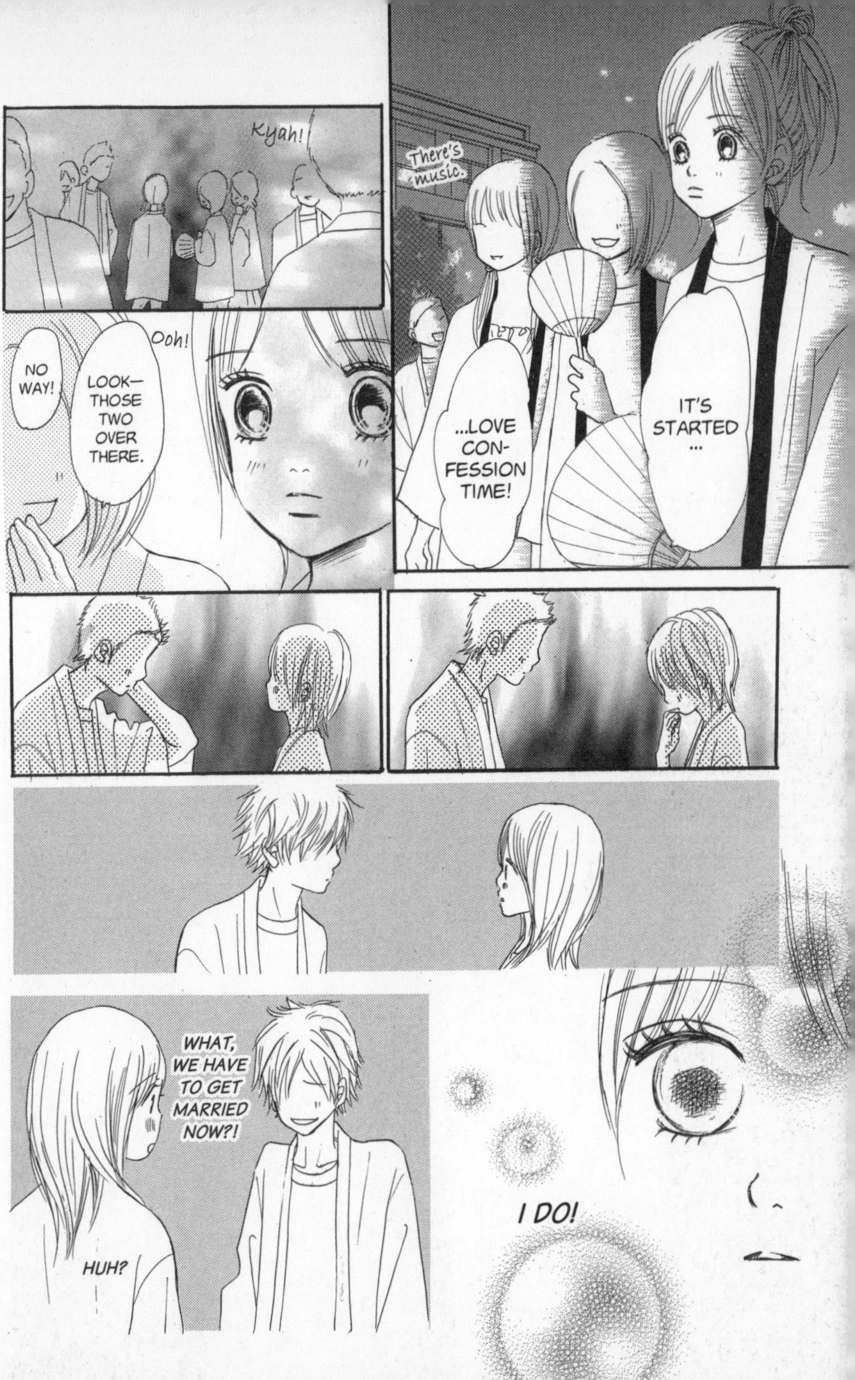
There's music.
IT'S STARTED ...
...LOVE CON-FESSION TIME!
Kyah!
Ooh!
LOOK— THOSE TWO OVER THERE.
NO WAY!
I DO!
WHAT, WE HAVE TO GET MARRIED NOW?!
HUH?

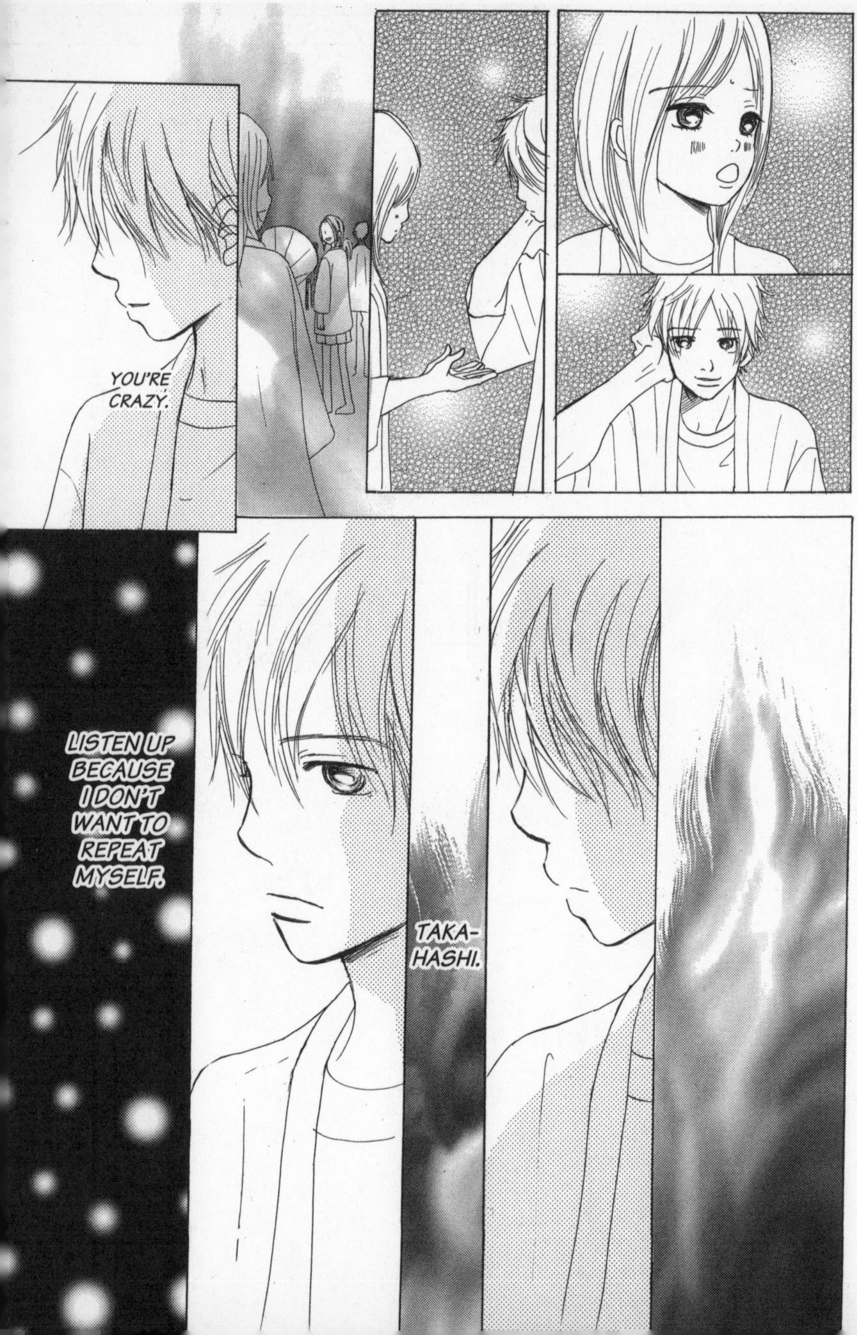
YOU'RE CRAZY.
TAKA-HASHI.
LISTEN UP BECAUSE I DON'T WANT TO REPEAT MYSELF.

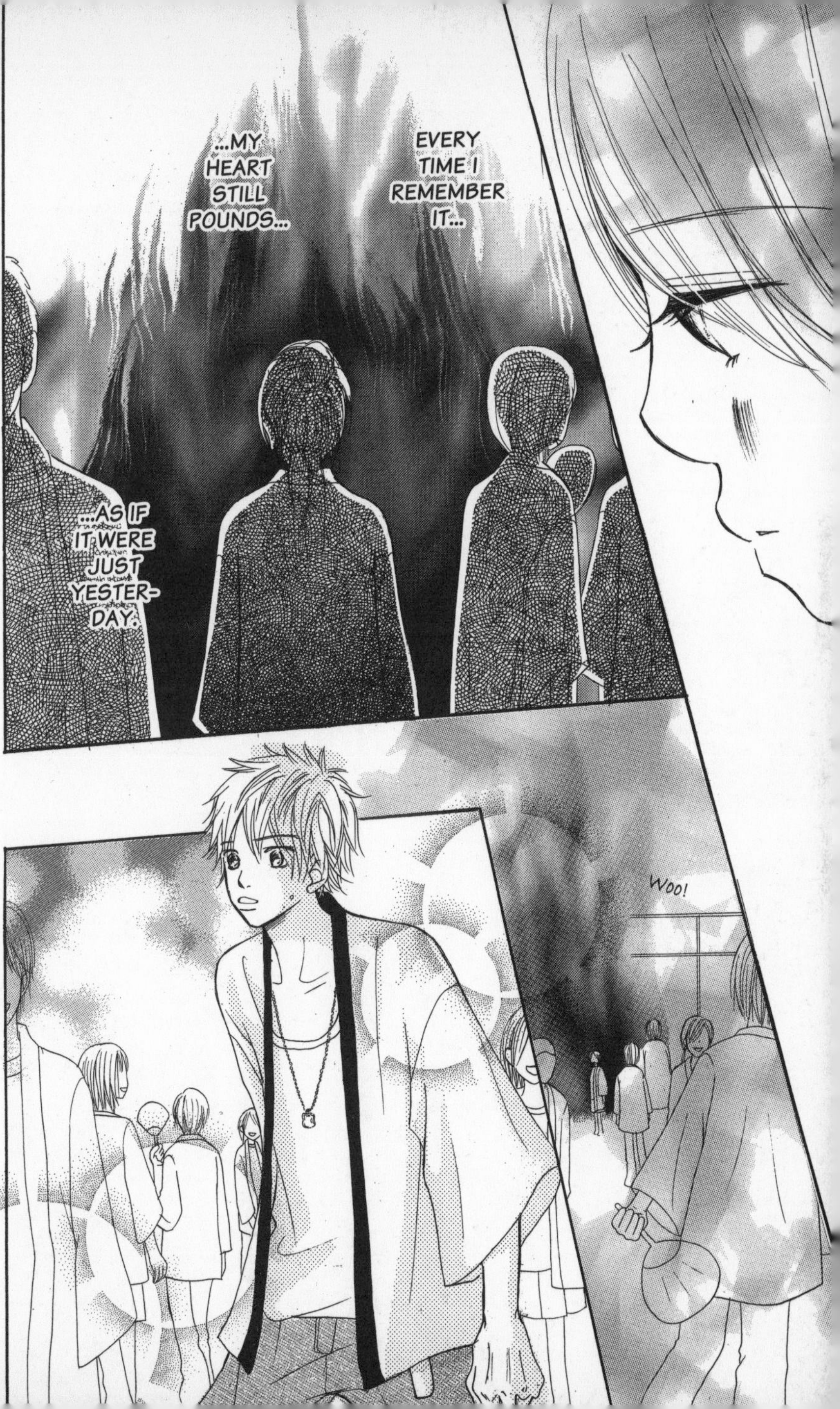
EVERY TIME I REMEMBER IT...
...MY HEART STILL POUNDS...
...AS IF IT WERE JUST YESTER-DAY.
Woo!

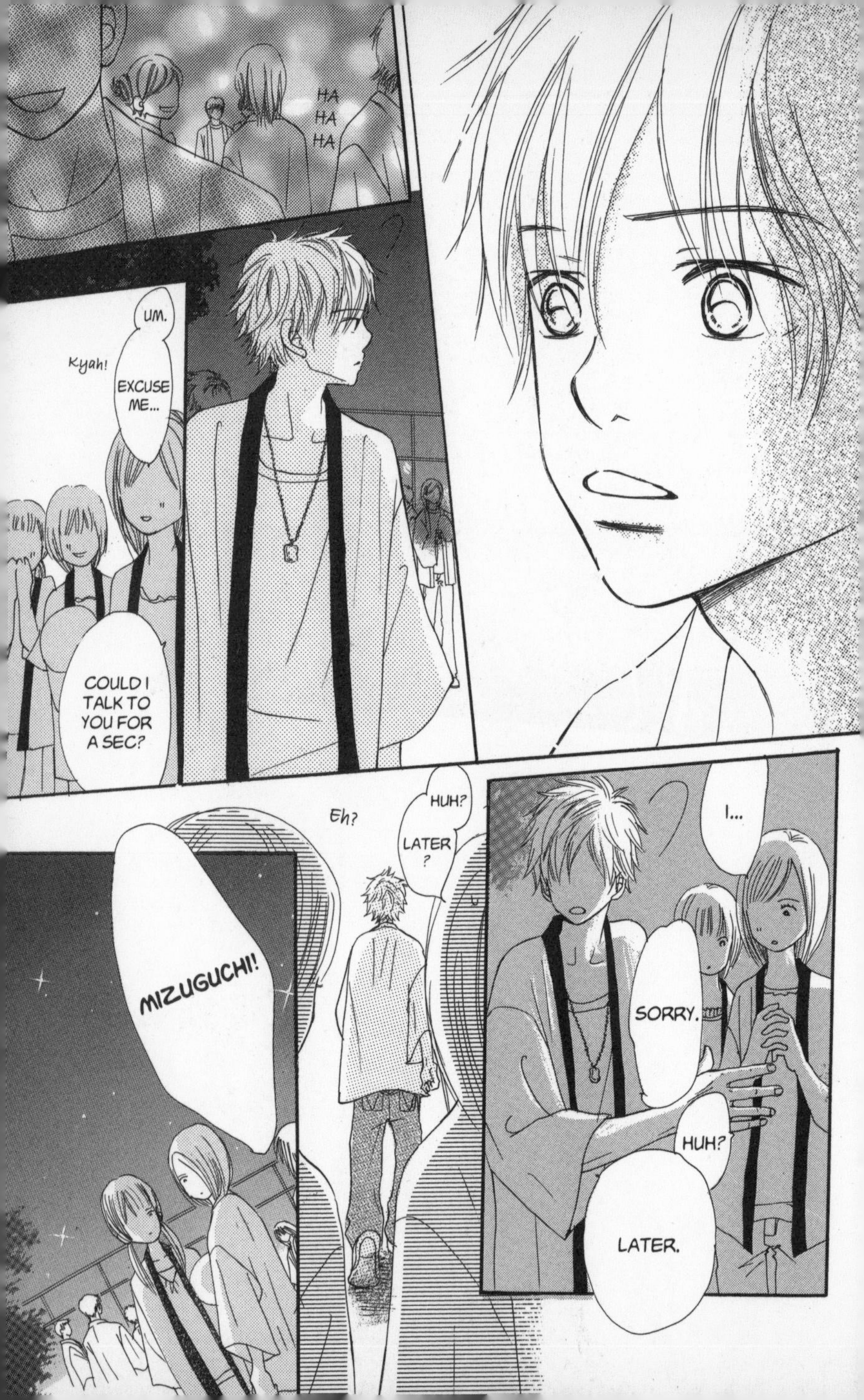
HA HA HA
UM. EXCUSE ME...
Kyah!
COULD I TALK TO YOU FOR A SEC?
I...
SORRY.
HUH?
LATER.
HUH? LATER?
Eh?
MIZUGUCHI!

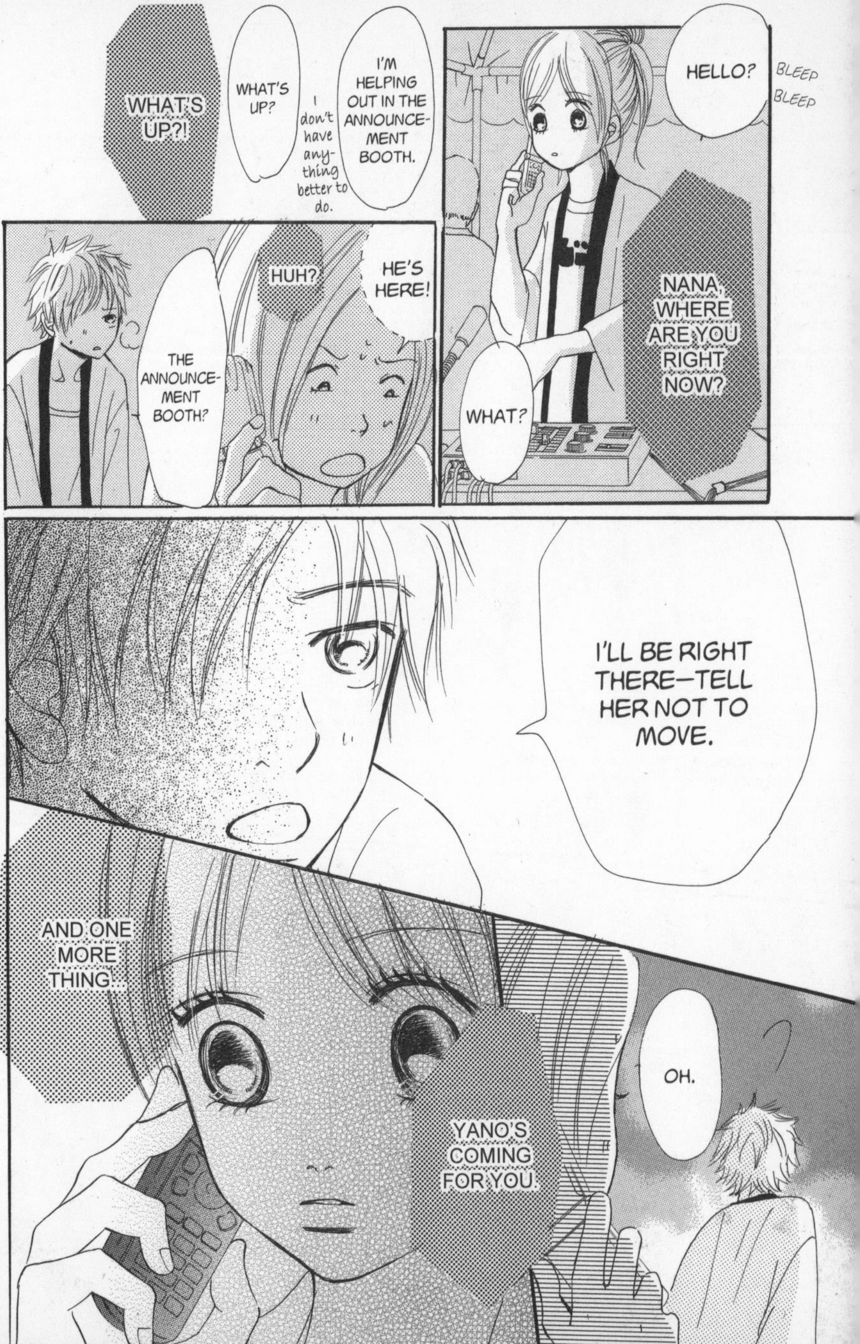
BLEEP
BLEEP
HELLO?
NANA, WHERE ARE YOU RIGHT NOW?
WHAT?
I'M HELPING OUT IN THE ANNOUNCEMENT BOOTH.
I don't have anything better to do.
WHAT'S UP?
WHAT'S UP?!
HE'S HERE!
HUH?
THE ANNOUNCEMENT BOOTH?
I'LL BE RIGHT THERE—TELL HER NOT TO MOVE.
OH.
AND ONE MORE THING...
YANO'S COMING FOR YOU.

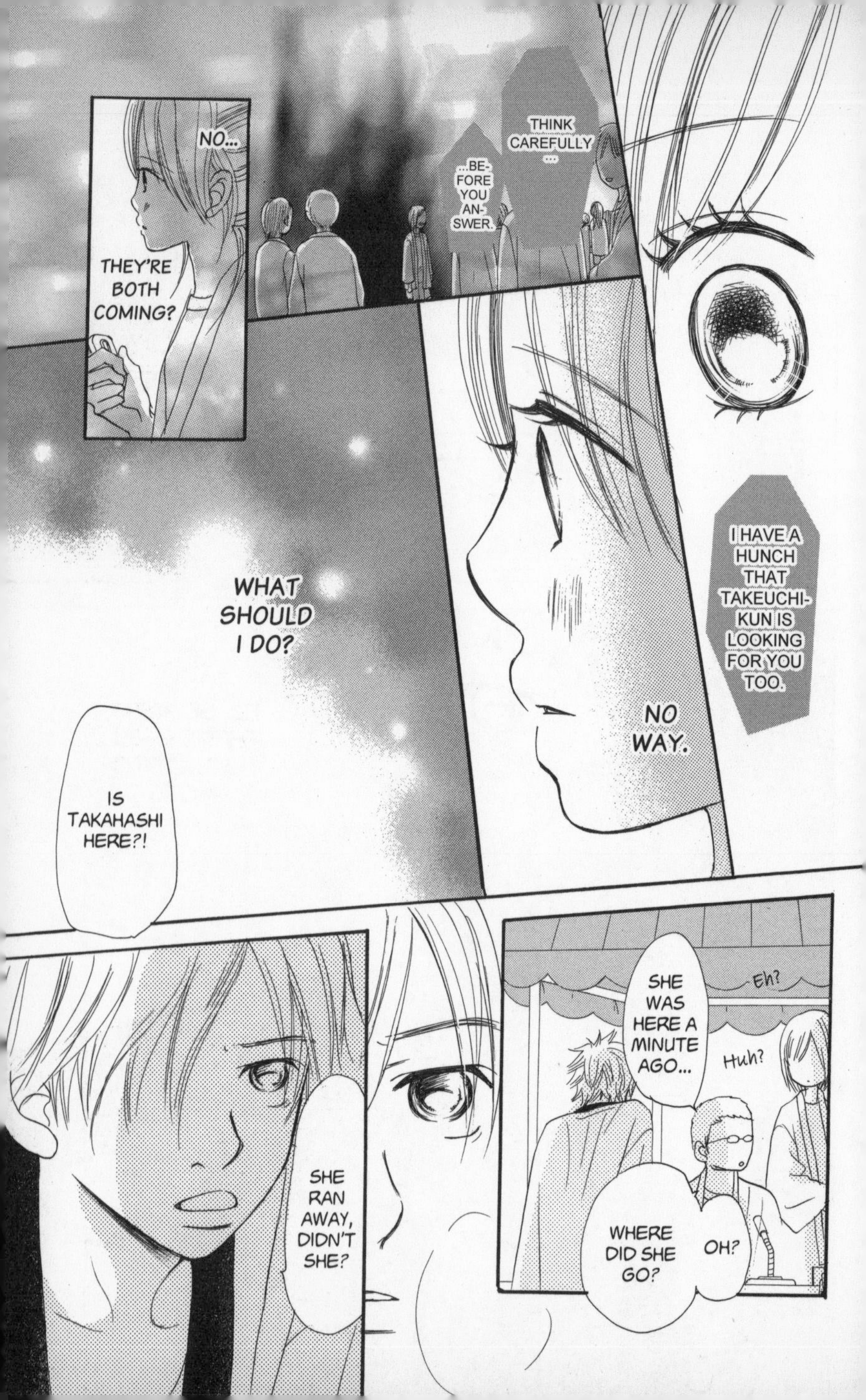
THINK CAREFULLY ...
...BE-FORE YOU AN-SWER.
I HAVE A HUNCH THAT TAKEUCHI-KUN IS LOOKING FOR YOU TOO.
NO WAY.
NO...
THEY'RE BOTH COMING?
WHAT SHOULD I DO?
IS TAKAHASHI HERE?!
SHE WAS HERE A MINUTE AGO...
Eh?
Huh?
WHERE DID SHE GO?
OH?
SHE RAN AWAY, DIDN'T SHE?

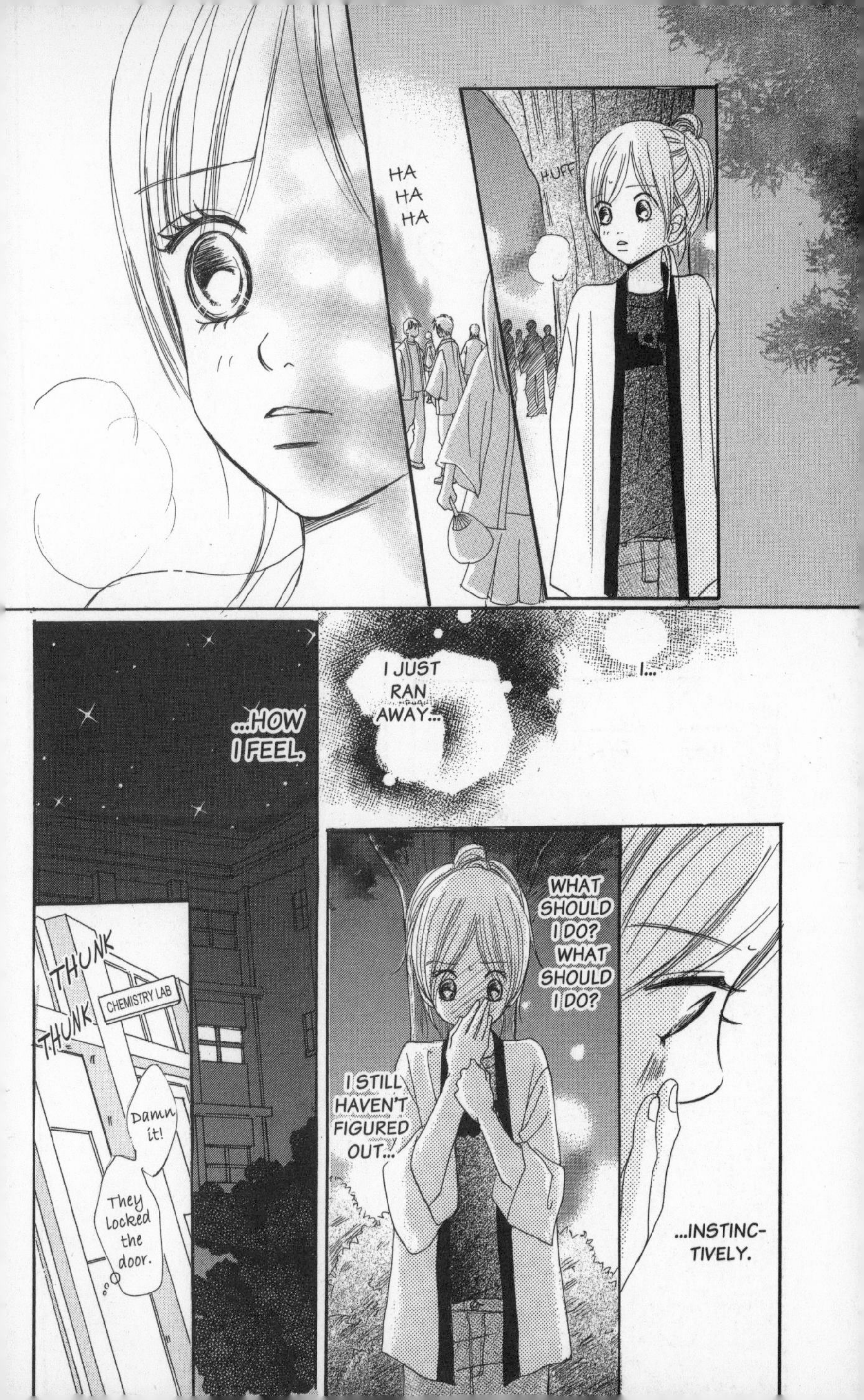
HUFF
HA HA HA
I...
I JUST RAN AWAY...
...INSTINCTIVELY.
WHAT SHOULD I DO? WHAT SHOULD I DO?
I STILL HAVEN'T FIGURED OUT...
...HOW I FEEL.
THUNK
THUNK
CHEMISTRY LAB
Damn it!
They locked the door.

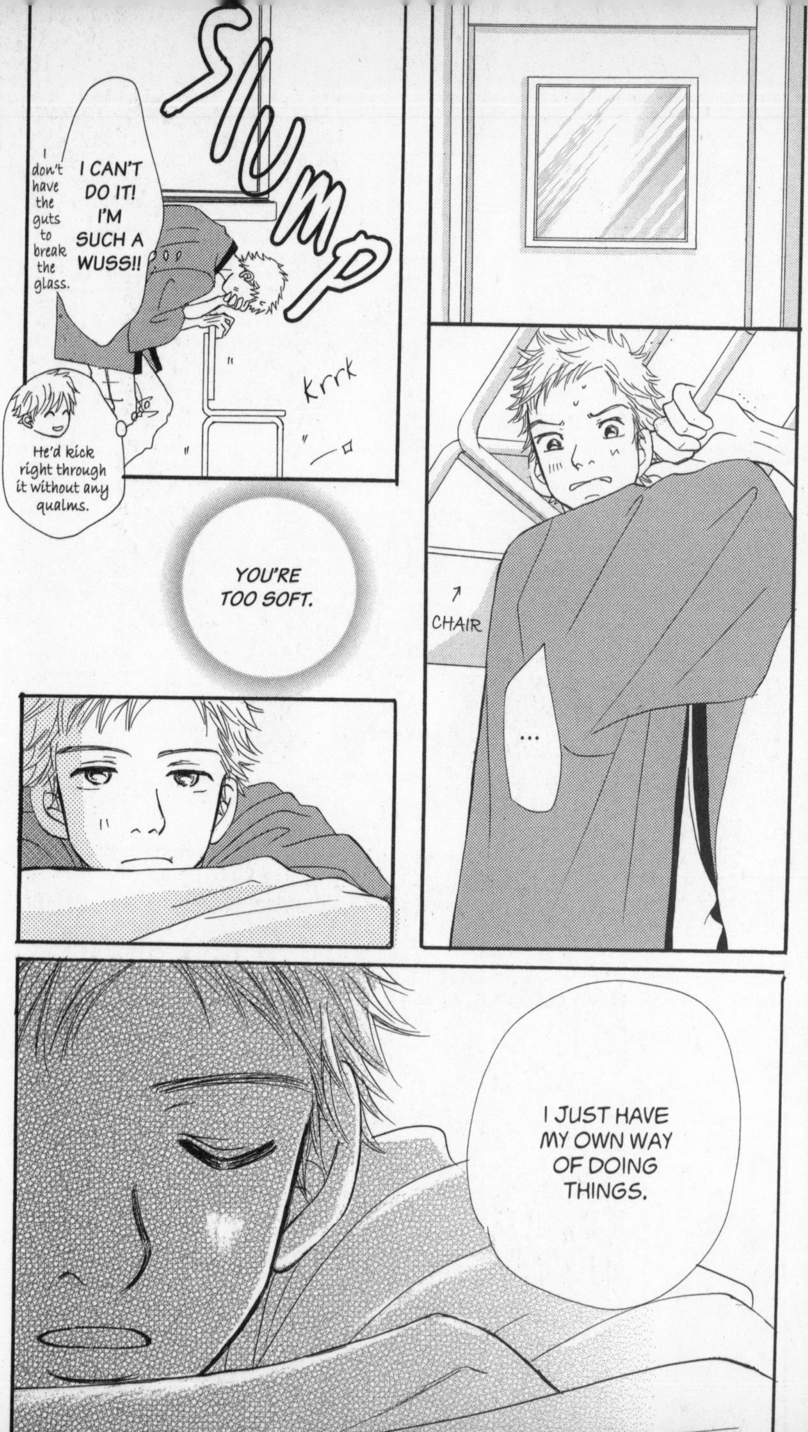
SLUMP
I CAN'T DO IT! I'M SUCH A WUSS!!
I don't have the guts to break the glass.
krrk
He'd kick right through it without any qualms.
CHAIR
...
YOU'RE TOO SOFT.
I JUST HAVE MY OWN WAY OF DOING THINGS.

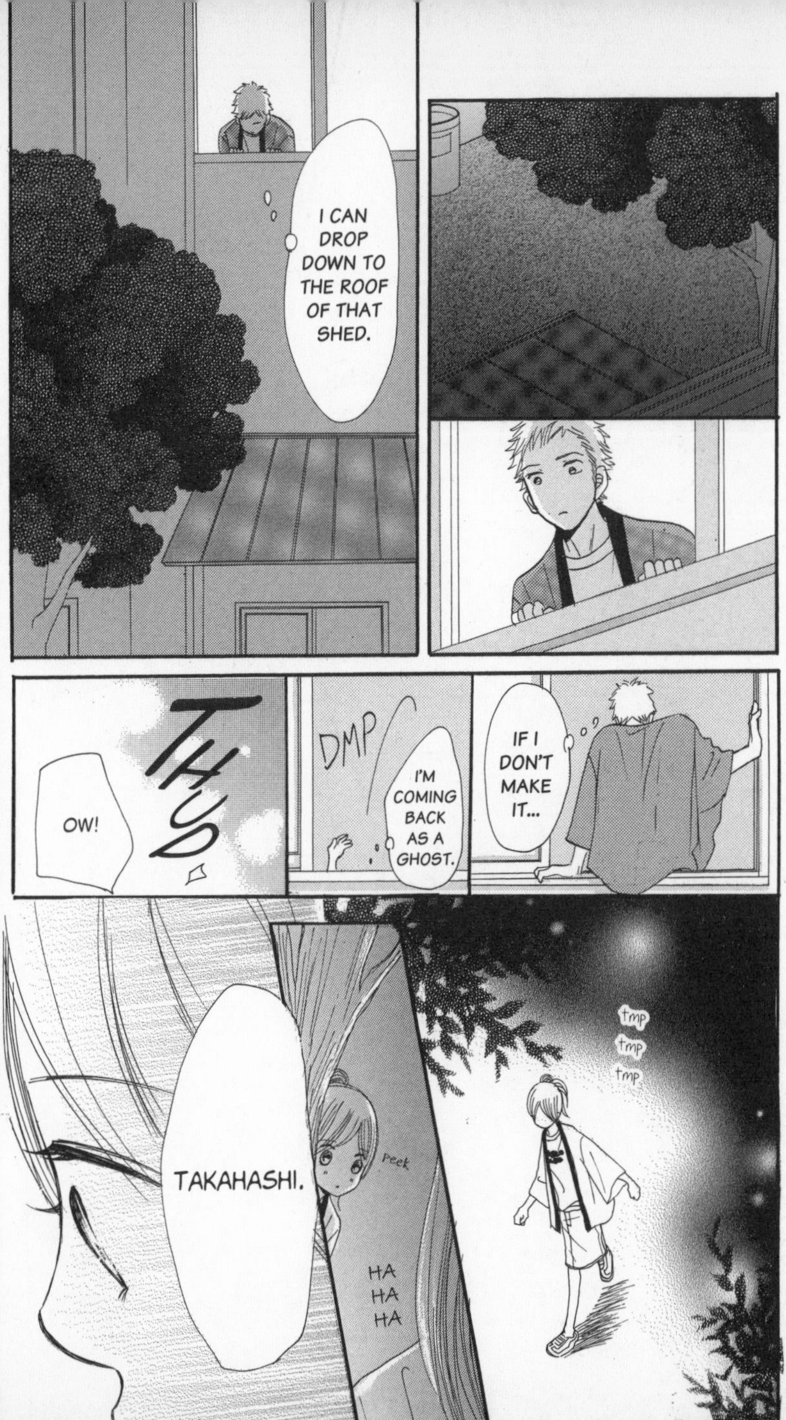
I CAN DROP DOWN TO THE ROOF OF THAT SHED.
IF I DON'T MAKE IT...
I'M COMING BACK AS A GHOST.
DMP
THUD
OW!
tmp
tmp
tmp
peek
TAKAHASHI.
HA HA HA

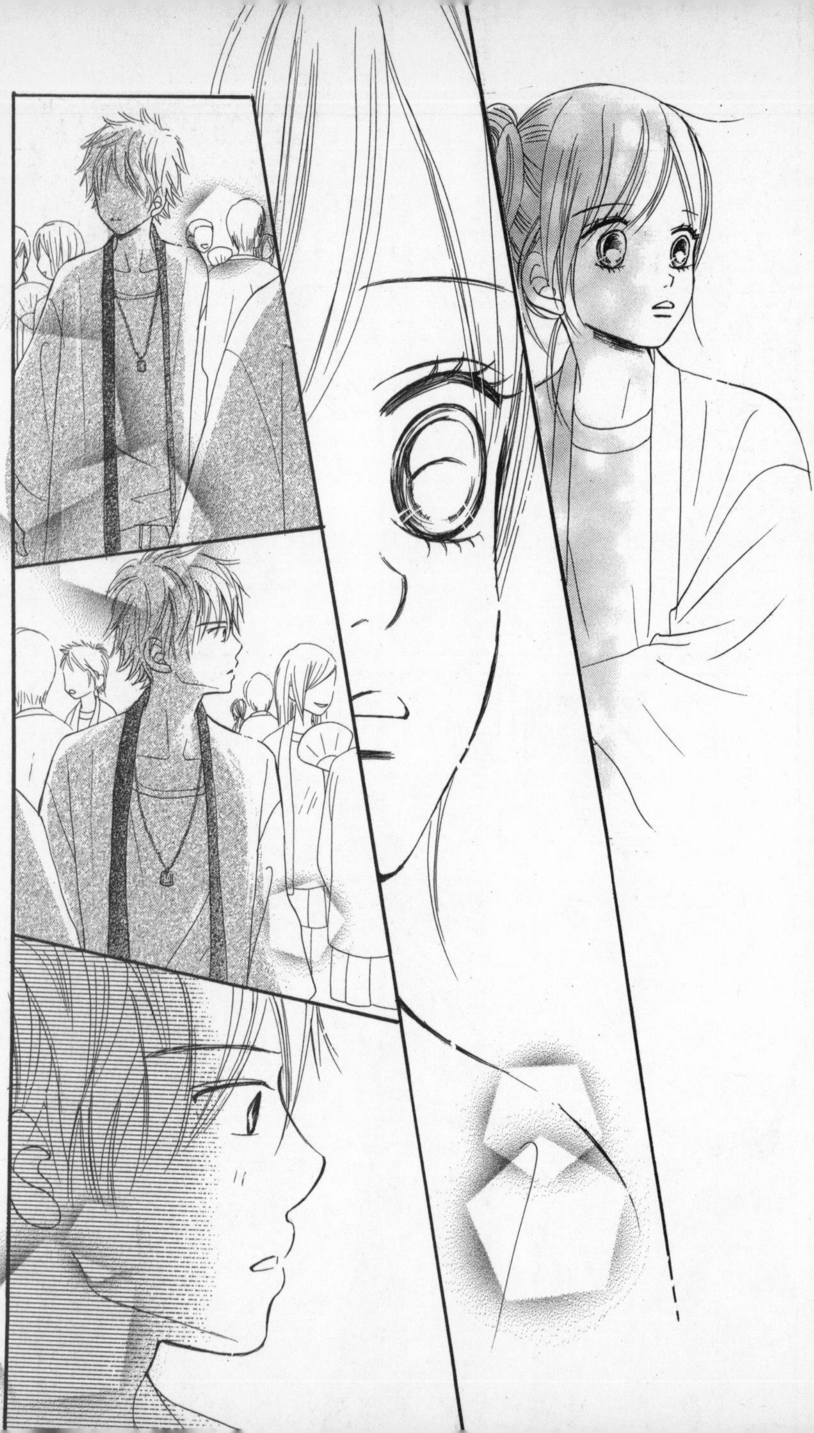

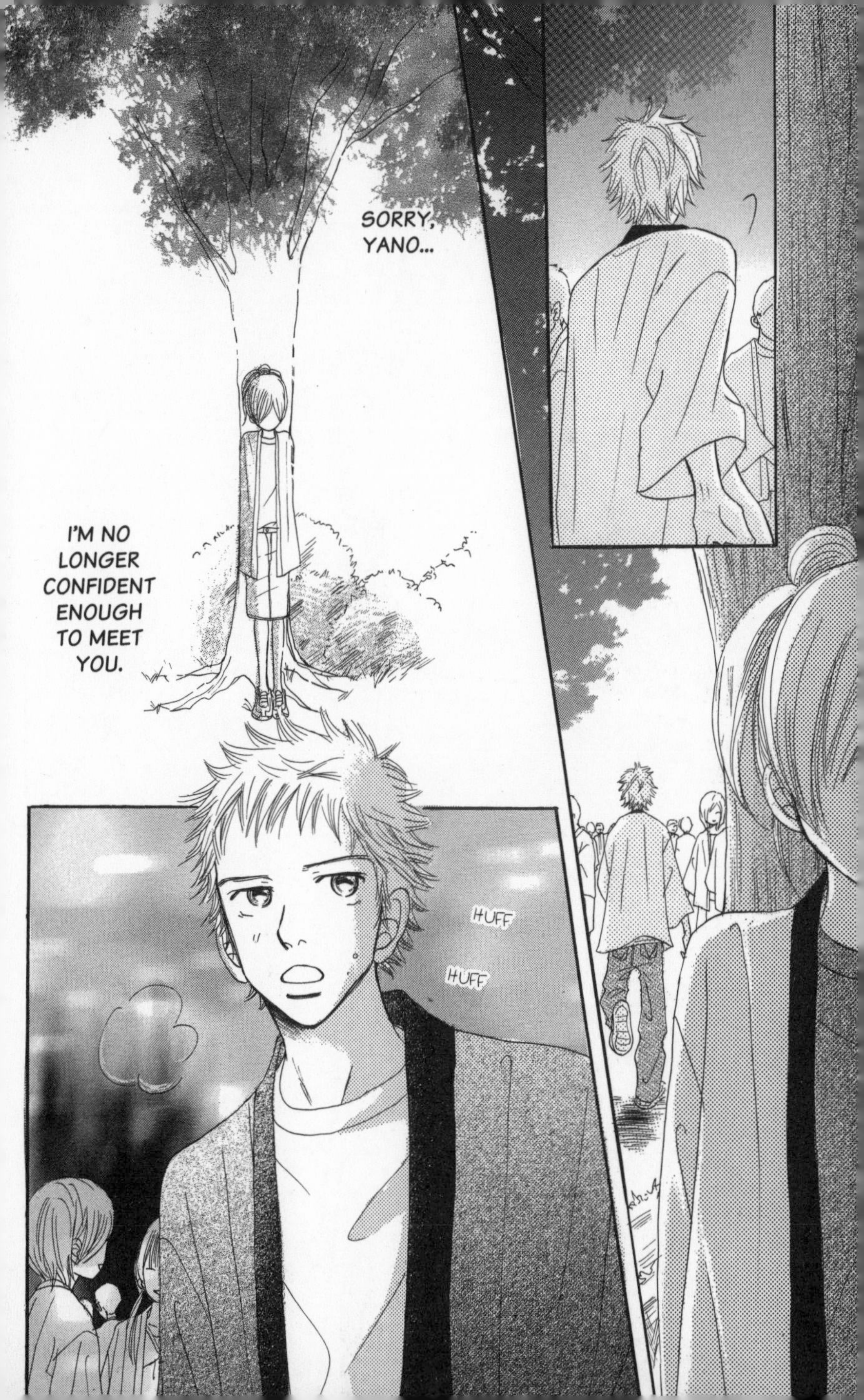
SORRY, YANO...
I'M NO LONGER CONFIDENT ENOUGH TO MEET YOU.
HUFF
HUFF

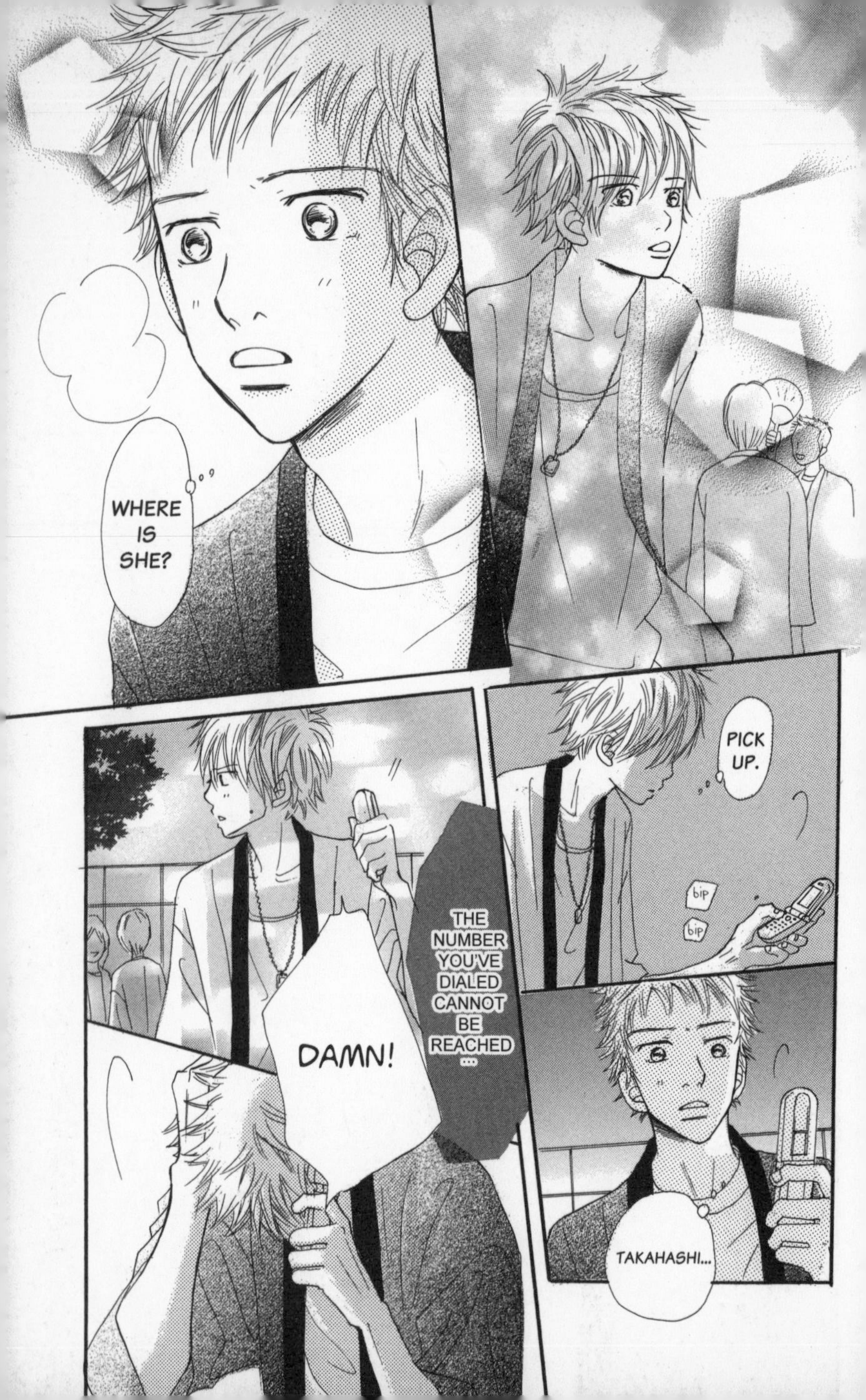

WHERE IS SHE?
PICK UP.
bip
bip
THE NUMBER YOU'VE DIALED CANNOT BE REACHED ...
DAMN!
TAKAHASHI...

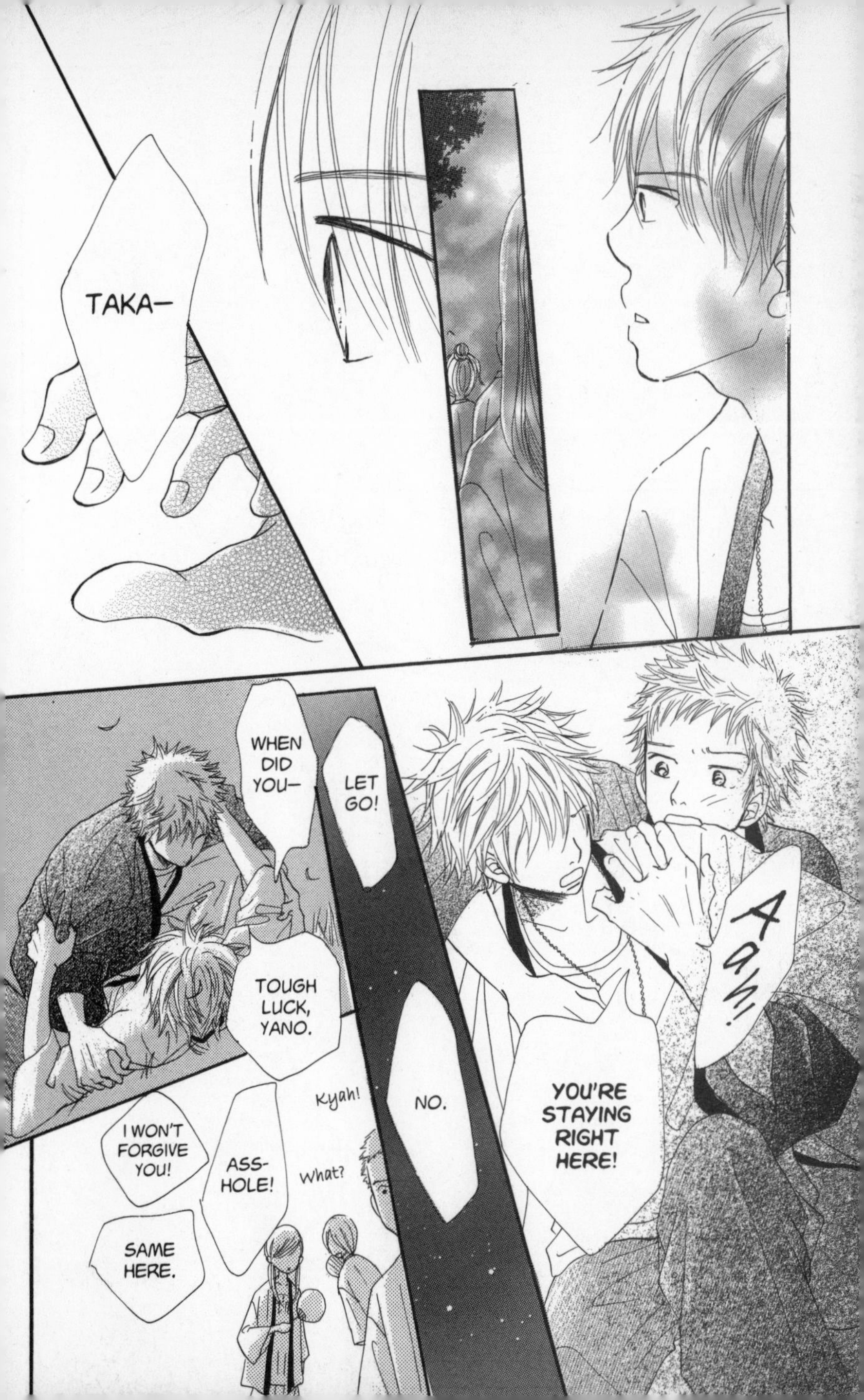
TAKA—
Aah!
LET GO!
YOU'RE STAYING RIGHT HERE!
NO.
WHEN DID YOU—
TOUGH LUCK, YANO.
Kyah!
What?
ASS-HOLE!
I WON'T FORGIVE YOU!
SAME HERE.

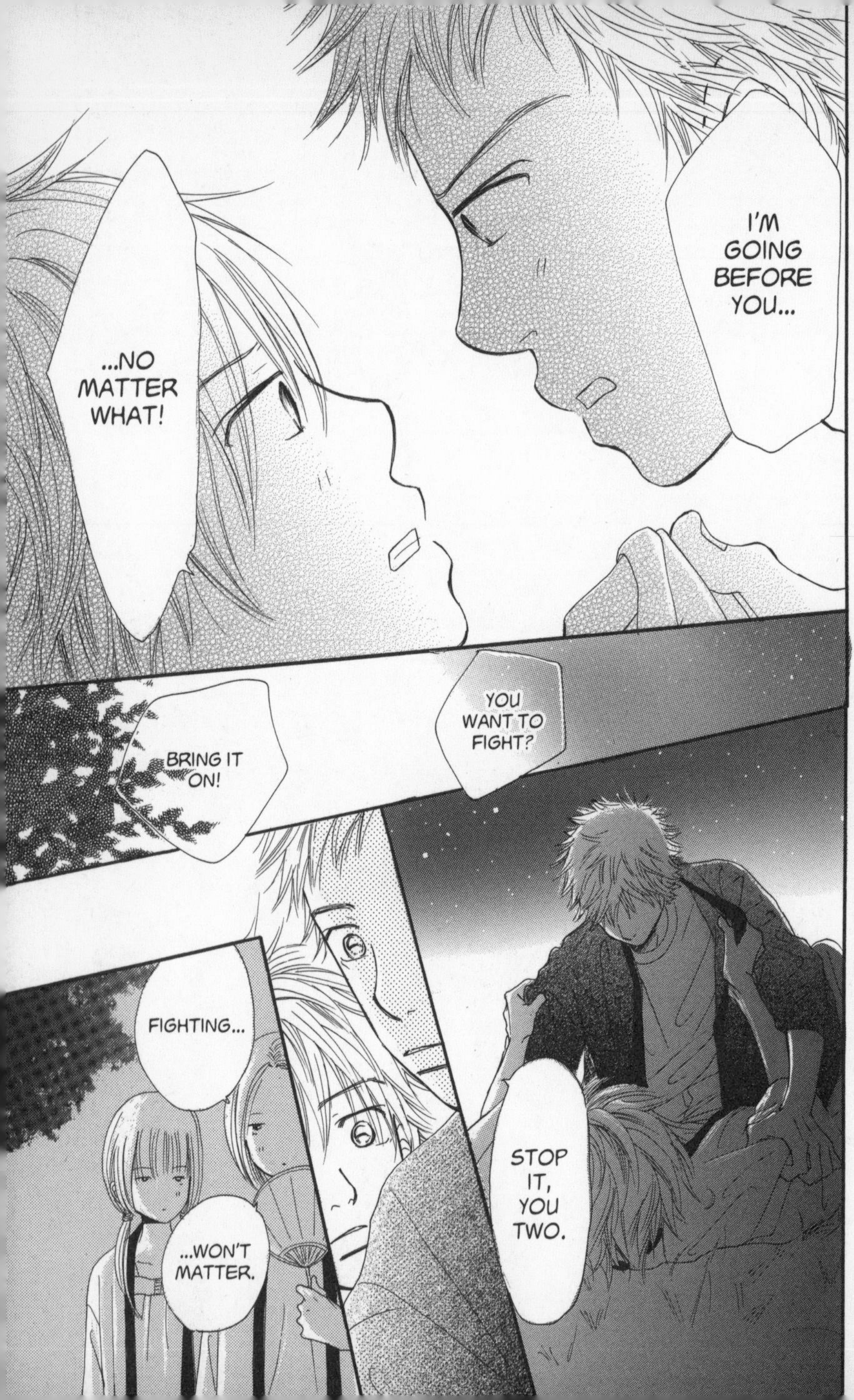
I'M GOING BEFORE YOU...
...NO MATTER WHAT!
YOU WANT TO FIGHT?
BRING IT ON!
STOP IT, YOU TWO.
FIGHTING...
...WON'T MATTER.

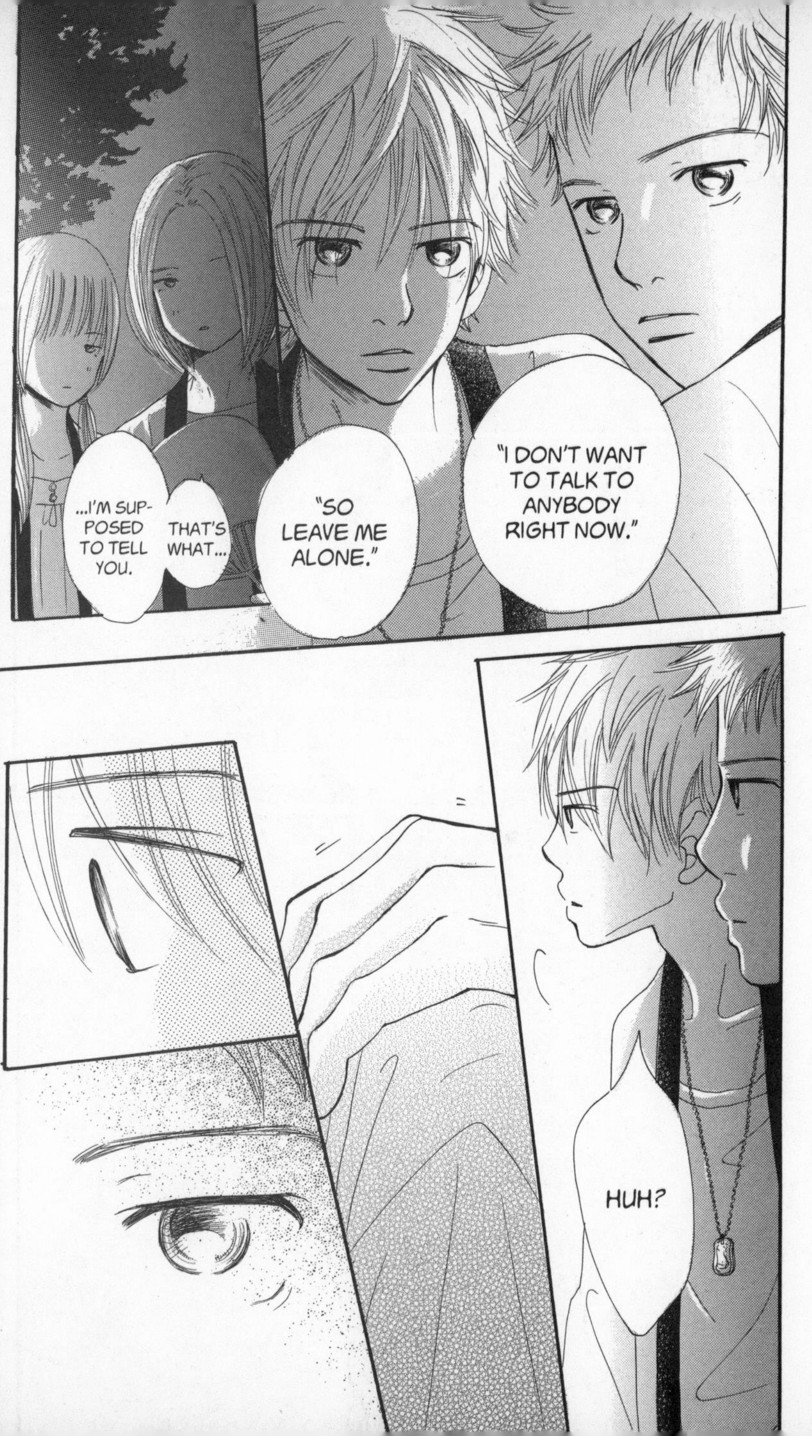
"I DON'T WANT TO TALK TO ANYBODY RIGHT NOW."
"SO LEAVE ME ALONE."
THAT'S WHAT...
...I'M SUP-POSED TO TELL YOU.
HUH?

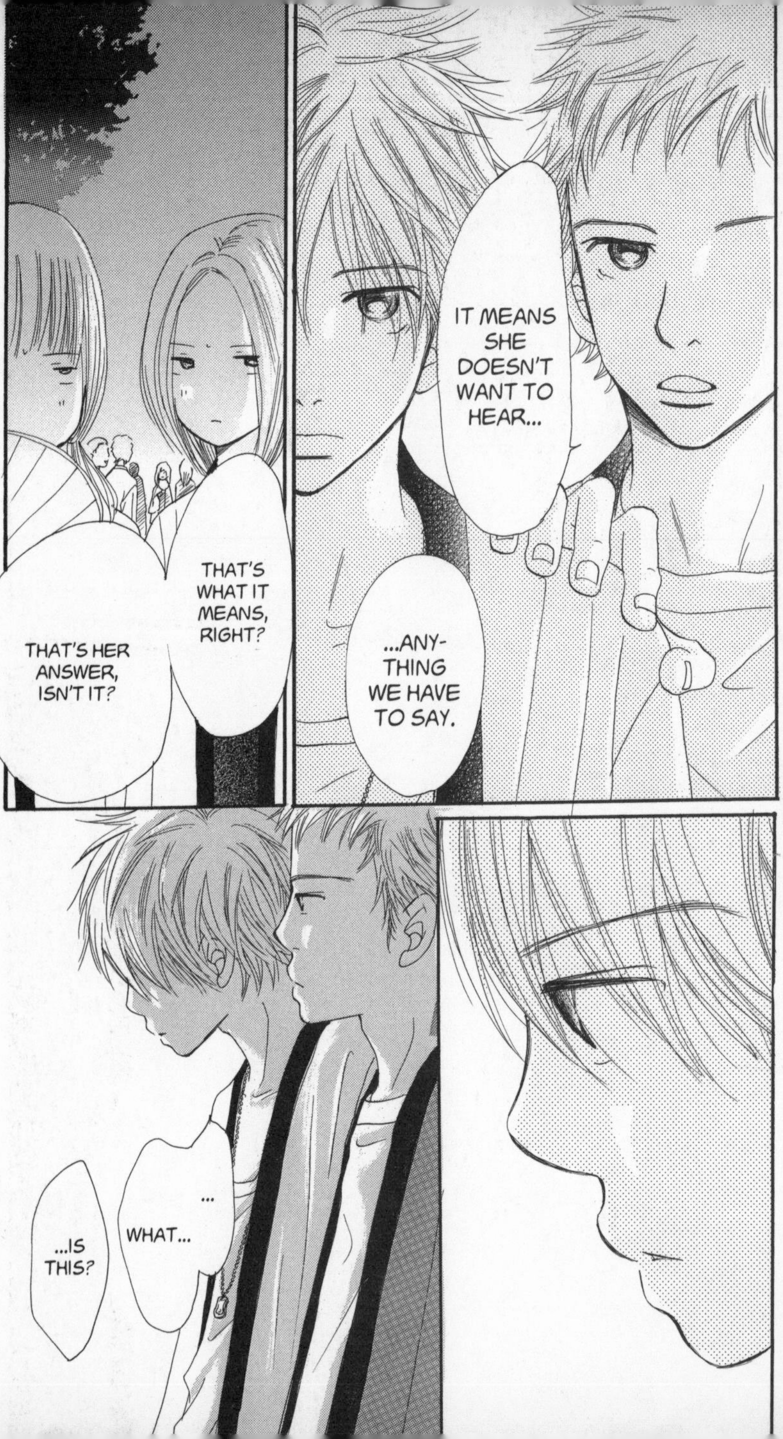
IT MEANS SHE DOESN'T WANT TO HEAR...
...ANY-THING WE HAVE TO SAY.
THAT'S WHAT IT MEANS, RIGHT?
THAT'S HER ANSWER, ISN'T IT?
...
WHAT...
...IS THIS?

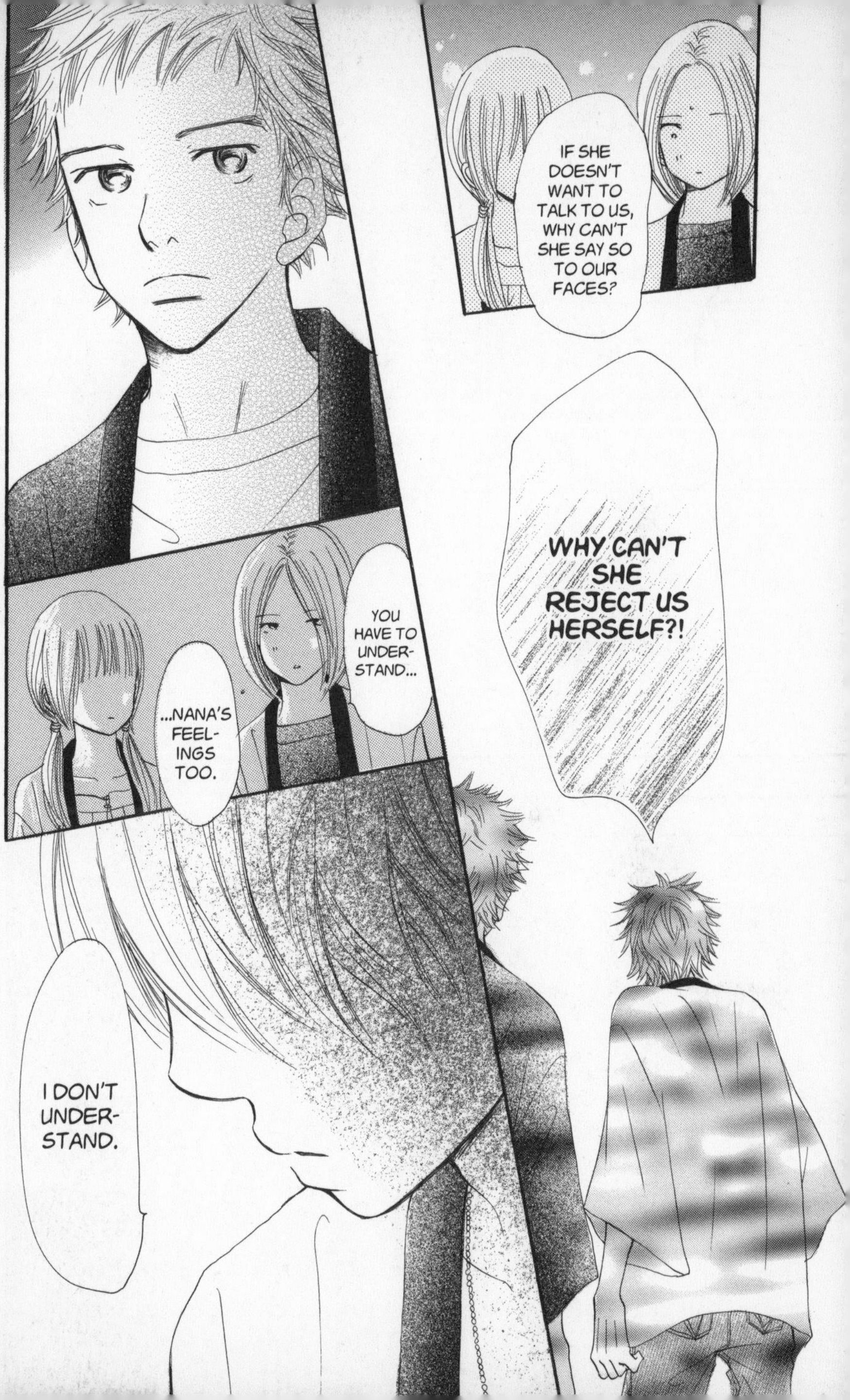
IF SHE DOESN'T WANT TO TALK TO US, WHY CAN'T SHE SAY SO TO OUR FACES?
WHY CAN'T SHE REJECT US HERSELF?!
YOU HAVE TO UNDER-STAND...
...NANA'S FEEL-INGS TOO.
I DON'T UNDER-STAND.

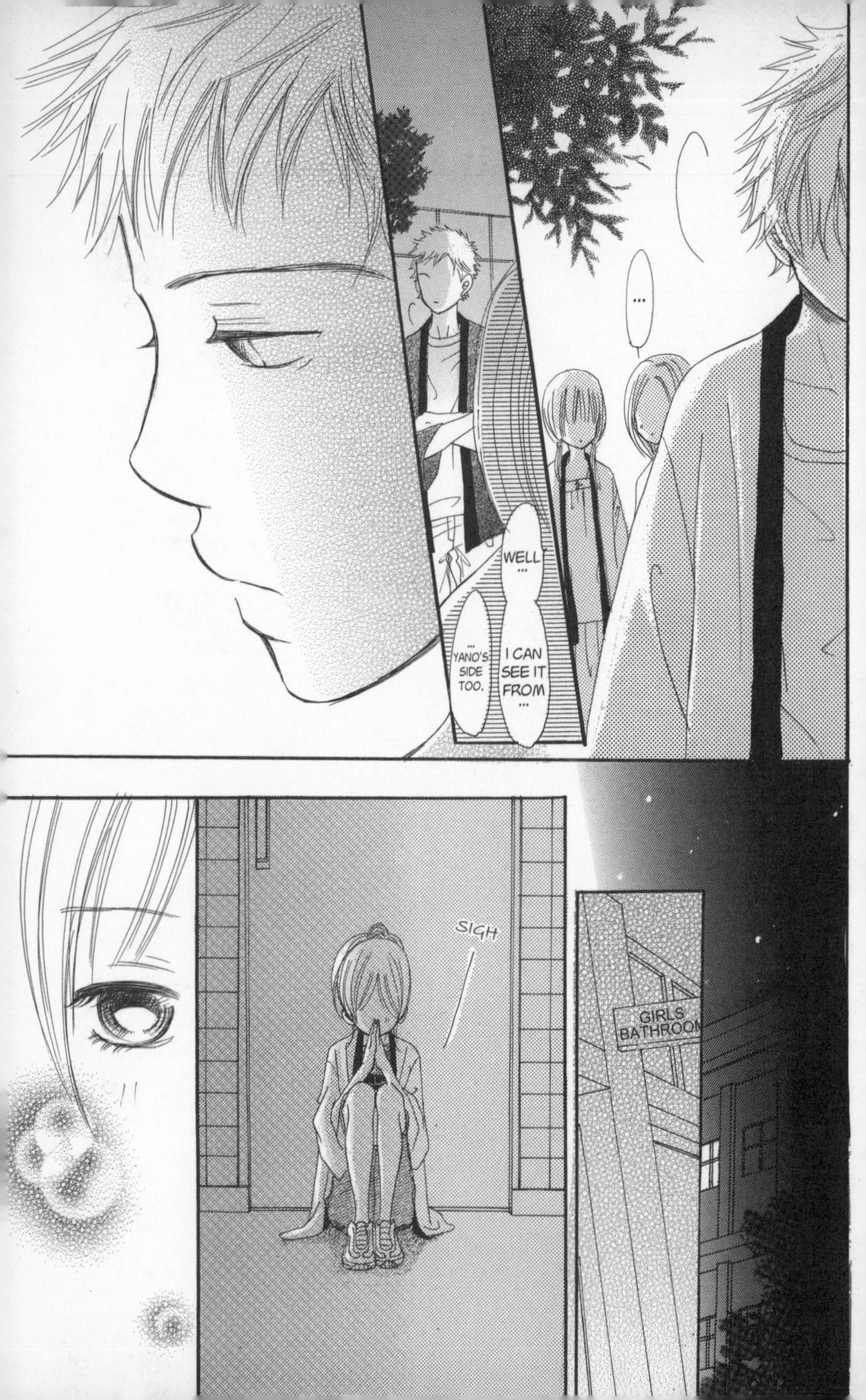
...
WELL ... I CAN SEE IT FROM ...
... YANO'S SIDE TOO.
GIRLS BATHROOM
SIGH

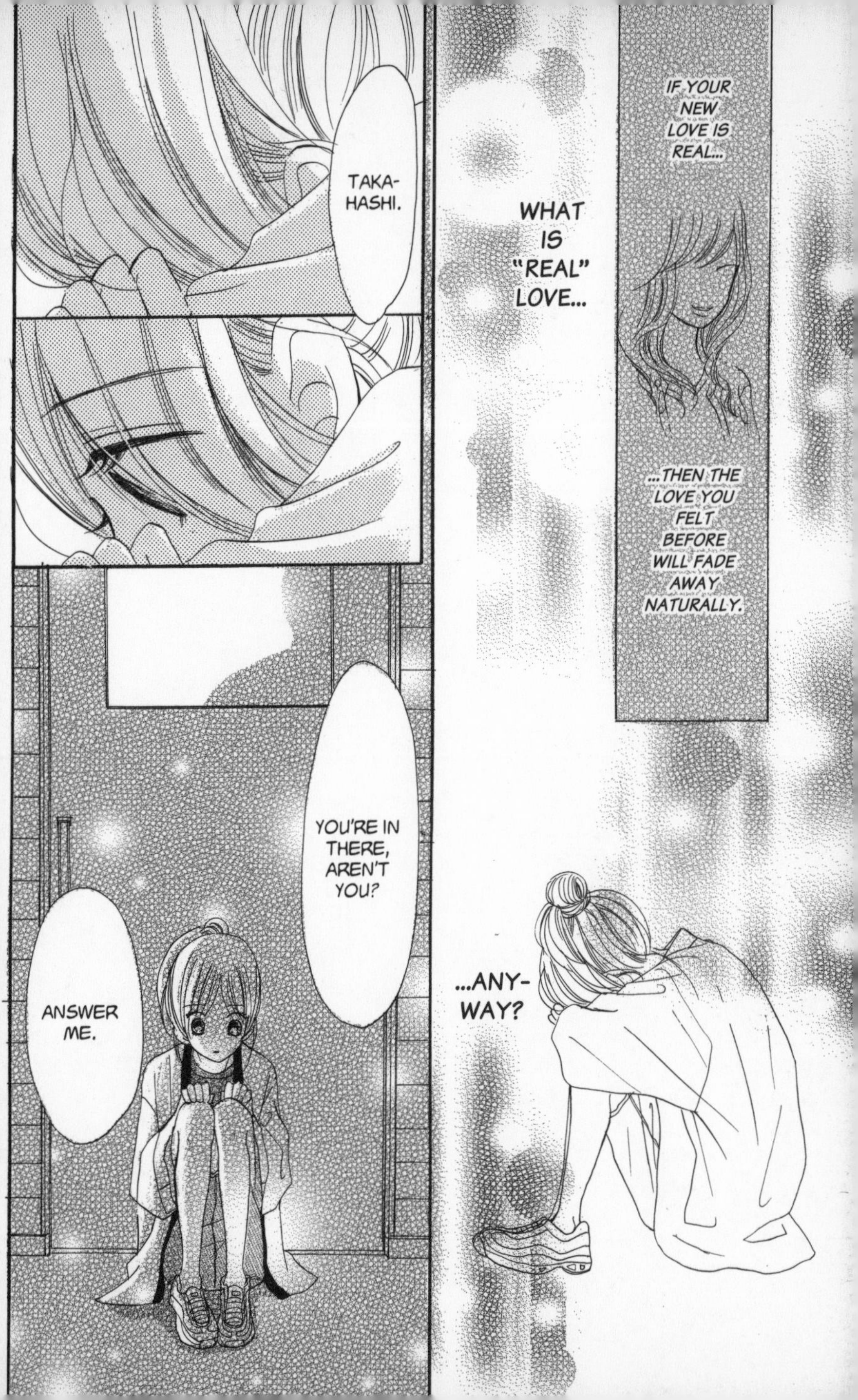
IF YOUR NEW LOVE IS REAL...
...THEN THE LOVE YOU FELT BEFORE WILL FADE AWAY NATURALLY.
WHAT IS "REAL" LOVE...
...ANY-WAY?
TAKA-HASHI.
YOU'RE IN THERE, AREN'T YOU?
ANSWER ME.

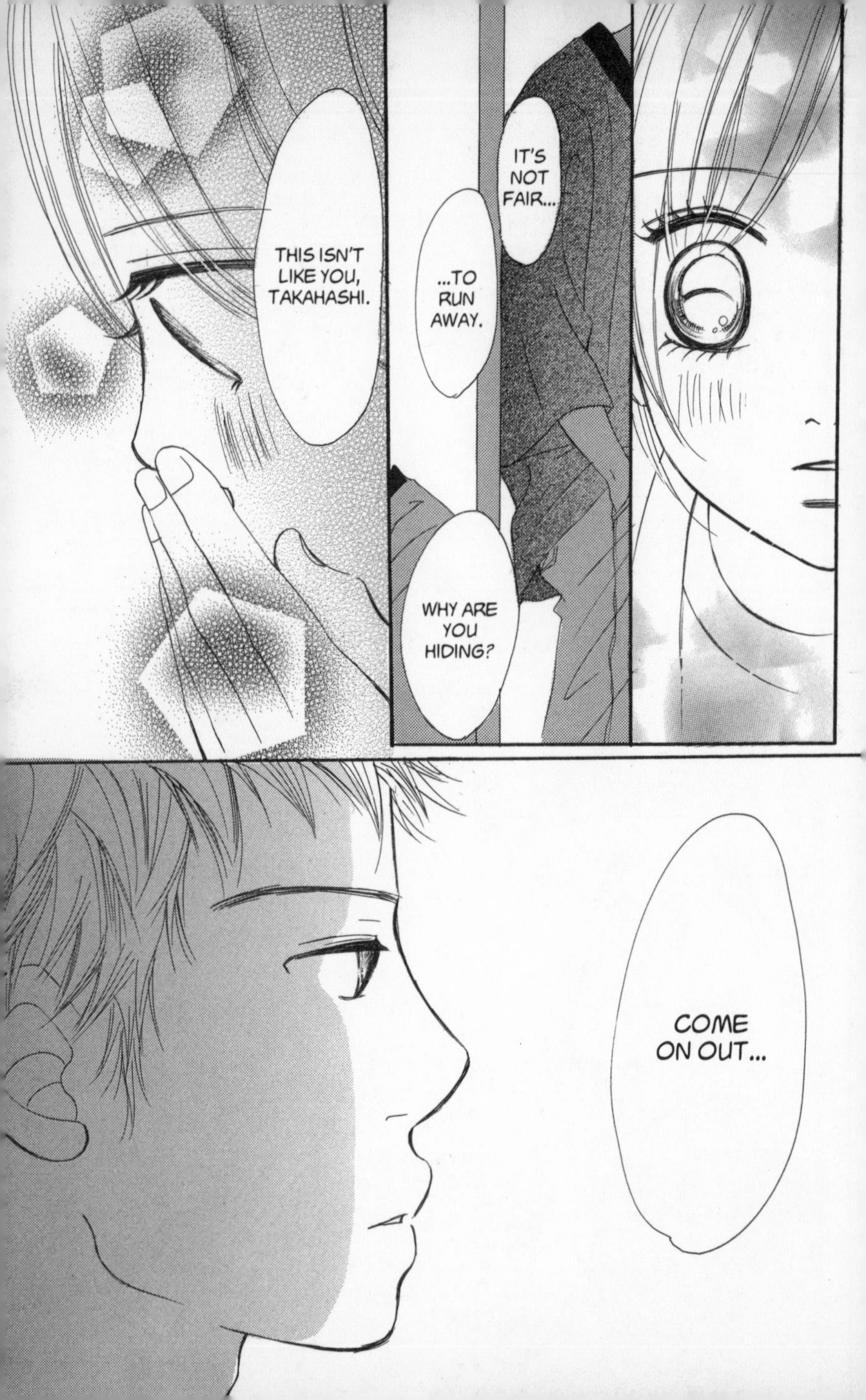
IT'S NOT FAIR...
...TO RUN AWAY.
WHY ARE YOU HIDING?
THIS ISN'T LIKE YOU, TAKAHASHI.
COME ON OUT...

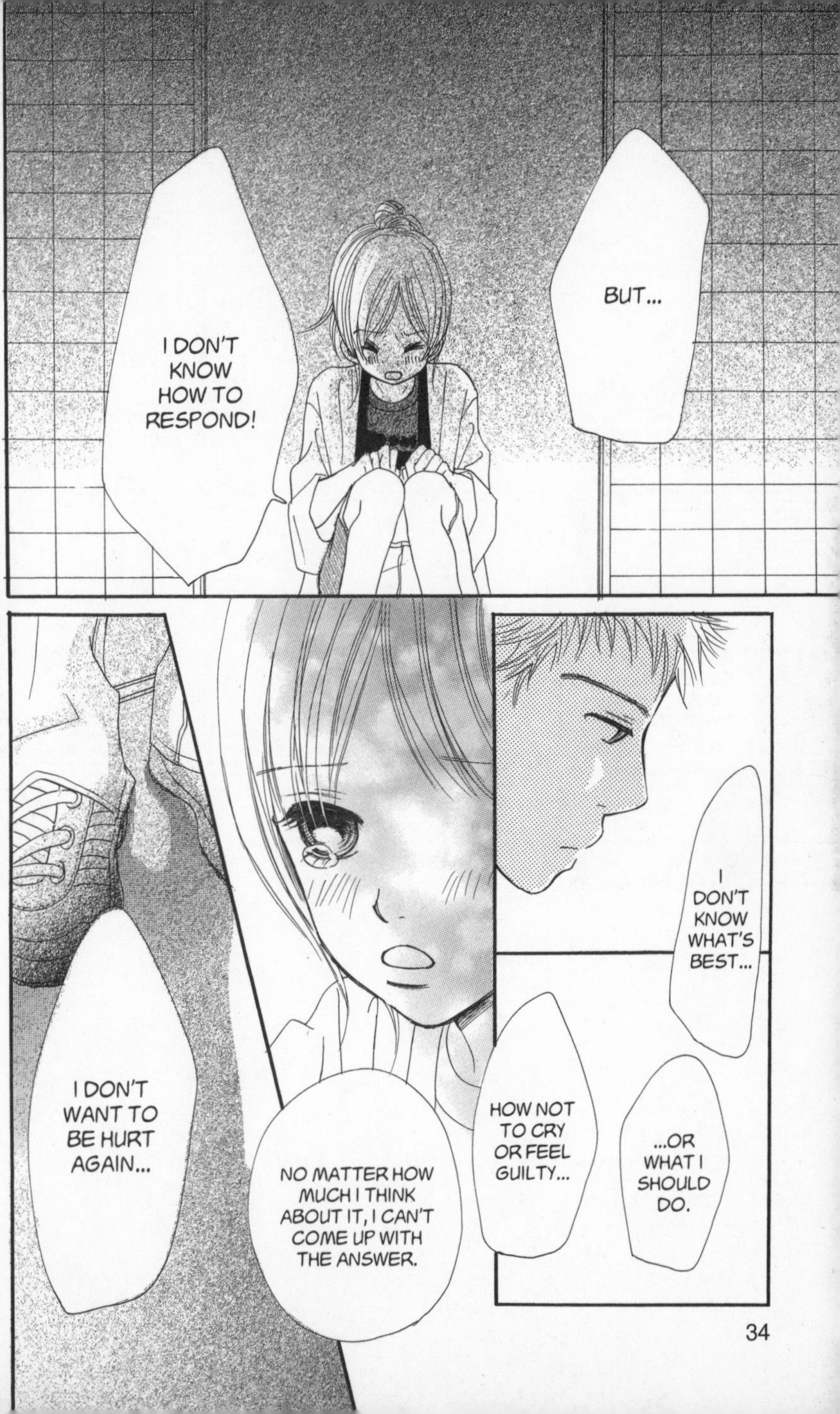
BUT...
I DON'T KNOW HOW TO RESPOND!
I DON'T KNOW WHAT'S BEST...
...OR WHAT I SHOULD DO.
HOW NOT TO CRY OR FEEL GUILTY...
NO MATTER HOW MUCH I THINK ABOUT IT, I CAN'T COME UP WITH THE ANSWER.
I DON'T WANT TO BE HURT AGAIN...

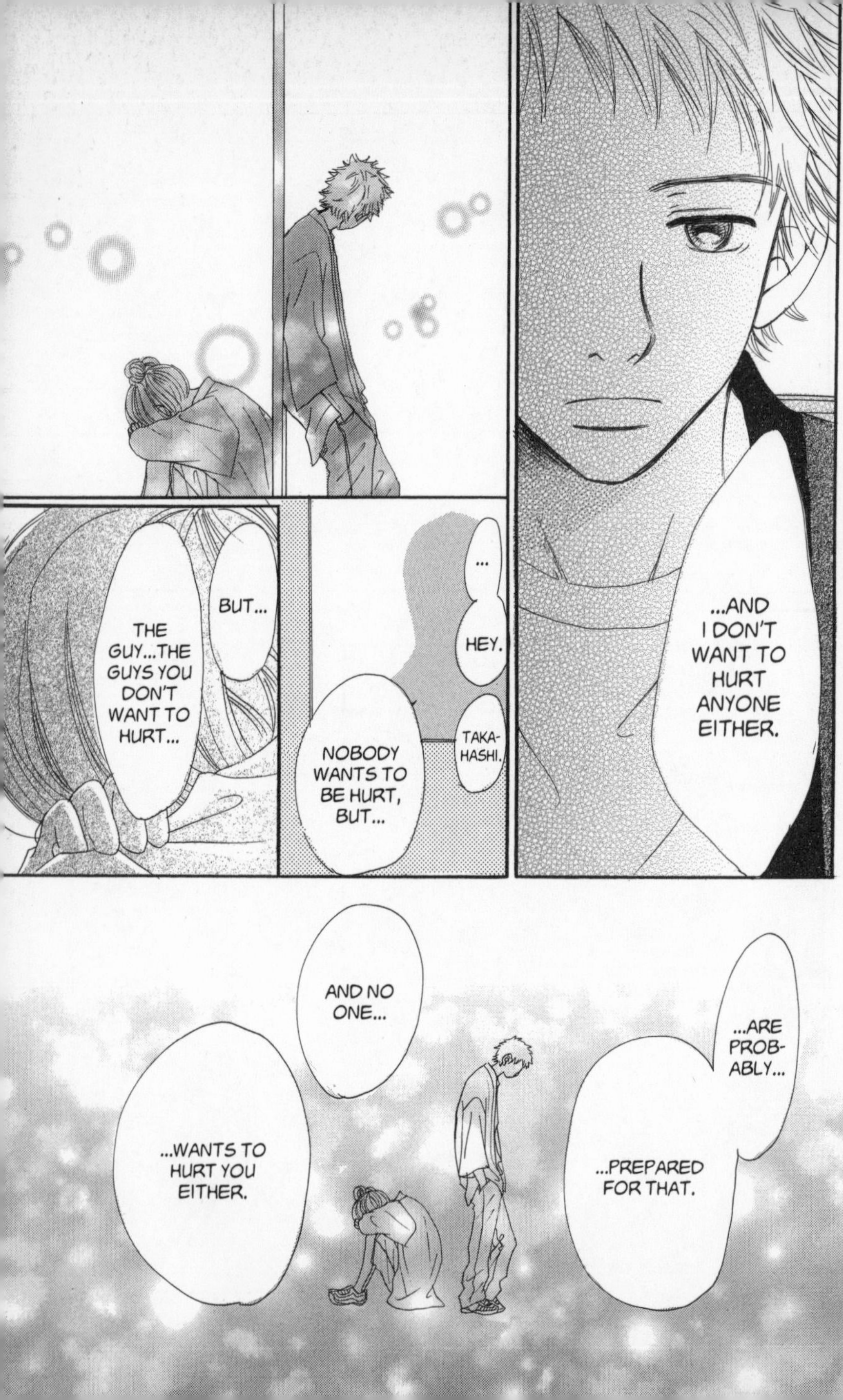
...AND I DON'T WANT TO HURT ANYONE EITHER.
...
HEY.
TAKAHASHI.
NOBODY WANTS TO BE HURT, BUT...
BUT...
THE GUY...THE GUYS YOU DON'T WANT TO HURT...
...ARE PROBABLY...
...PREPARED FOR THAT.
AND NO ONE...
...WANTS TO HURT YOU EITHER.

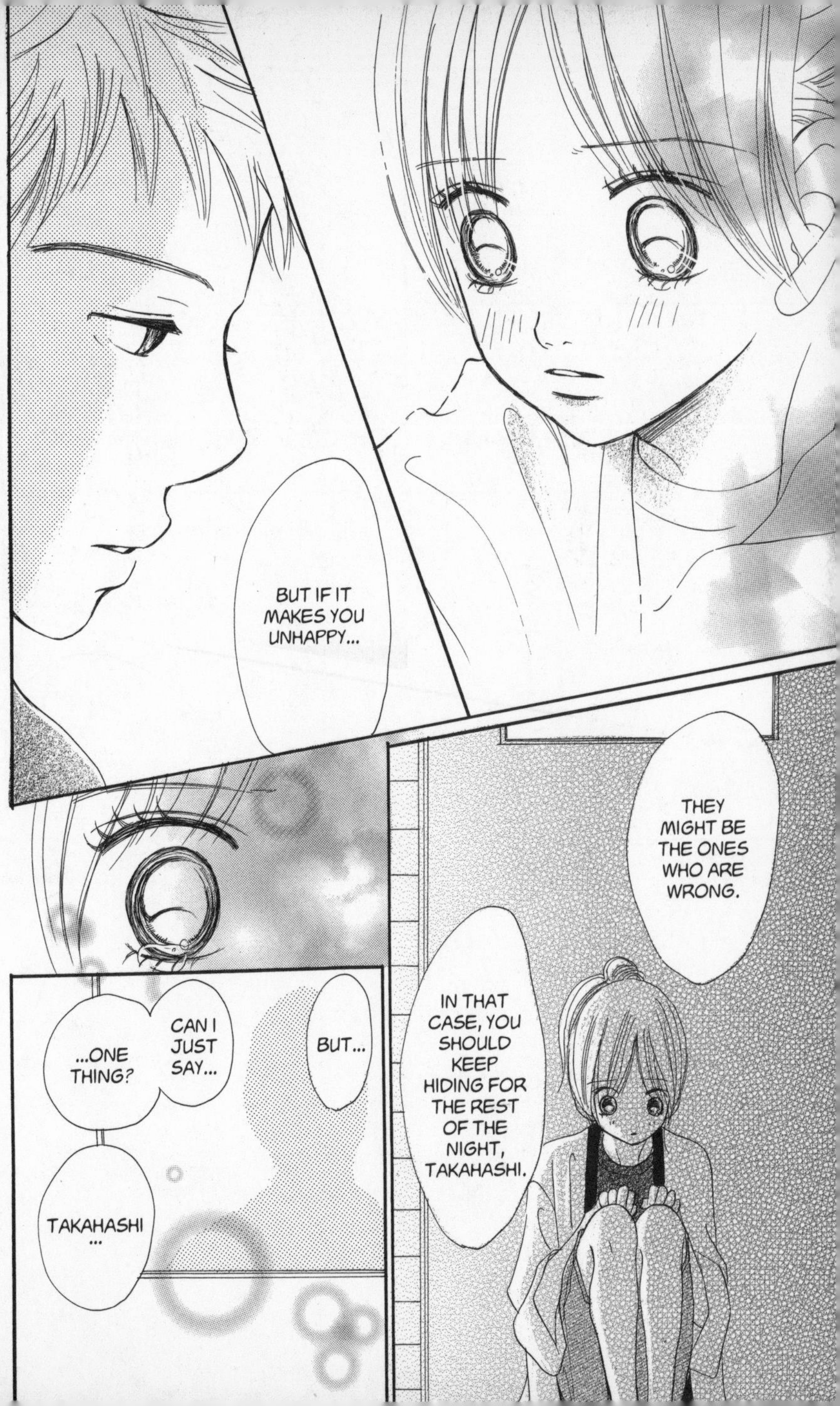
BUT IF IT MAKES YOU UNHAPPY...
THEY MIGHT BE THE ONES WHO ARE WRONG.
IN THAT CASE, YOU SHOULD KEEP HIDING FOR THE REST OF THE NIGHT, TAKAHASHI.
BUT...
CAN I JUST SAY...
...ONE THING?
TAKAHASHI
...

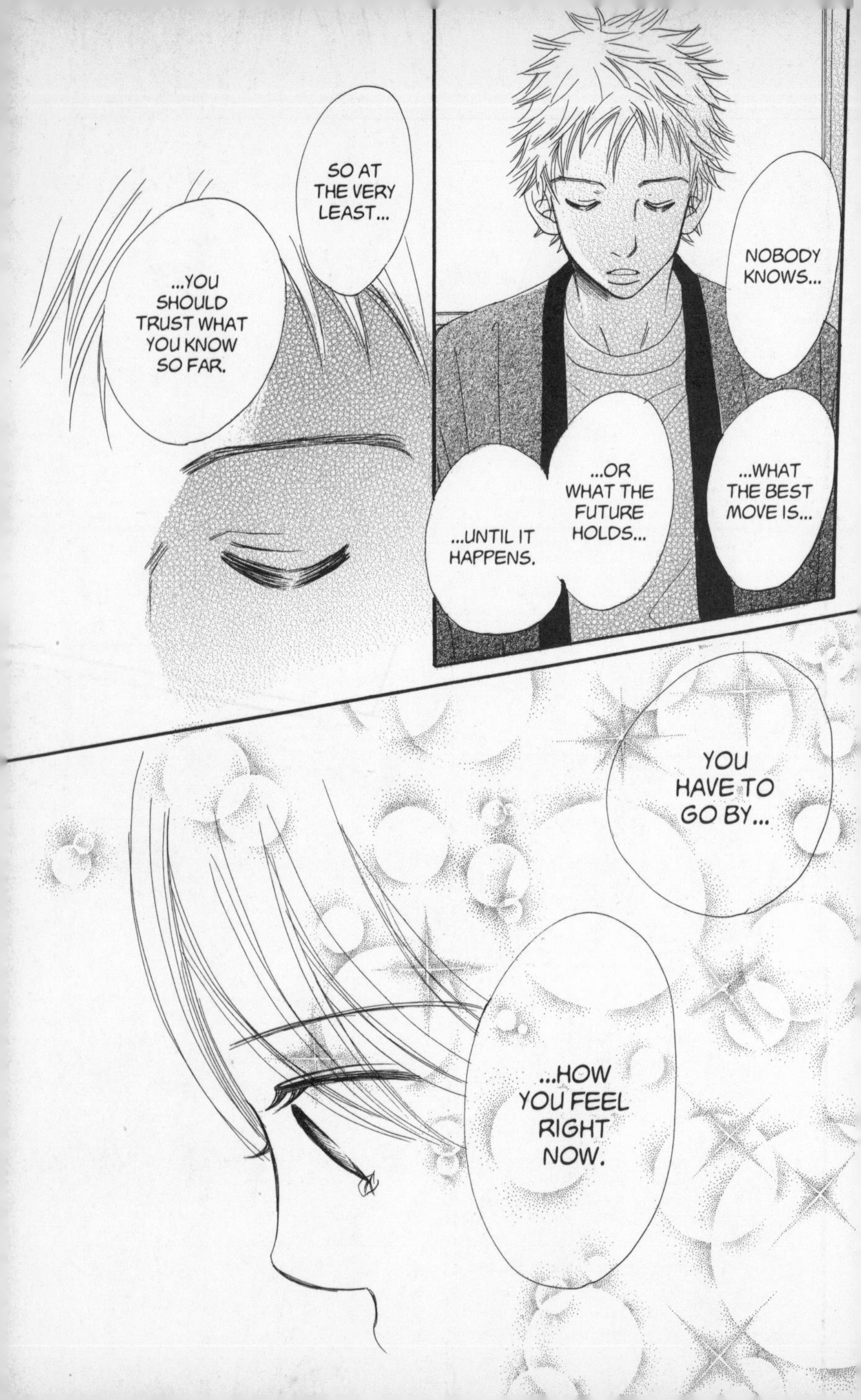
NOBODY KNOWS...
...WHAT THE BEST MOVE IS...
...OR WHAT THE FUTURE HOLDS...
...UNTIL IT HAPPENS.
SO AT THE VERY LEAST...
...YOU SHOULD TRUST WHAT YOU KNOW SO FAR.
YOU HAVE TO GO BY...
...HOW YOU FEEL RIGHT NOW.

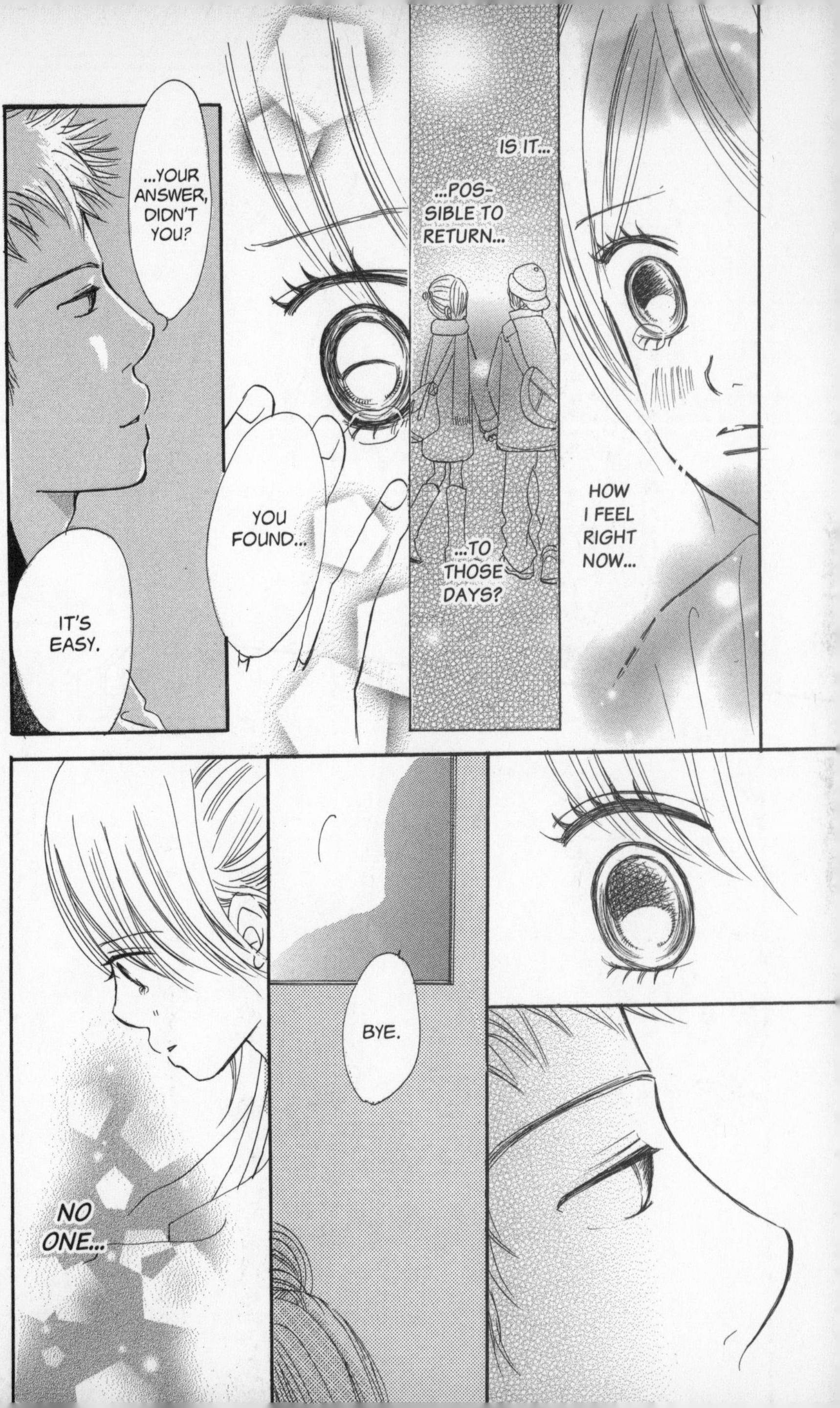
HOW I FEEL RIGHT NOW...
IS IT...
...POS-SIBLE TO RETURN...
...TO THOSE DAYS?
YOU FOUND...
...YOUR ANSWER, DIDN'T YOU?
IT'S EASY.
BYE.
NO ONE...

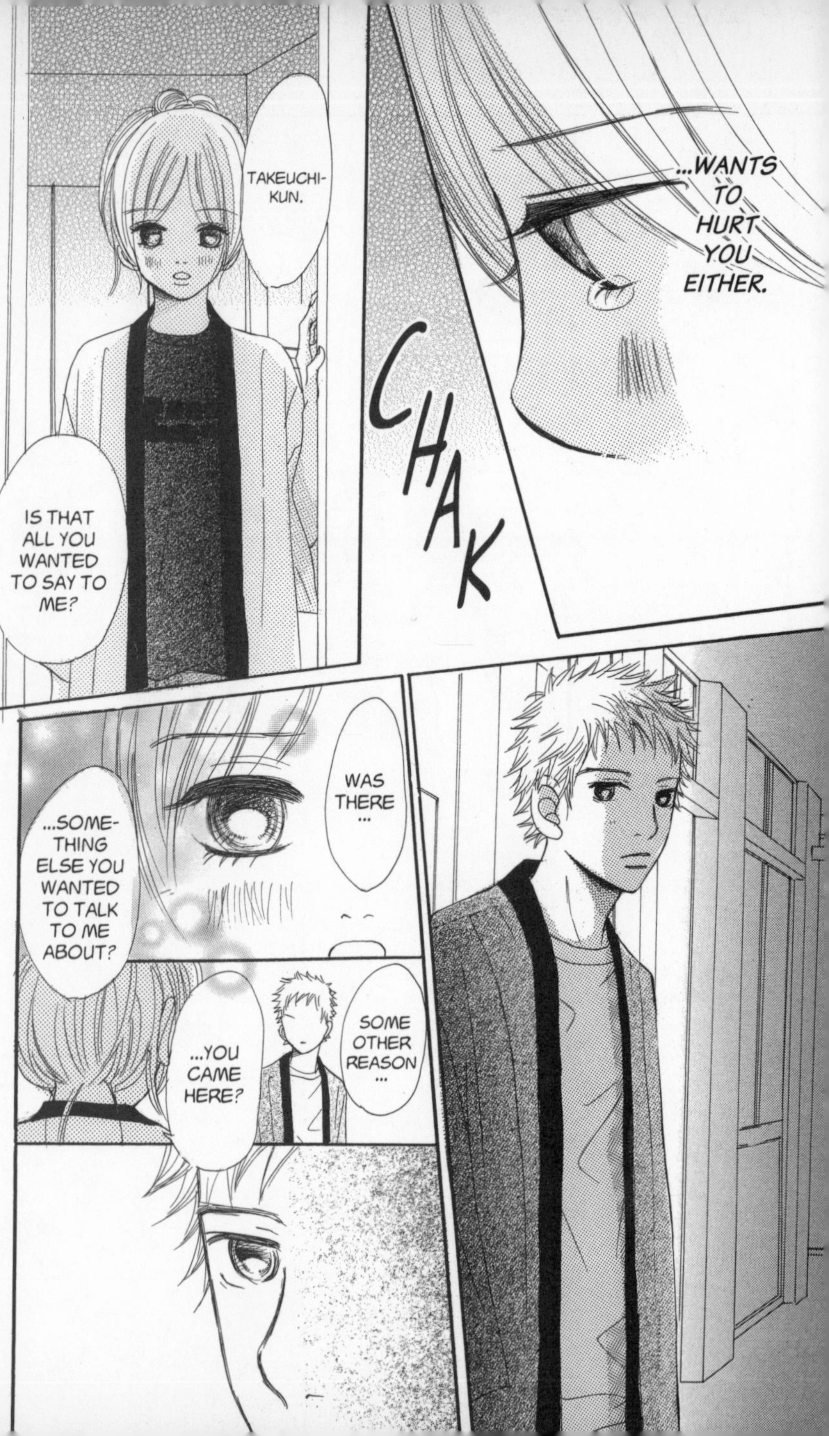
...WANTS TO HURT YOU EITHER.
CHAK
TAKEUCHI-KUN.
IS THAT ALL YOU WANTED TO SAY TO ME?
WAS THERE...
...SOME-THING ELSE YOU WANTED TO TALK TO ME ABOUT?
SOME OTHER REASON...
...YOU CAME HERE?

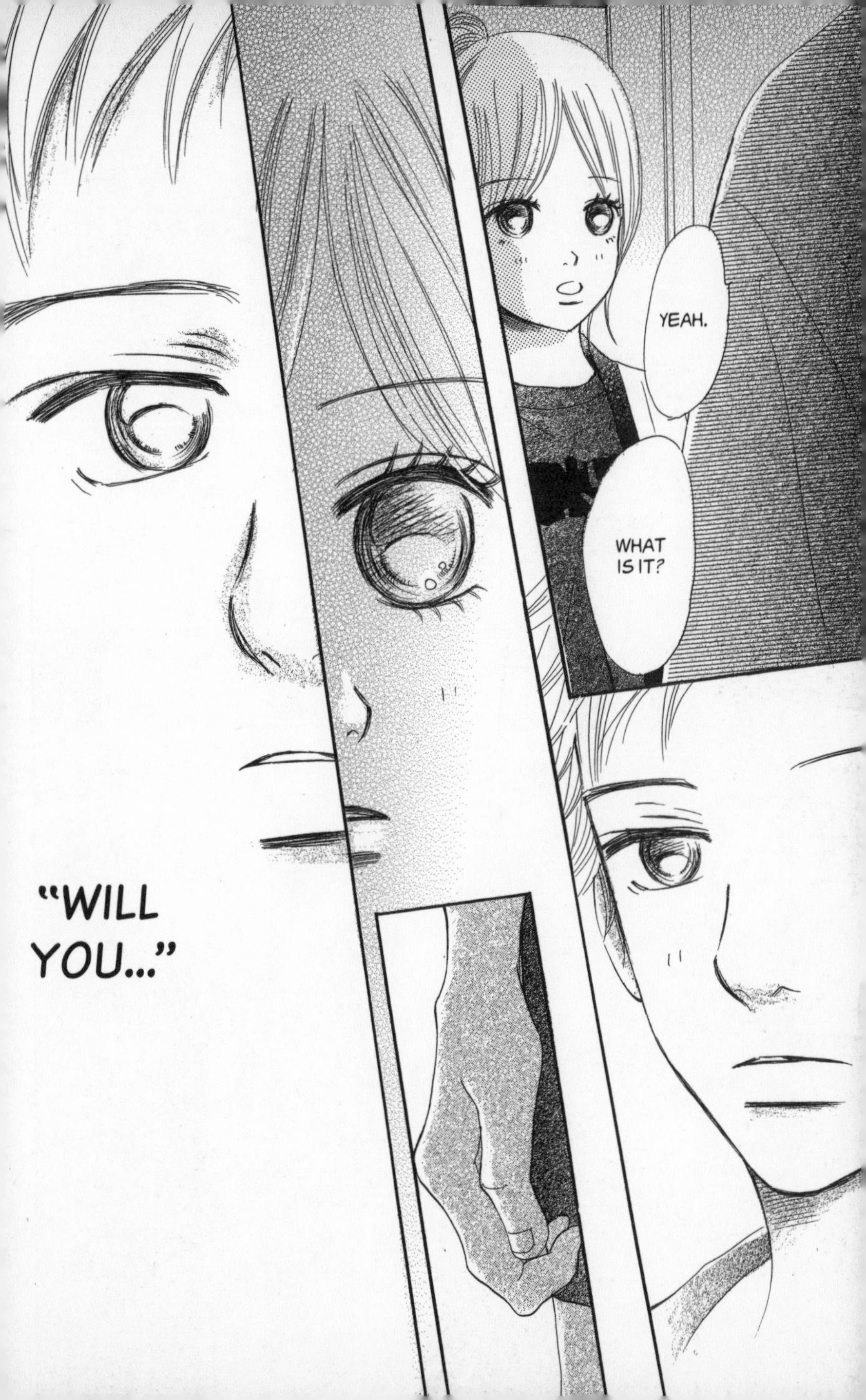
YEAH.
WHAT IS IT?
"WILL YOU..."

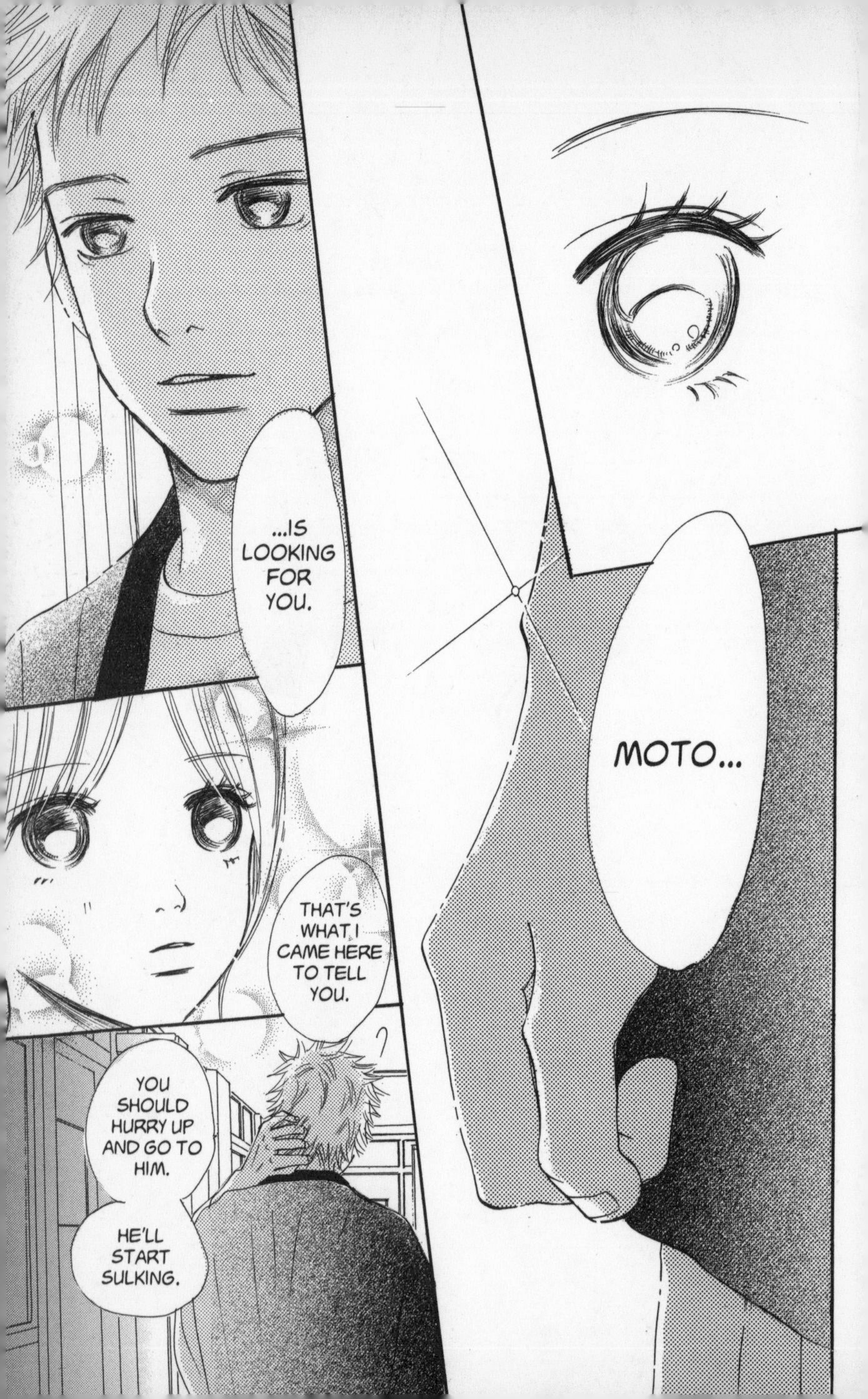
MOTO...
...IS LOOKING FOR YOU.
THAT'S WHAT I CAME HERE TO TELL YOU.
YOU SHOULD HURRY UP AND GO TO HIM.
HE'LL START SULKING.

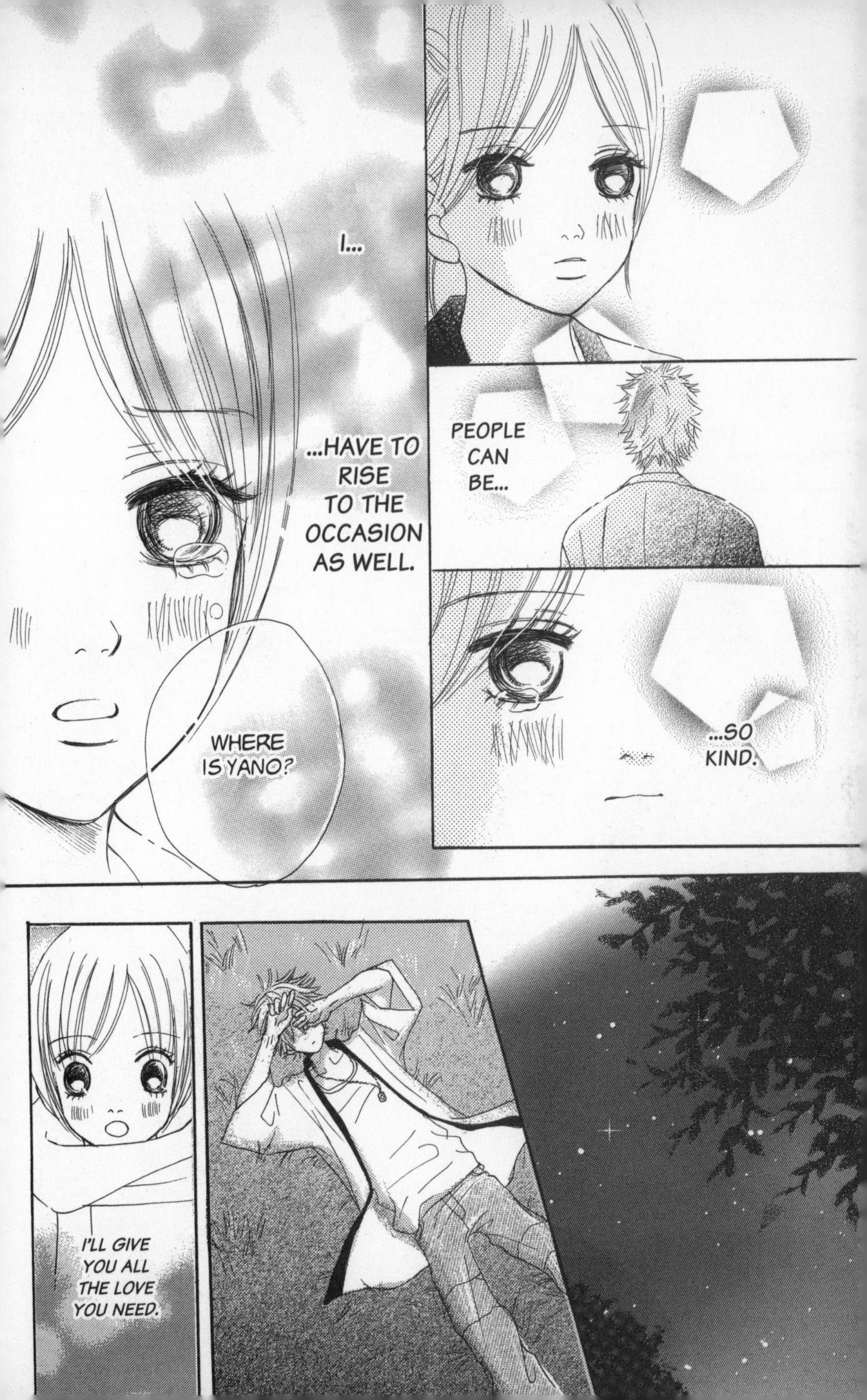
PEOPLE CAN BE...
...SO KIND.
I...
...HAVE TO RISE TO THE OCCASION AS WELL.
WHERE IS YANO?
I'LL GIVE YOU ALL THE LOVE YOU NEED.

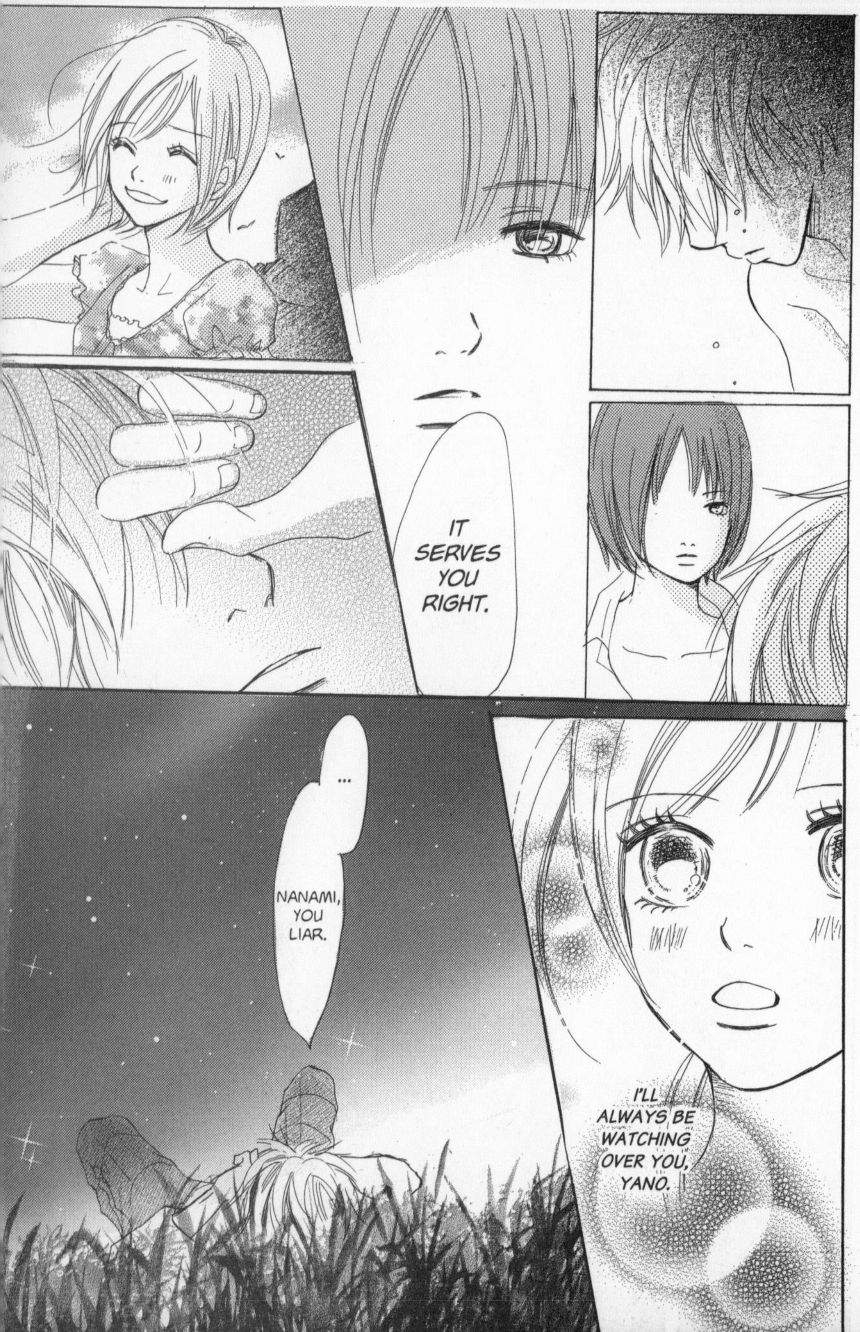
IT SERVES YOU RIGHT.
I'LL ALWAYS BE WATCHING OVER YOU, YANO.
...
NANAMI, YOU LIAR.

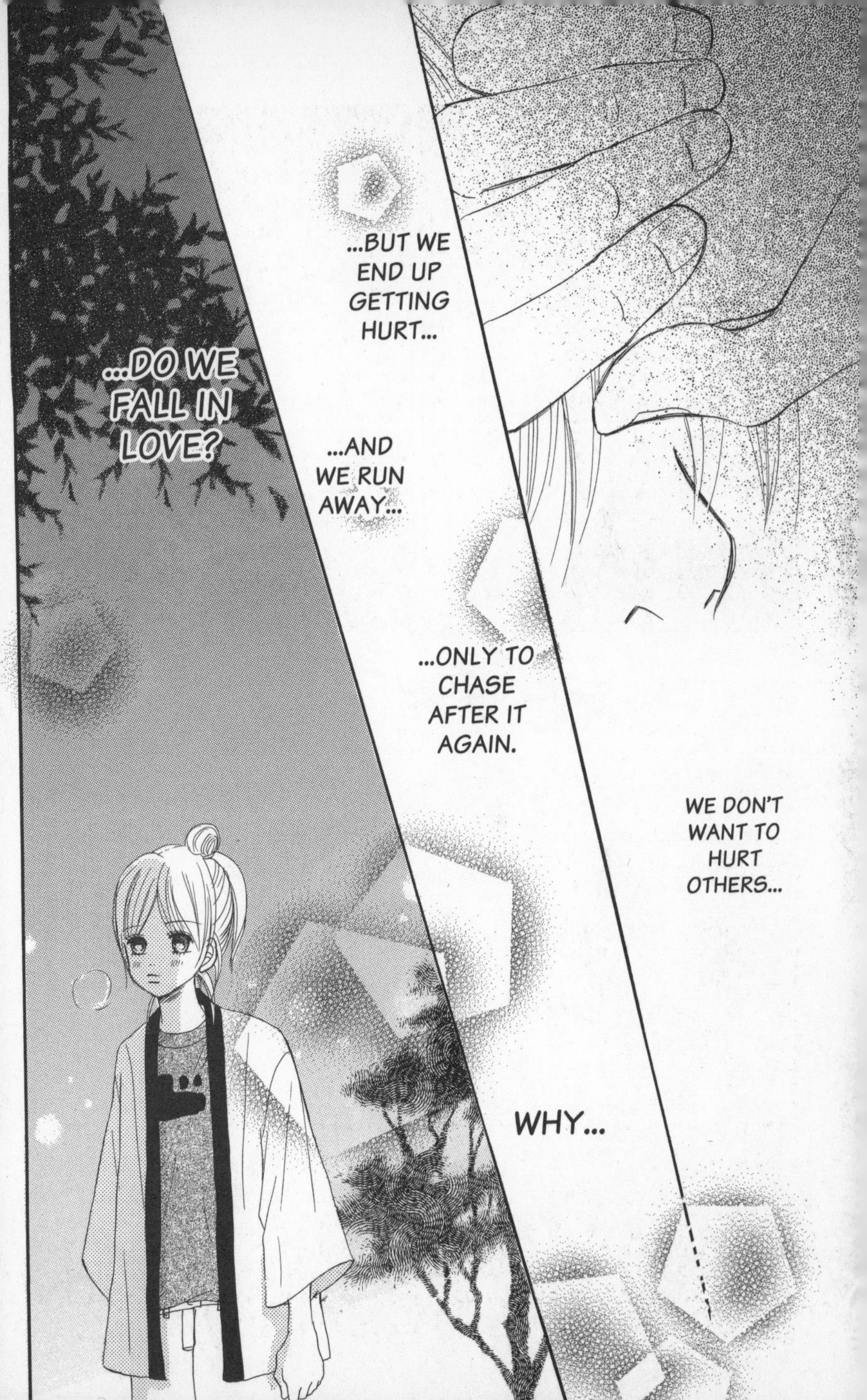
WE DON'T WANT TO HURT OTHERS...
...BUT WE END UP GETTING HURT...
...AND WE RUN AWAY...
...ONLY TO CHASE AFTER IT AGAIN.
WHY...
...DO WE FALL IN LOVE?

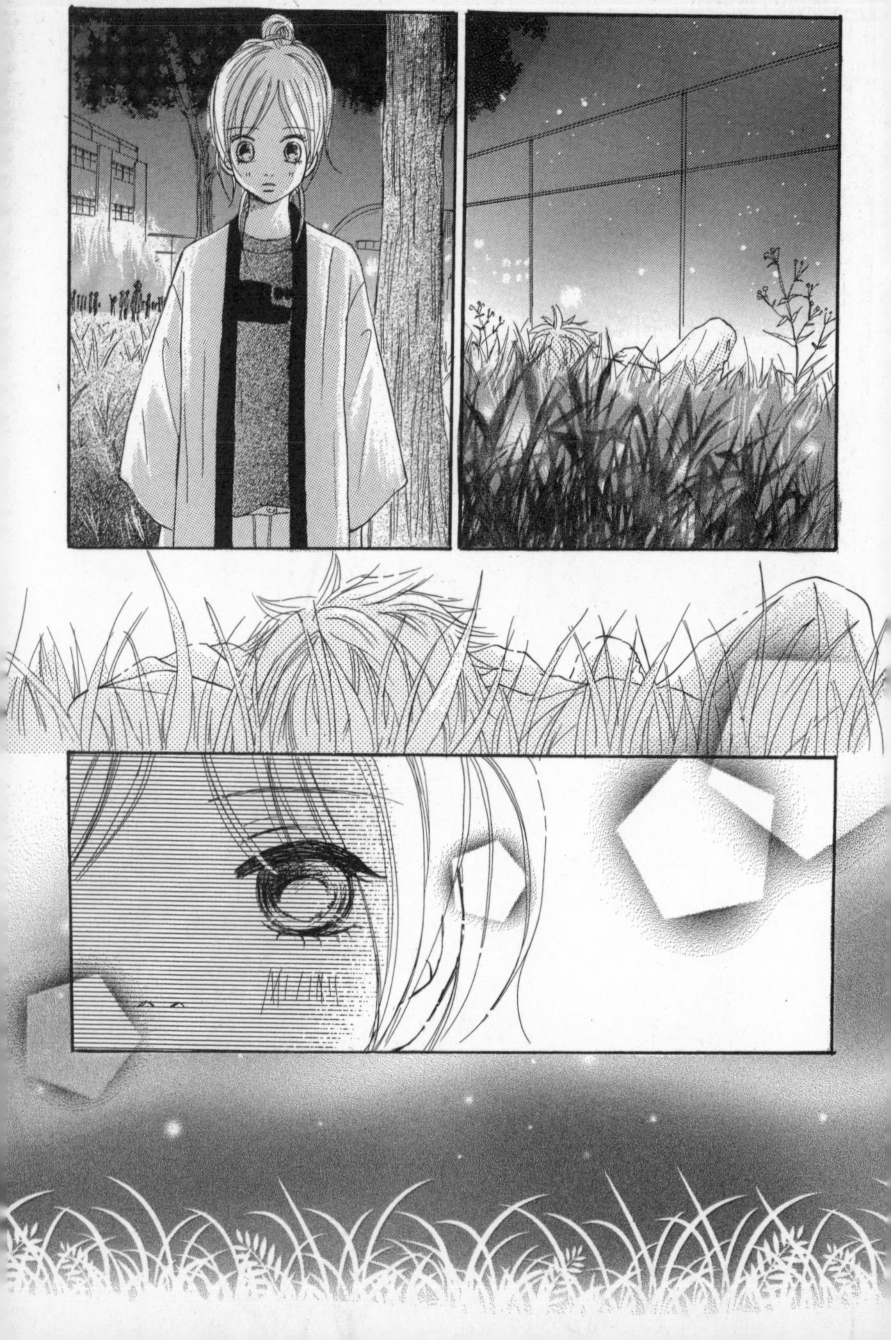

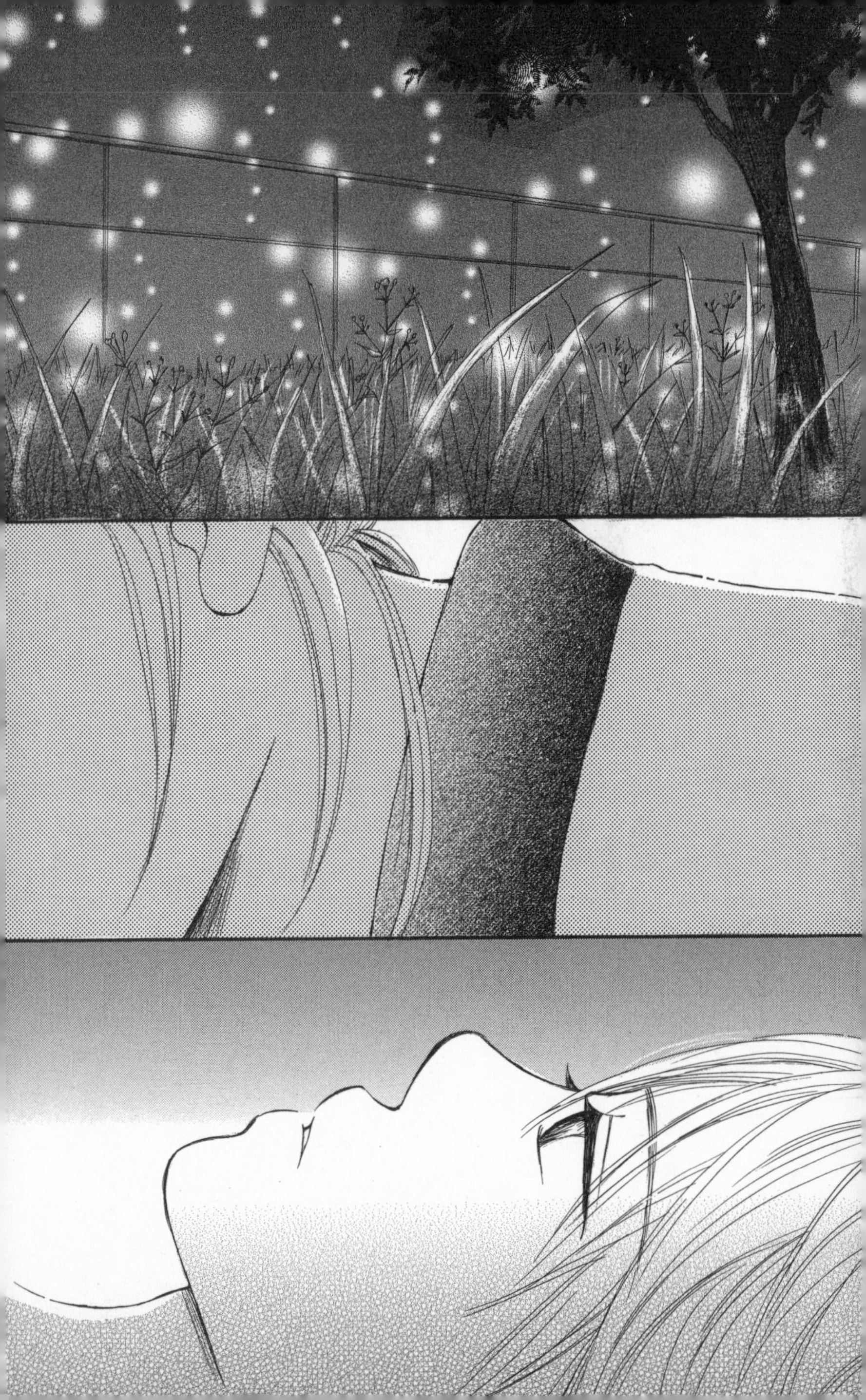

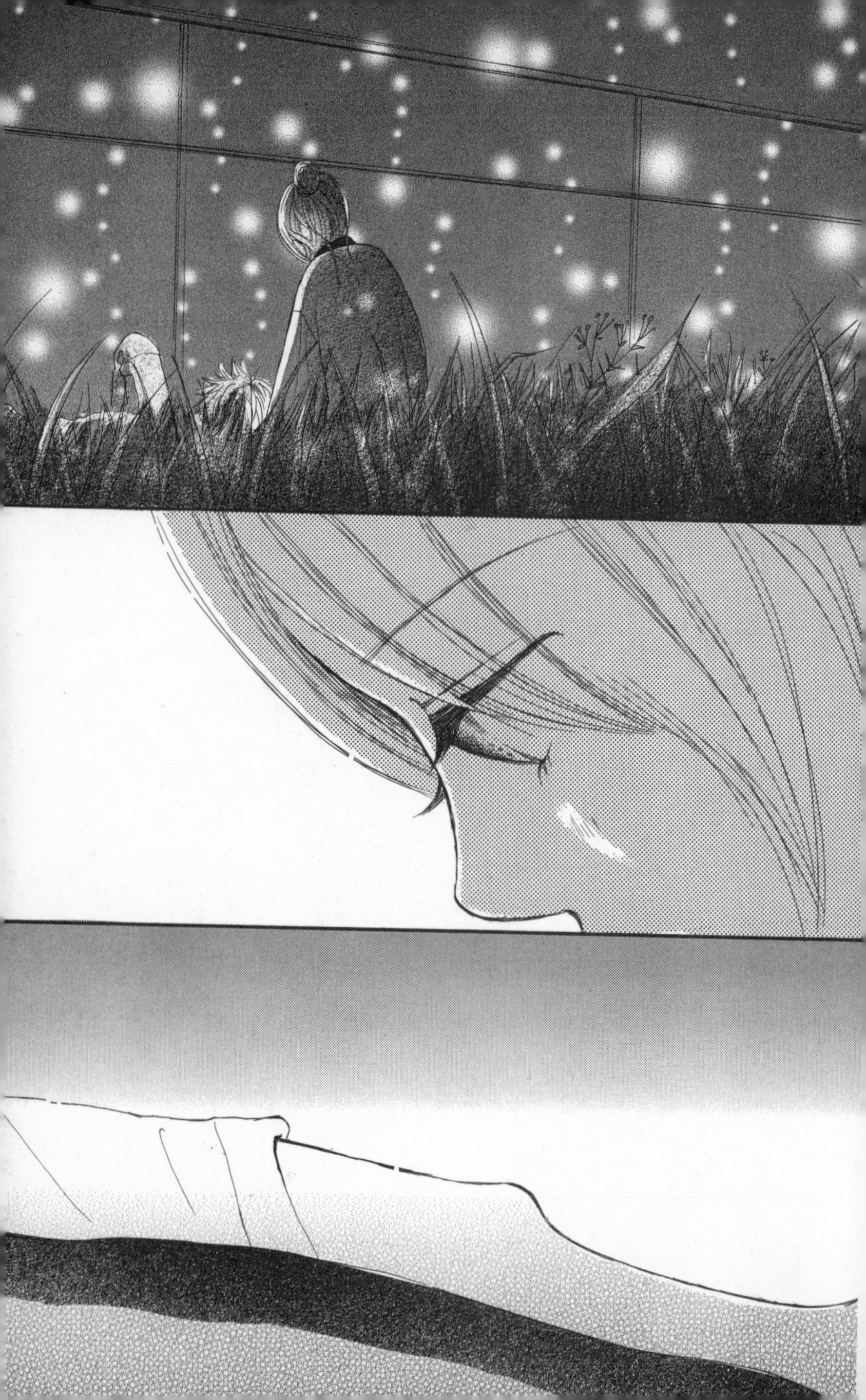

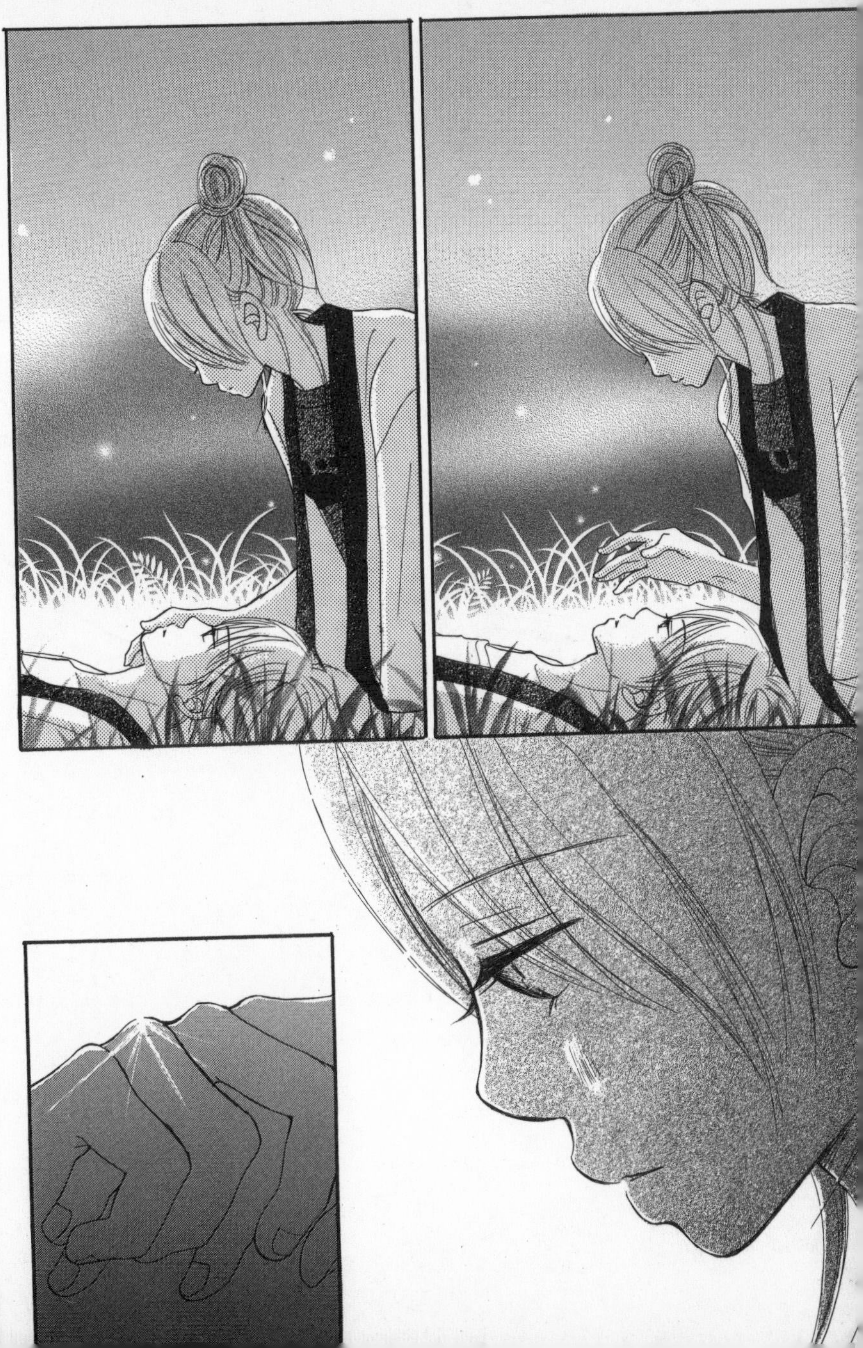

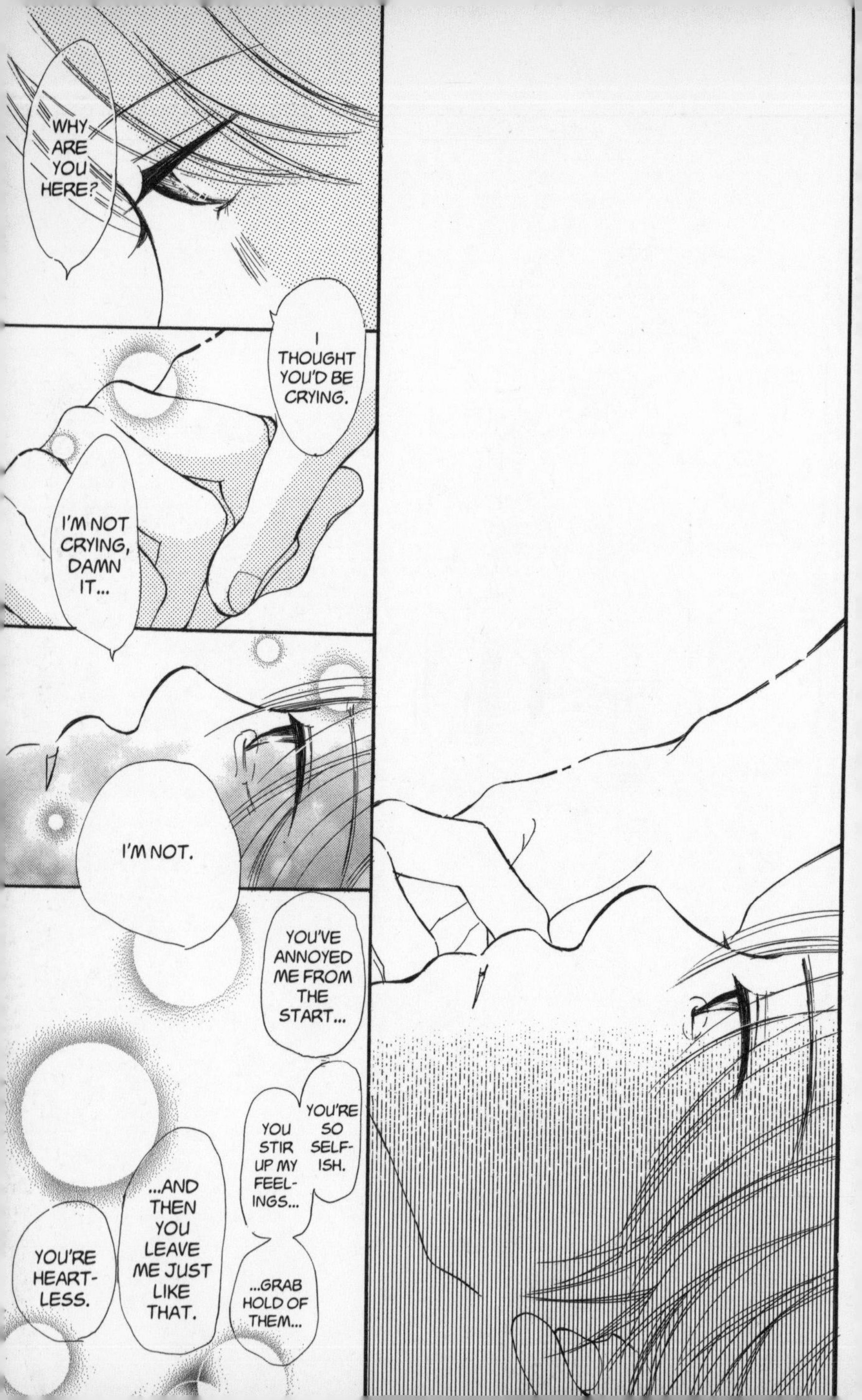
WHY ARE YOU HERE?
I THOUGHT YOU'D BE CRYING.
I'M NOT CRYING, DAMN IT...
I'M NOT.
YOU'VE ANNOYED ME FROM THE START...
YOU'RE SO SELF-ISH.
YOU STIR UP MY FEEL-INGS...
...GRAB HOLD OF THEM...
...AND THEN YOU LEAVE ME JUST LIKE THAT.
YOU'RE HEART-LESS.

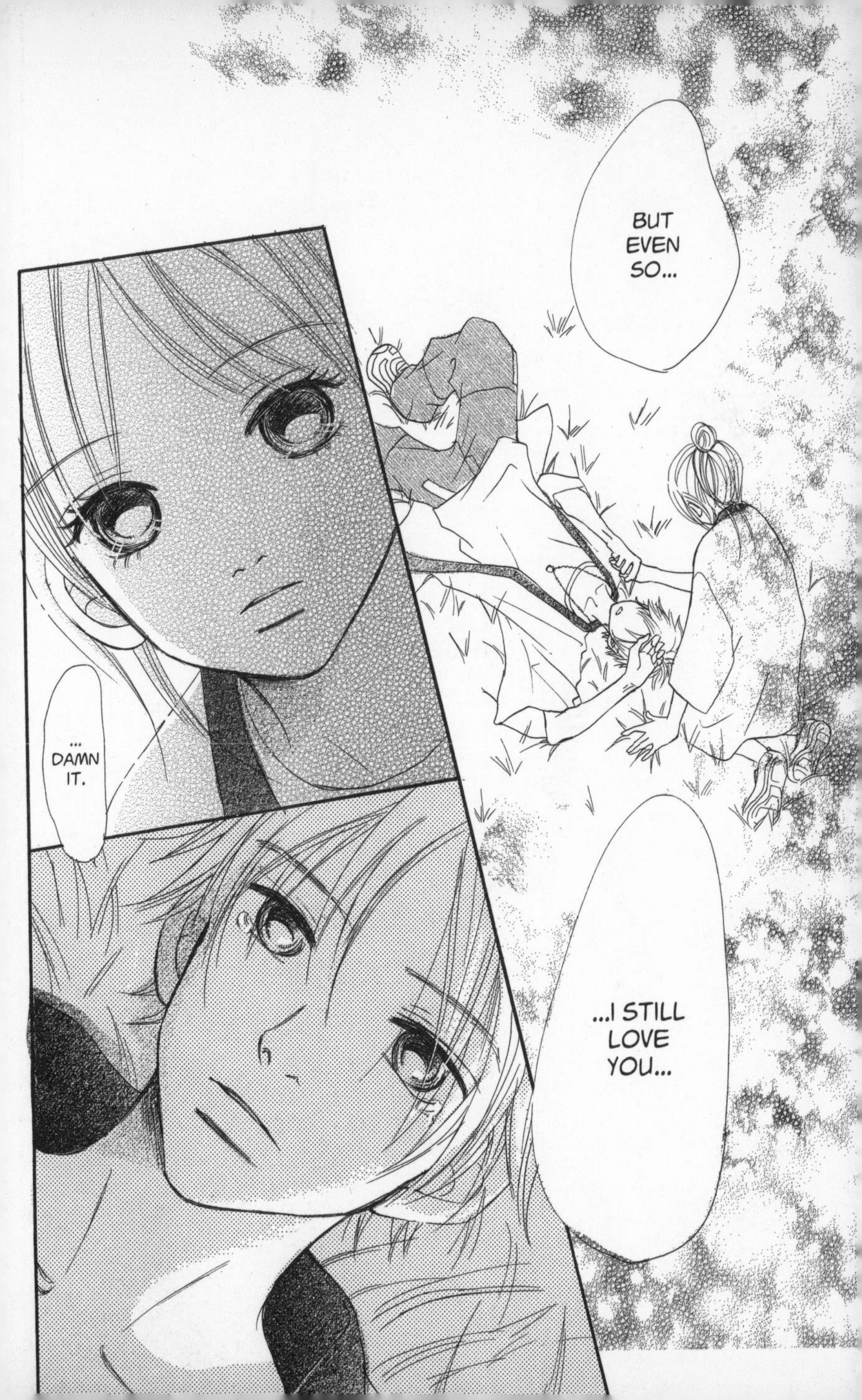
BUT EVEN SO...
...I STILL LOVE YOU...
...DAMN IT.

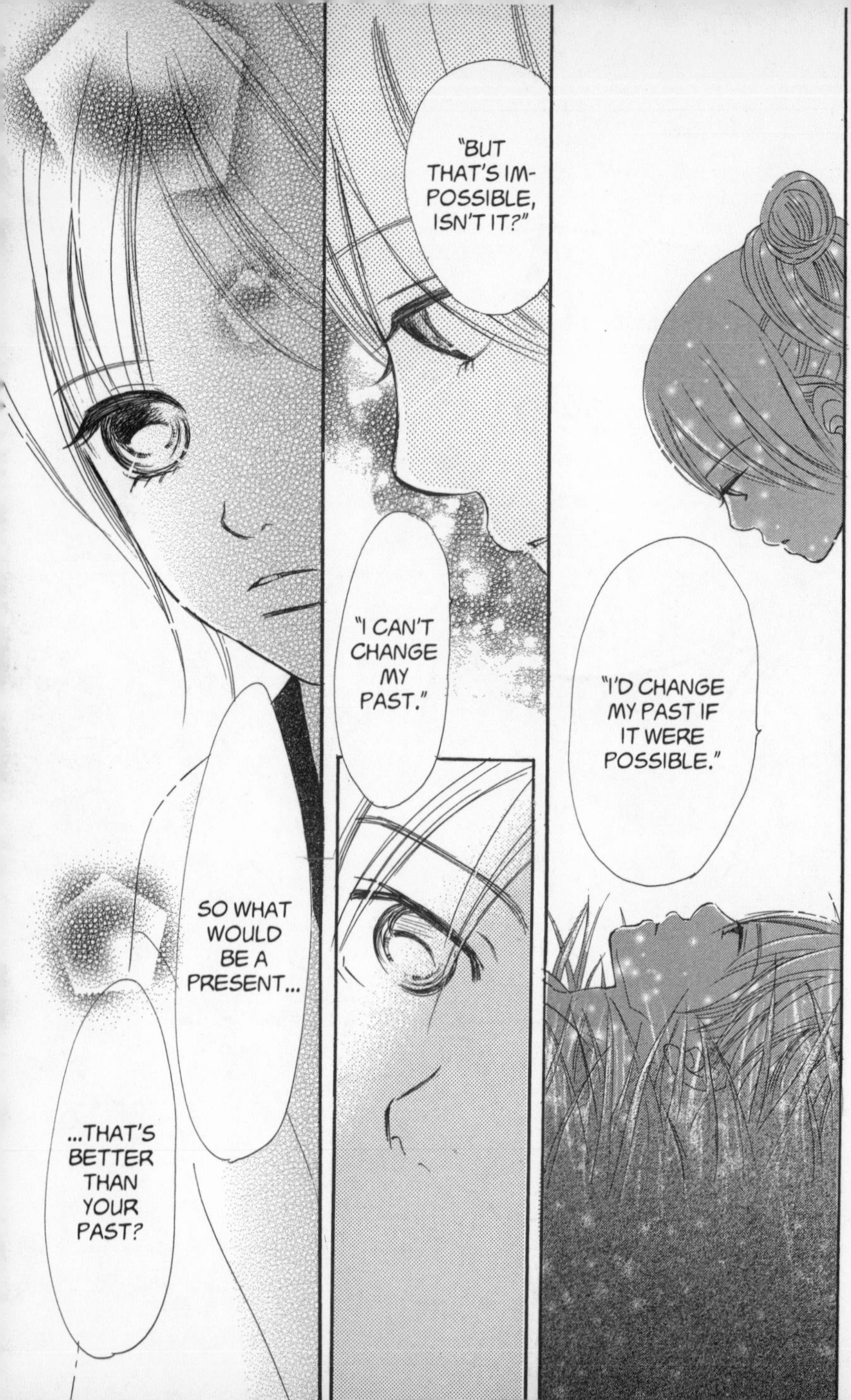
"I'D CHANGE MY PAST IF IT WERE POSSIBLE."
"BUT THAT'S IMPOSSIBLE, ISN'T IT?"
"I CAN'T CHANGE MY PAST."
SO WHAT WOULD BE A PRESENT...
...THAT'S BETTER THAN YOUR PAST?

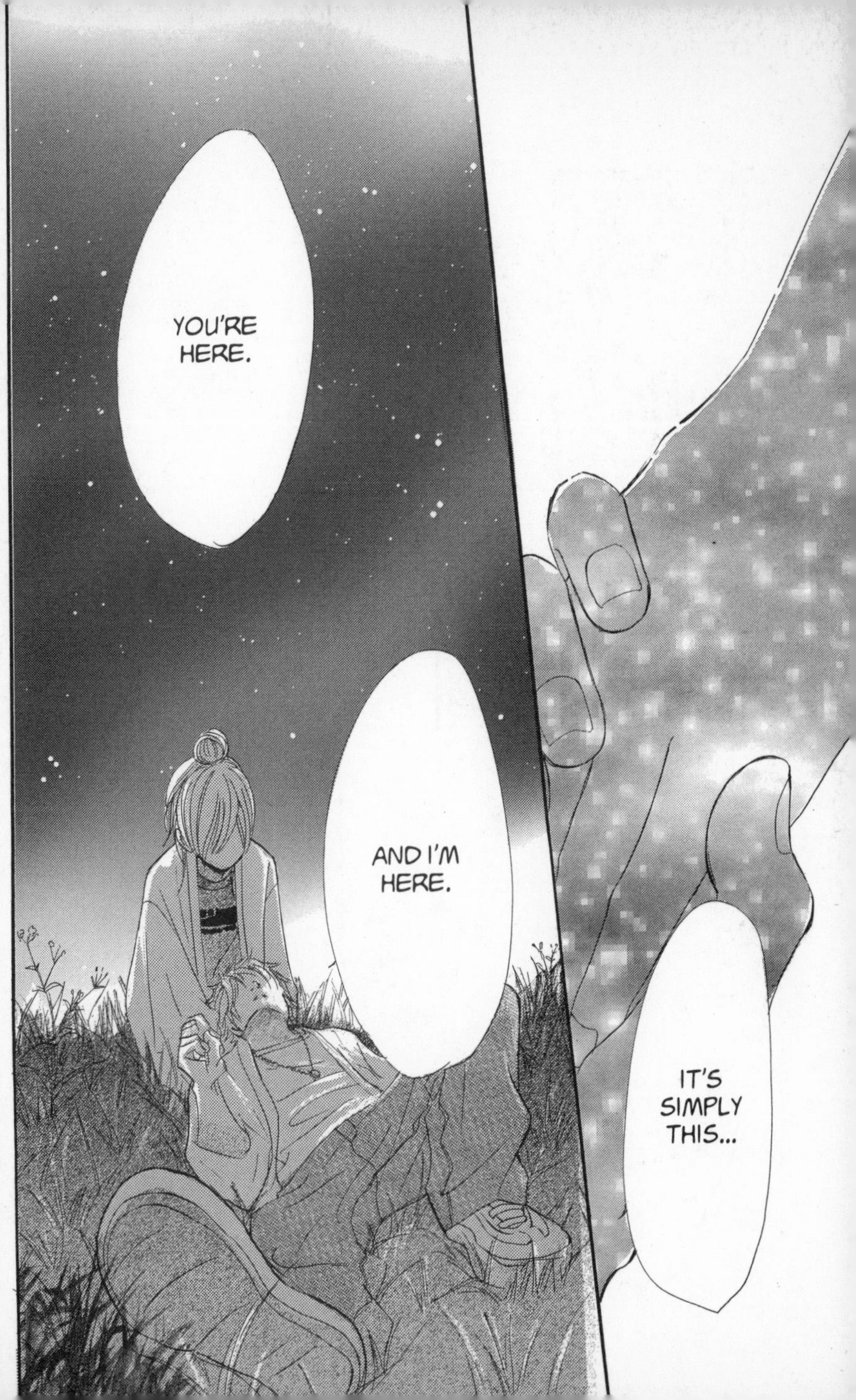
IT'S SIMPLY THIS...
YOU'RE HERE.
AND I'M HERE.

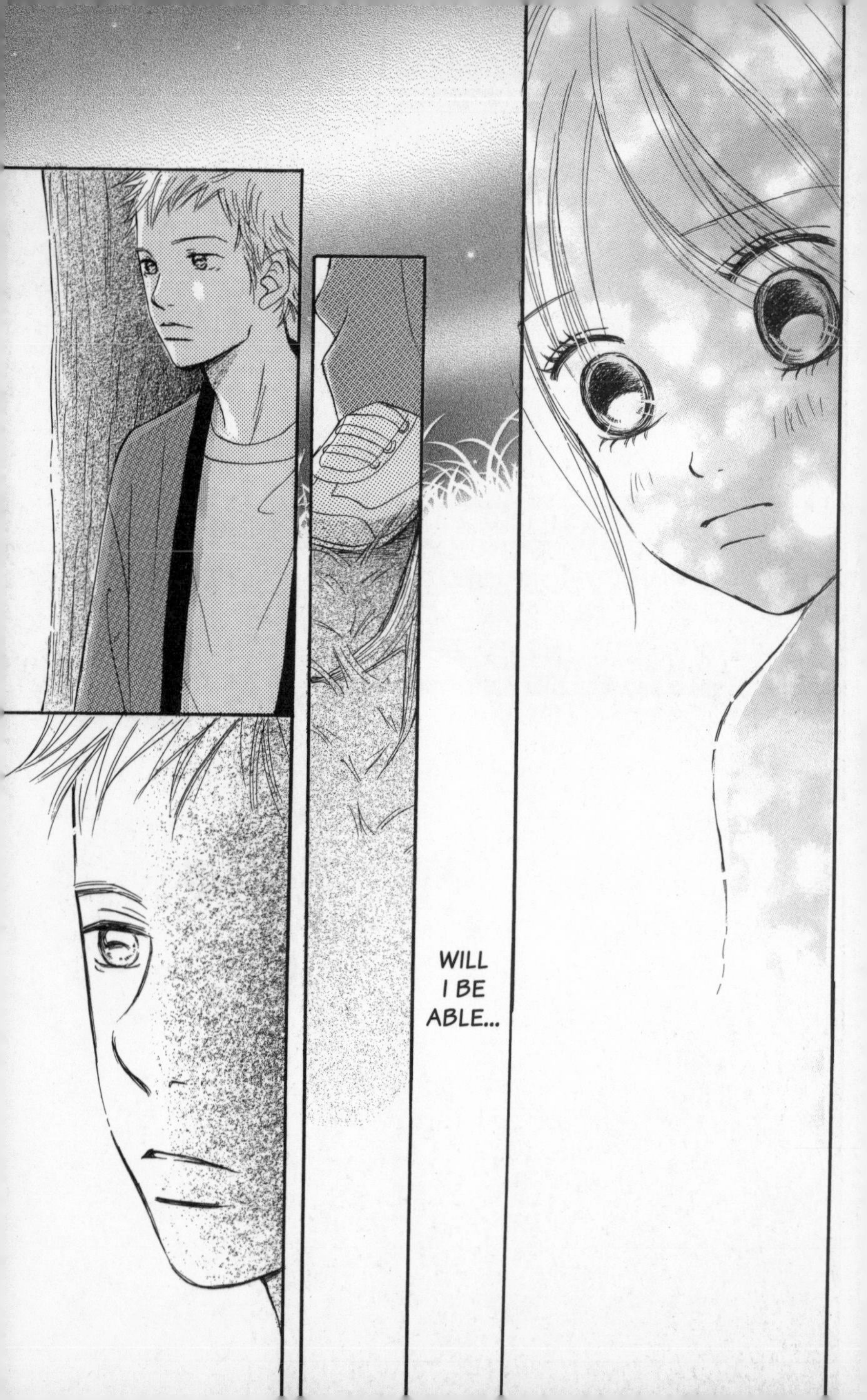
WILL
I BE
ABLE...

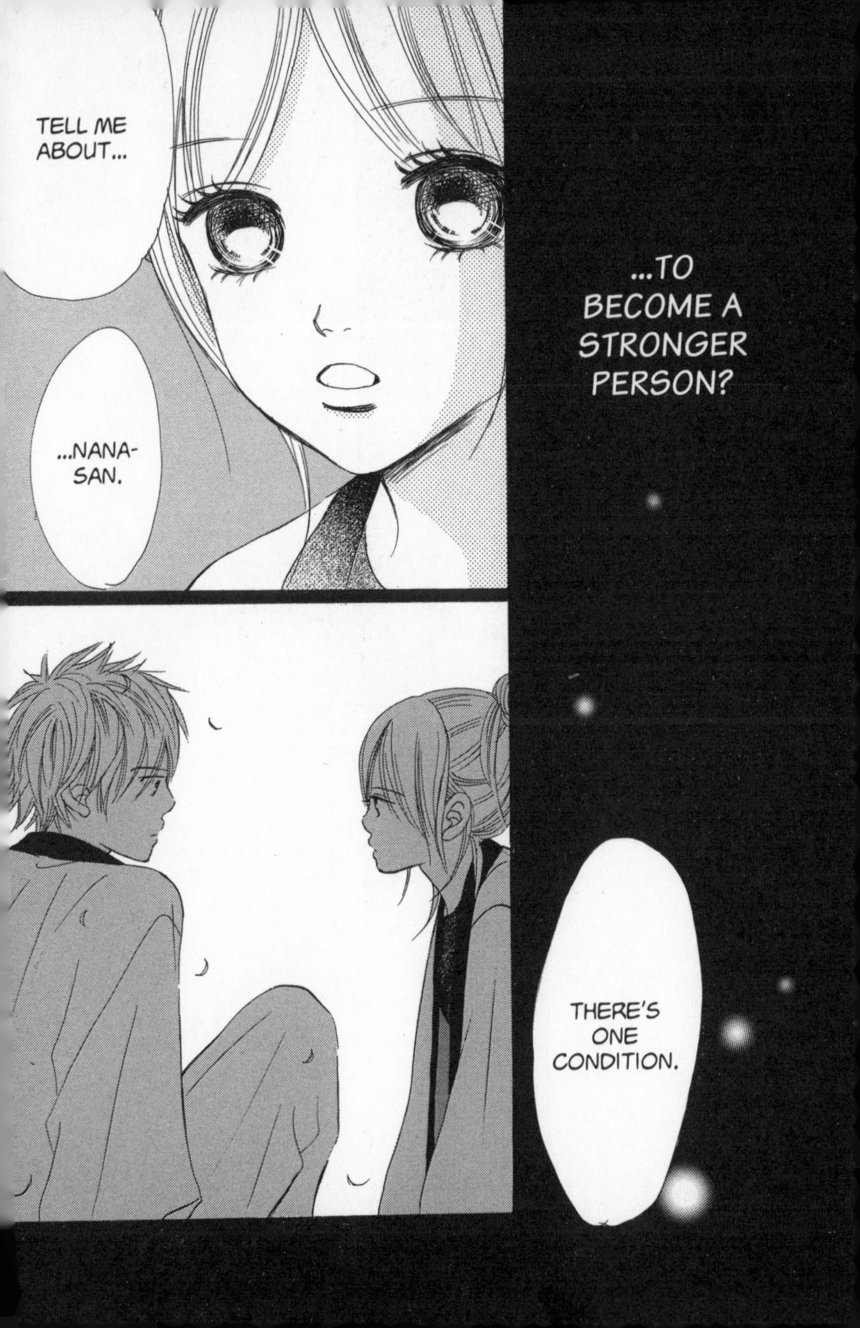
TELL ME ABOUT...
...NANA-SAN.
...TO BECOME A STRONGER PERSON?
THERE'S ONE CONDITION.

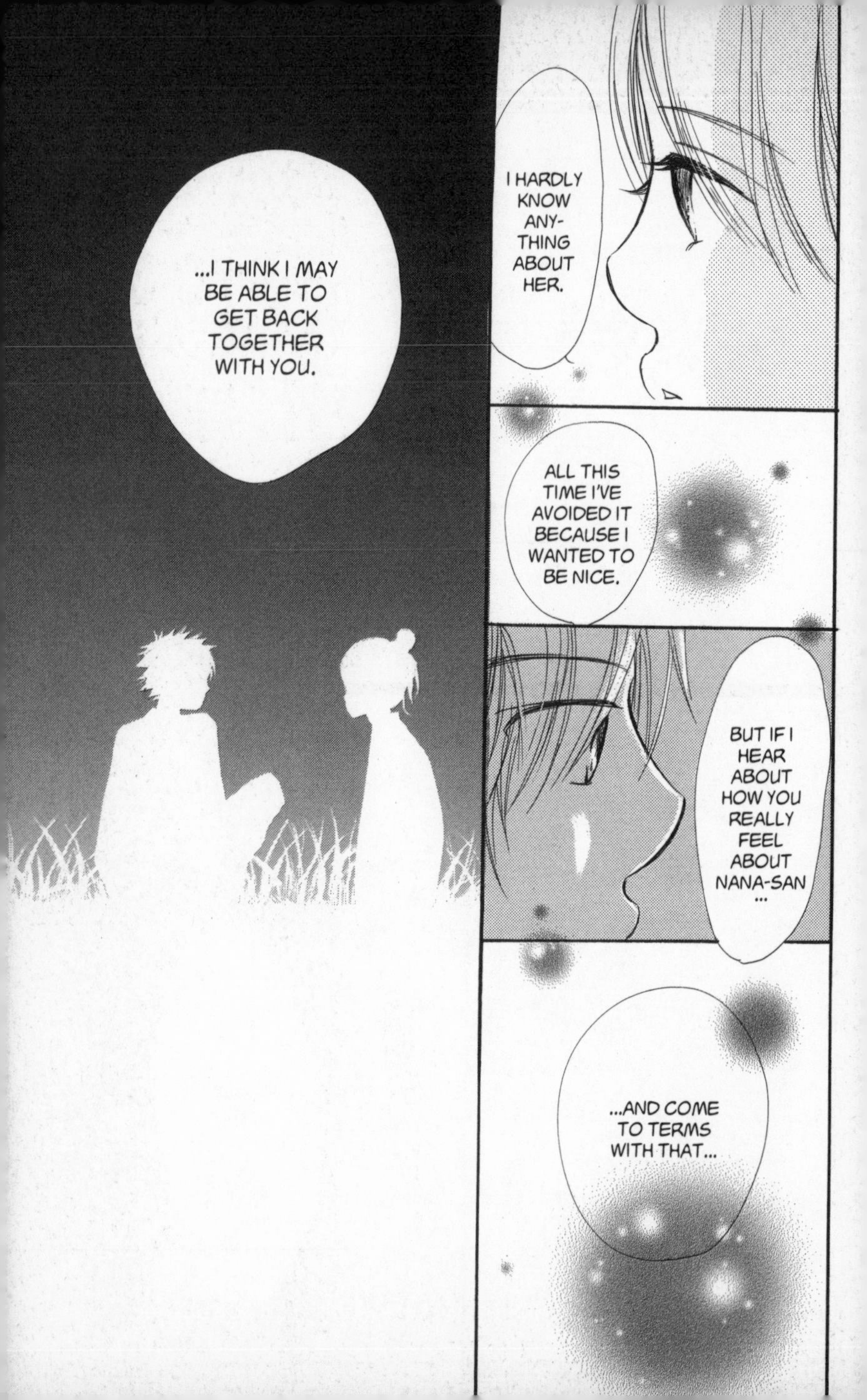
I HARDLY KNOW ANY-THING ABOUT HER.
ALL THIS TIME I'VE AVOIDED IT BECAUSE I WANTED TO BE NICE.
BUT IF I HEAR ABOUT HOW YOU REALLY FEEL ABOUT NANA-SAN...
...AND COME TO TERMS WITH THAT...
...I THINK I MAY BE ABLE TO GET BACK TOGETHER WITH YOU.

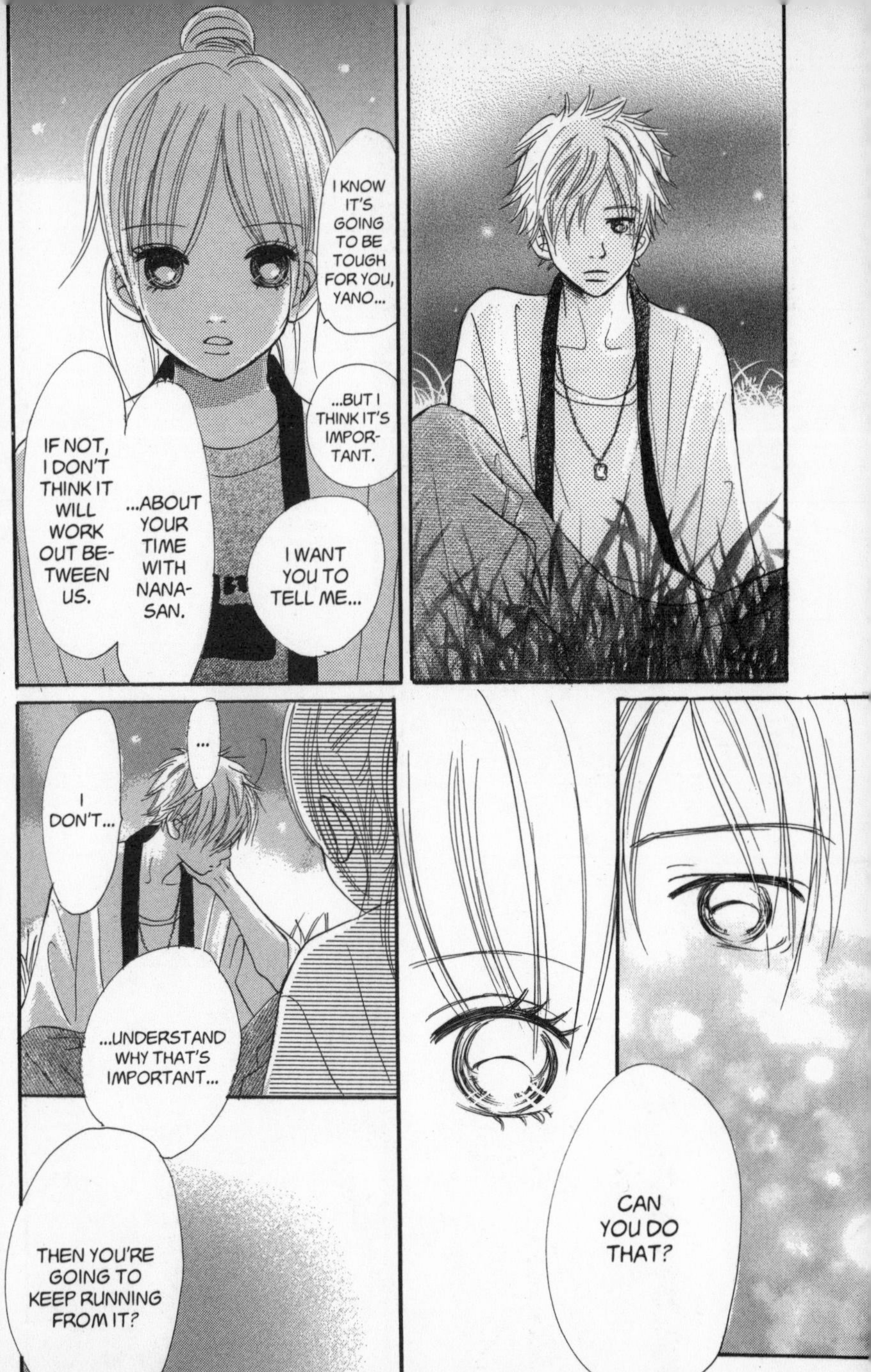
I KNOW IT'S GOING TO BE TOUGH FOR YOU, YANO...
...BUT I THINK IT'S IMPORTANT.
I WANT YOU TO TELL ME...
...ABOUT YOUR TIME WITH NANA-SAN.
IF NOT, I DON'T THINK IT WILL WORK OUT BE-TWEEN US.
...
I DON'T...
...UNDERSTAND WHY THAT'S IMPORTANT...
THEN YOU'RE GOING TO KEEP RUNNING FROM IT?
CAN YOU DO THAT?

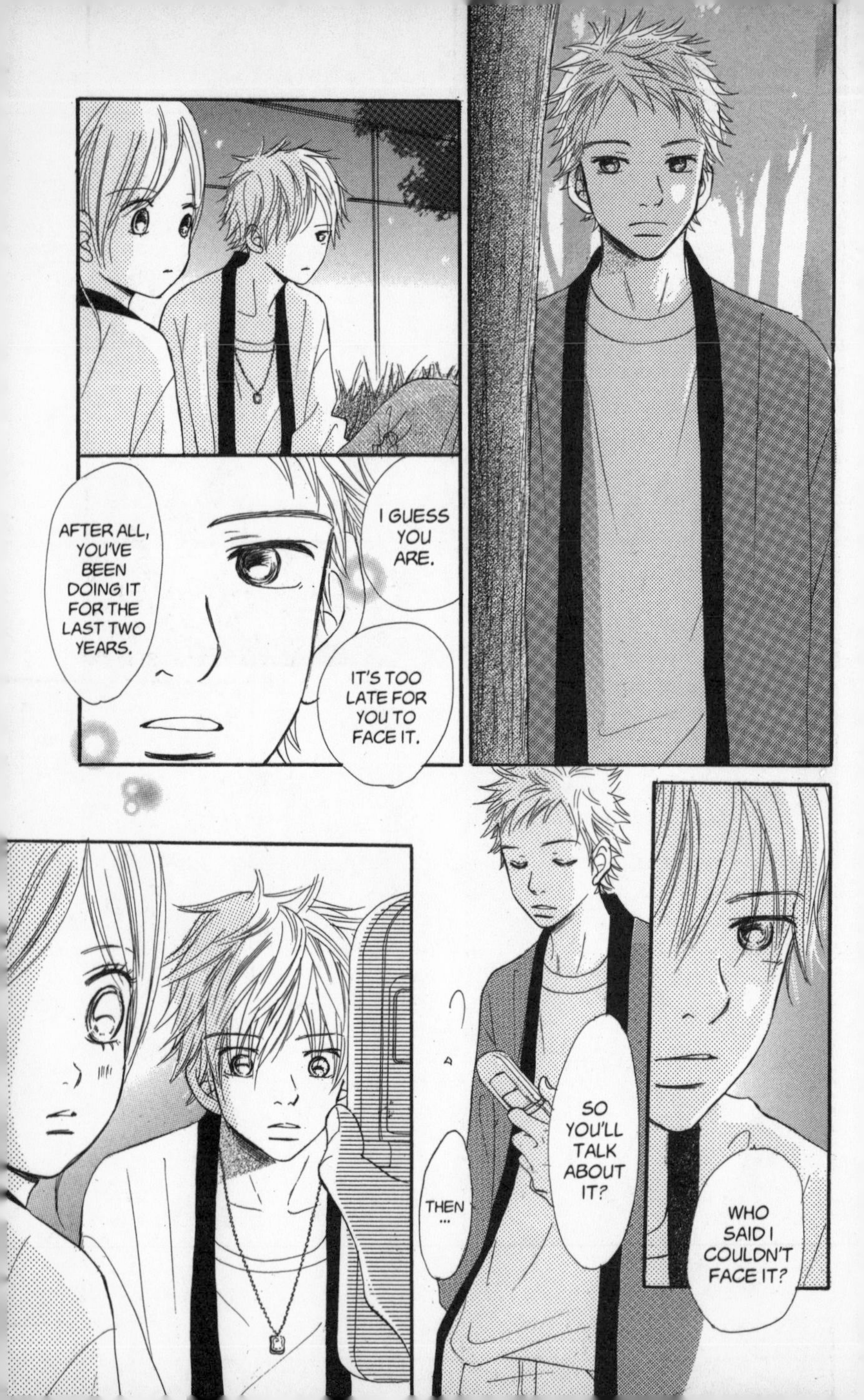
I GUESS YOU ARE.
AFTER ALL, YOU'VE BEEN DOING IT FOR THE LAST TWO YEARS.
IT'S TOO LATE FOR YOU TO FACE IT.
WHO SAID I COULDN'T FACE IT?
SO YOU'LL TALK ABOUT IT?
THEN...

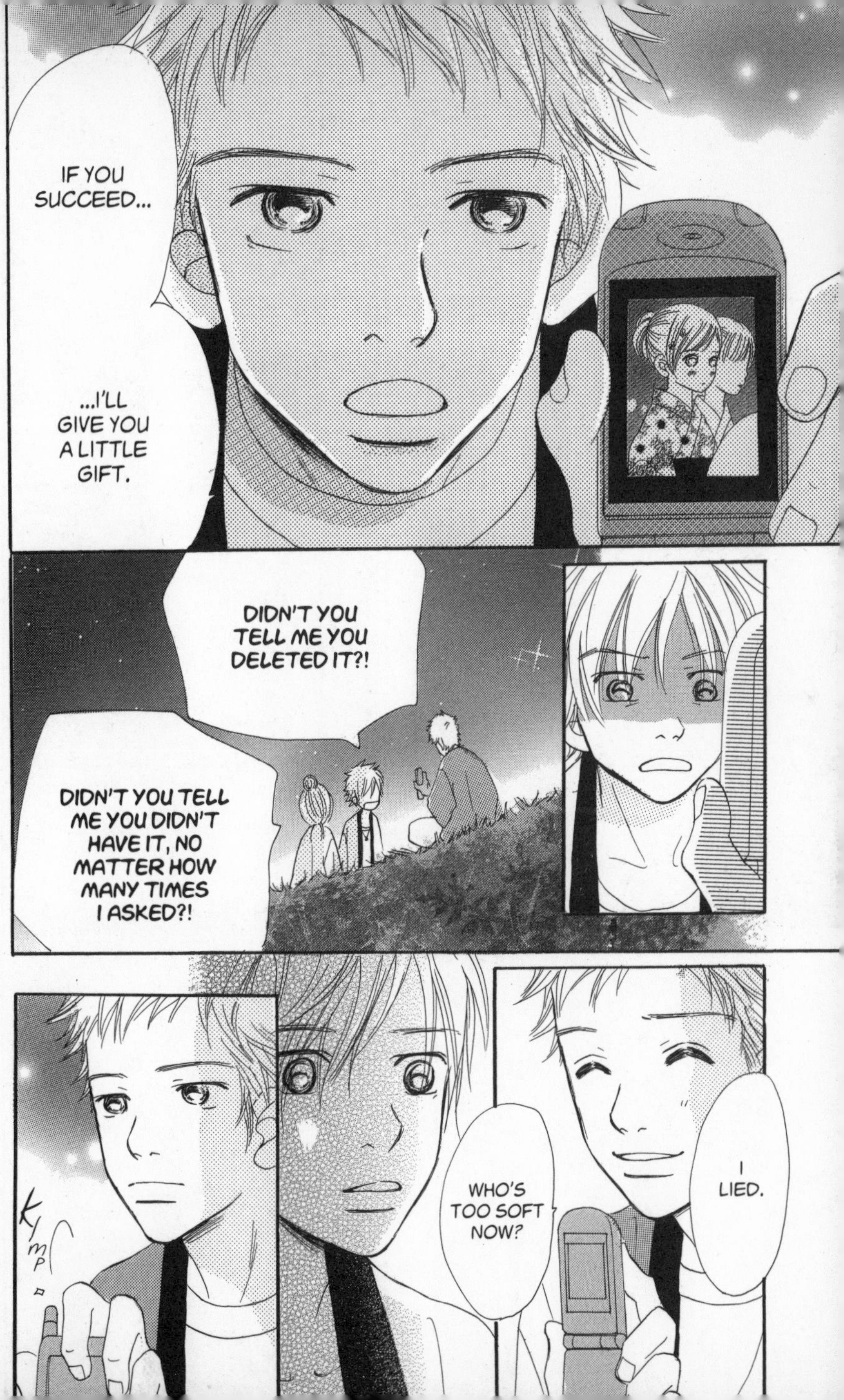
IF YOU SUCCEED...
...I'LL GIVE YOU A LITTLE GIFT.
DIDN'T YOU TELL ME YOU DELETED IT?!
DIDN'T YOU TELL ME YOU DIDN'T HAVE IT, NO MATTER HOW MANY TIMES I ASKED?!
I LIED.
WHO'S TOO SOFT NOW?
KLMP

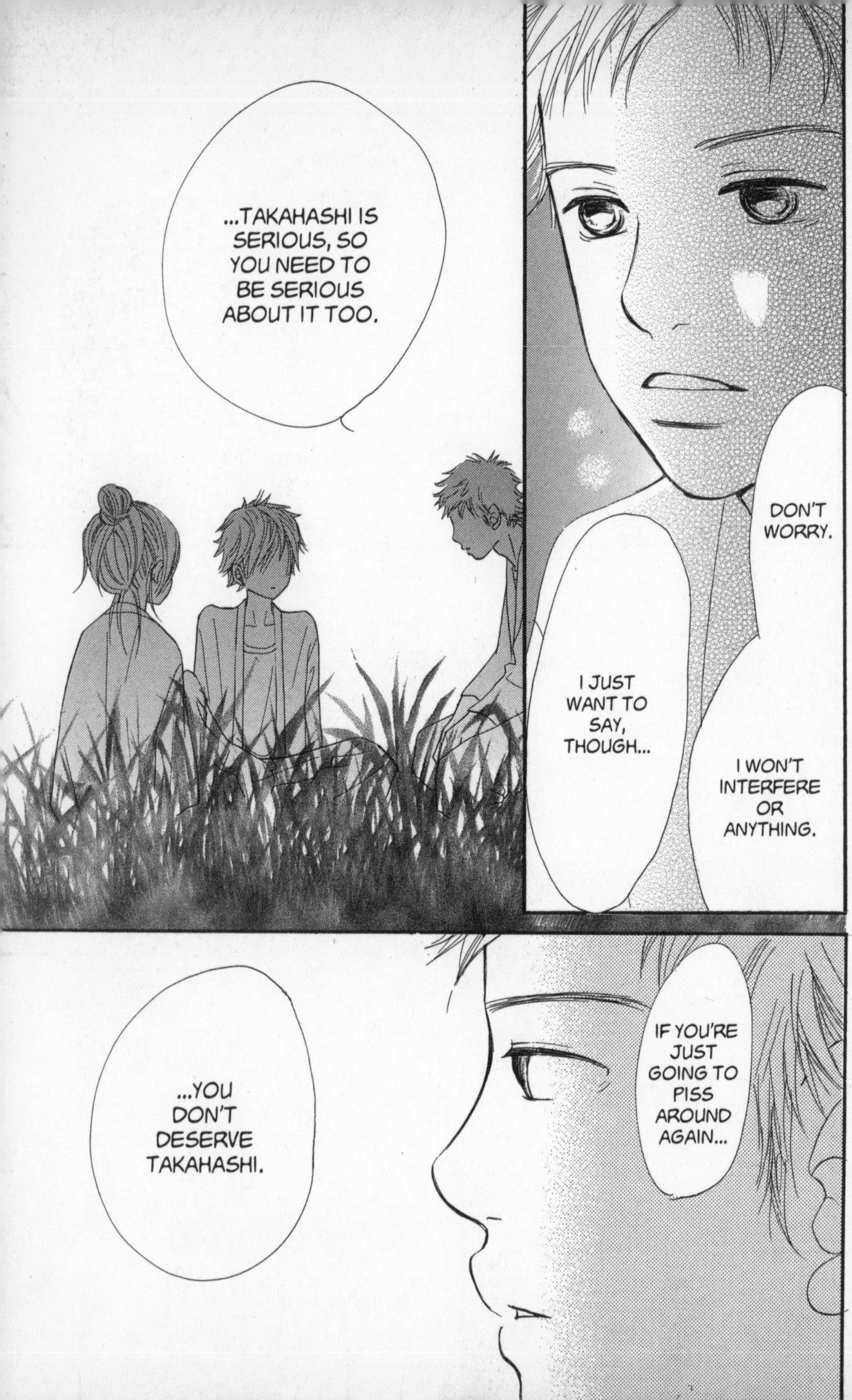
DON'T WORRY.
I WON'T INTERFERE OR ANYTHING.
I JUST WANT TO SAY, THOUGH...
...TAKAHASHI IS SERIOUS, SO YOU NEED TO BE SERIOUS ABOUT IT TOO.
IF YOU'RE JUST GOING TO PISS AROUND AGAIN...
...YOU DON'T DESERVE TAKAHASHI.

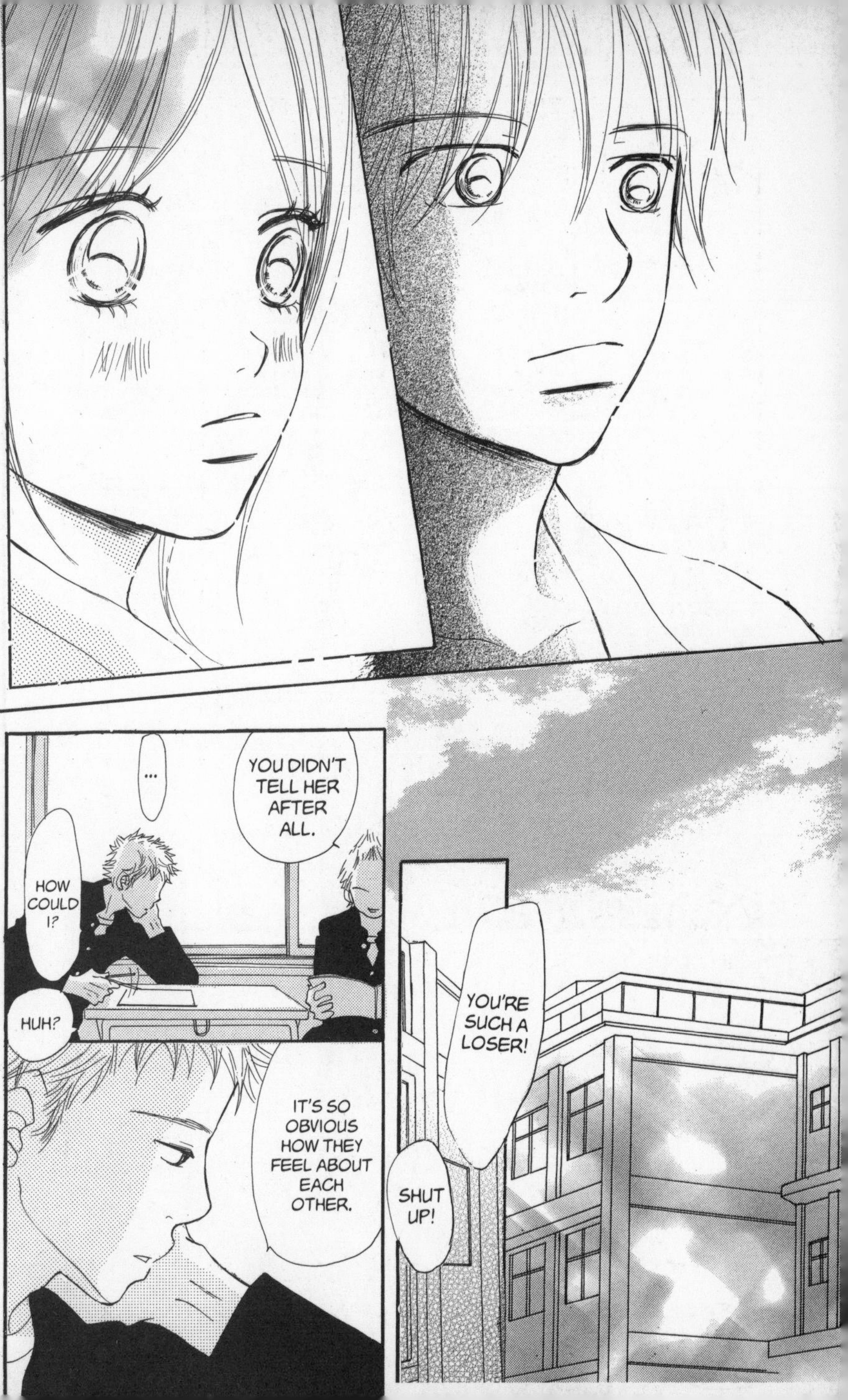
YOU DIDN'T TELL HER AFTER ALL.
...
HOW COULD I?
HUH?
IT'S SO OBVIOUS HOW THEY FEEL ABOUT EACH OTHER.
YOU'RE SUCH A LOSER!
SHUT UP!

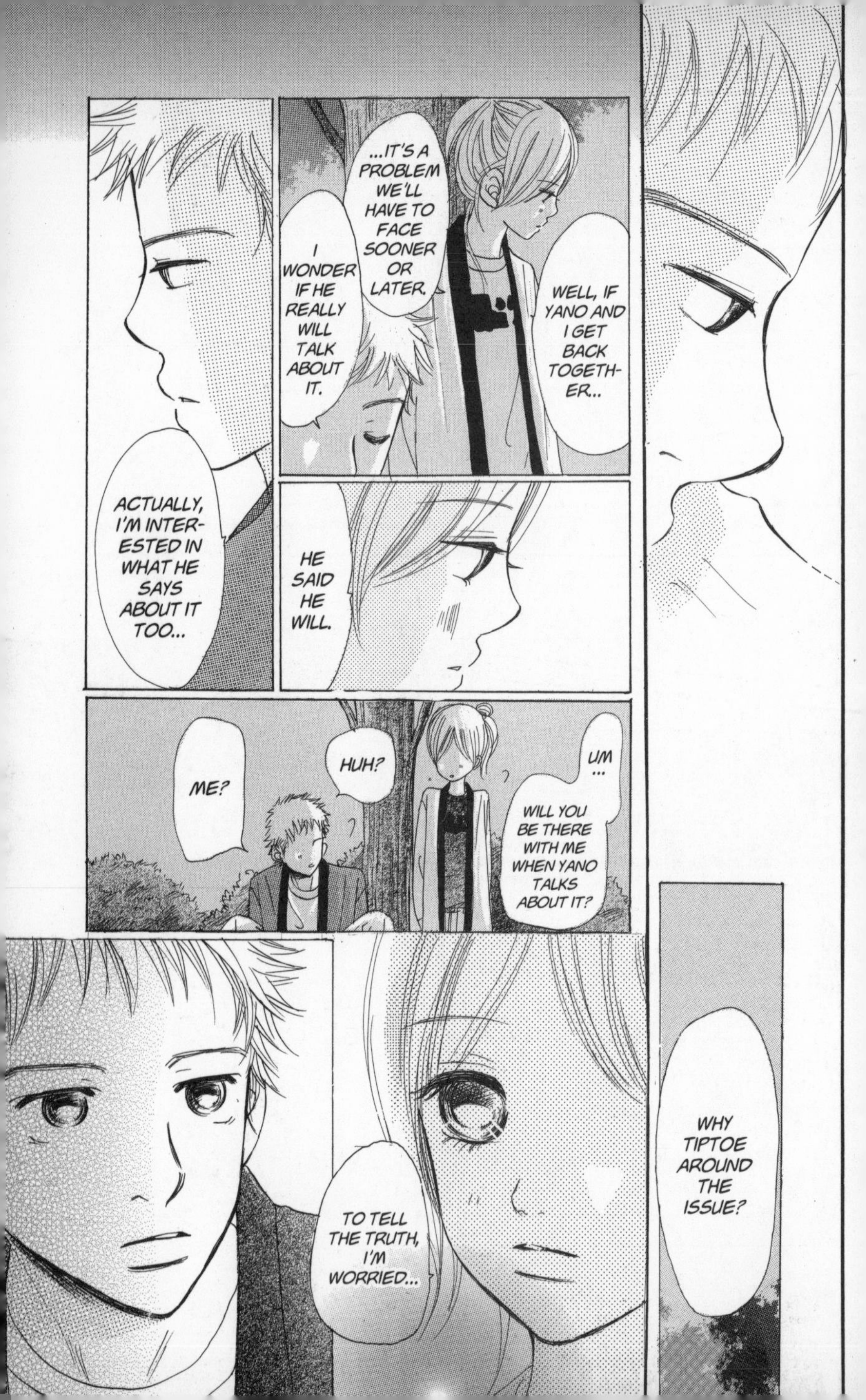
WELL, IF YANO AND I GET BACK TOGETH-ER...
...IT'S A PROBLEM WE'LL HAVE TO FACE SOONER OR LATER.
I WONDER IF HE REALLY WILL TALK ABOUT IT.
HE SAID HE WILL.
ACTUALLY, I'M INTER-ESTED IN WHAT HE SAYS ABOUT IT TOO...
UM...
WILL YOU BE THERE WITH ME WHEN YANO TALKS ABOUT IT?
HUH?
ME?
WHY TIPTOE AROUND THE ISSUE?
TO TELL THE TRUTH, I'M WORRIED...

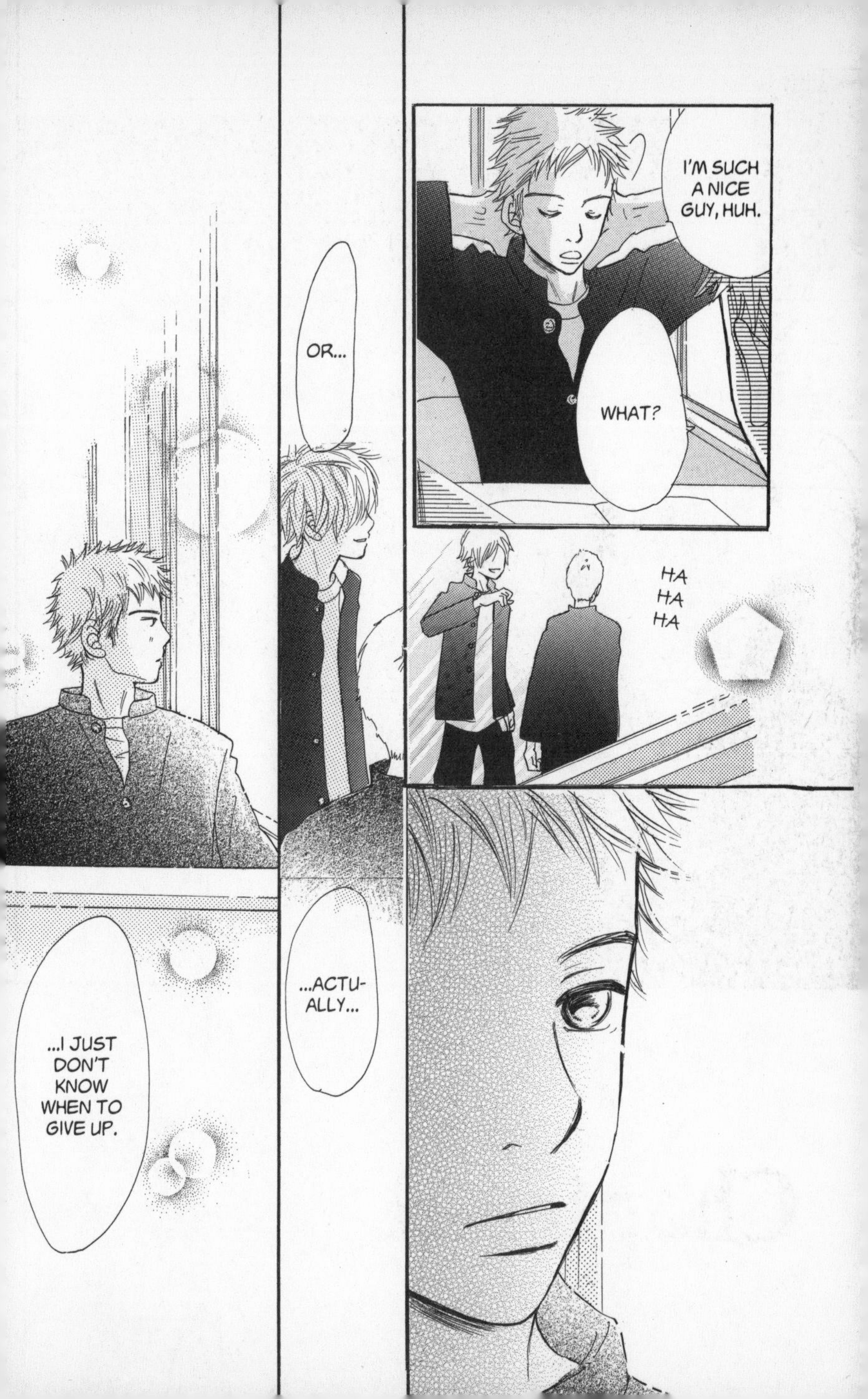
I'M SUCH A NICE GUY, HUH.
WHAT?
HA HA HA
OR...
...ACTU-ALLY...
...I JUST DON'T KNOW WHEN TO GIVE UP.

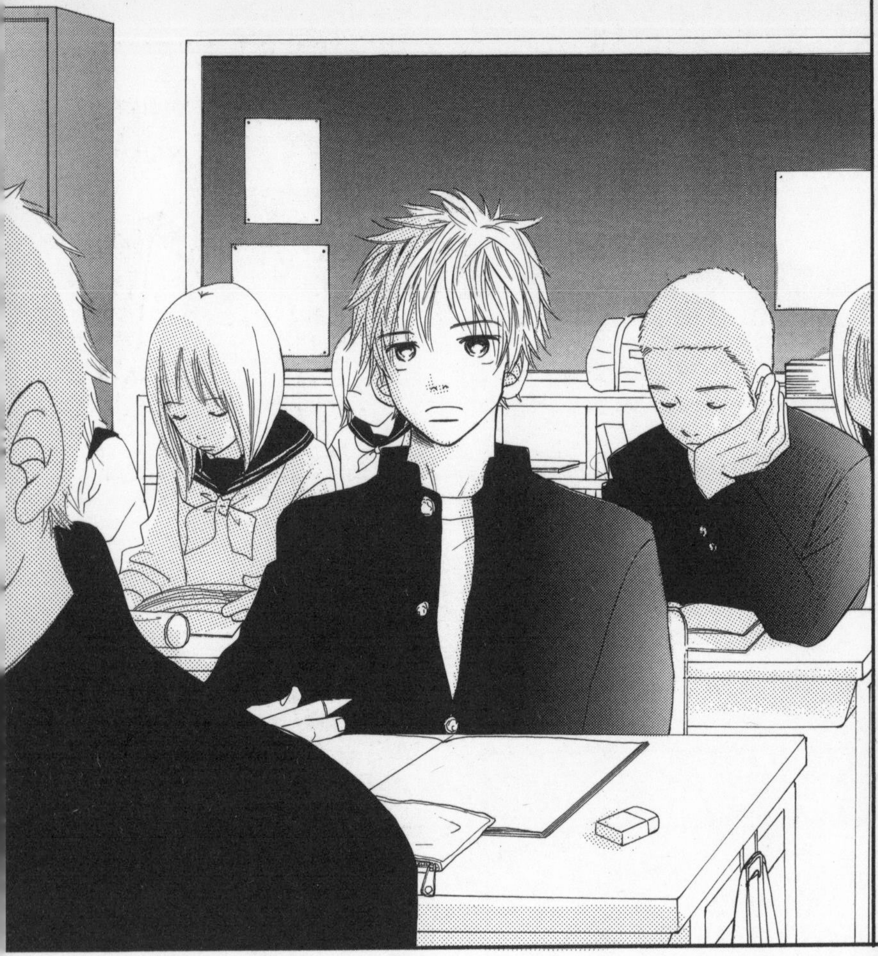

# Chapter 21

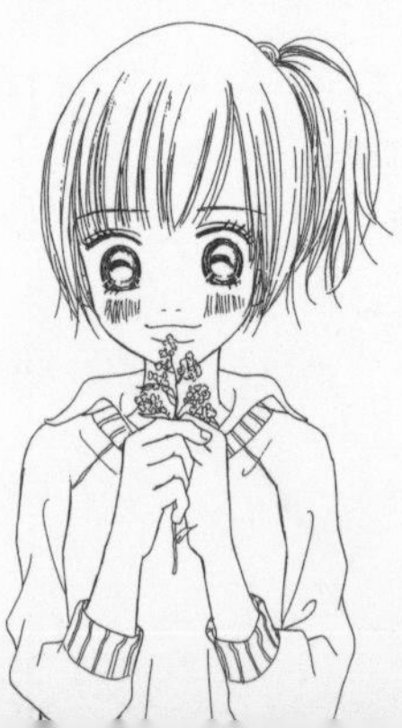

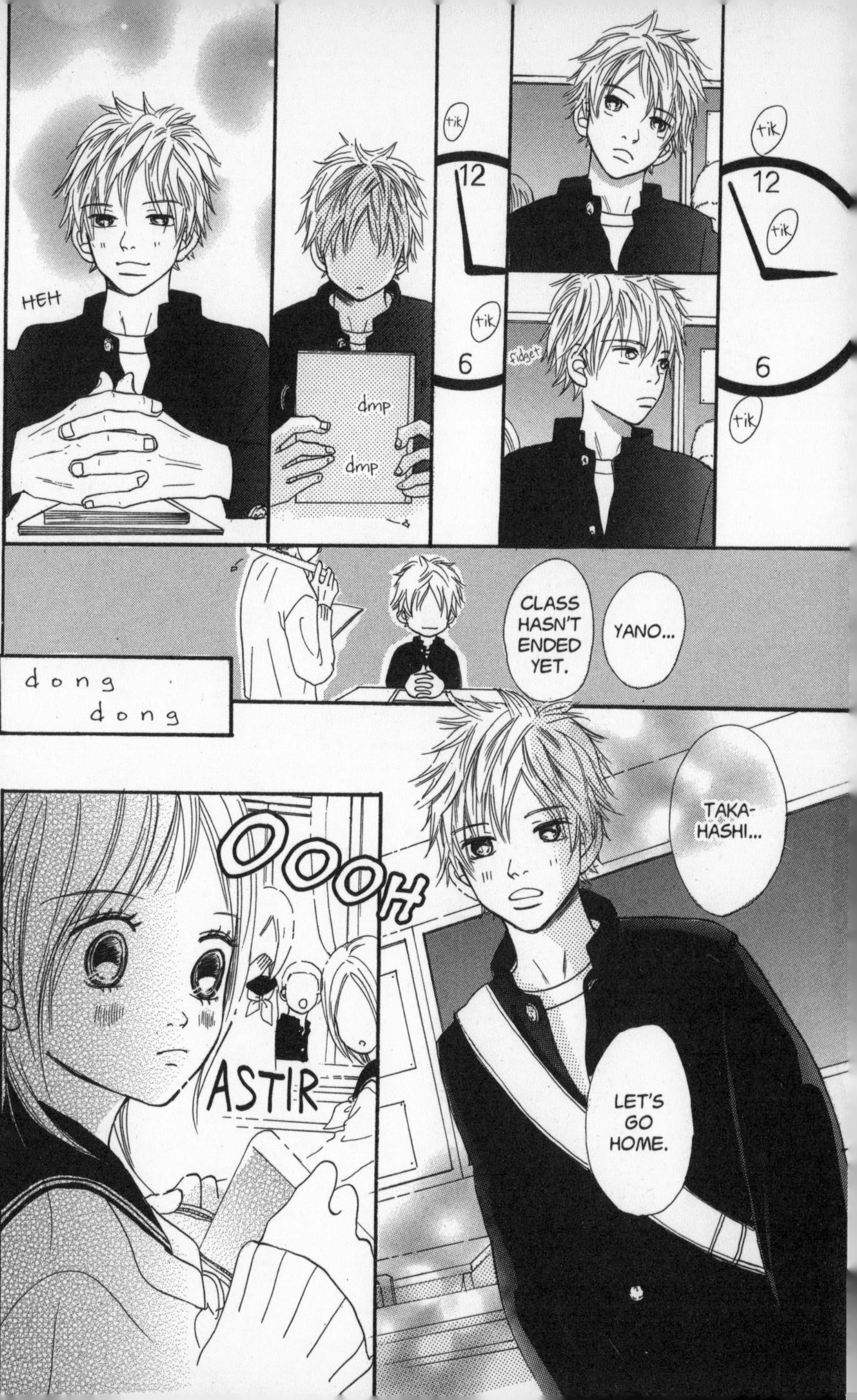
tik
12
tik
6
tik
fidget
tik
12
tik
6
dmp
dmp
HEH
YANO...
CLASS HASN'T ENDED YET.
dong dong
TAKA-HASHI...
LET'S GO HOME.
OOOH
ASTIR

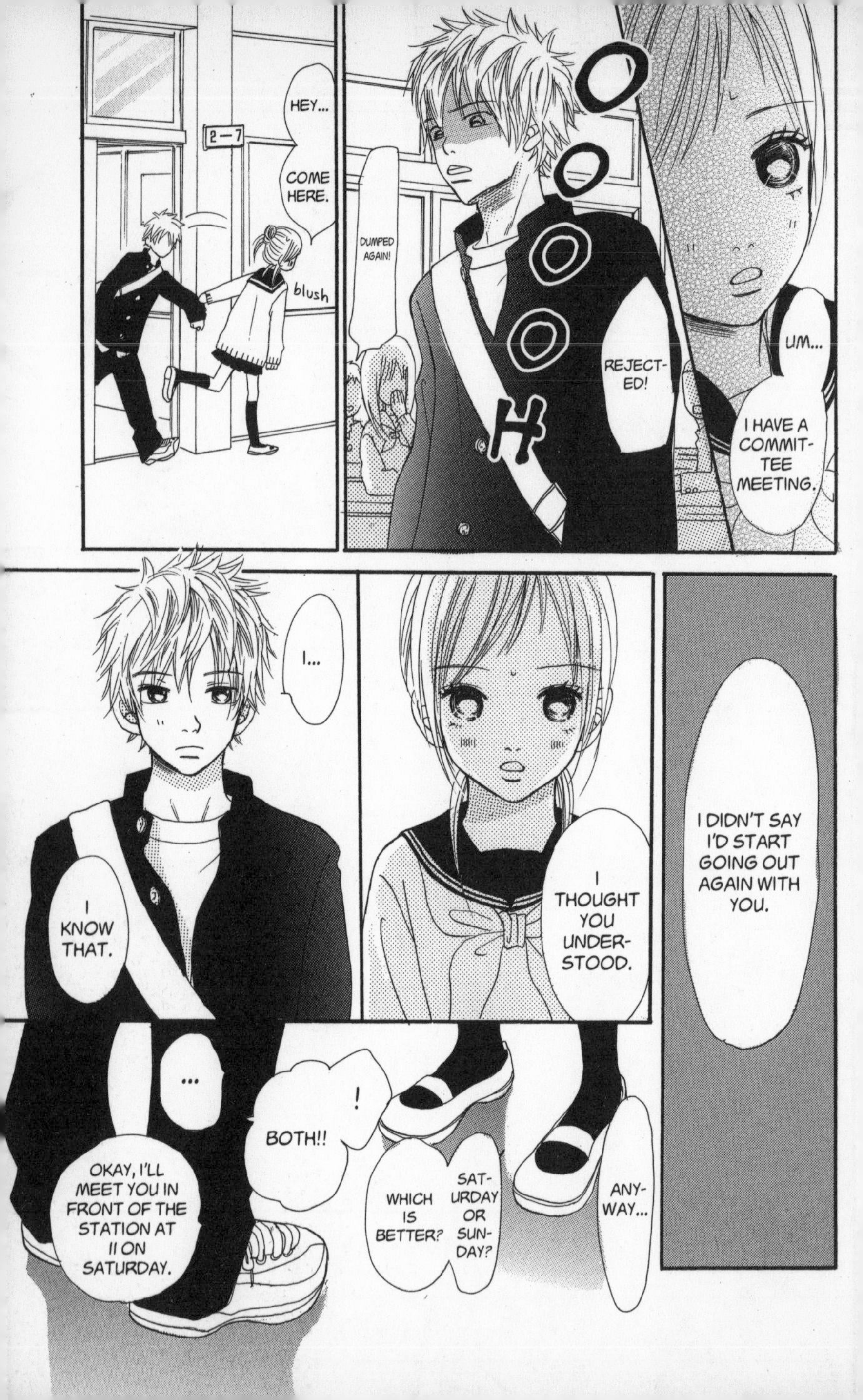
UM...
I HAVE A COMMITTEE MEETING.
REJECTED!
DUMPED AGAIN!
2-7
HEY... COME HERE.
blush
I DIDN'T SAY I'D START GOING OUT AGAIN WITH YOU.
I THOUGHT YOU UNDERSTOOD.
I...
I KNOW THAT.
ANYWAY...
SATURDAY OR SUNDAY?
WHICH IS BETTER?
!
BOTH!!
...
OKAY, I'LL MEET YOU IN FRONT OF THE STATION AT 11 ON SATURDAY.

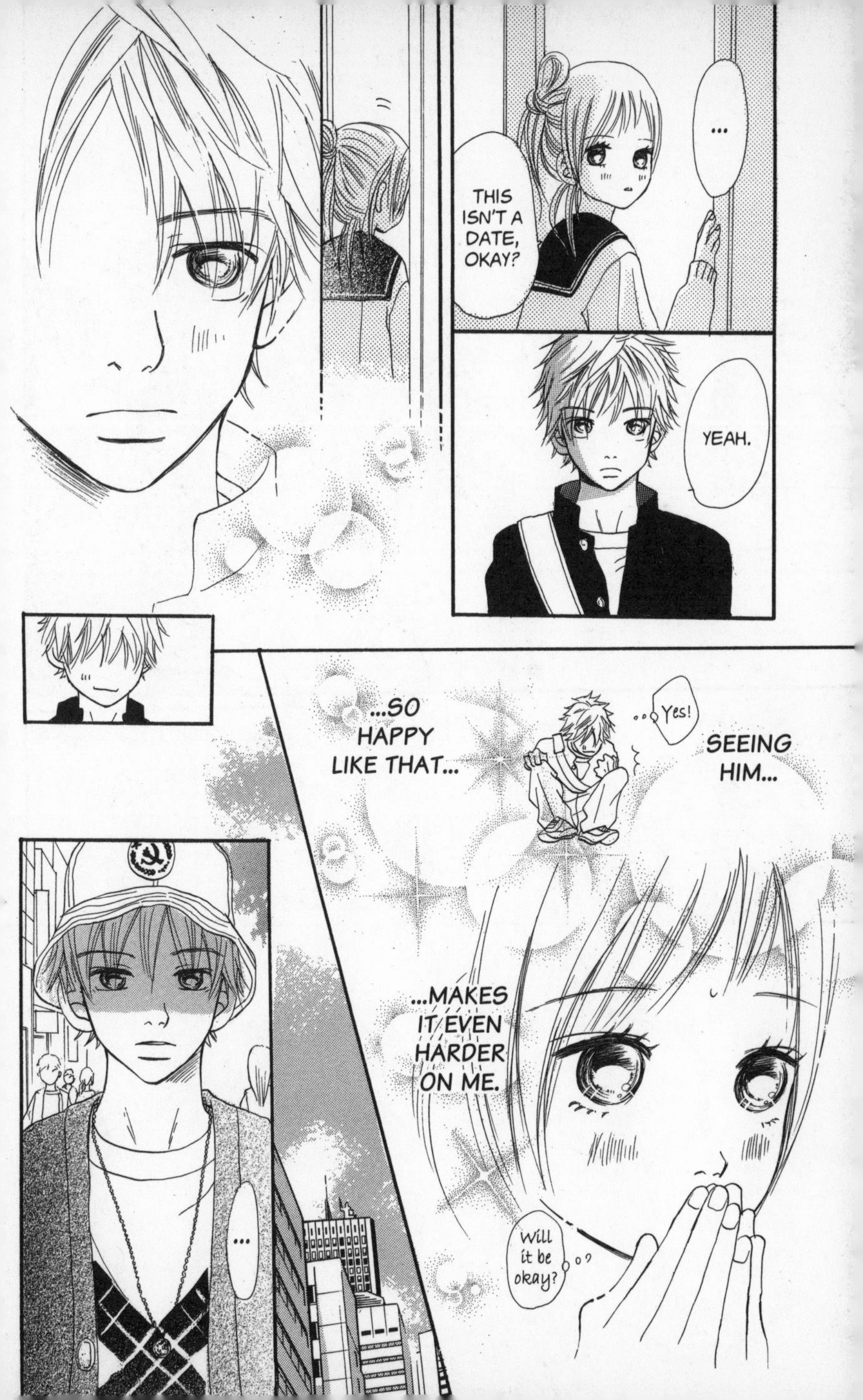
...
THIS ISN'T A DATE, OKAY?
YEAH.
SEEING HIM...
Yes!
...SO HAPPY LIKE THAT...
...MAKES IT EVEN HARDER ON ME.
Will it be okay?
...

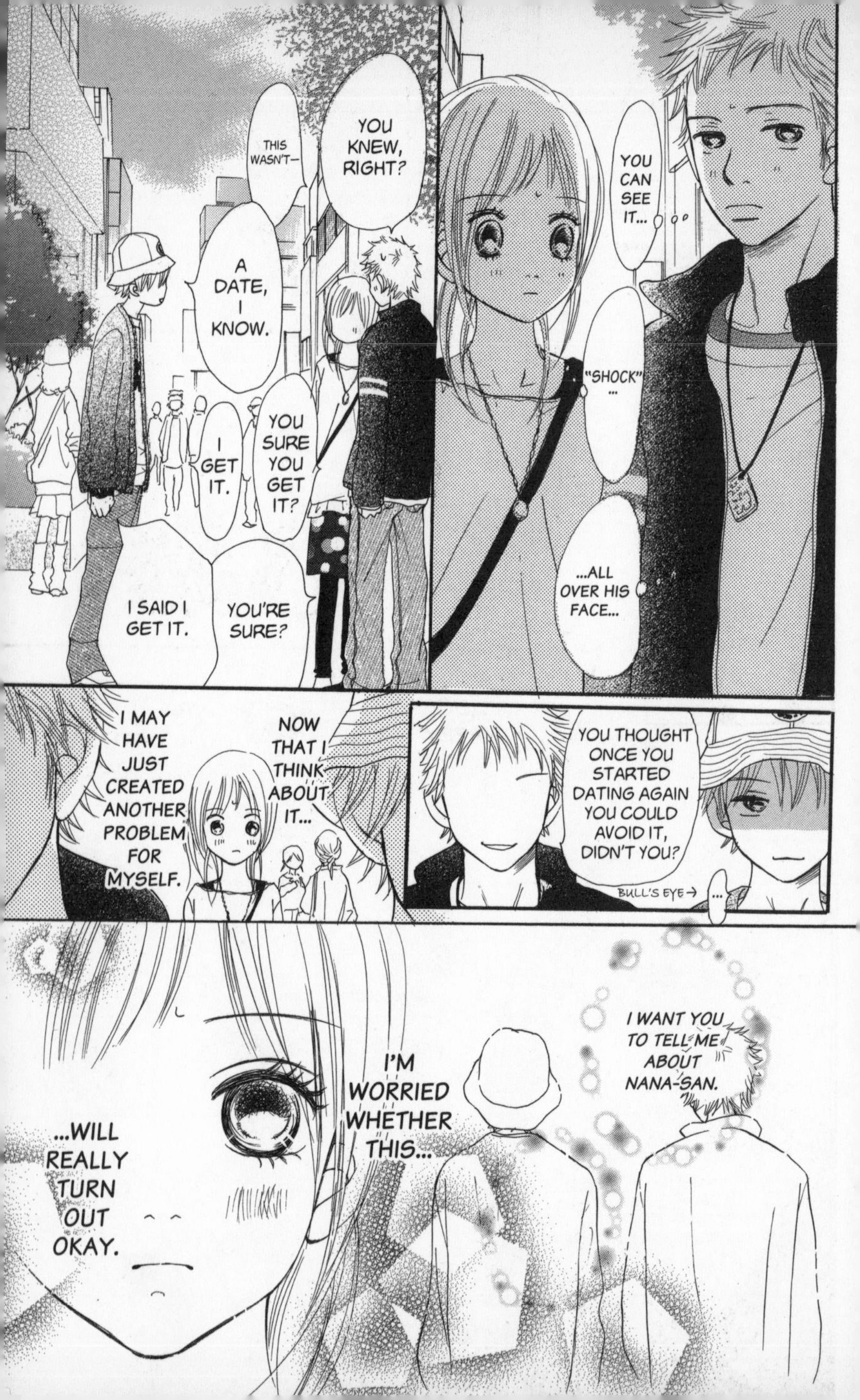
YOU CAN SEE IT...
"SHOCK"...
...ALL OVER HIS FACE...
YOU KNEW, RIGHT?
THIS WASN'T—
A DATE, I KNOW.
YOU SURE YOU GET IT?
I GET IT.
YOU'RE SURE?
I SAID I GET IT.
YOU THOUGHT ONCE YOU STARTED DATING AGAIN YOU COULD AVOID IT, DIDN'T YOU?
BULL'S EYE →
...
NOW THAT I THINK ABOUT IT...
I MAY HAVE JUST CREATED ANOTHER PROBLEM FOR MYSELF.
I WANT YOU TO TELL ME ABOUT NANA-SAN.
I'M WORRIED WHETHER THIS...
...WILL REALLY TURN OUT OKAY.

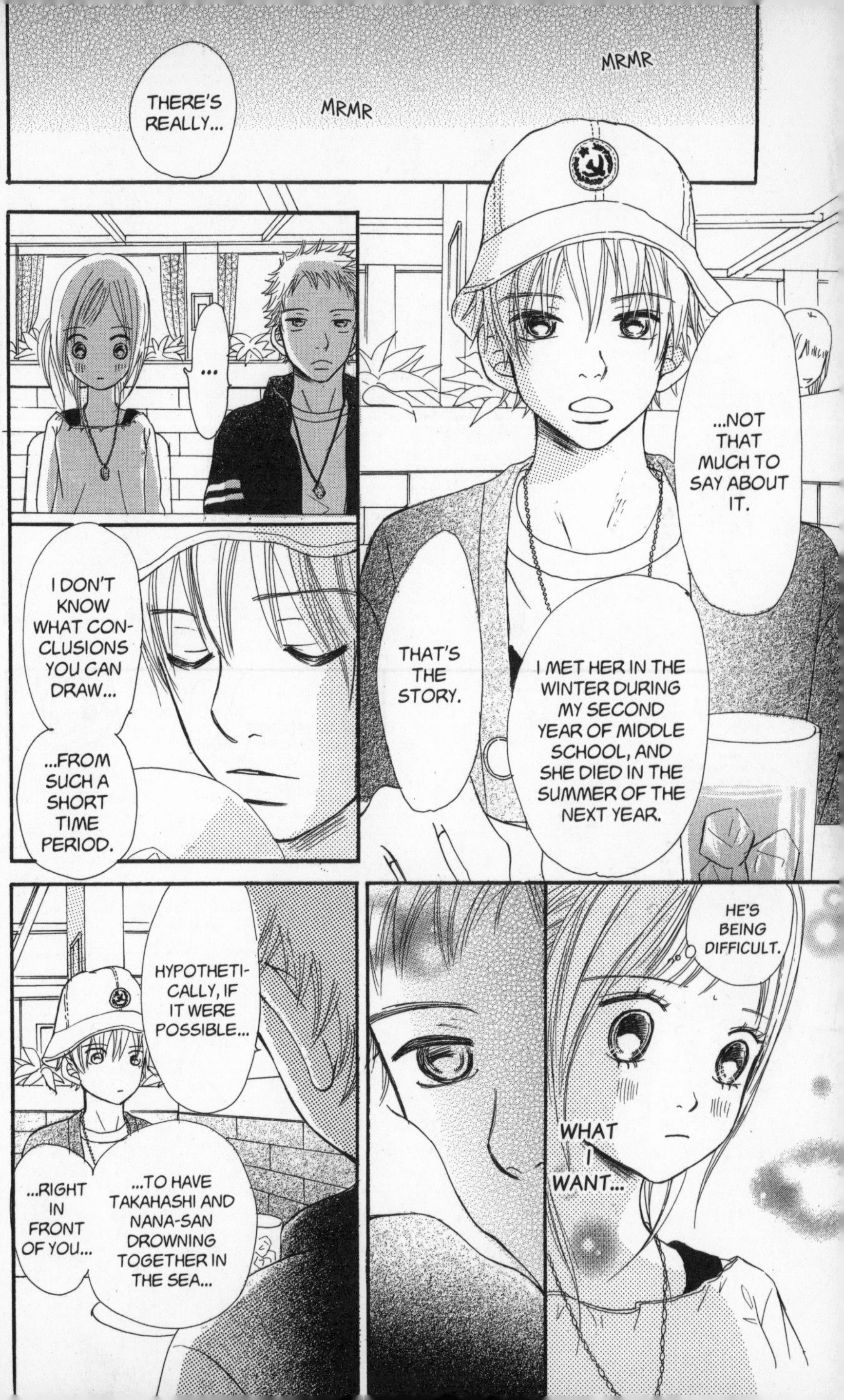
MRMR
MRMR
THERE'S REALLY...
...NOT THAT MUCH TO SAY ABOUT IT.
I MET HER IN THE WINTER DURING MY SECOND YEAR OF MIDDLE SCHOOL, AND SHE DIED IN THE SUMMER OF THE NEXT YEAR.
THAT'S THE STORY.
...
I DON'T KNOW WHAT CON-CLUSIONS YOU CAN DRAW...
...FROM SUCH A SHORT TIME PERIOD.
HE'S BEING DIFFICULT.
WHAT I WANT...
HYPOTHETI-CALLY, IF IT WERE POSSIBLE...
...TO HAVE TAKAHASHI AND NANA-SAN DROWNING TOGETHER IN THE SEA...
...RIGHT IN FRONT OF YOU...

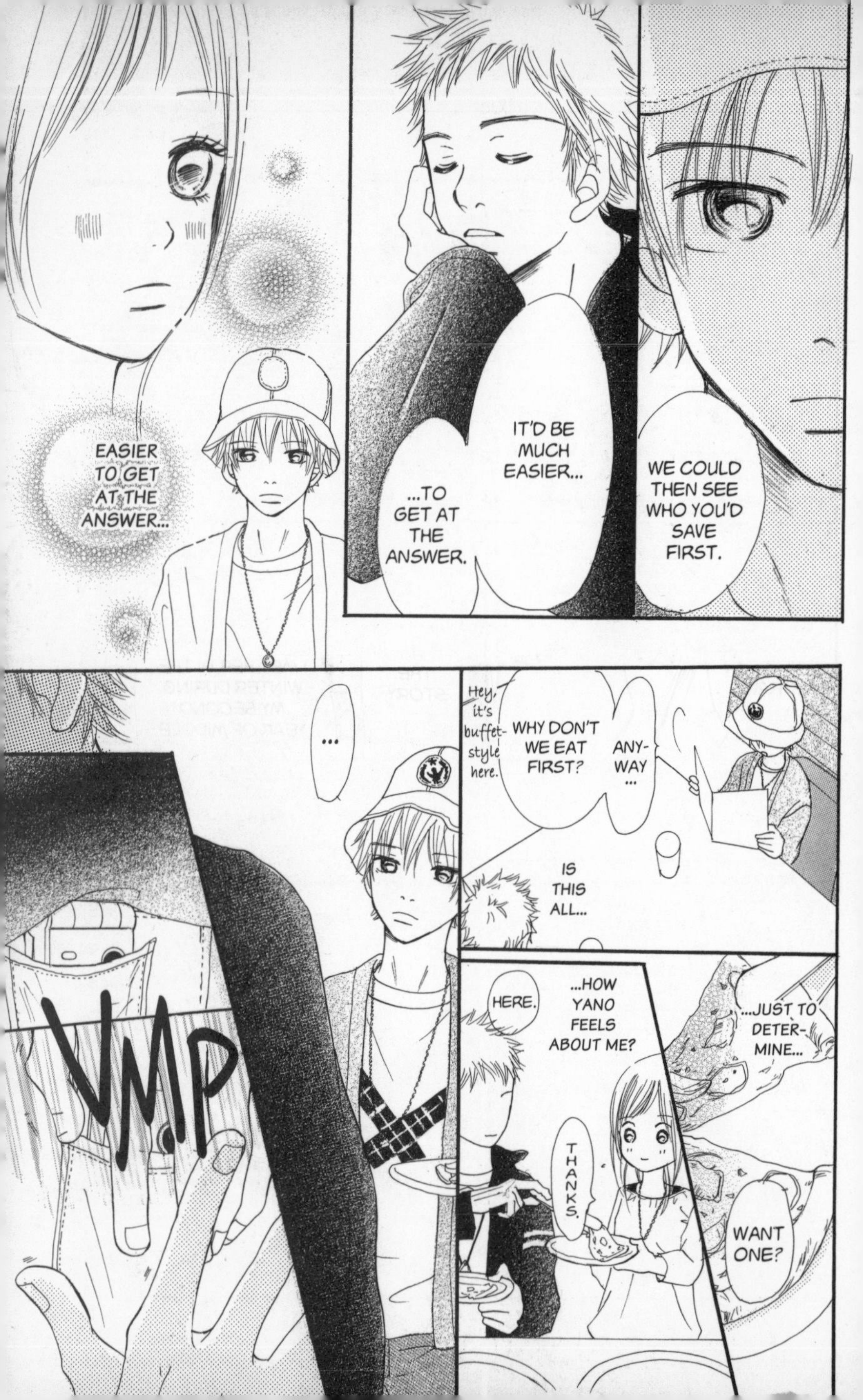
WE COULD THEN SEE WHO YOU'D SAVE FIRST.
IT'D BE MUCH EASIER...
...TO GET AT THE ANSWER.
EASIER TO GET AT THE ANSWER...
ANY-WAY...
WHY DON'T WE EAT FIRST?
Hey, it's buffet-style here.
IS THIS ALL...
...JUST TO DETER-MINE...
WANT ONE?
...HOW YANO FEELS ABOUT ME?
HERE.
THANKS.
...
VMP

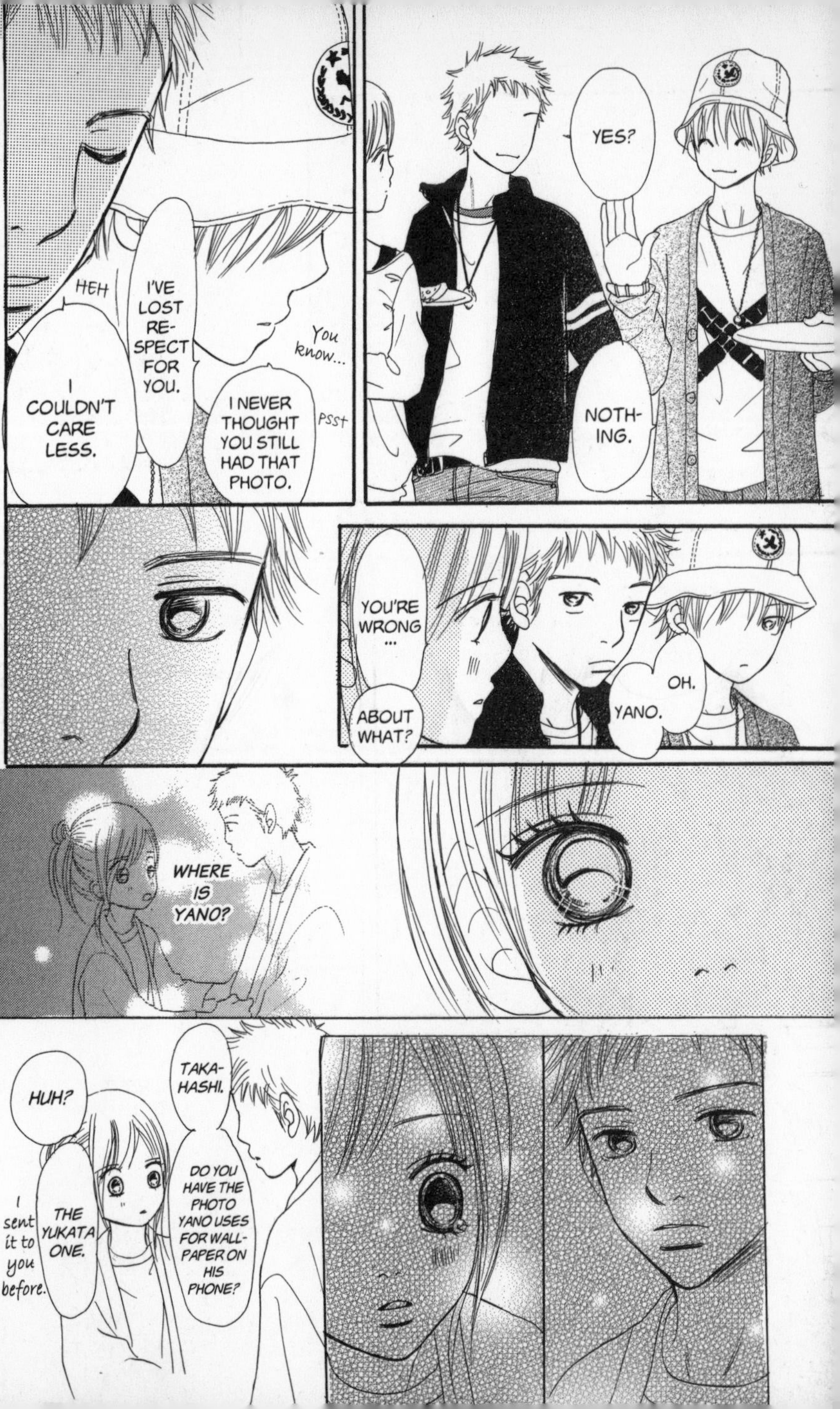
YES?
NOTHING.
You know...
PSST
I NEVER THOUGHT YOU STILL HAD THAT PHOTO.
I'VE LOST RESPECT FOR YOU.
HEH
I COULDN'T CARE LESS.
OH.
YANO.
YOU'RE WRONG...
ABOUT WHAT?
WHERE IS YANO?
TAKAHASHI.
DO YOU HAVE THE PHOTO YANO USES FOR WALLPAPER ON HIS PHONE?
HUH?
THE YUKATA ONE.
I sent it to you before.

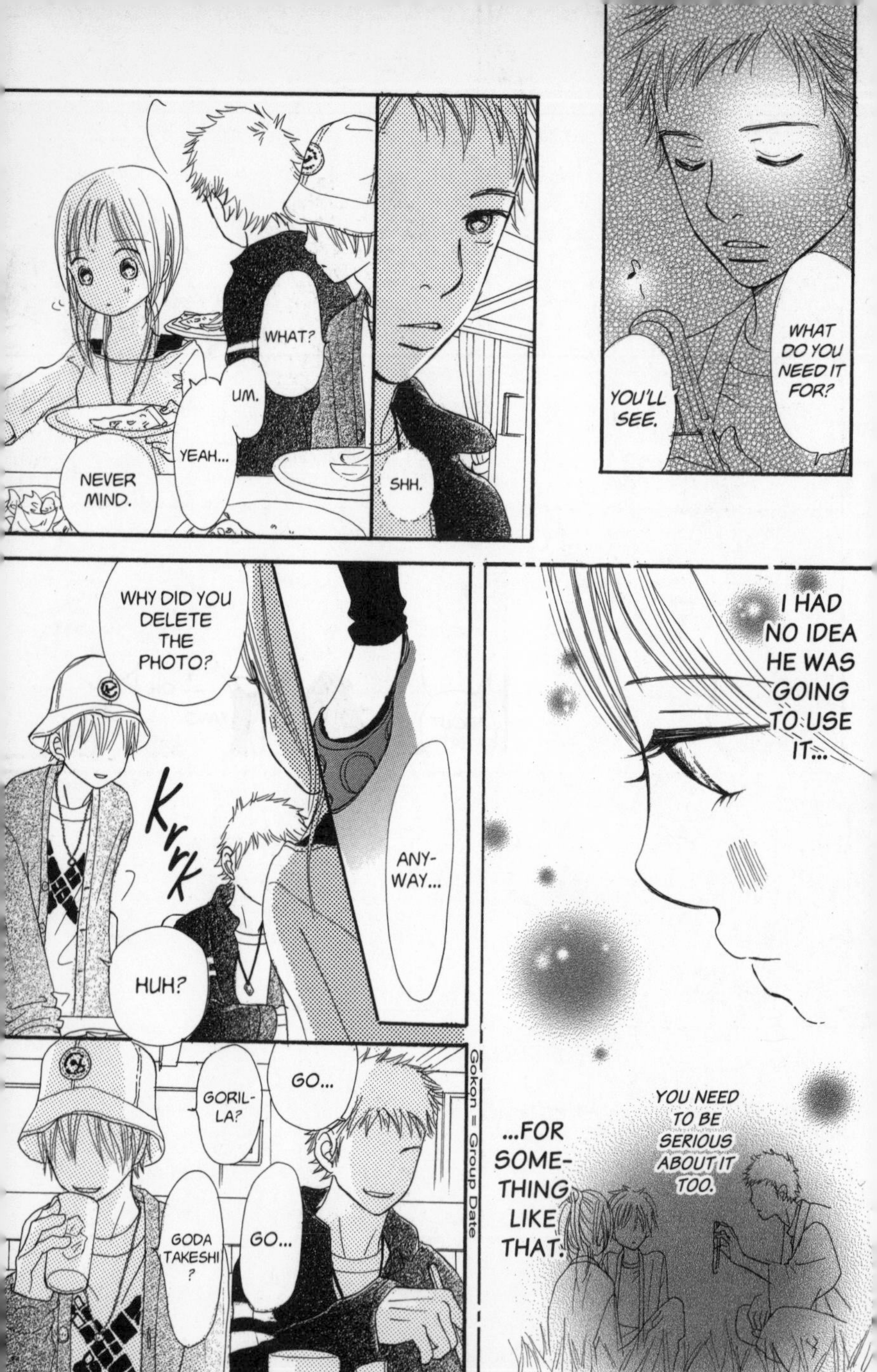
WHAT DO YOU NEED IT FOR?
YOU'LL SEE.
SHH.
WHAT?
UM.
YEAH...
NEVER MIND.
I HAD NO IDEA HE WAS GOING TO USE IT...
YOU NEED TO BE SERIOUS ABOUT IT TOO.
...FOR SOME-THING LIKE THAT.
WHY DID YOU DELETE THE PHOTO?
ANY-WAY...
Krrk
HUH?
Gokon = Group Date
GO...
GORIL-LA?
GO...
GODA TAKESHI?

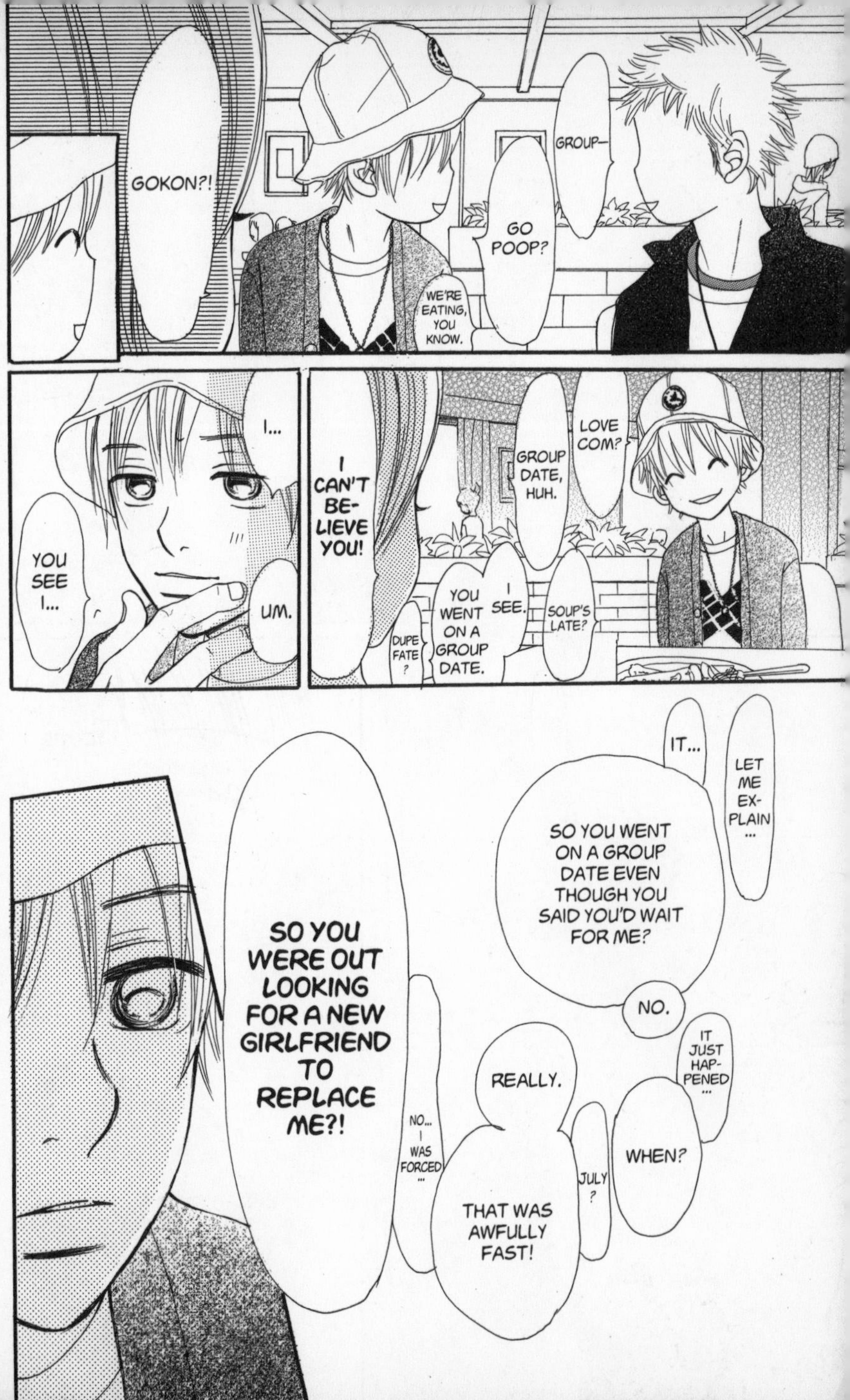
GROUP—
GO POOP?
WE'RE EATING, YOU KNOW.
GOKON?!
LOVE COM?
GROUP DATE, HUH.
SOUP'S LATE?
I SEE.
YOU WENT ON A GROUP DATE.
DUPE FATE?
I CAN'T BE-LIEVE YOU!
I...
UM.
YOU SEE I...
LET ME EX-PLAIN...
IT...
SO YOU WENT ON A GROUP DATE EVEN THOUGH YOU SAID YOU'D WAIT FOR ME?
NO.
IT JUST HAP-PENED...
WHEN?
JULY?
REALLY.
THAT WAS AWFULLY FAST!
NO... I WAS FORCED...
SO YOU WERE OUT LOOKING FOR A NEW GIRLFRIEND TO REPLACE ME?!

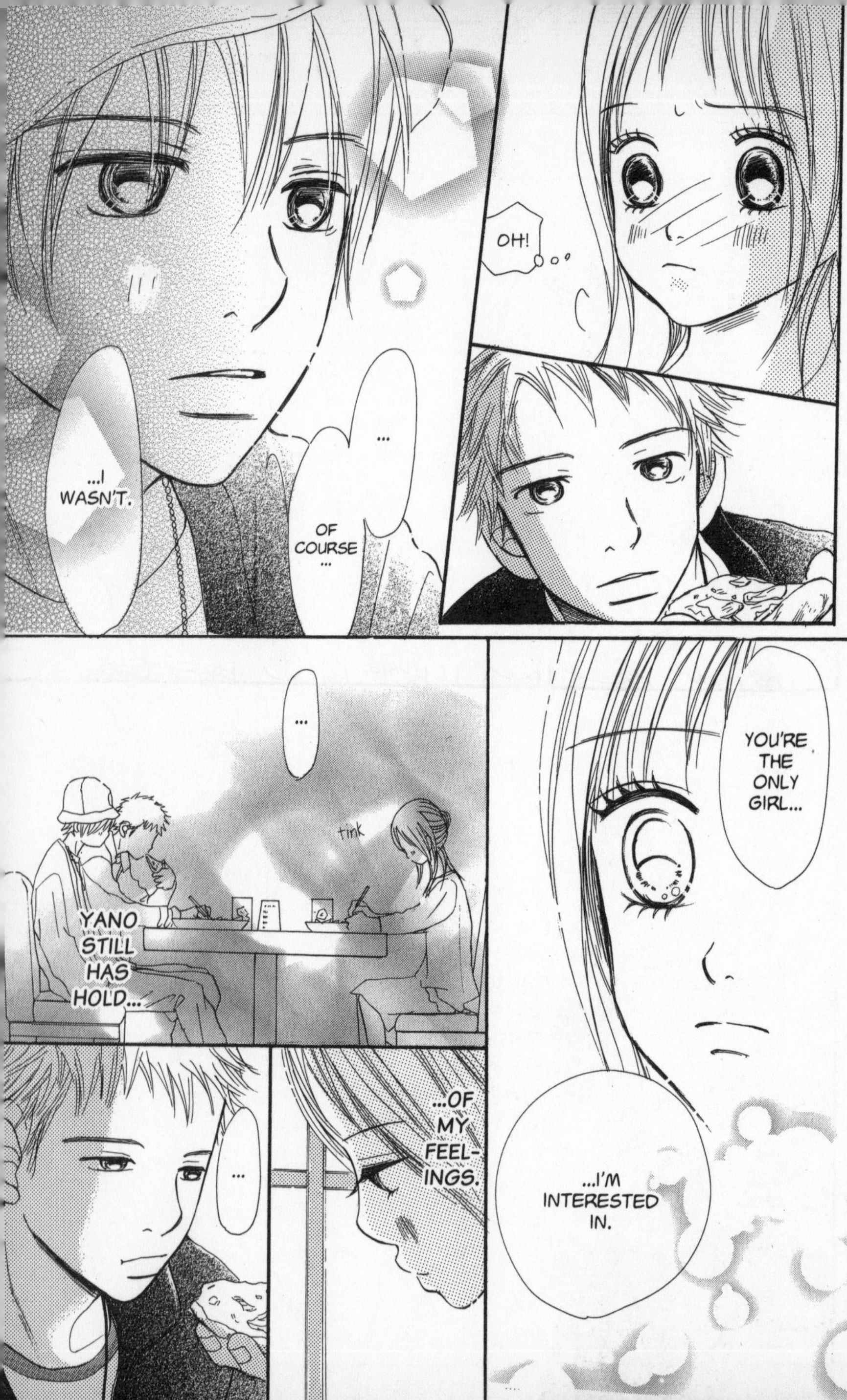
OH!
...
OF COURSE ...
...I WASN'T.
YOU'RE THE ONLY GIRL...
...I'M INTERESTED IN.
...
tink
YANO STILL HAS HOLD...
...OF MY FEEL-INGS.
...

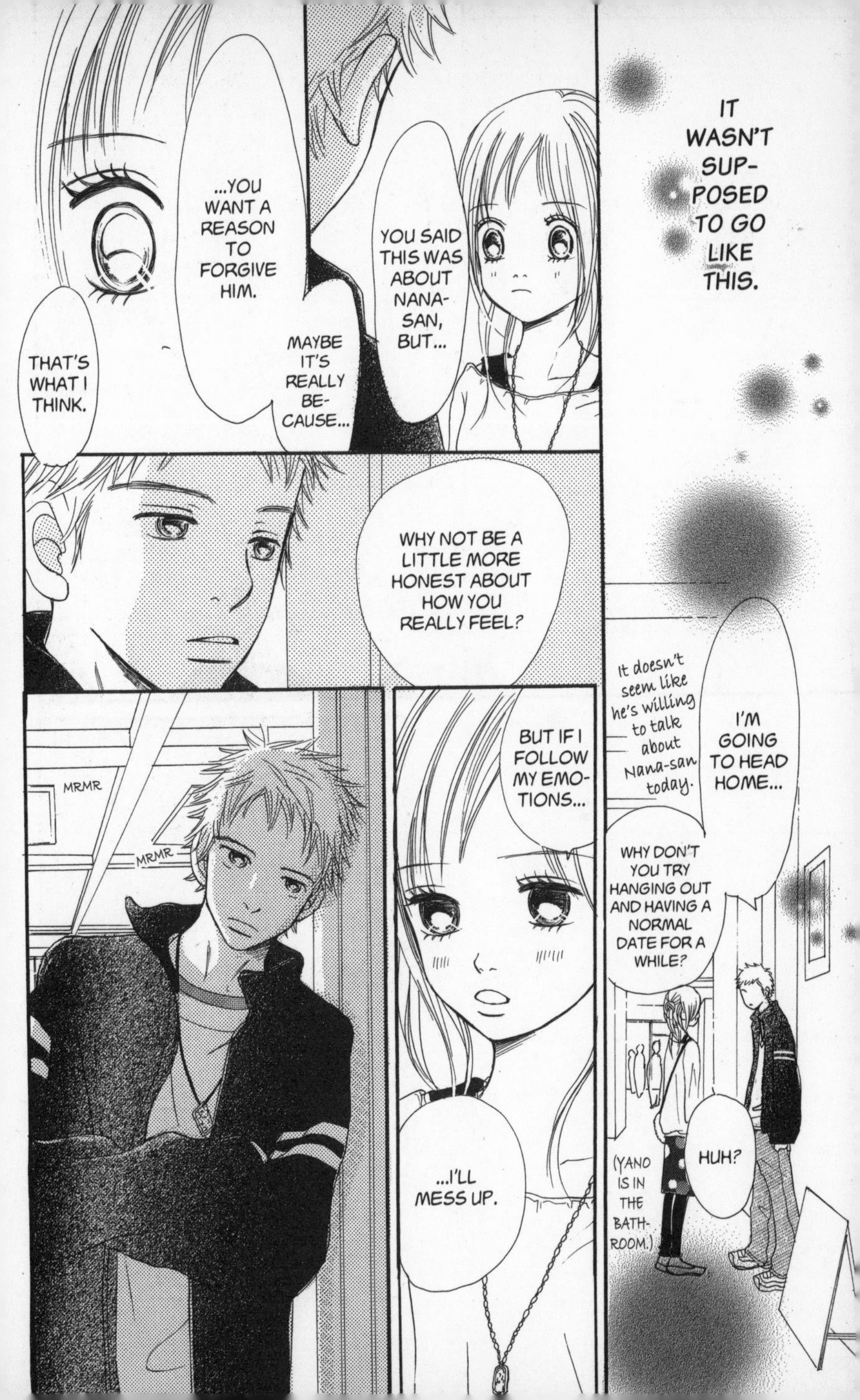
IT WASN'T SUP-POSED TO GO LIKE THIS.
I'M GOING TO HEAD HOME...
It doesn't seem like he's willing to talk about Nana-san today.
WHY DON'T YOU TRY HANGING OUT AND HAVING A NORMAL DATE FOR A WHILE?
HUH?
(YANO IS IN THE BATH-ROOM.)
YOU SAID THIS WAS ABOUT NANA-SAN, BUT...
MAYBE IT'S REALLY BE-CAUSE...
...YOU WANT A REASON TO FORGIVE HIM.
THAT'S WHAT I THINK.
WHY NOT BE A LITTLE MORE HONEST ABOUT HOW YOU REALLY FEEL?
BUT IF I FOLLOW MY EMO-TIONS...
...I'LL MESS UP.
MRMR
MRMR

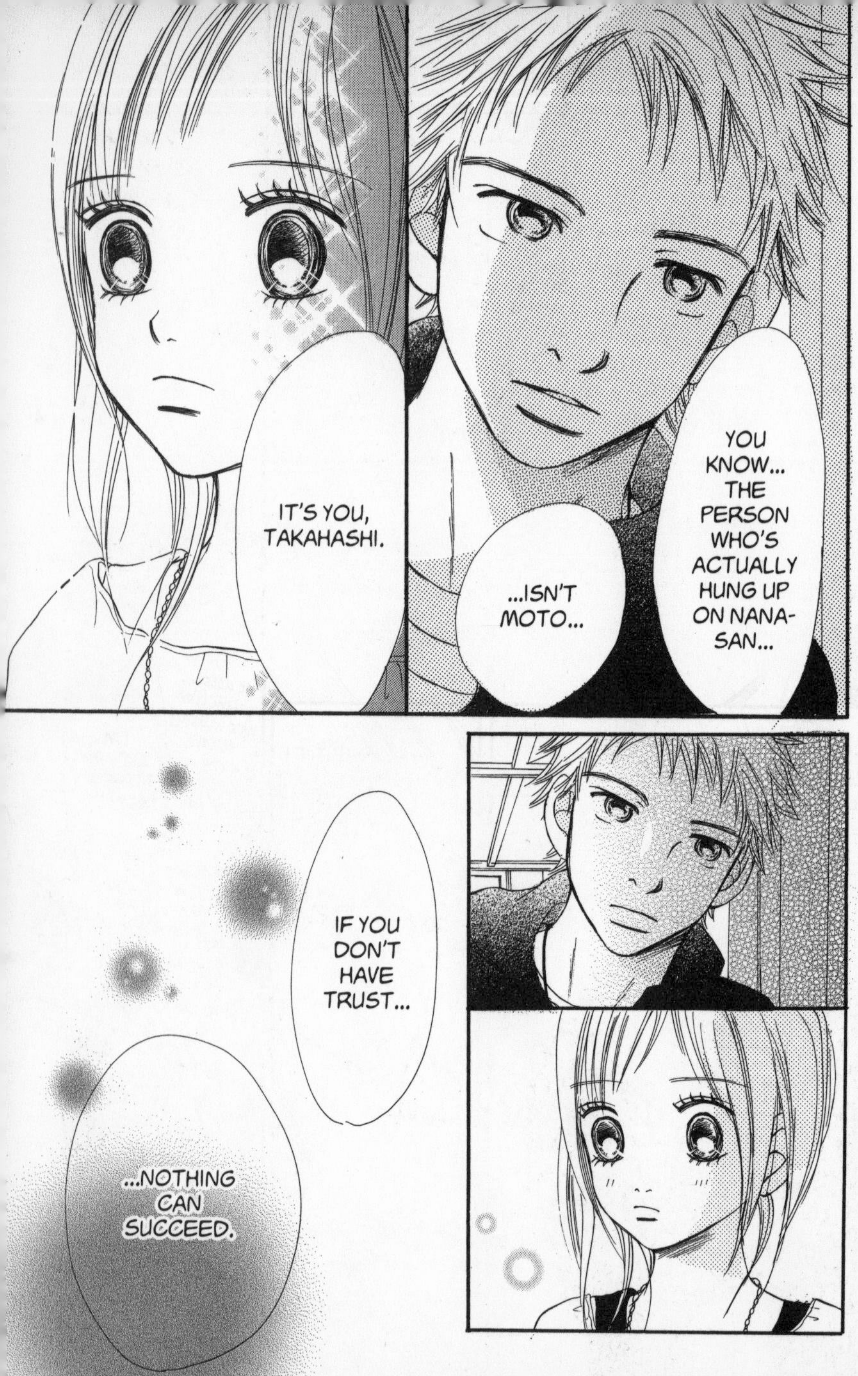
YOU KNOW... THE PERSON WHO'S ACTUALLY HUNG UP ON NANA-SAN...
...ISN'T MOTO...
IT'S YOU, TAKAHASHI.
IF YOU DON'T HAVE TRUST...
...NOTHING CAN SUCCEED.

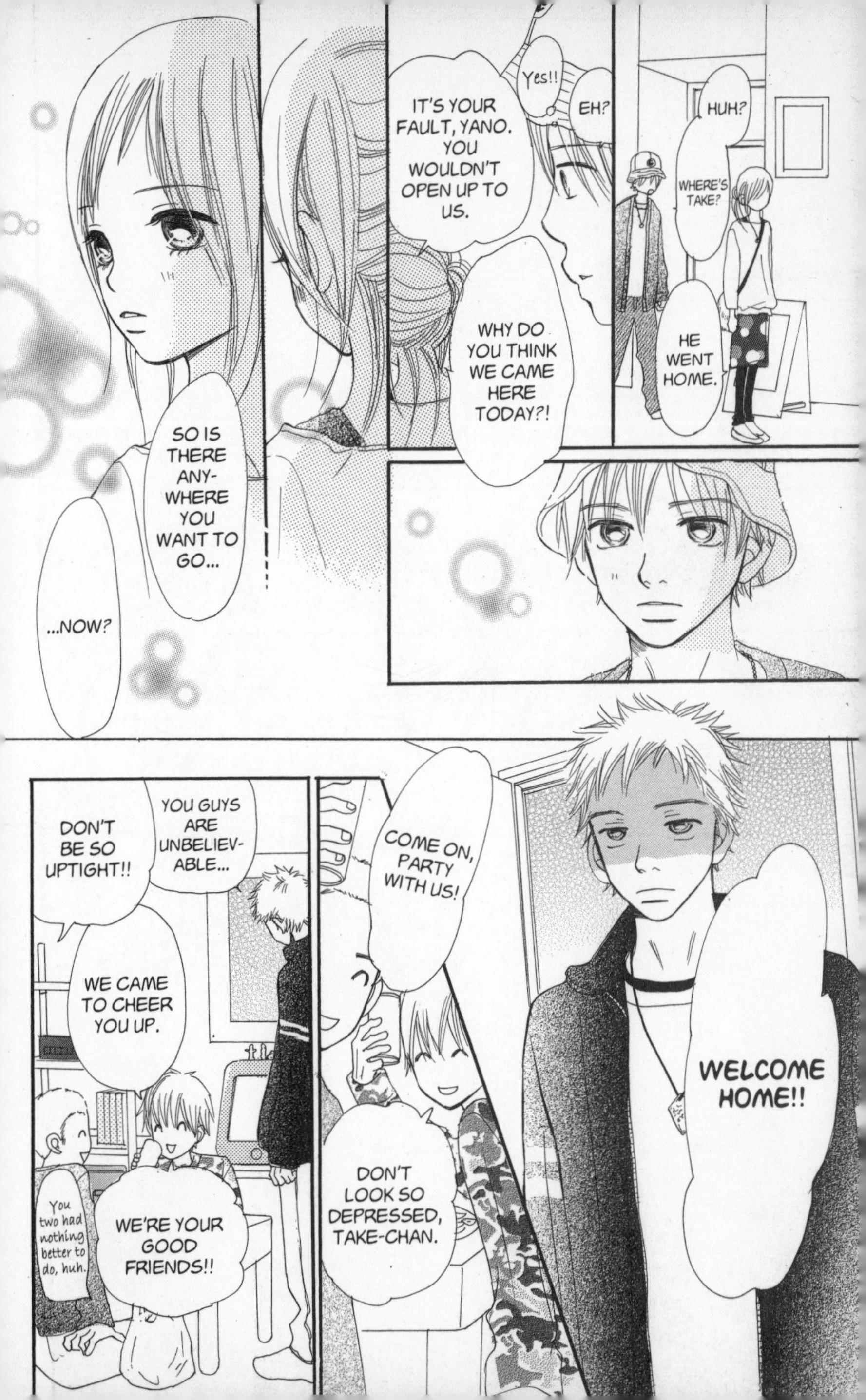
HUH?
WHERE'S TAKE?
HE WENT HOME.
EH?
Yes!!
IT'S YOUR FAULT, YANO. YOU WOULDN'T OPEN UP TO US.
WHY DO YOU THINK WE CAME HERE TODAY?!
SO IS THERE ANYWHERE YOU WANT TO GO...
...NOW?
WELCOME HOME!!
COME ON, PARTY WITH US!
DON'T LOOK SO DEPRESSED, TAKE-CHAN.
YOU GUYS ARE UNBELIEVABLE...
DON'T BE SO UPTIGHT!!
WE CAME TO CHEER YOU UP.
WE'RE YOUR GOOD FRIENDS!!
You two had nothing better to do, huh.

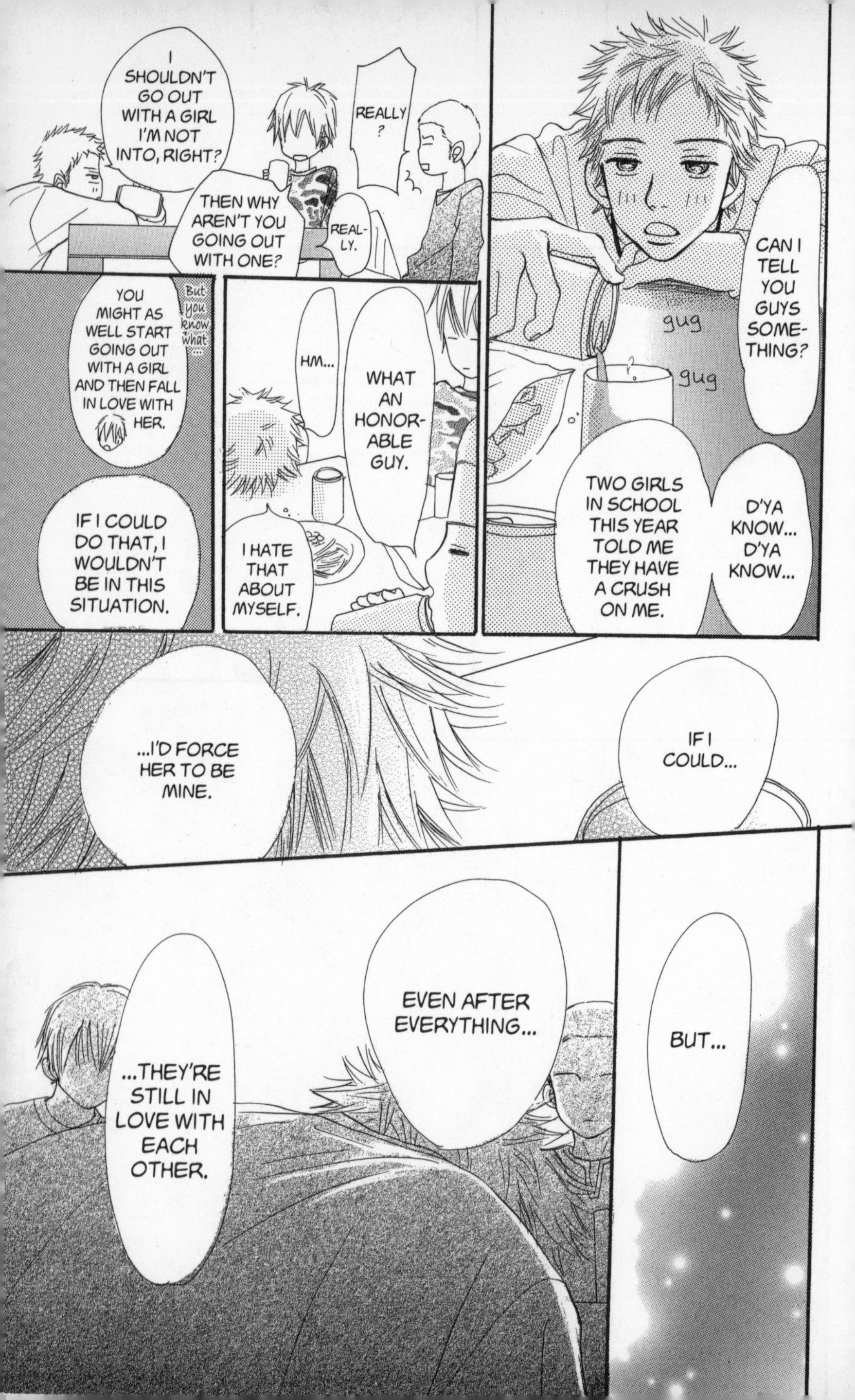
CAN I TELL YOU GUYS SOME-THING?
gug
gug
D'YA KNOW... D'YA KNOW...
TWO GIRLS IN SCHOOL THIS YEAR TOLD ME THEY HAVE A CRUSH ON ME.
I SHOULDN'T GO OUT WITH A GIRL I'M NOT INTO, RIGHT?
REALLY?
REAL-LY.
THEN WHY AREN'T YOU GOING OUT WITH ONE?
HM...
WHAT AN HONOR-ABLE GUY.
I HATE THAT ABOUT MYSELF.
YOU MIGHT AS WELL START GOING OUT WITH A GIRL AND THEN FALL IN LOVE WITH HER.
But you know what...
IF I COULD DO THAT, I WOULDN'T BE IN THIS SITUATION.
IF I COULD...
...I'D FORCE HER TO BE MINE.
BUT...
EVEN AFTER EVERYTHING...
...THEY'RE STILL IN LOVE WITH EACH OTHER.

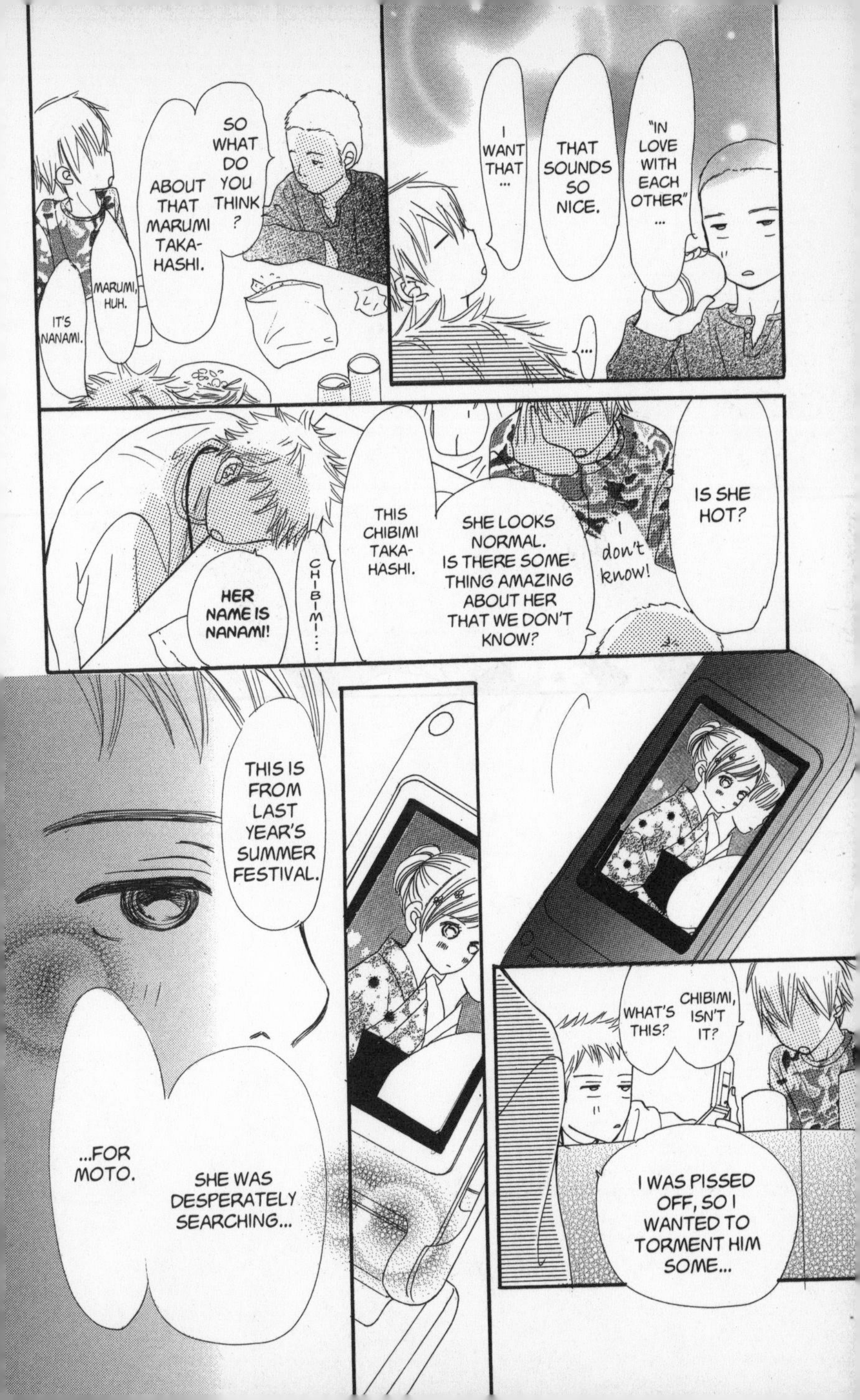
"IN LOVE WITH EACH OTHER"...
THAT SOUNDS SO NICE.
I WANT THAT...
...
SO WHAT DO YOU THINK ABOUT THAT MARUMI TAKA-HASHI?
MARUMI, HUH.
IT'S NANAMI.
IS SHE HOT?
I don't know!
SHE LOOKS NORMAL. IS THERE SOME-THING AMAZING ABOUT HER THAT WE DON'T KNOW?
THIS CHIBIMI TAKA-HASHI.
CHIBIMI...
HER NAME IS NANAMI!
CHIBIMI, ISN'T IT?
WHAT'S THIS?
I WAS PISSED OFF, SO I WANTED TO TORMENT HIM SOME...
THIS IS FROM LAST YEAR'S SUMMER FESTIVAL.
SHE WAS DESPERATELY SEARCHING...
...FOR MOTO.

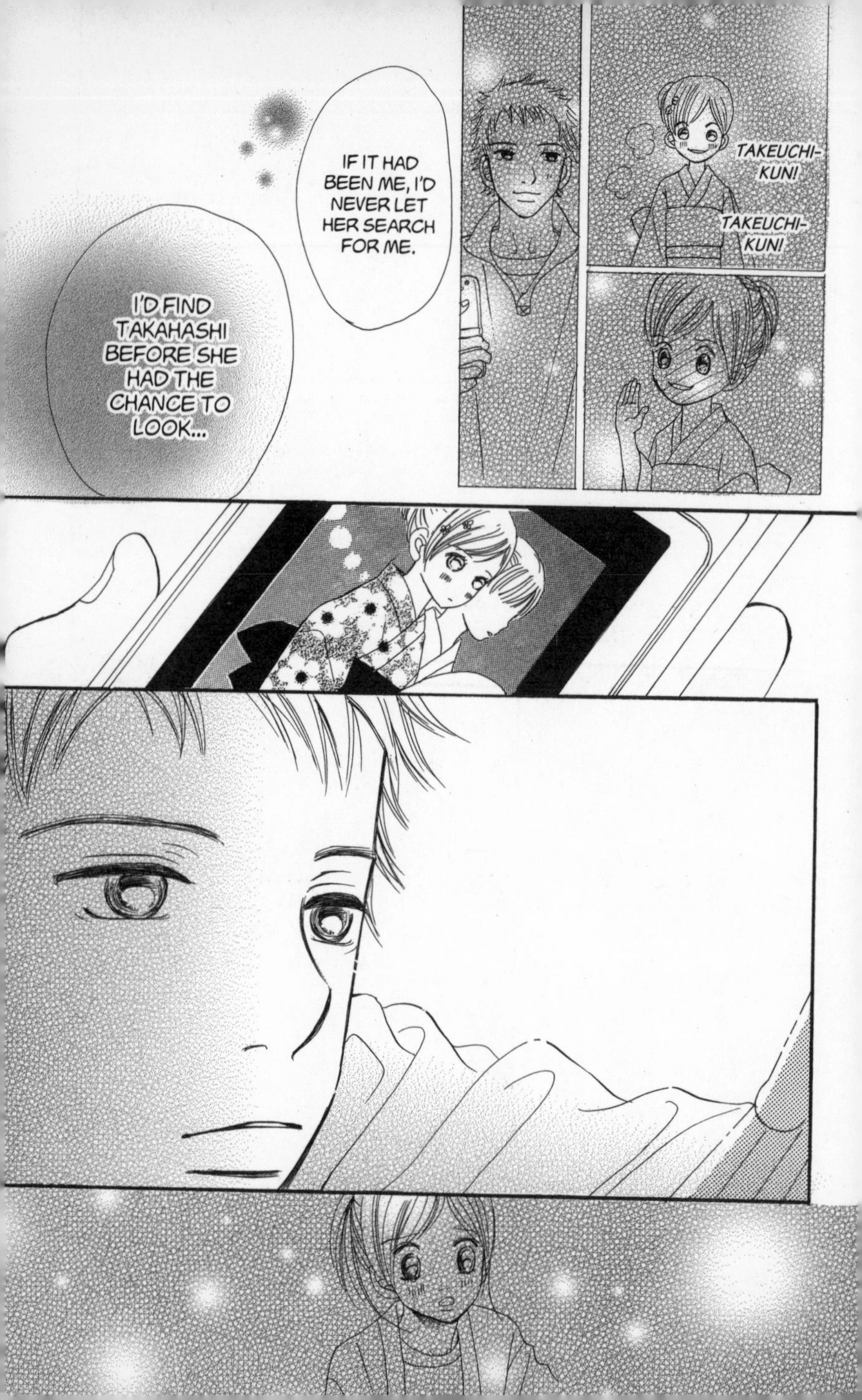
TAKEUCHI-KUN!
TAKEUCHI-KUN!
IF IT HAD BEEN ME, I'D NEVER LET HER SEARCH FOR ME.
I'D FIND TAKAHASHI BEFORE SHE HAD THE CHANCE TO LOOK...

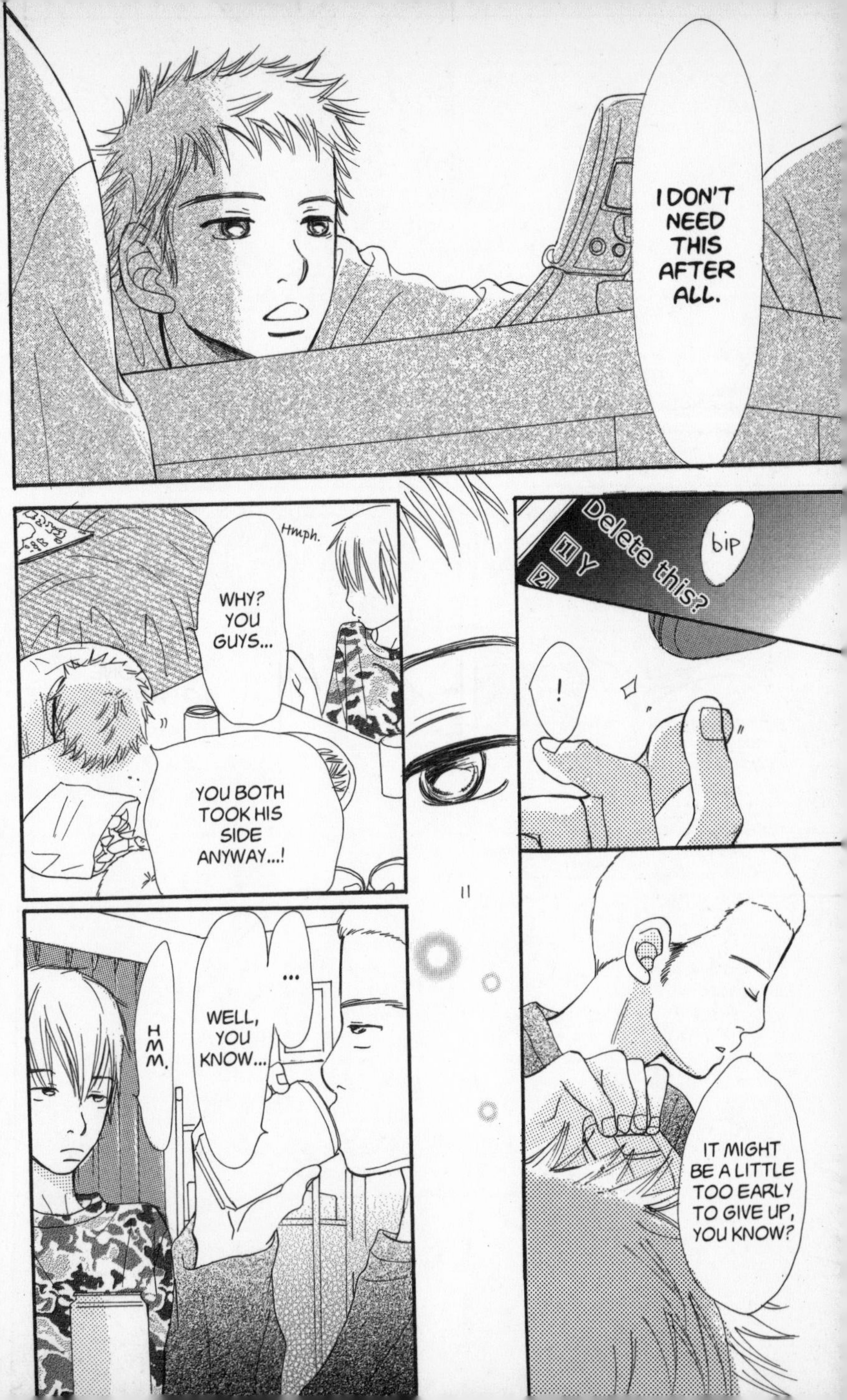
I DON'T NEED THIS AFTER ALL.
Delete this?
1 Y
2
bip
!
Hmph.
WHY? YOU GUYS...
YOU BOTH TOOK HIS SIDE ANYWAY...!
IT MIGHT BE A LITTLE TOO EARLY TO GIVE UP, YOU KNOW?
...
WELL, YOU KNOW...
HMM.

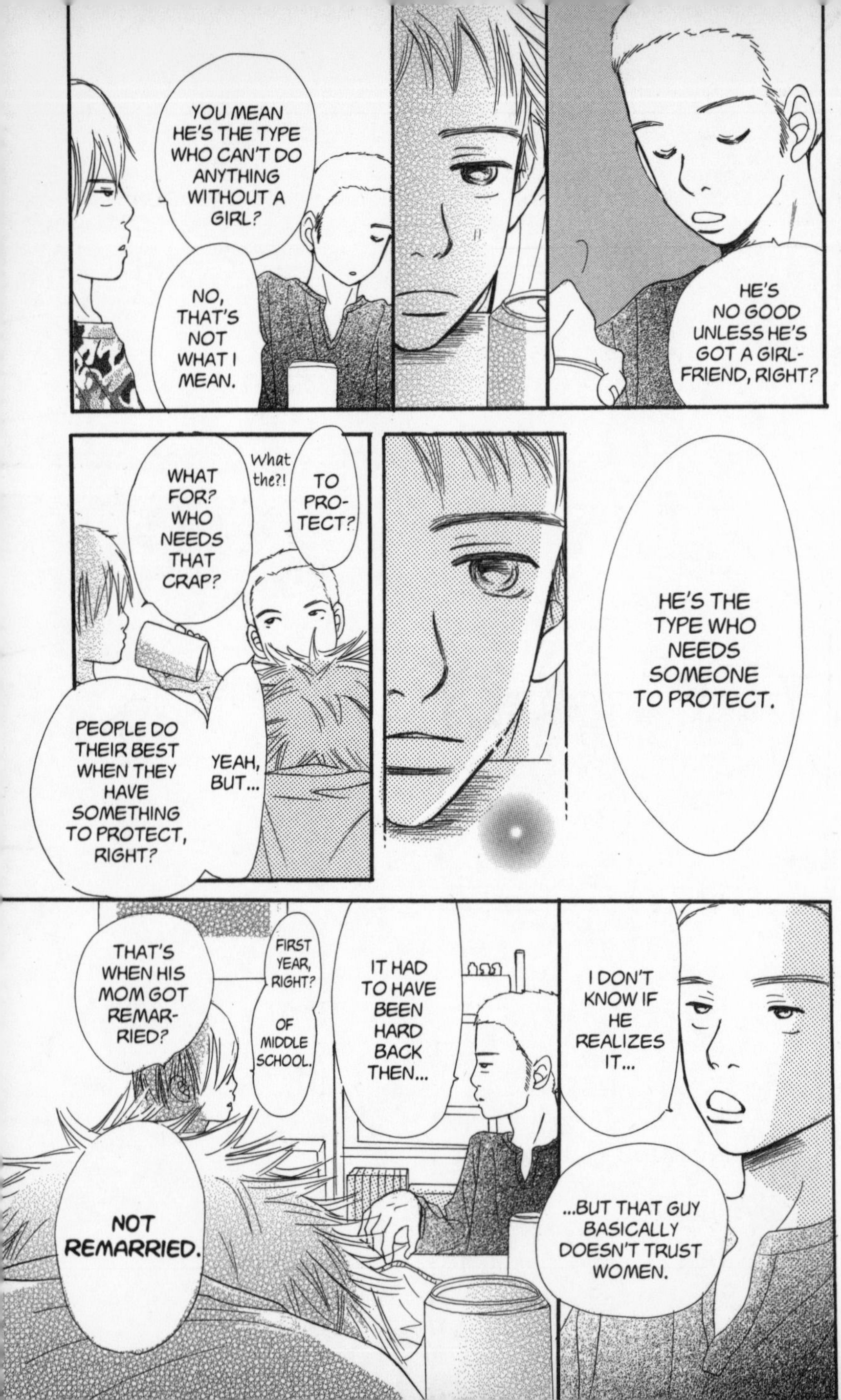
HE'S NO GOOD UNLESS HE'S GOT A GIRL-FRIEND, RIGHT?
YOU MEAN HE'S THE TYPE WHO CAN'T DO ANYTHING WITHOUT A GIRL?
NO, THAT'S NOT WHAT I MEAN.
HE'S THE TYPE WHO NEEDS SOMEONE TO PROTECT.
TO PRO-TECT?
What the?!
WHAT FOR? WHO NEEDS THAT CRAP?
YEAH, BUT...
PEOPLE DO THEIR BEST WHEN THEY HAVE SOMETHING TO PROTECT, RIGHT?
I DON'T KNOW IF HE REALIZES IT...
...BUT THAT GUY BASICALLY DOESN'T TRUST WOMEN.
IT HAD TO HAVE BEEN HARD BACK THEN...
FIRST YEAR, RIGHT?
OF MIDDLE SCHOOL.
THAT'S WHEN HIS MOM GOT REMAR-RIED?
NOT REMARRIED.

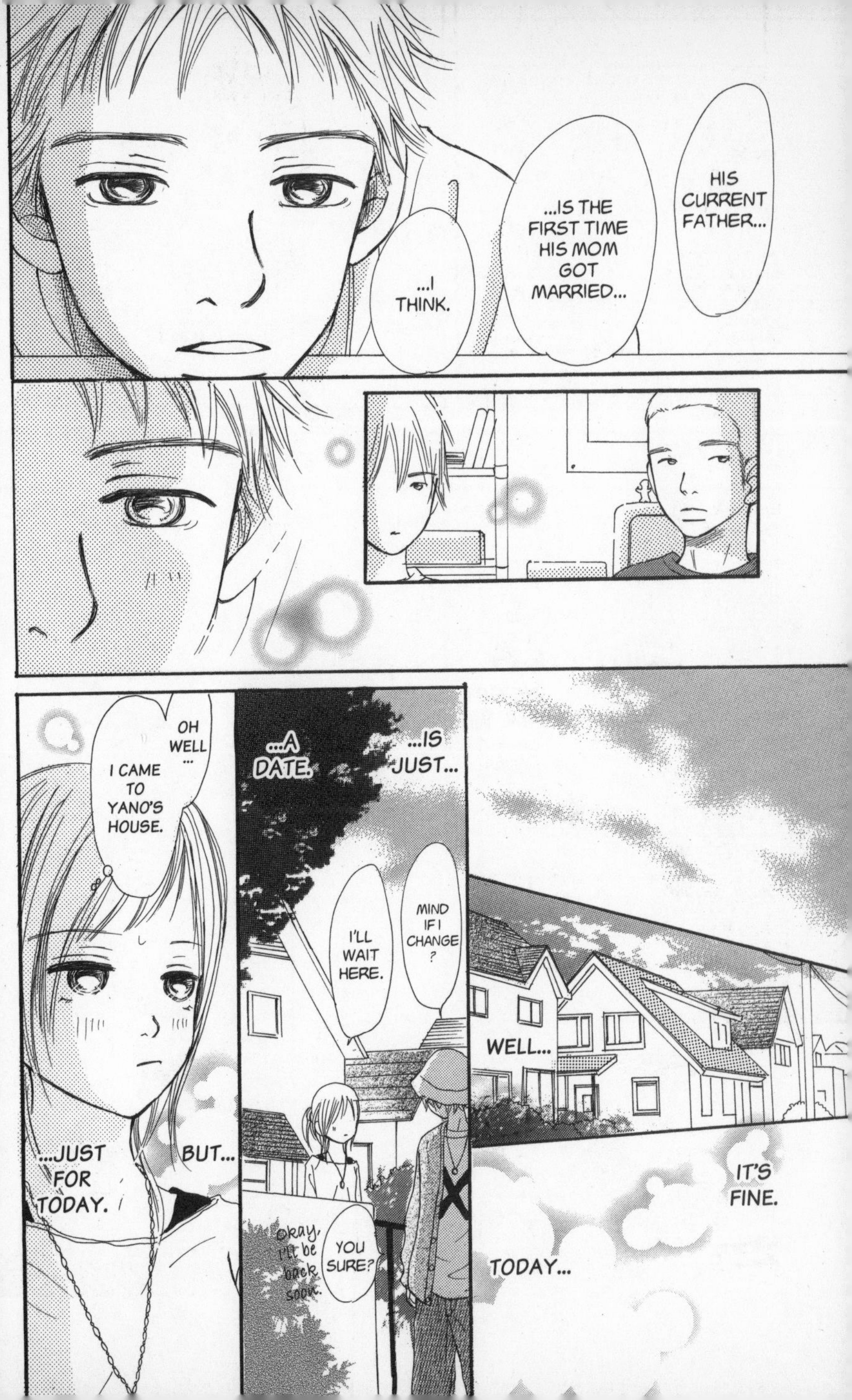
HIS CURRENT FATHER...
...IS THE FIRST TIME HIS MOM GOT MARRIED...
...I THINK.
WELL...
IT'S FINE.
TODAY...
...IS JUST...
...A DATE.
MIND IF I CHANGE?
I'LL WAIT HERE.
YOU SURE?
Okay, I'll be back soon.
OH WELL...
I CAME TO YANO'S HOUSE.
BUT...
...JUST FOR TODAY.

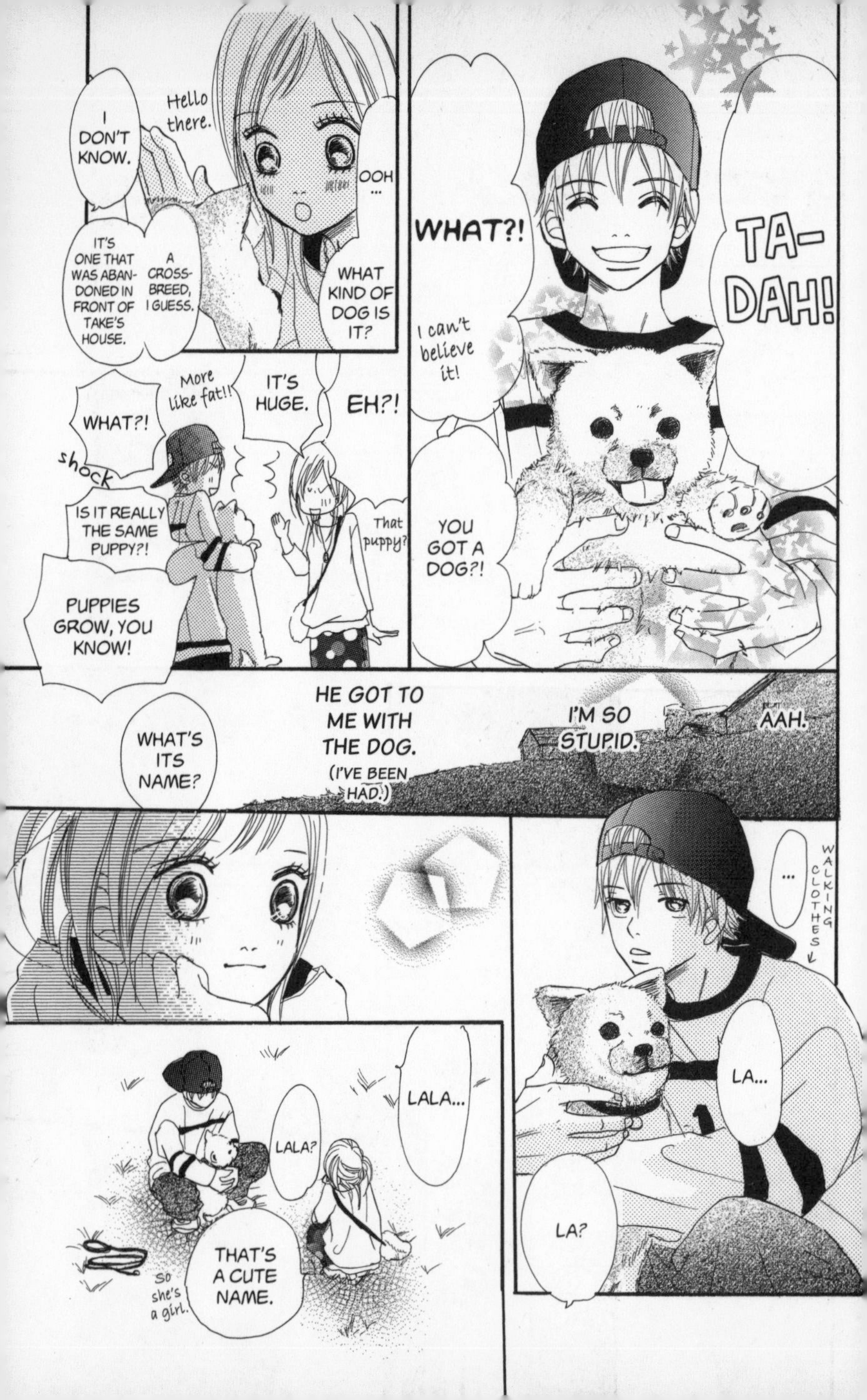
TA-DAH!
WHAT?!
I can't believe it!
YOU GOT A DOG?!
OOH ...
Hello there.
I DON'T KNOW.
WHAT KIND OF DOG IS IT?
A CROSS-BREED, I GUESS.
IT'S ONE THAT WAS ABANDONED IN FRONT OF TAKE'S HOUSE.
EH?!
That puppy?
IT'S HUGE.
More like fat!!
WHAT?!
shock
IS IT REALLY THE SAME PUPPY?!
PUPPIES GROW, YOU KNOW!
AAH.
I'M SO STUPID.
HE GOT TO ME WITH THE DOG.
(I'VE BEEN HAD.)
WHAT'S ITS NAME?
...
WALKING CLOTHES
LA...
LA?
LALA...
LALA?
THAT'S A CUTE NAME.
So she's a girl.

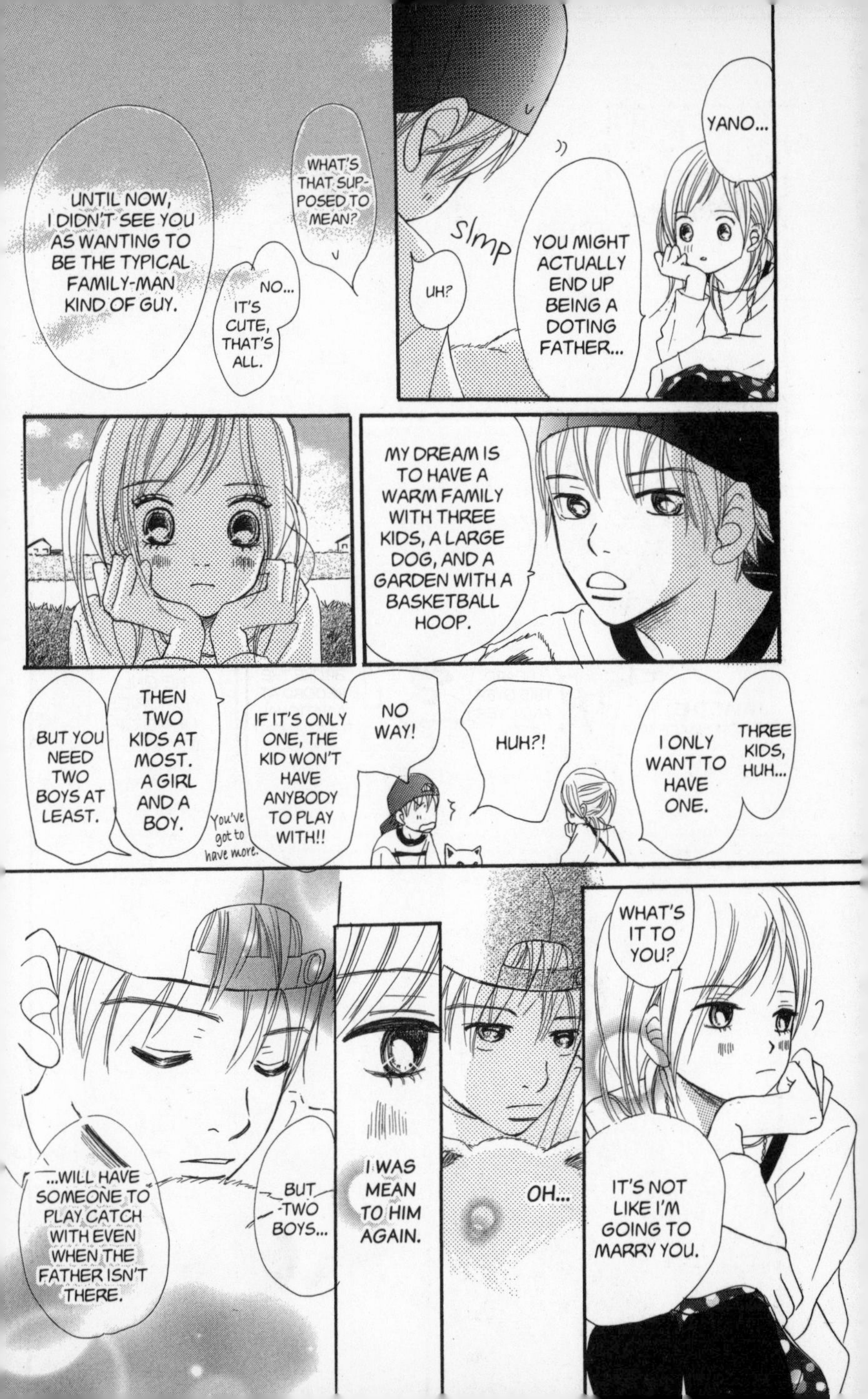
YANO...
YOU MIGHT ACTUALLY END UP BEING A DOTING FATHER...
slmp
UH?
WHAT'S THAT SUPPOSED TO MEAN?
NO... IT'S CUTE, THAT'S ALL.
UNTIL NOW, I DIDN'T SEE YOU AS WANTING TO BE THE TYPICAL FAMILY-MAN KIND OF GUY.
MY DREAM IS TO HAVE A WARM FAMILY WITH THREE KIDS, A LARGE DOG, AND A GARDEN WITH A BASKETBALL HOOP.
THREE KIDS, HUH...
I ONLY WANT TO HAVE ONE.
HUH?!
NO WAY!
IF IT'S ONLY ONE, THE KID WON'T HAVE ANYBODY TO PLAY WITH!!
You've got to have more.
THEN TWO KIDS AT MOST. A GIRL AND A BOY.
BUT YOU NEED TWO BOYS AT LEAST.
WHAT'S IT TO YOU?
IT'S NOT LIKE I'M GOING TO MARRY YOU.
OH...
I WAS MEAN TO HIM AGAIN.
BUT TWO BOYS...
...WILL HAVE SOMEONE TO PLAY CATCH WITH EVEN WHEN THE FATHER ISN'T THERE.

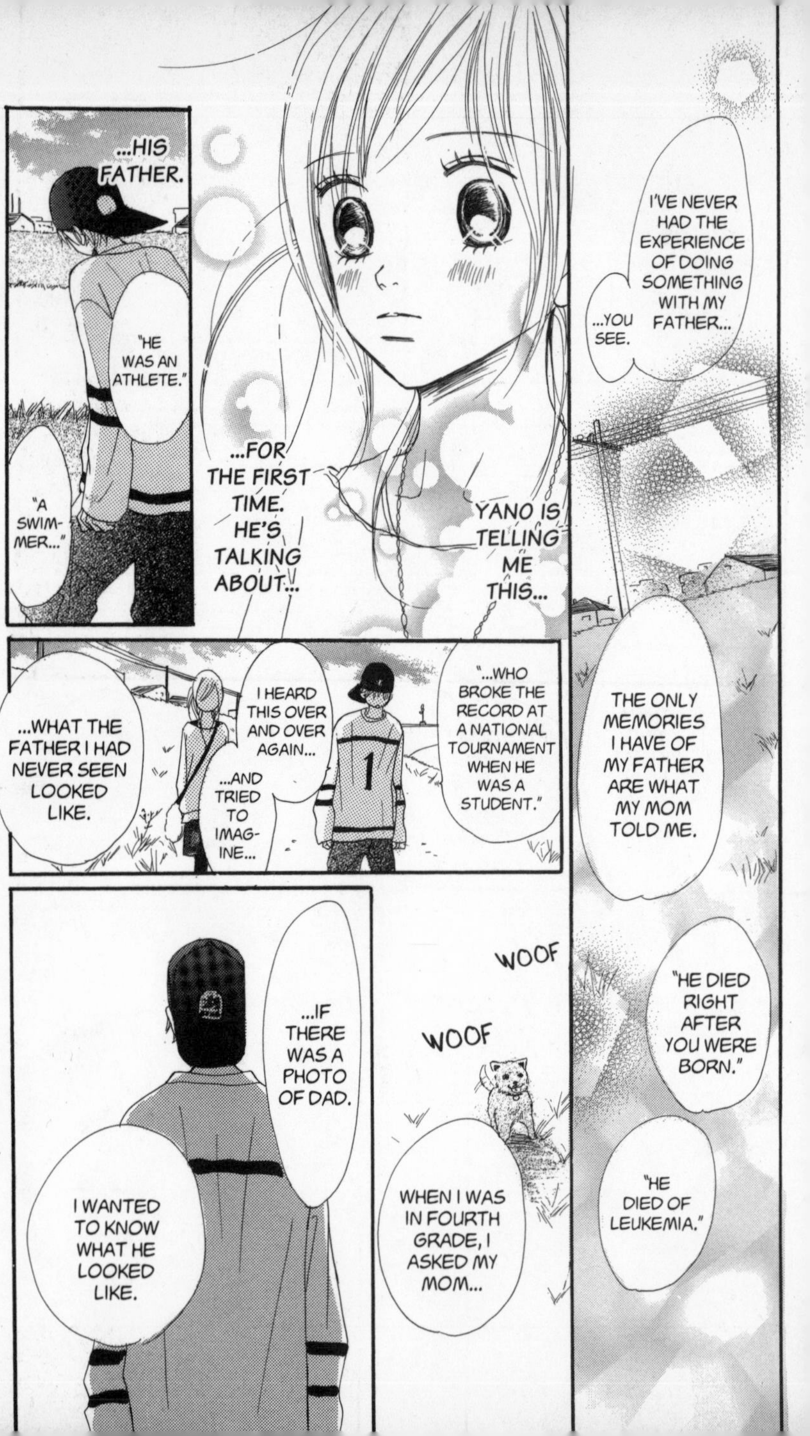
I'VE NEVER HAD THE EXPERIENCE OF DOING SOMETHING WITH MY FATHER...
...YOU SEE.
THE ONLY MEMORIES I HAVE OF MY FATHER ARE WHAT MY MOM TOLD ME.
"HE DIED RIGHT AFTER YOU WERE BORN."
"HE DIED OF LEUKEMIA."
YANO IS TELLING ME THIS...
...FOR THE FIRST TIME. HE'S TALKING ABOUT...
...HIS FATHER.
"HE WAS AN ATHLETE."
"A SWIMMER..."
"...WHO BROKE THE RECORD AT A NATIONAL TOURNAMENT WHEN HE WAS A STUDENT."
I HEARD THIS OVER AND OVER AGAIN...
...AND TRIED TO IMAGINE...
...WHAT THE FATHER I HAD NEVER SEEN LOOKED LIKE.
WOOF
WOOF
WHEN I WAS IN FOURTH GRADE, I ASKED MY MOM...
...IF THERE WAS A PHOTO OF DAD.
I WANTED TO KNOW WHAT HE LOOKED LIKE.

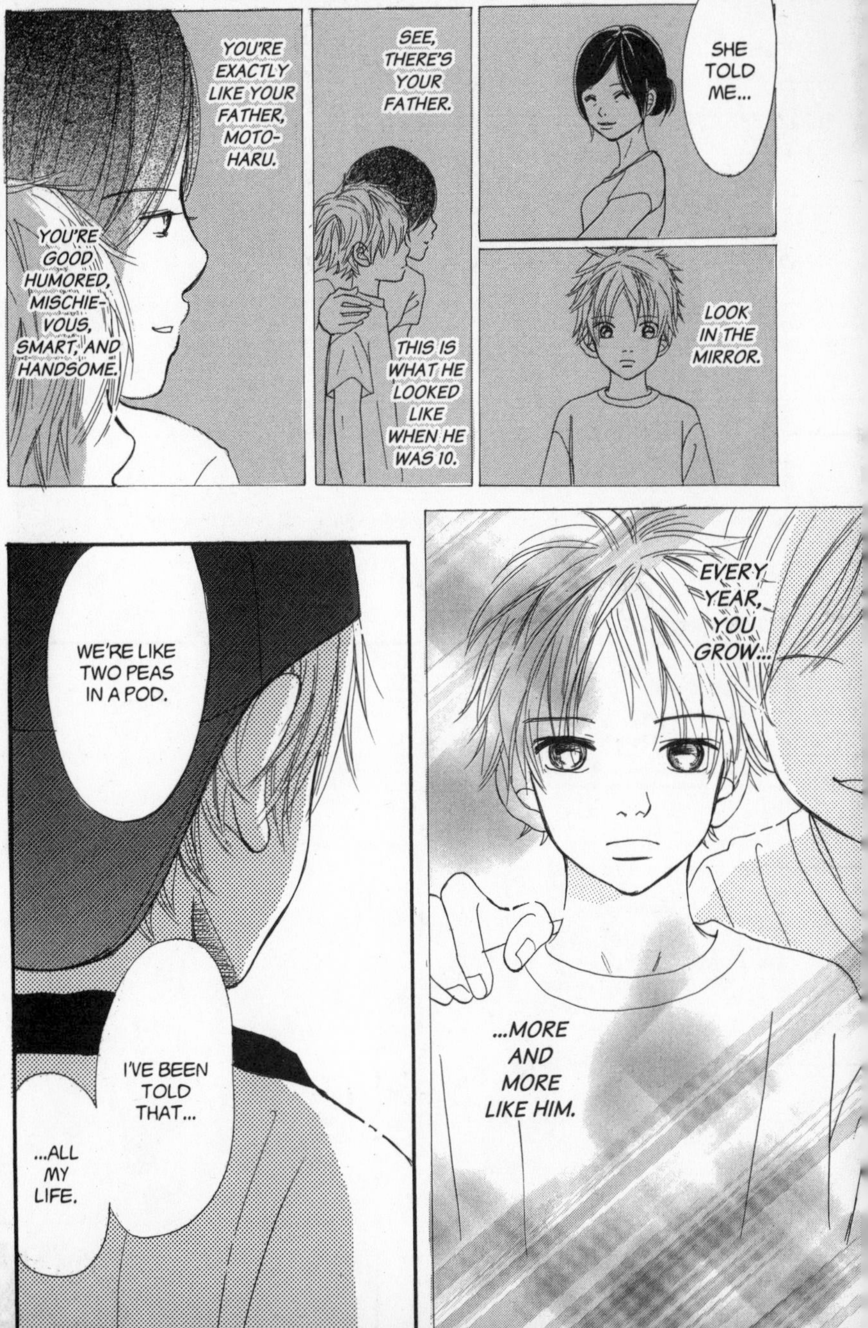
SHE TOLD ME...
LOOK IN THE MIRROR.
SEE, THERE'S YOUR FATHER.
THIS IS WHAT HE LOOKED LIKE WHEN HE WAS 10.
YOU'RE EXACTLY LIKE YOUR FATHER, MOTO-HARU.
YOU'RE GOOD HUMORED, MISCHIE-VOUS, SMART, AND HANDSOME.
EVERY YEAR, YOU GROW...
...MORE AND MORE LIKE HIM.
WE'RE LIKE TWO PEAS IN A POD.
I'VE BEEN TOLD THAT...
...ALL MY LIFE.

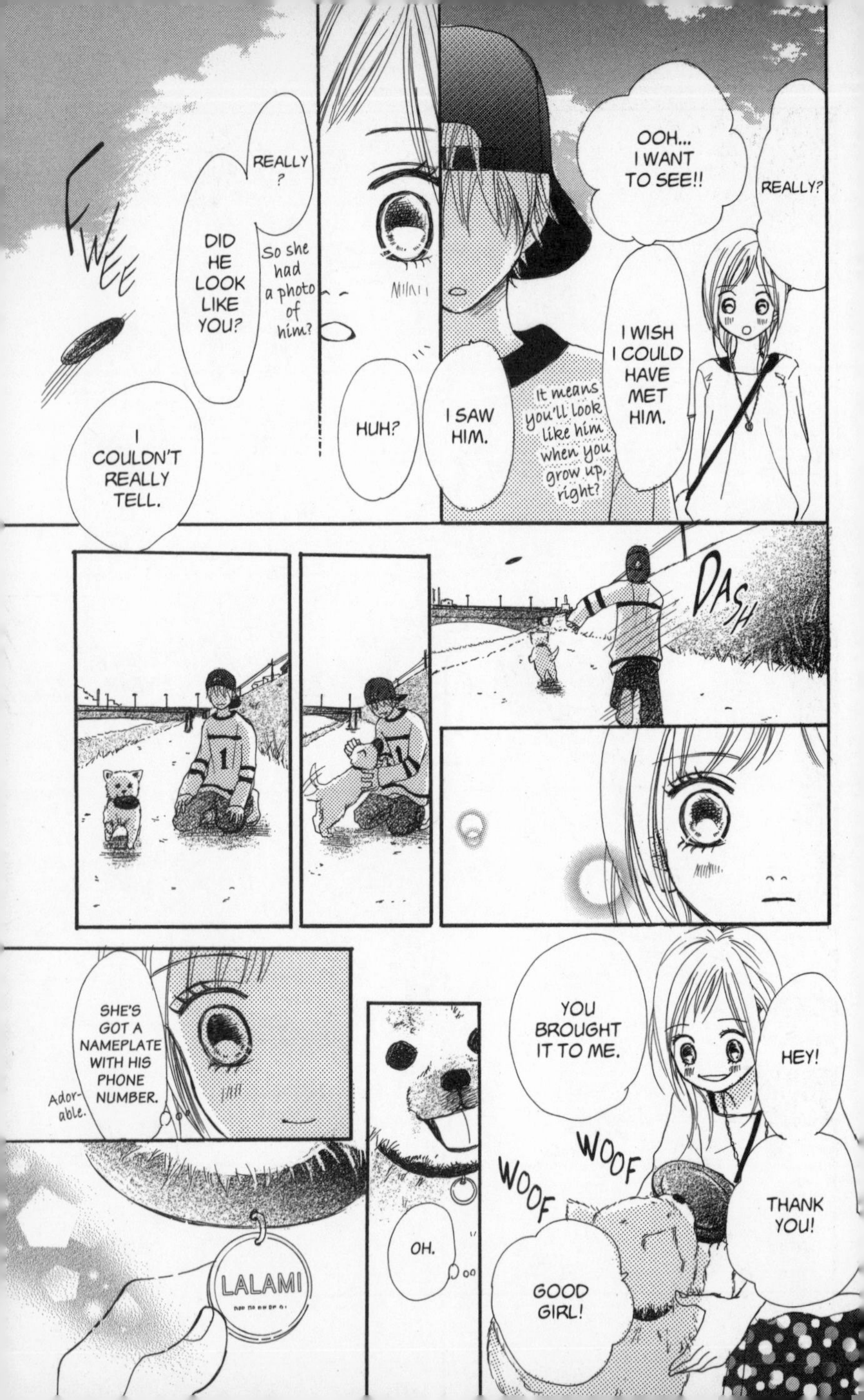
REALLY?
OOH... I WANT TO SEE!!
I WISH I COULD HAVE MET HIM.
It means you'll look like him when you grow up, right?
I SAW HIM.
HUH?
REALLY?
So she had a photo of him?
DID HE LOOK LIKE YOU?
FWEE
I COULDN'T REALLY TELL.
DASH
HEY!
YOU BROUGHT IT TO ME.
THANK YOU!
WOOF
WOOF
GOOD GIRL!
OH.
SHE'S GOT A NAMEPLATE WITH HIS PHONE NUMBER.
Ador-able.
LALAMI

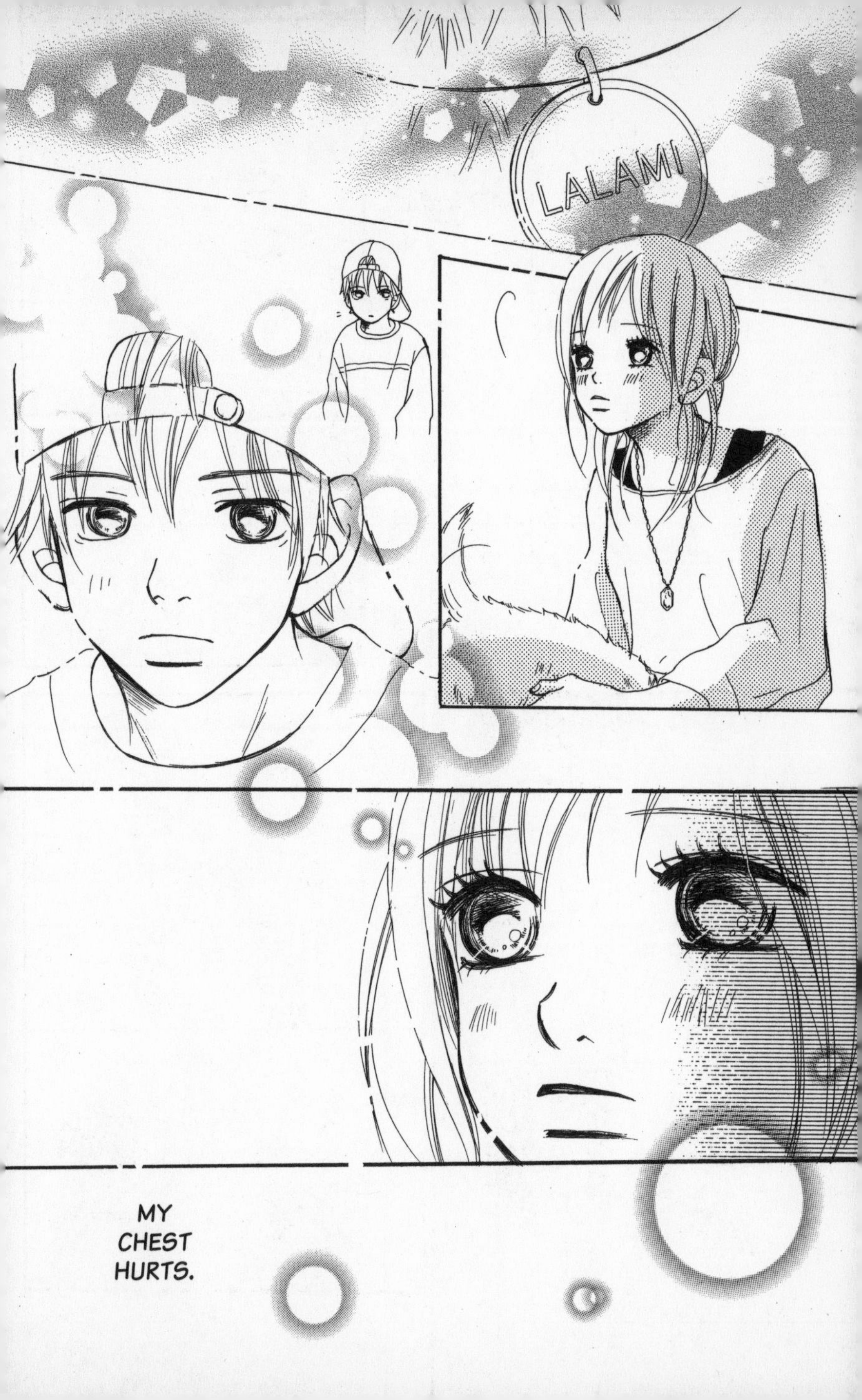
LALAMI
MY CHEST HURTS.

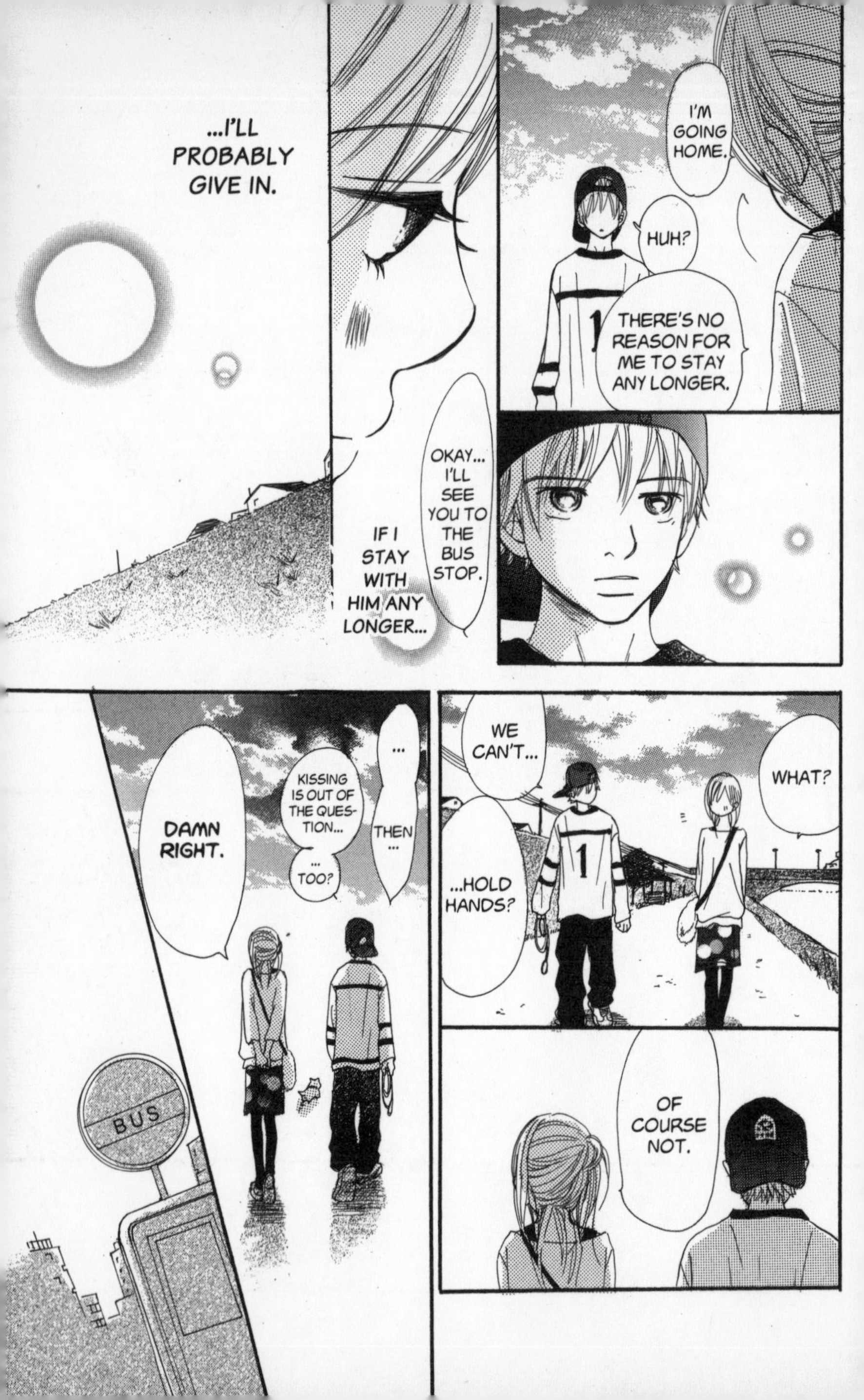
I'M GOING HOME.
HUH?
THERE'S NO REASON FOR ME TO STAY ANY LONGER.
OKAY... I'LL SEE YOU TO THE BUS STOP.
IF I STAY WITH HIM ANY LONGER...
...I'LL PROBABLY GIVE IN.
WHAT?
WE CAN'T...
...HOLD HANDS?
OF COURSE NOT.
...
THEN...
KISSING IS OUT OF THE QUES- TION...
...TOO?
DAMN RIGHT.
BUS

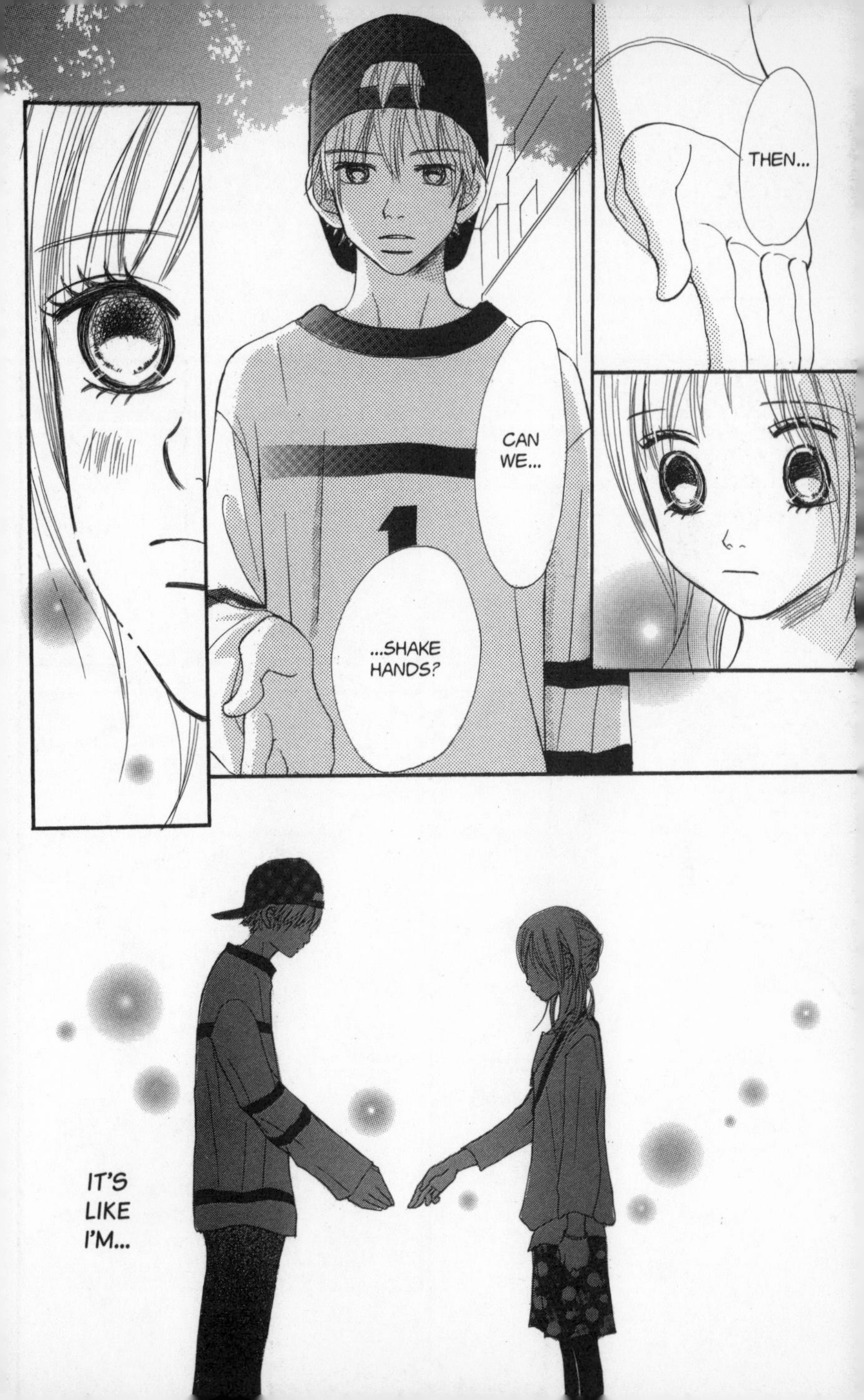
THEN...
CAN WE...
...SHAKE HANDS?
IT'S LIKE I'M...

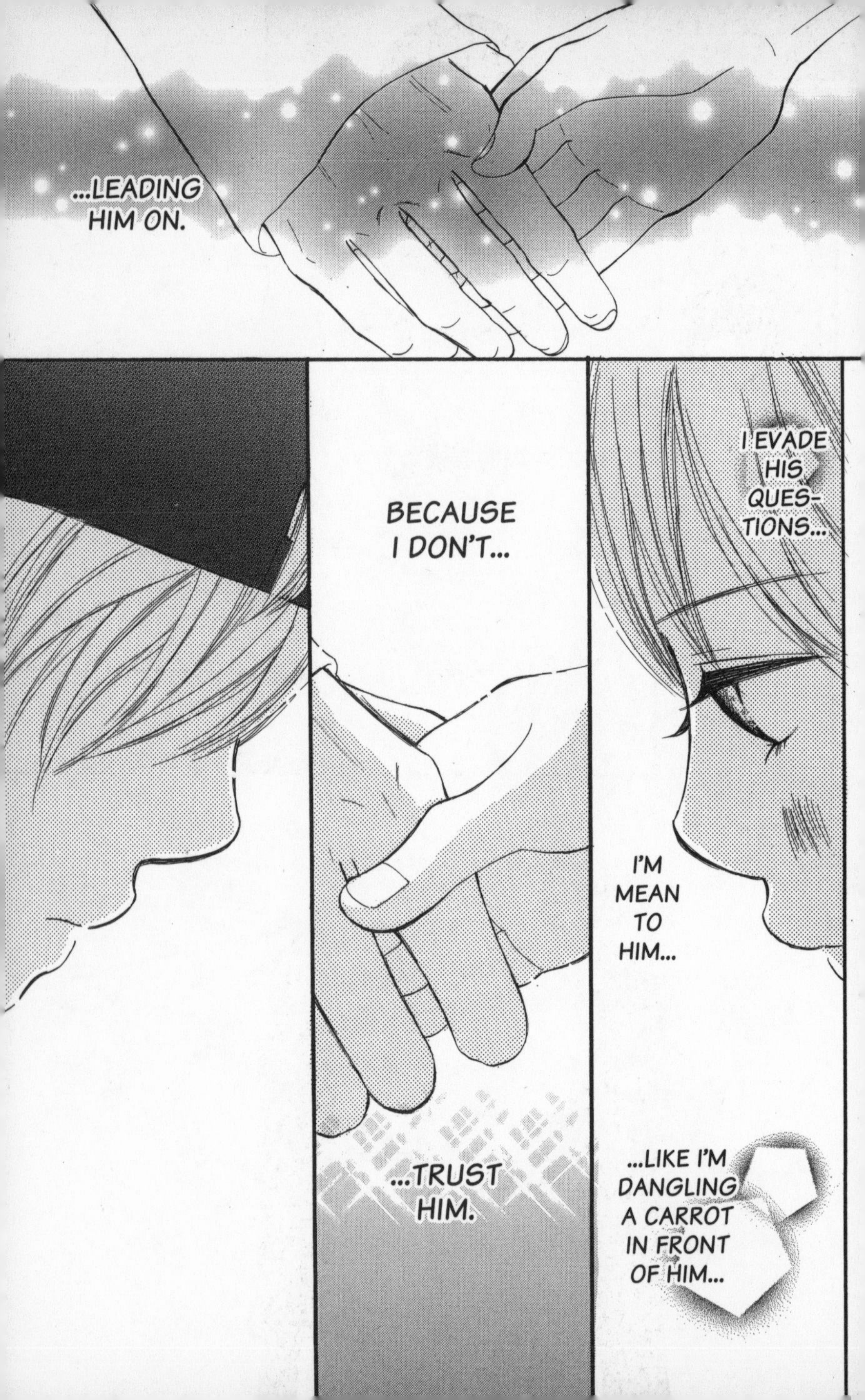
...LEADING HIM ON.
I EVADE HIS QUES-TIONS...
I'M MEAN TO HIM...
...LIKE I'M DANGLING A CARROT IN FRONT OF HIM...
BECAUSE I DON'T...
...TRUST HIM.

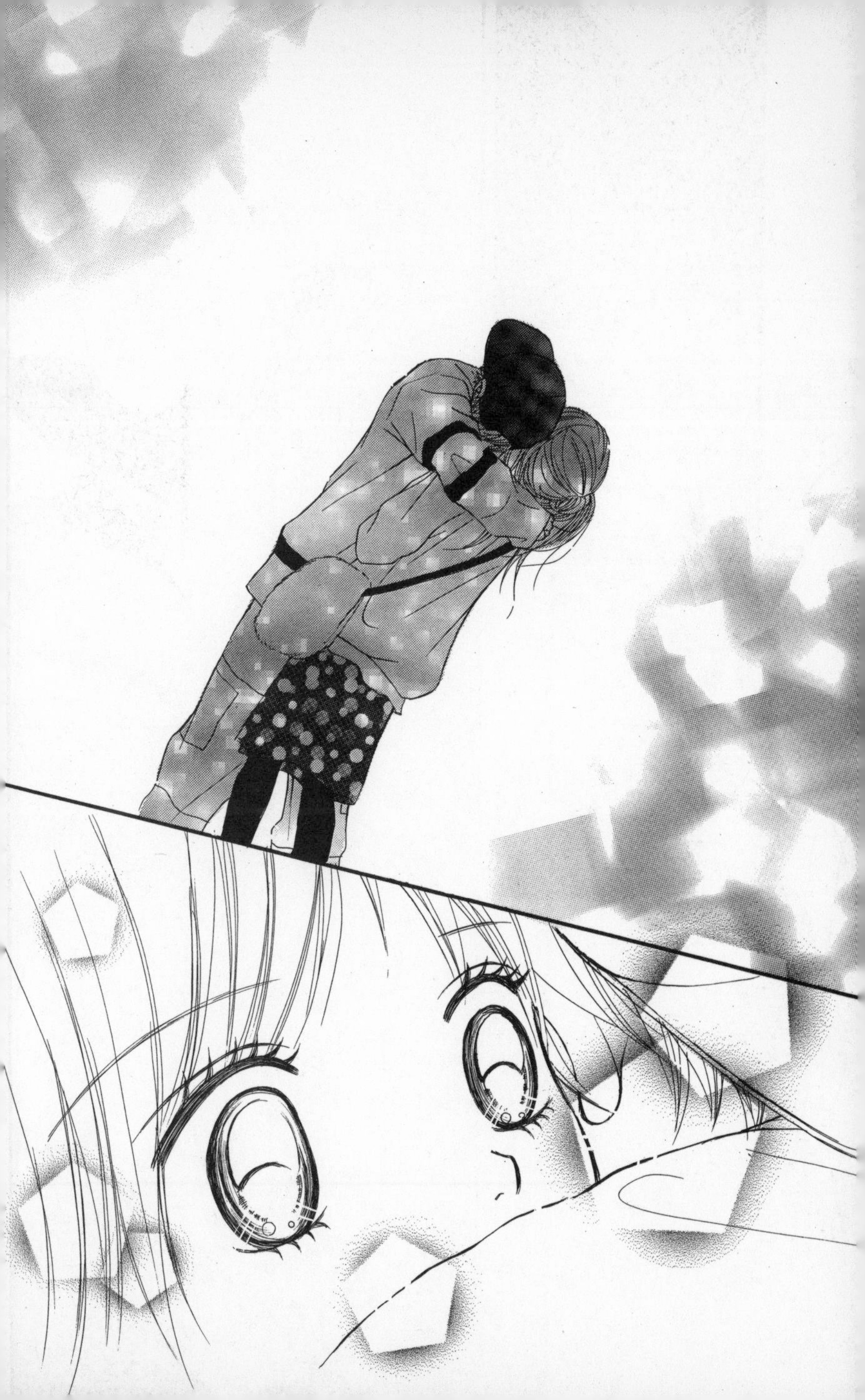

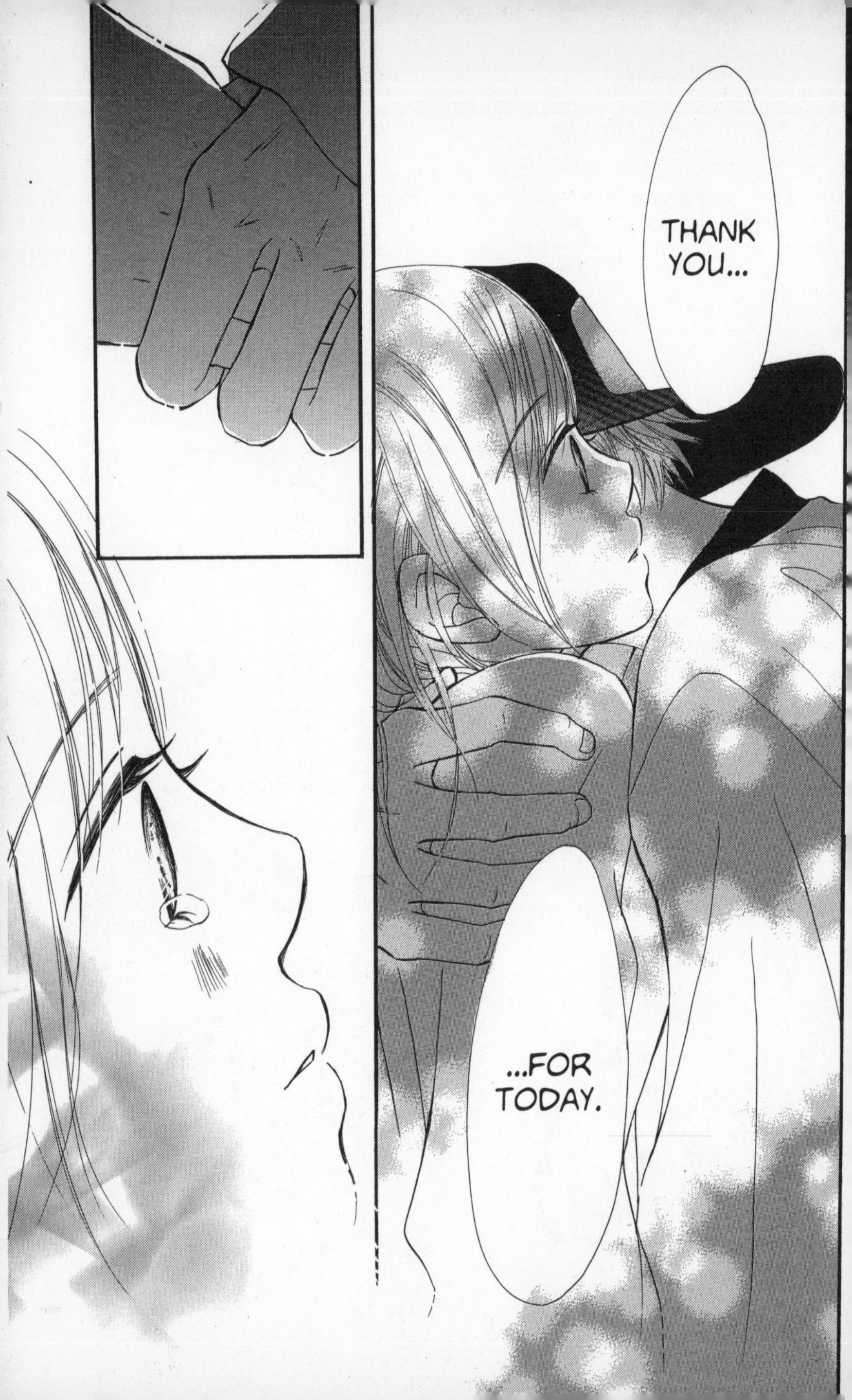
THANK YOU...
...FOR TODAY.

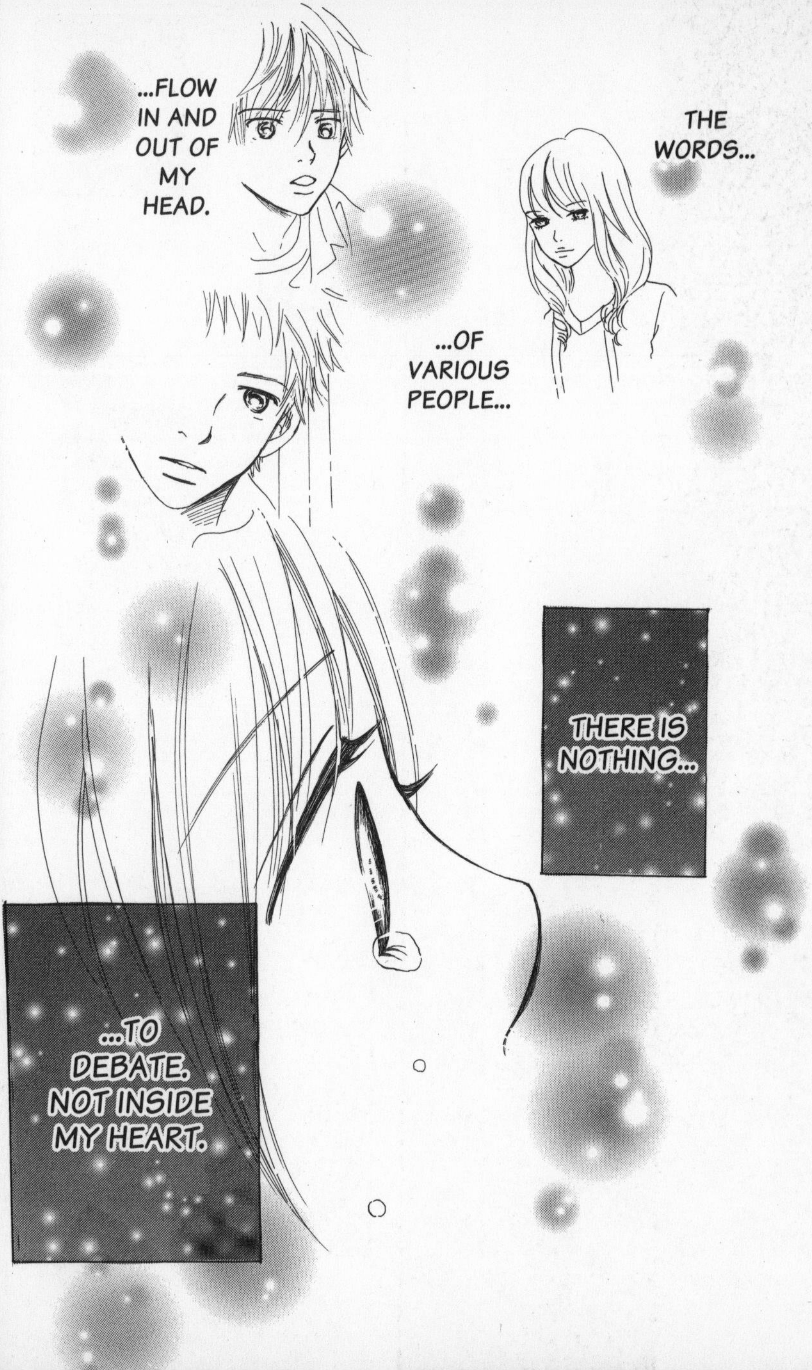
THE WORDS...
...OF VARIOUS PEOPLE...
...FLOW IN AND OUT OF MY HEAD.
THERE IS NOTHING...
...TO DEBATE. NOT INSIDE MY HEART.

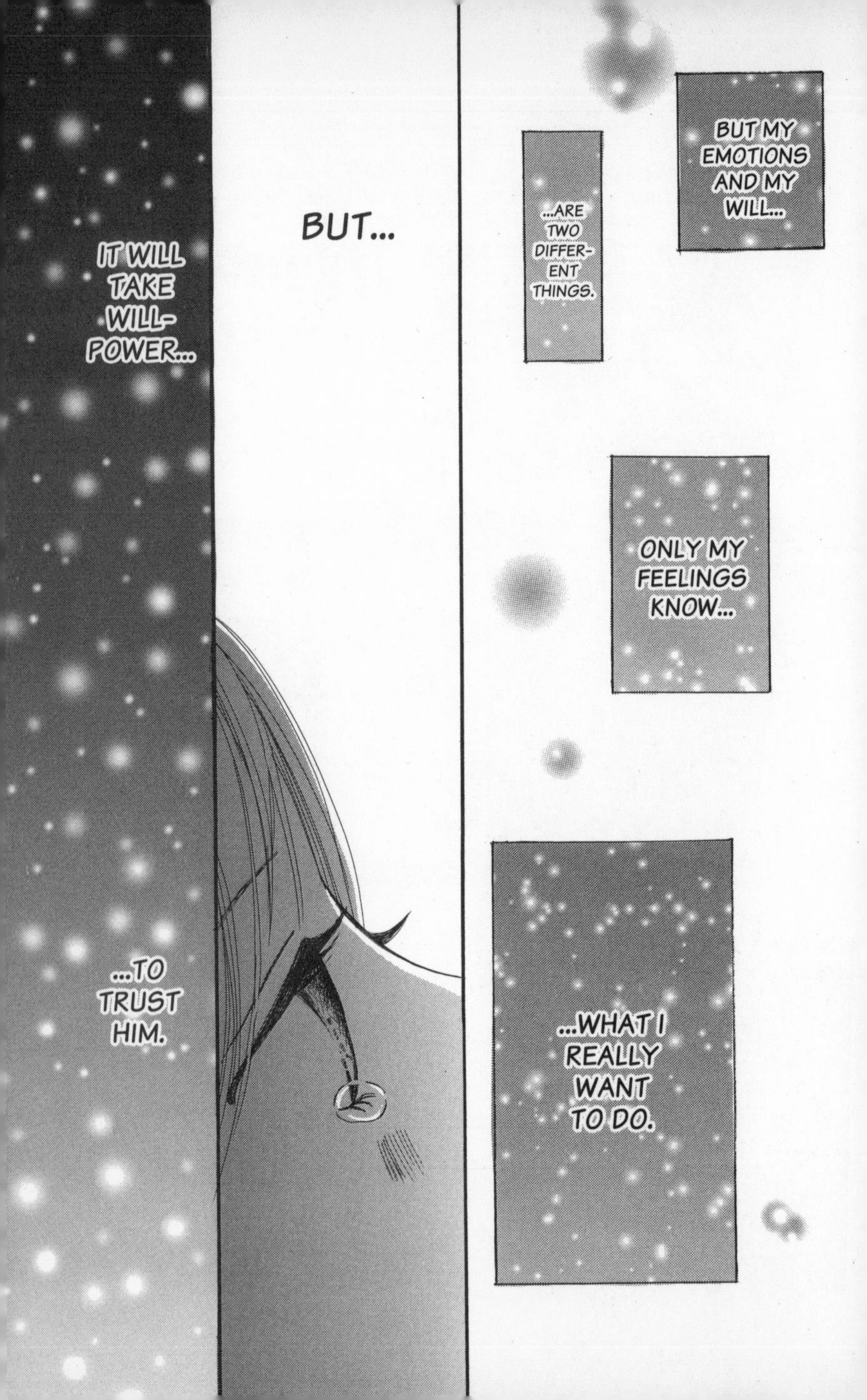
BUT MY EMOTIONS AND MY WILL...
...ARE TWO DIFFER-ENT THINGS.
ONLY MY FEELINGS KNOW...
...WHAT I REALLY WANT TO DO.
BUT...
IT WILL TAKE WILL-POWER...
...TO TRUST HIM.

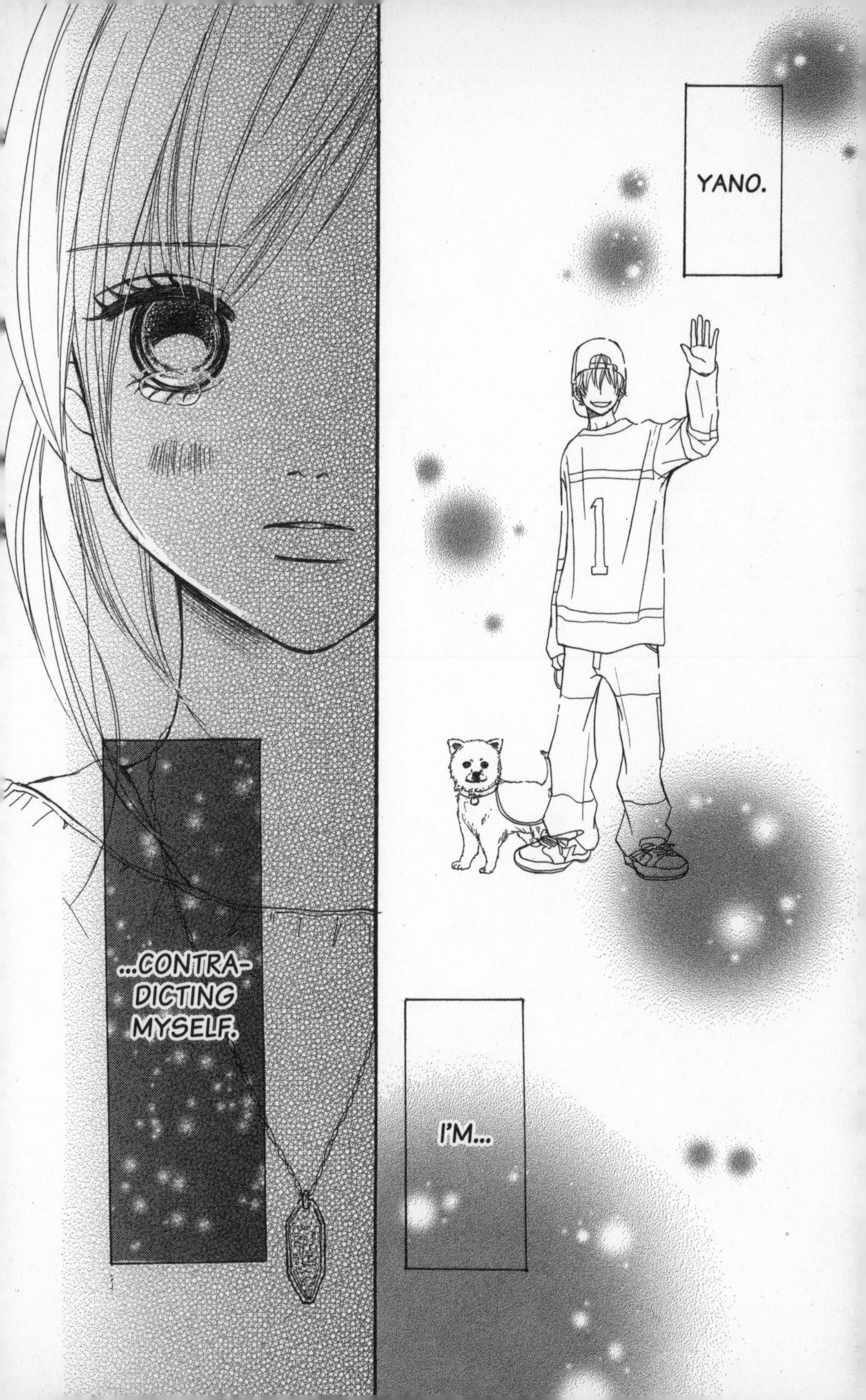
YANO.
I'M...
...CONTRA-DICTING MYSELF.

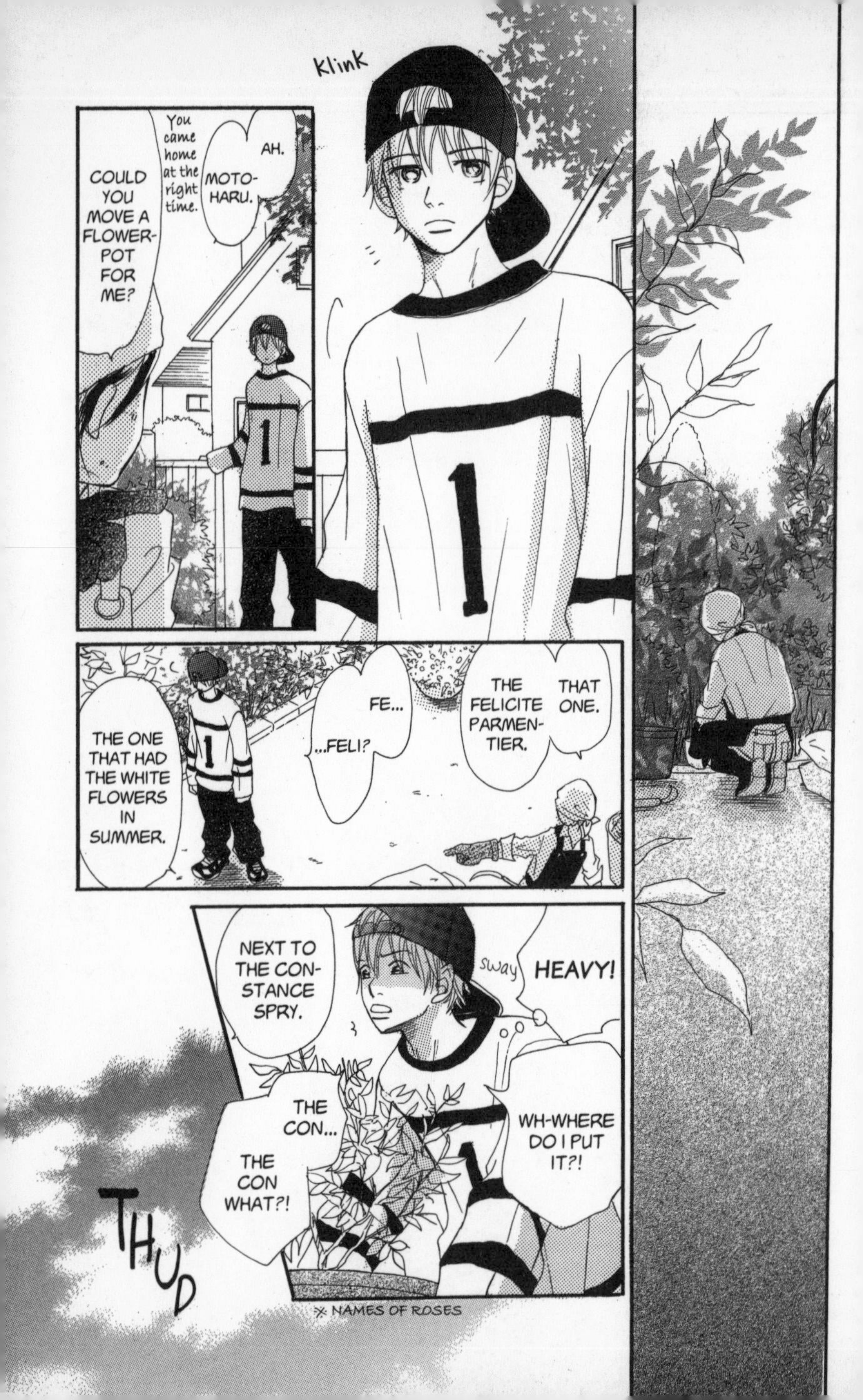
Klink
AH. MOTOHARU.
You came home at the right time.
COULD YOU MOVE A FLOWERPOT FOR ME?
THAT ONE.
THE FELICITE PARMENTIER.
FE...
...FELI?
THE ONE THAT HAD THE WHITE FLOWERS IN SUMMER.
HEAVY!
sway
WH-WHERE DO I PUT IT?!
NEXT TO THE CONSTANCE SPRY.
THE CON...
THE CON WHAT?!
THUD
※ NAMES OF ROSES

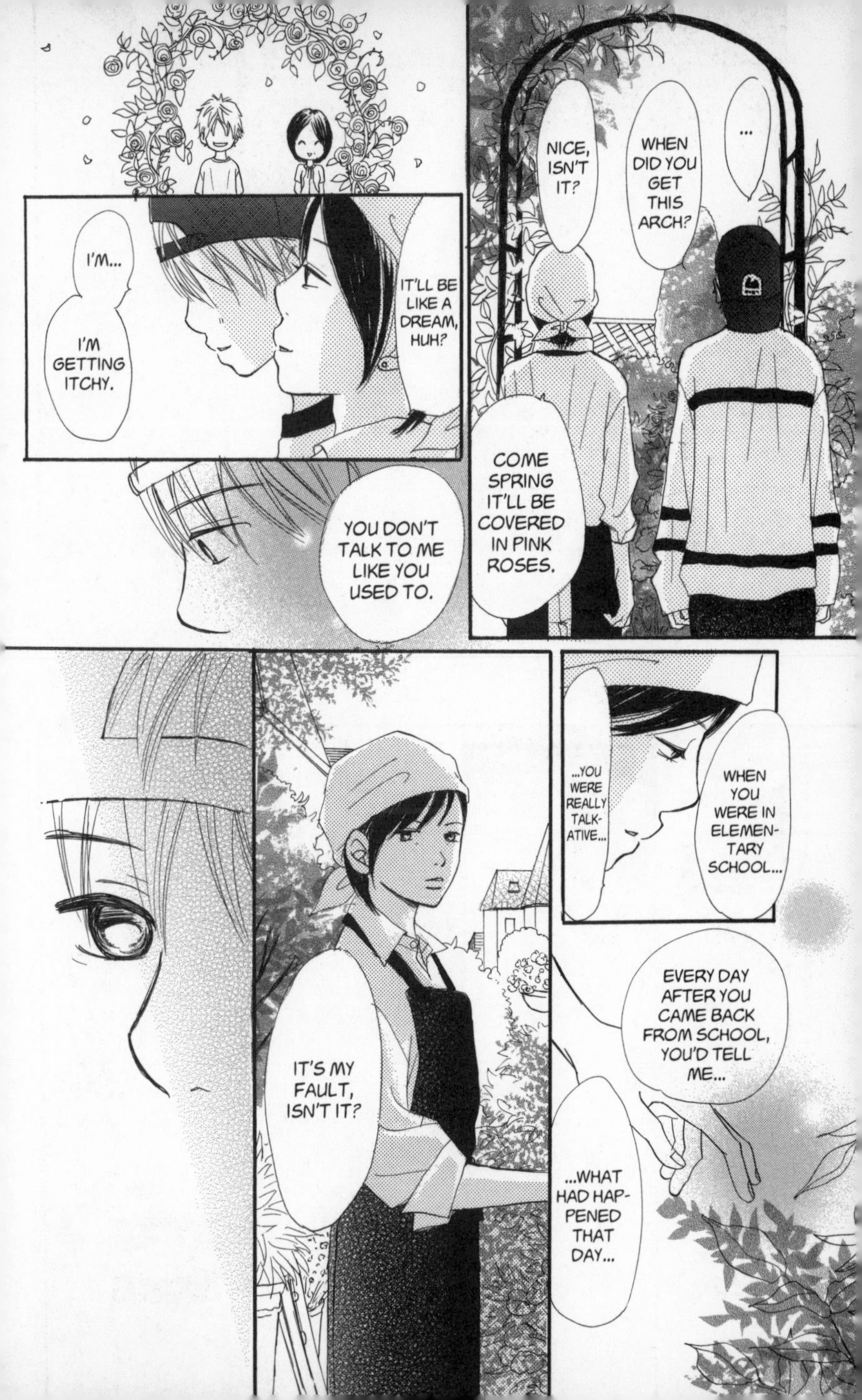
...
WHEN DID YOU GET THIS ARCH?
NICE, ISN'T IT?
COME SPRING IT'LL BE COVERED IN PINK ROSES.
IT'LL BE LIKE A DREAM, HUH?
I'M...
I'M GETTING ITCHY.
YOU DON'T TALK TO ME LIKE YOU USED TO.
WHEN YOU WERE IN ELEMENTARY SCHOOL...
...YOU WERE REALLY TALK-ATIVE...
EVERY DAY AFTER YOU CAME BACK FROM SCHOOL, YOU'D TELL ME...
...WHAT HAD HAP-PENED THAT DAY...
IT'S MY FAULT, ISN'T IT?

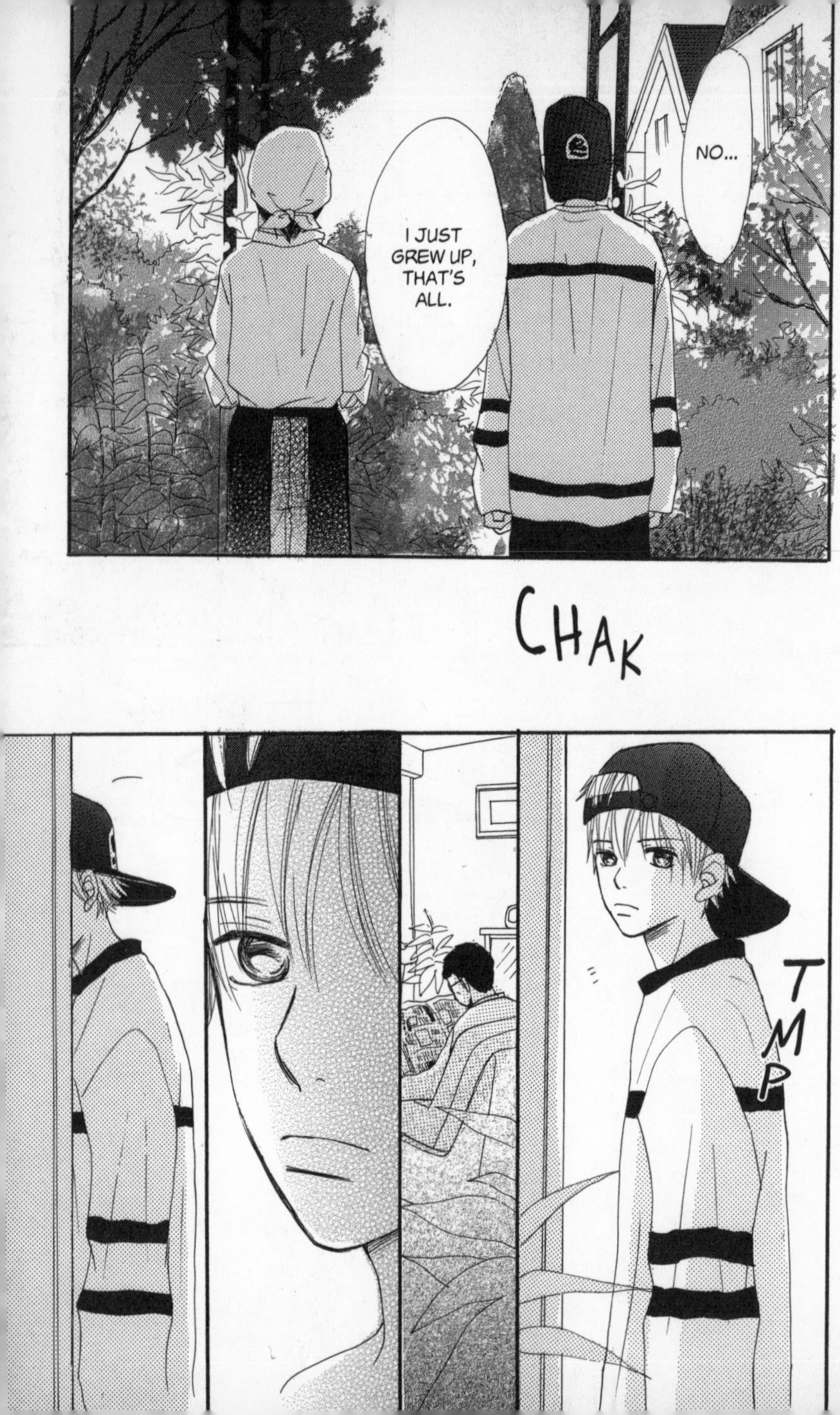
NO...
I JUST GREW UP, THAT'S ALL.
CHAK
TMP

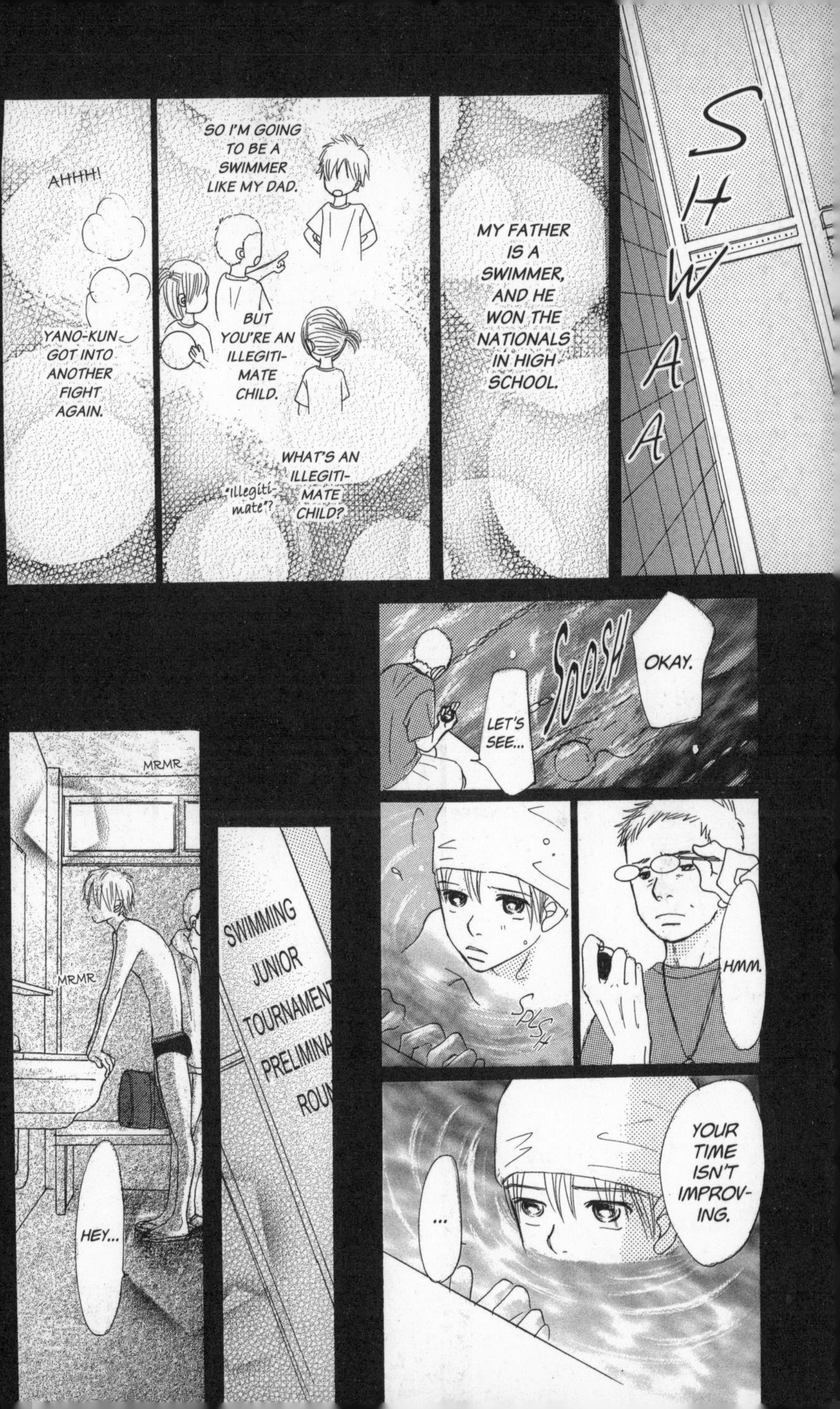
SHWAAA
MY FATHER IS A SWIMMER, AND HE WON THE NATIONALS IN HIGH SCHOOL.
SO I'M GOING TO BE A SWIMMER LIKE MY DAD.
BUT YOU'RE AN ILLEGITIMATE CHILD.
WHAT'S AN ILLEGITIMATE CHILD?
"illegitimate"?
AHHHH!
YANO-KUN GOT INTO ANOTHER FIGHT AGAIN.
OKAY.
SOOSH
LET'S SEE...
HMM.
SPLSH
YOUR TIME ISN'T IMPROVING.
...
SWIMMING JUNIOR TOURNAMENT PRELIMINA ROUN
MRMR
MRMR
HEY...

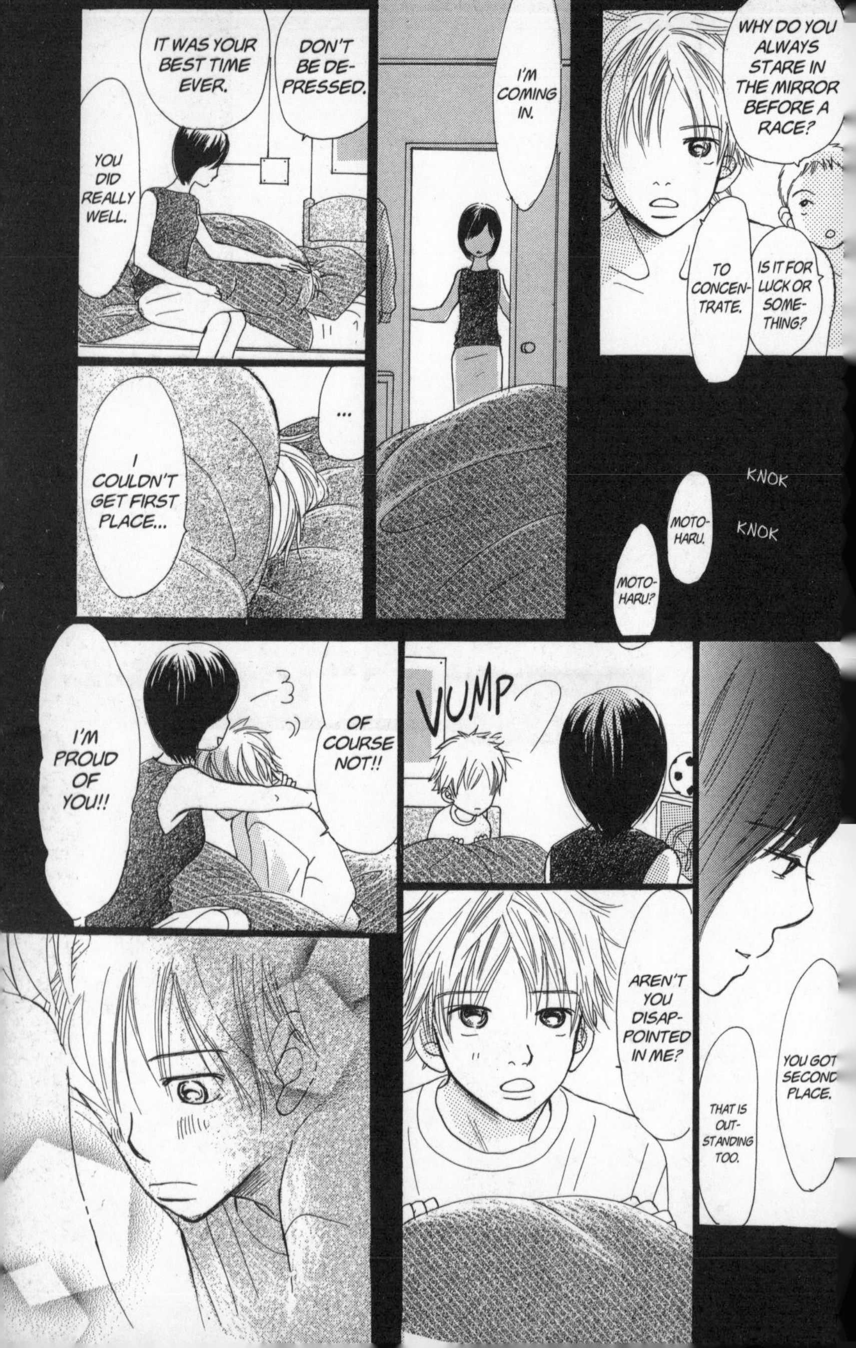
WHY DO YOU ALWAYS STARE IN THE MIRROR BEFORE A RACE?
IS IT FOR LUCK OR SOME-THING?
TO CONCEN-TRATE.
KNOK
KNOK
MOTO-HARU.
MOTO-HARU?
I'M COMING IN.
DON'T BE DE-PRESSED.
IT WAS YOUR BEST TIME EVER.
YOU DID REALLY WELL.
...
I COULDN'T GET FIRST PLACE...
YOU GOT SECOND PLACE.
THAT IS OUT-STANDING TOO.
VUMP
AREN'T YOU DISAP-POINTED IN ME?
OF COURSE NOT!!
I'M PROUD OF YOU!!

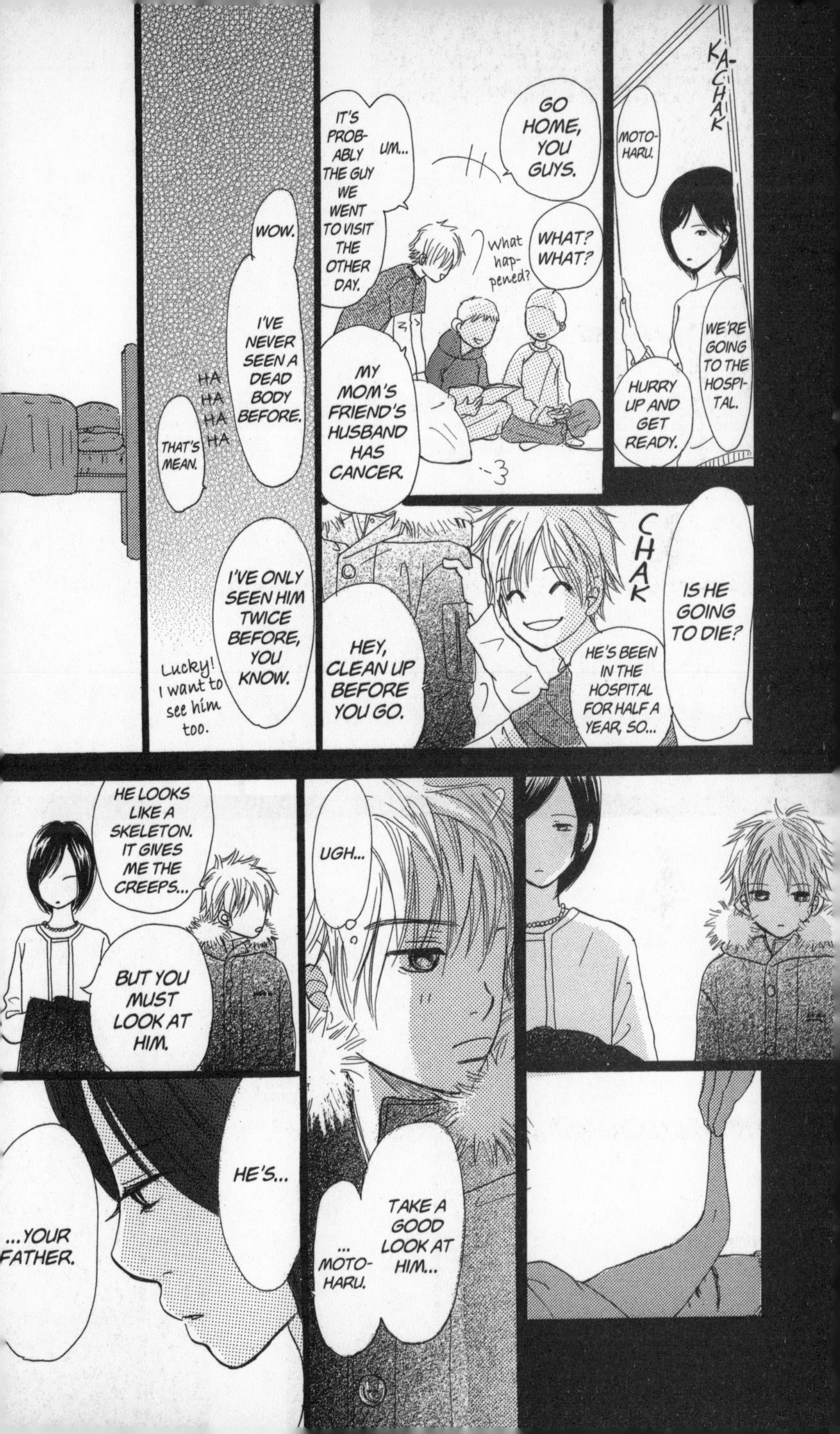
KA-CHAK
MOTO-HARU.
WE'RE GOING TO THE HOSPITAL.
HURRY UP AND GET READY.
GO HOME, YOU GUYS.
WHAT? WHAT?
What happened?
UM...
IT'S PROBABLY THE GUY WE WENT TO VISIT THE OTHER DAY.
MY MOM'S FRIEND'S HUSBAND HAS CANCER.
CHAK
IS HE GOING TO DIE?
HE'S BEEN IN THE HOSPITAL FOR HALF A YEAR, SO...
HEY, CLEAN UP BEFORE YOU GO.
WOW.
I'VE NEVER SEEN A DEAD BODY BEFORE.
HA HA HA HA
THAT'S MEAN.
I'VE ONLY SEEN HIM TWICE BEFORE, YOU KNOW.
Lucky! I want to see him too.
UGH...
HE LOOKS LIKE A SKELETON. IT GIVES ME THE CREEPS...
BUT YOU MUST LOOK AT HIM.
TAKE A GOOD LOOK AT HIM...
... MOTO-HARU.
HE'S...
...YOUR FATHER.

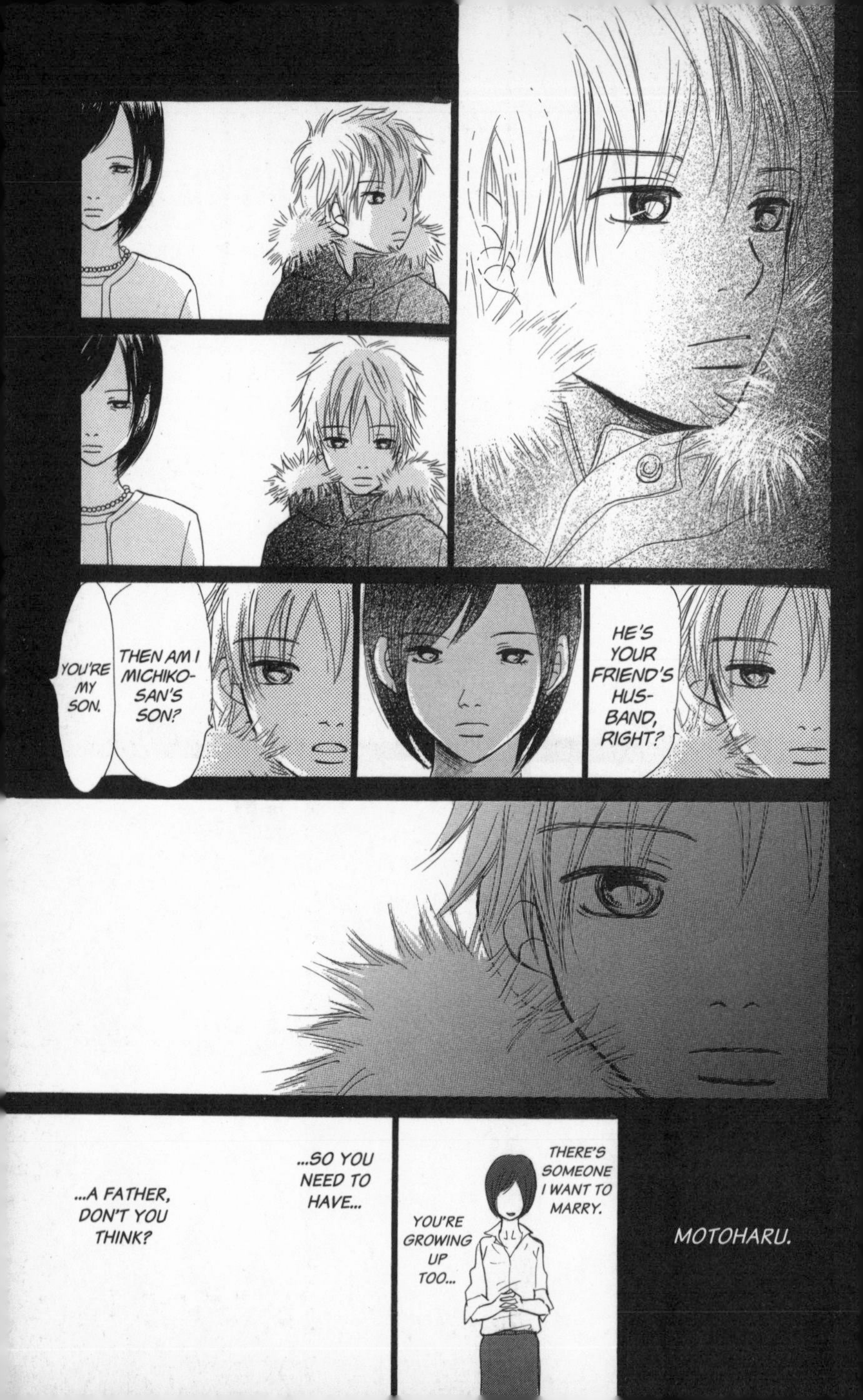
HE'S YOUR FRIEND'S HUS-BAND, RIGHT?
THEN AM I MICHIKO-SAN'S SON?
YOU'RE MY SON.
MOTOHARU.
THERE'S SOMEONE I WANT TO MARRY.
YOU'RE GROWING UP TOO...
...SO YOU NEED TO HAVE...
...A FATHER, DON'T YOU THINK?

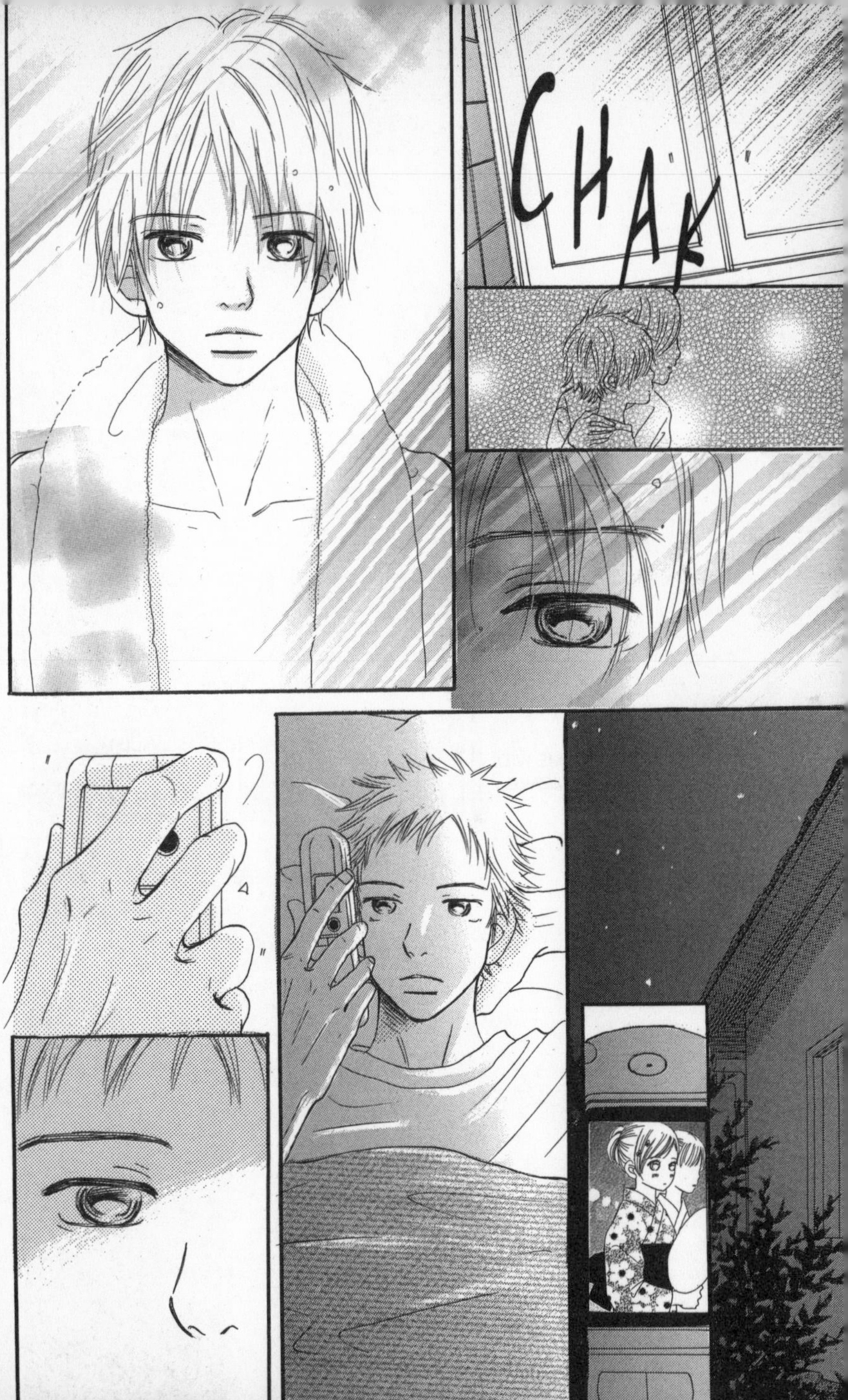
CHAK

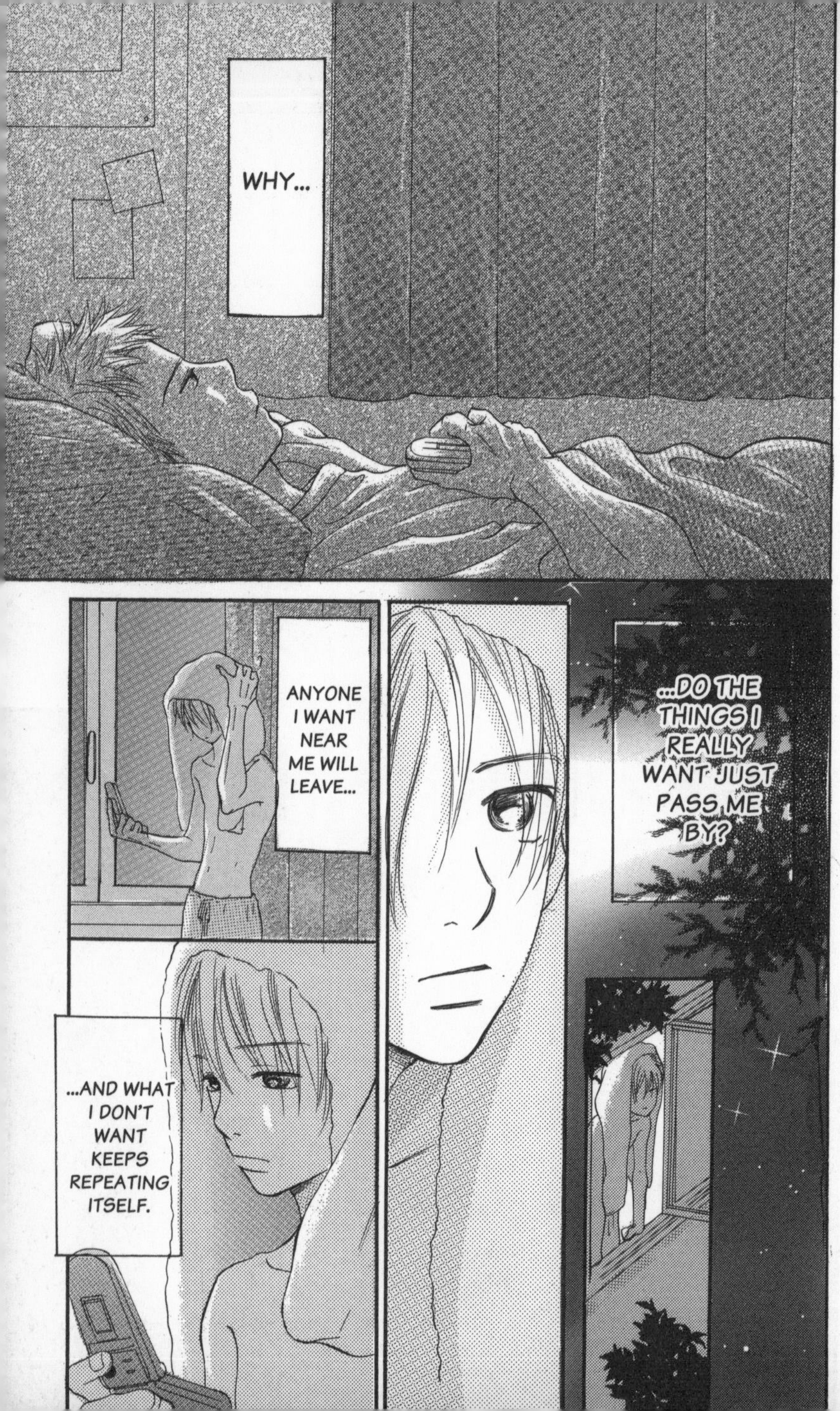
WHY...
...DO THE THINGS I REALLY WANT JUST PASS ME BY?
ANYONE I WANT NEAR ME WILL LEAVE...
...AND WHAT I DON'T WANT KEEPS REPEATING ITSELF.

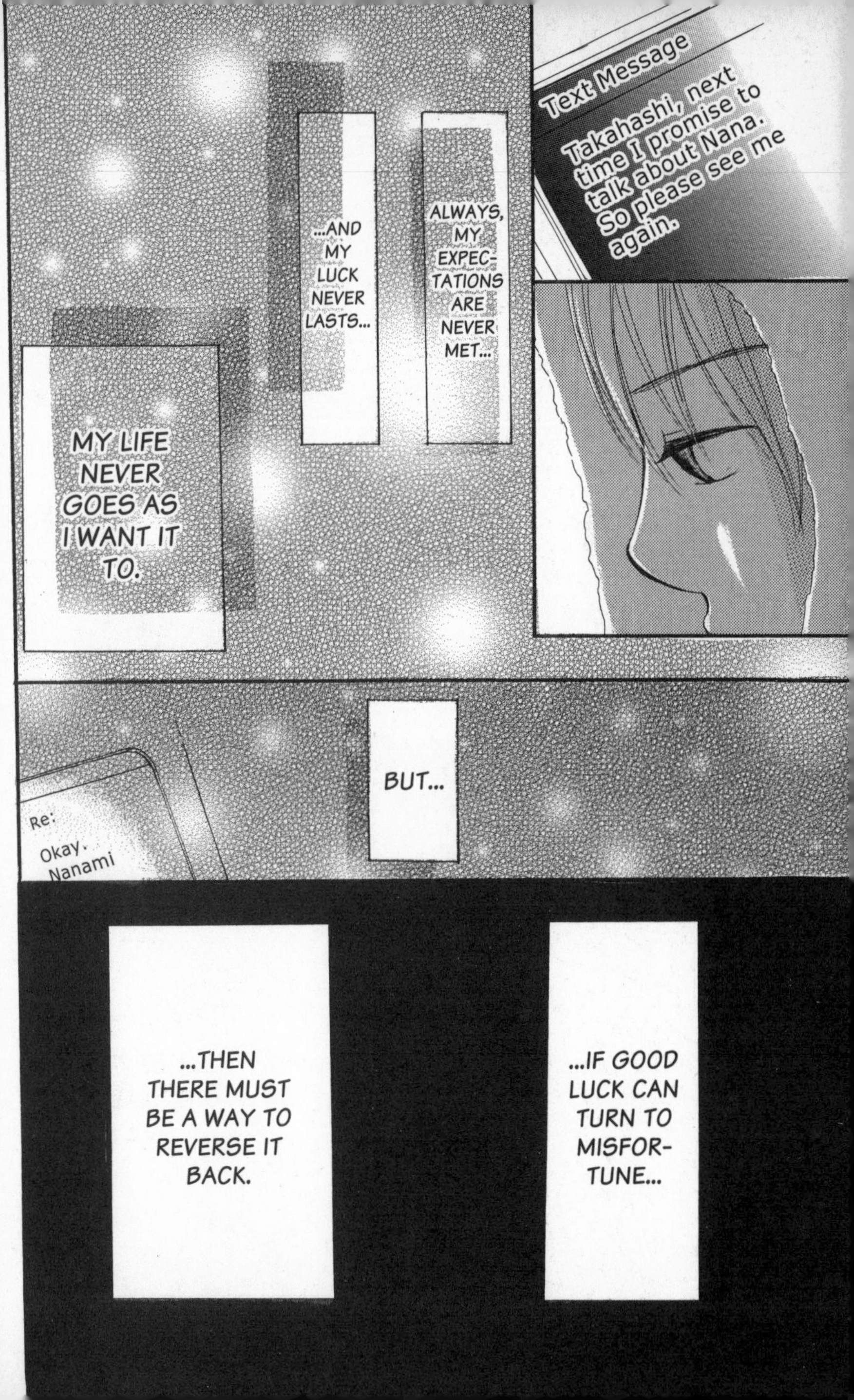
Text Message
Takahashi, next time I promise to talk about Nana. So please see me again.
ALWAYS, MY EXPECTATIONS ARE NEVER MET...
...AND MY LUCK NEVER LASTS...
MY LIFE NEVER GOES AS I WANT IT TO.
BUT...
Re:
Okay. Nanami
...IF GOOD LUCK CAN TURN TO MISFORTUNE...
...THEN THERE MUST BE A WAY TO REVERSE IT BACK.

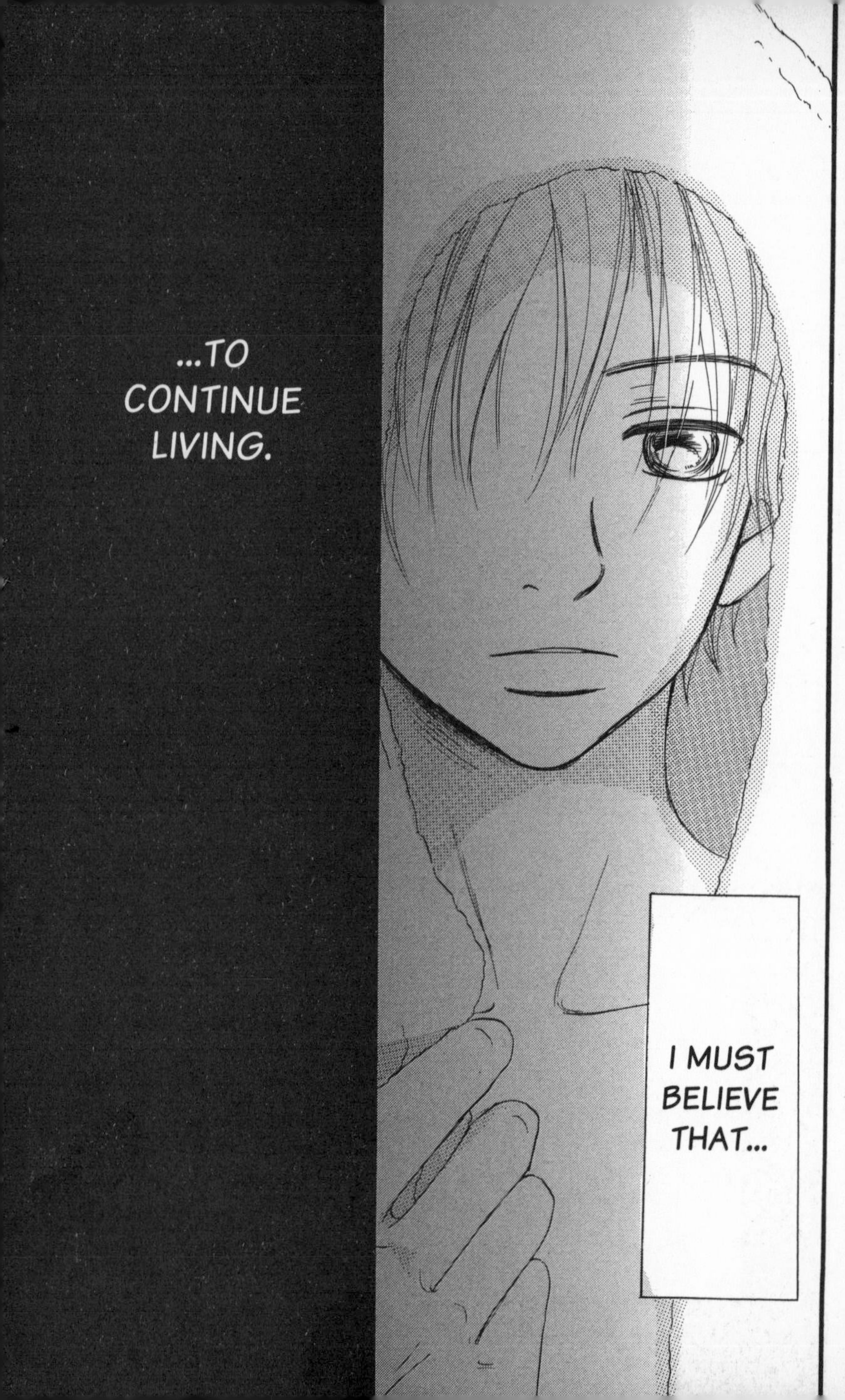
I MUST BELIEVE THAT...
...TO CONTINUE LIVING.

# Nanami's School Life

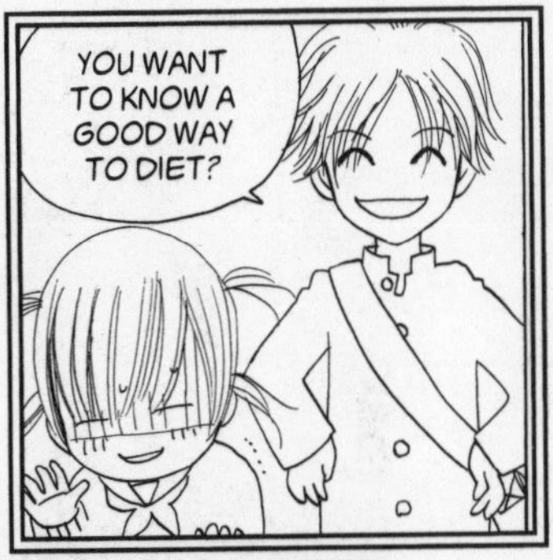
YOU WANT TO KNOW A GOOD WAY TO DIET?

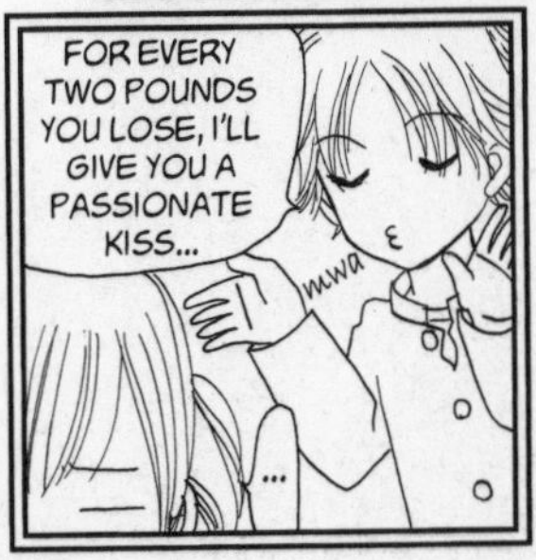
FOR EVERY TWO POUNDS YOU LOSE, I'LL GIVE YOU A PASSIONATE KISS...
mwa
...

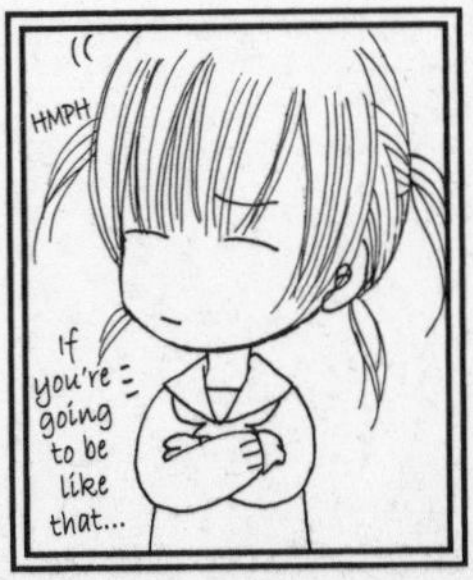
HMPH
If you're going to be like that...

Continued on page 110...

# Chapter 22

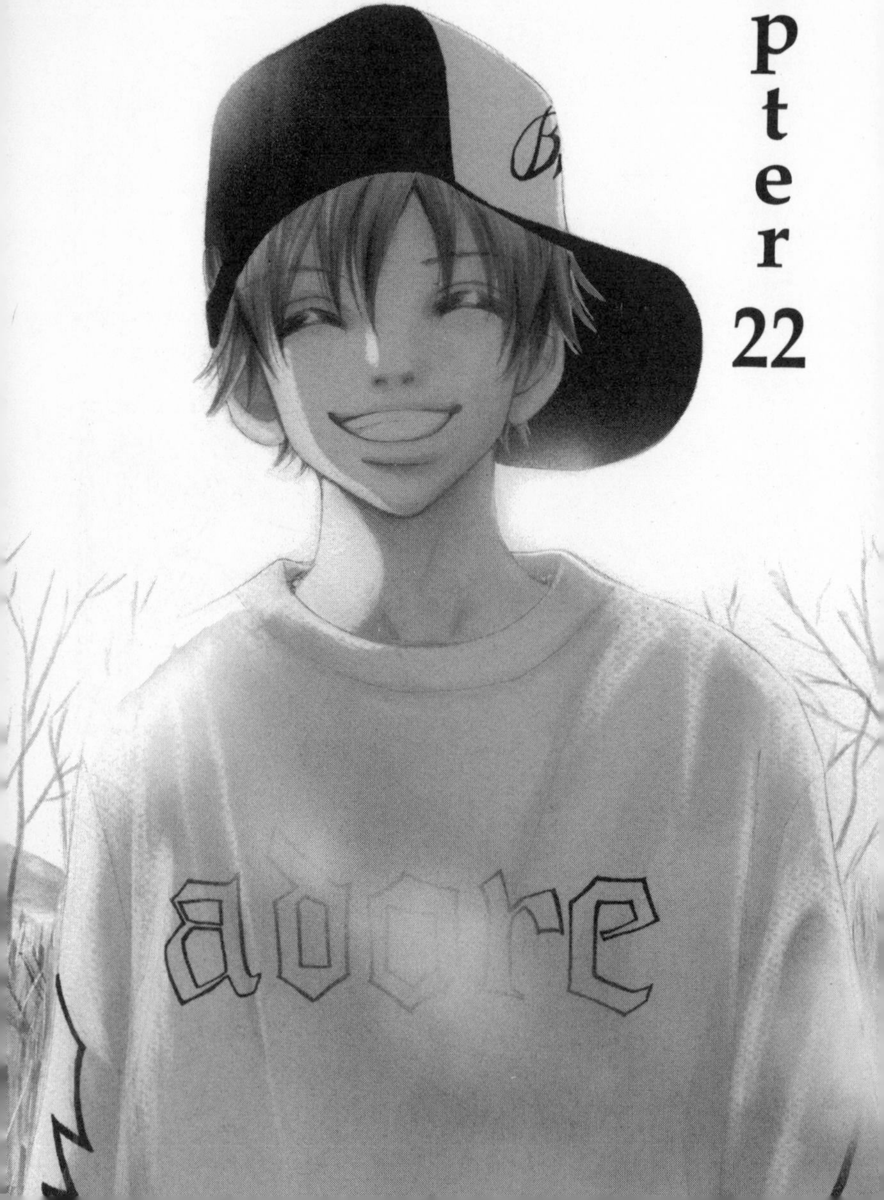

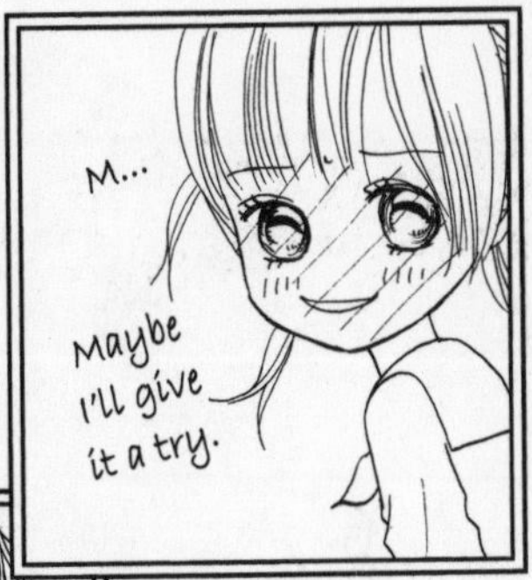
M...
Maybe I'll give it a try.

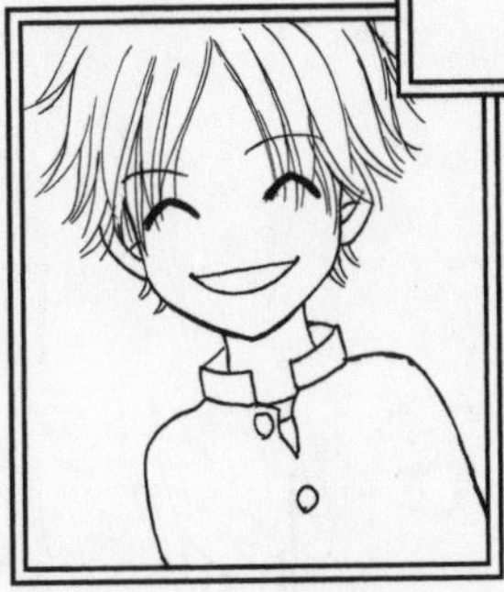

Nanami's School Life

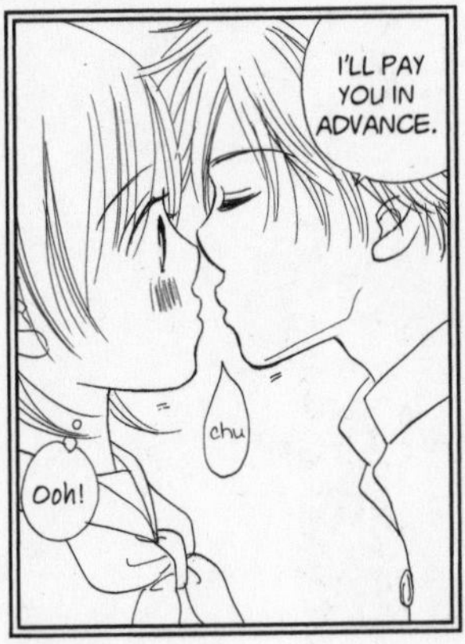
I'LL PAY YOU IN ADVANCE.
chu
Ooh!

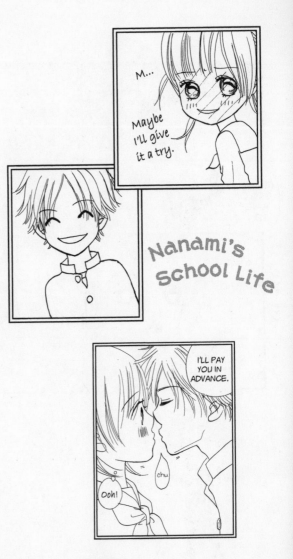

Fin

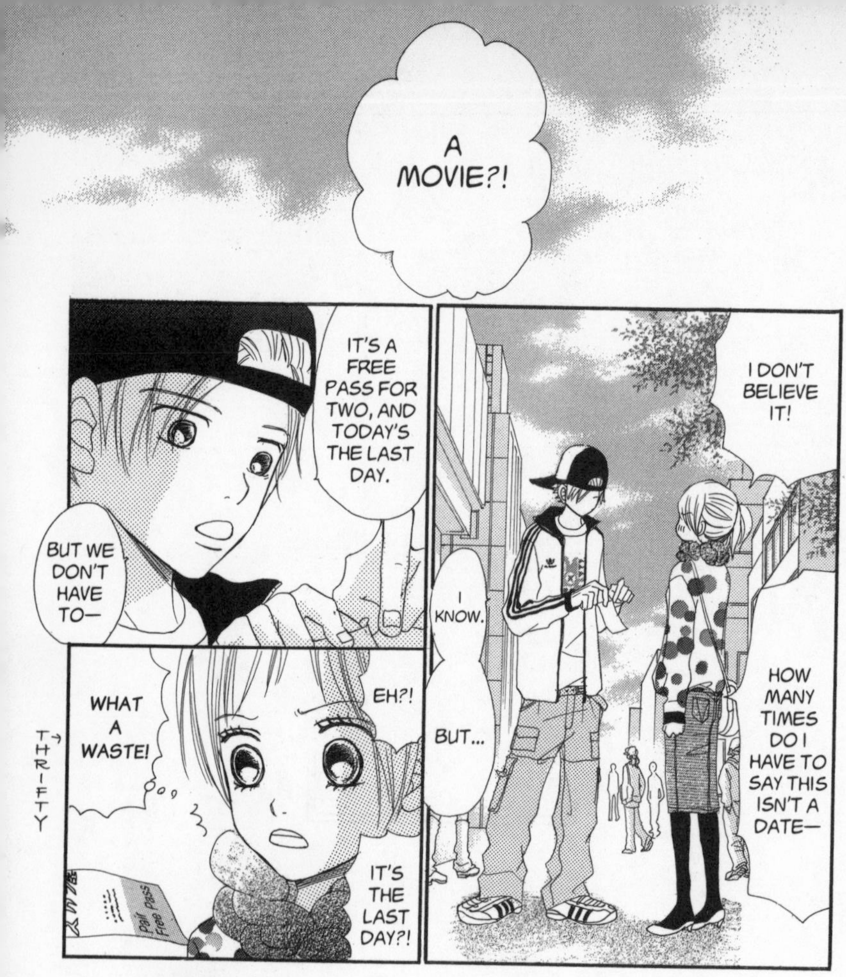
A MOVIE?!
I DON'T BELIEVE IT!
HOW MANY TIMES DO I HAVE TO SAY THIS ISN'T A DATE—
I KNOW.
BUT...
IT'S A FREE PASS FOR TWO, AND TODAY'S THE LAST DAY.
BUT WE DON'T HAVE TO—
EH?!
IT'S THE LAST DAY?!
WHAT A WASTE!
THRIFTY
Pair Free Pass

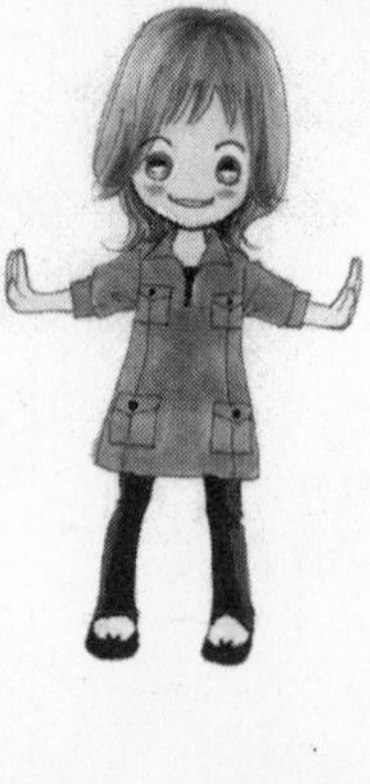

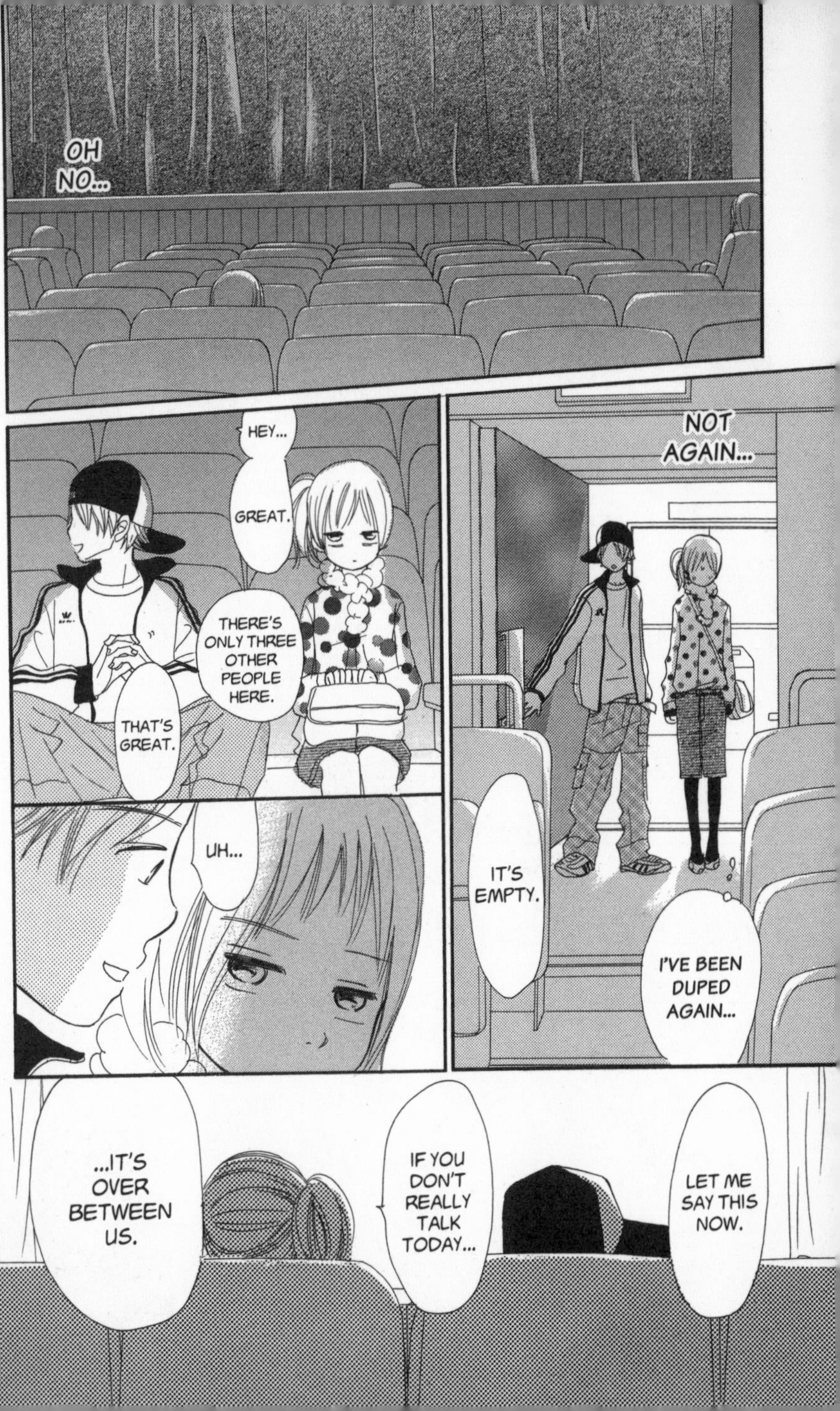
OH NO...
NOT AGAIN...
IT'S EMPTY.
I'VE BEEN DUPED AGAIN...
HEY...
GREAT.
THERE'S ONLY THREE OTHER PEOPLE HERE.
THAT'S GREAT.
UH...
LET ME SAY THIS NOW.
IF YOU DON'T REALLY TALK TODAY...
...IT'S OVER BETWEEN US.

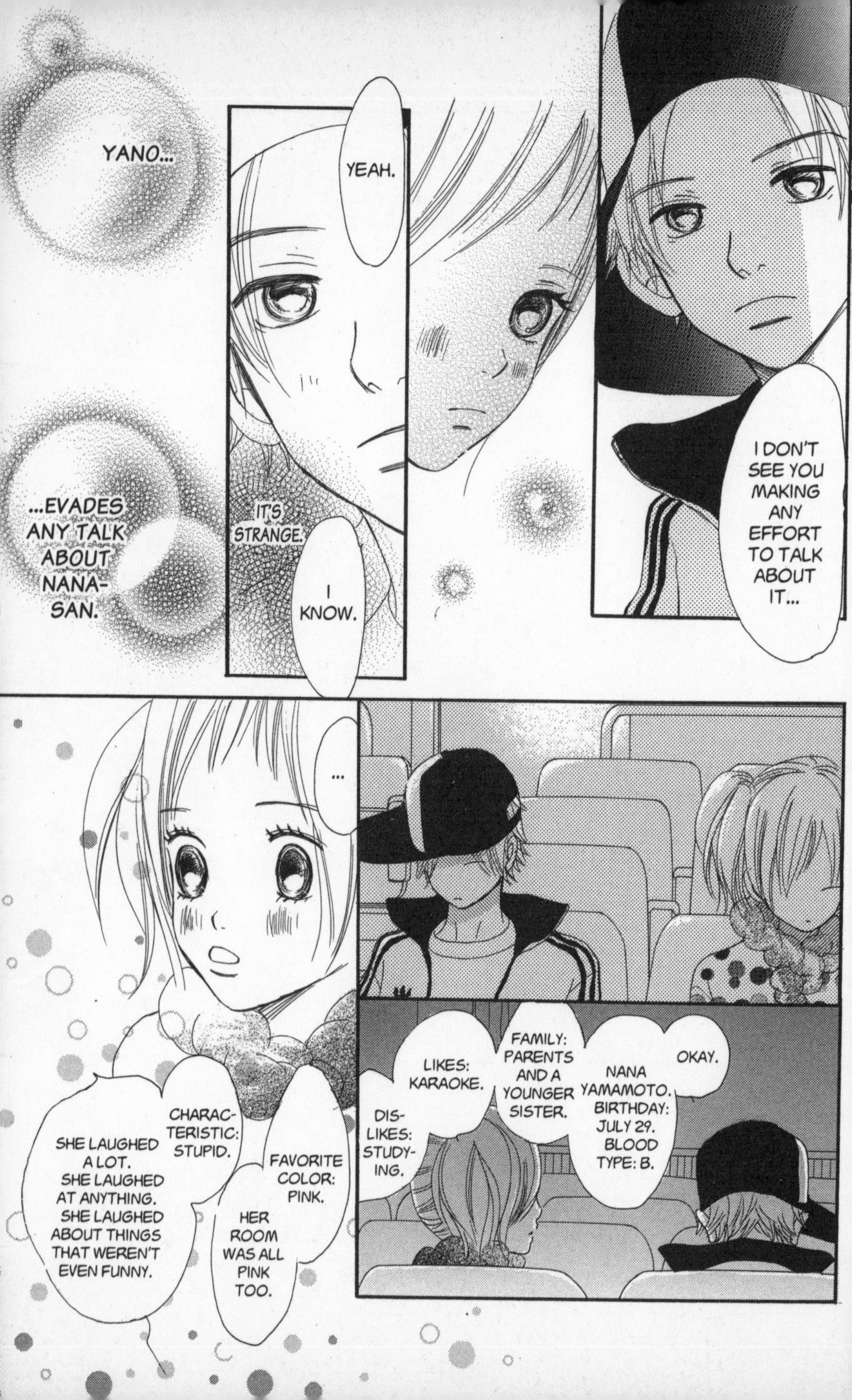
I DON'T SEE YOU MAKING ANY EFFORT TO TALK ABOUT IT...
YEAH.
IT'S STRANGE.
I KNOW.
YANO...
...EVADES ANY TALK ABOUT NANA-SAN.
OKAY.
NANA YAMAMOTO. BIRTHDAY: JULY 29. BLOOD TYPE: B.
FAMILY: PARENTS AND A YOUNGER SISTER.
LIKES: KARAOKE.
DIS-LIKES: STUDY-ING.
...
FAVORITE COLOR: PINK.
HER ROOM WAS ALL PINK TOO.
CHARAC-TERISTIC: STUPID.
SHE LAUGHED A LOT. SHE LAUGHED AT ANYTHING. SHE LAUGHED ABOUT THINGS THAT WEREN'T EVEN FUNNY.

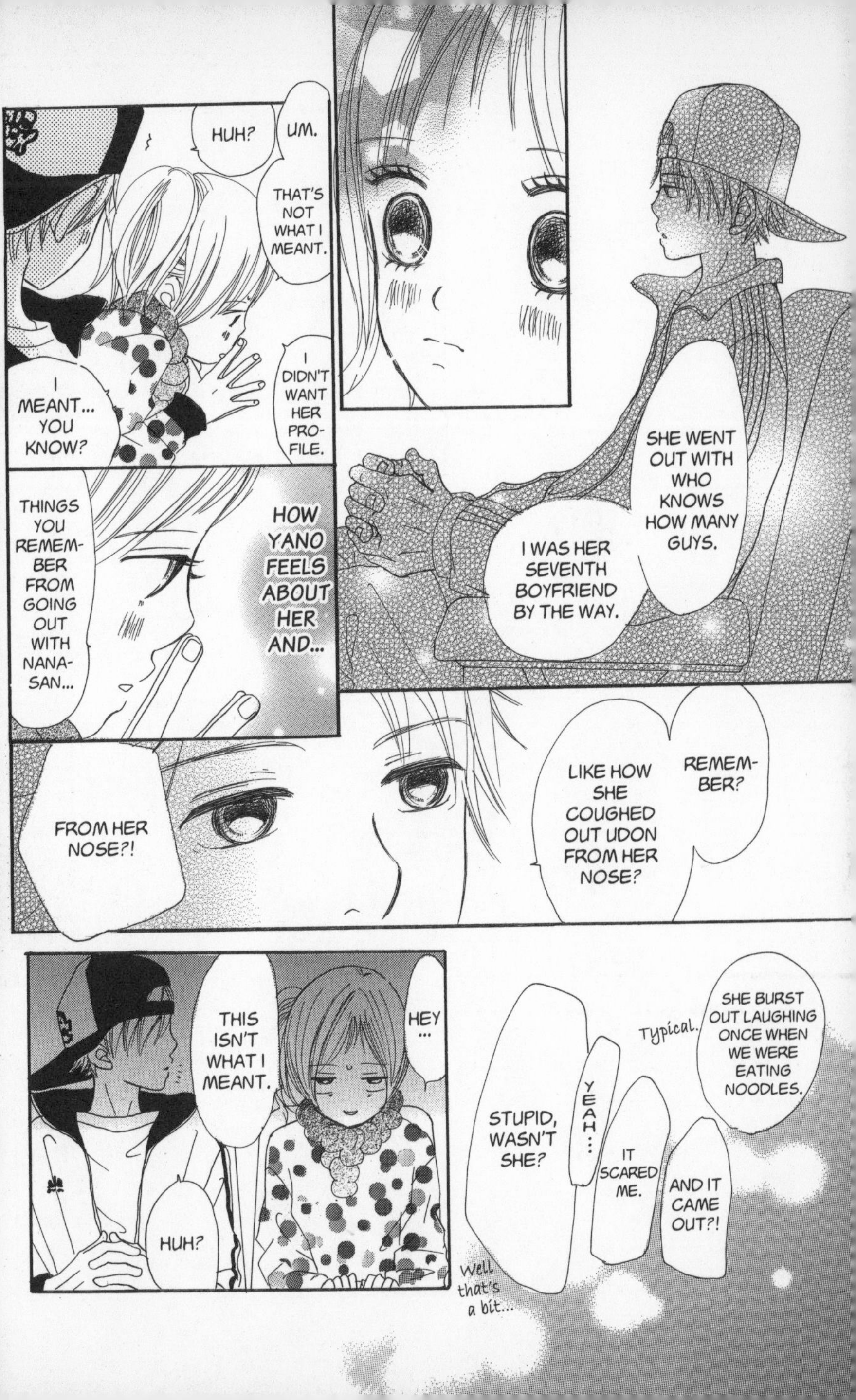
SHE WENT OUT WITH WHO KNOWS HOW MANY GUYS.
I WAS HER SEVENTH BOYFRIEND BY THE WAY.
UM.
HUH?
THAT'S NOT WHAT I MEANT.
I DIDN'T WANT HER PRO-FILE.
I MEANT... YOU KNOW?
HOW YANO FEELS ABOUT HER AND...
THINGS YOU REMEM-BER FROM GOING OUT WITH NANA-SAN...
REMEM-BER?
LIKE HOW SHE COUGHED OUT UDON FROM HER NOSE?
FROM HER NOSE?!
SHE BURST OUT LAUGHING ONCE WHEN WE WERE EATING NOODLES.
Typical.
AND IT CAME OUT?!
IT SCARED ME.
YEAH...
STUPID, WASN'T SHE?
Well that's a bit...
HEY...
THIS ISN'T WHAT I MEANT.
HUH?

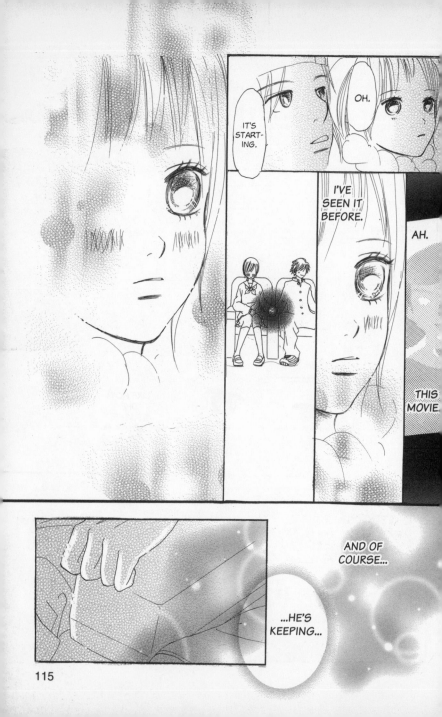

IT'S START- ING.

OH.

I'VE SEEN IT BEFORE.

AH.

THIS MOVIE.

AND OF COURSE...

...HE'S KEEPING...

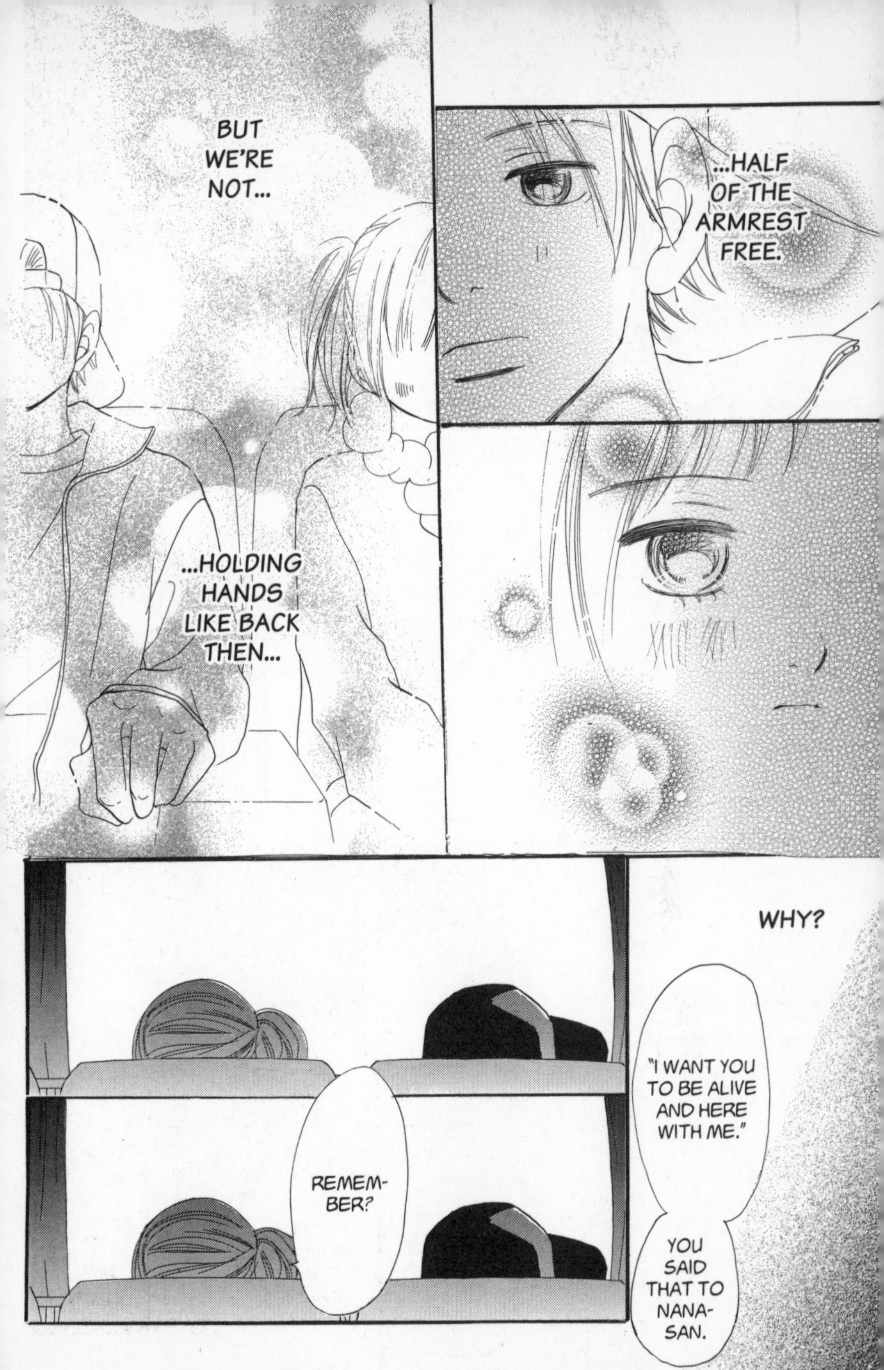
...HALF OF THE ARMREST FREE.
BUT WE'RE NOT...
...HOLDING HANDS LIKE BACK THEN...
WHY?
"I WANT YOU TO BE ALIVE AND HERE WITH ME."
YOU SAID THAT TO NANA-SAN.
REMEM-BER?

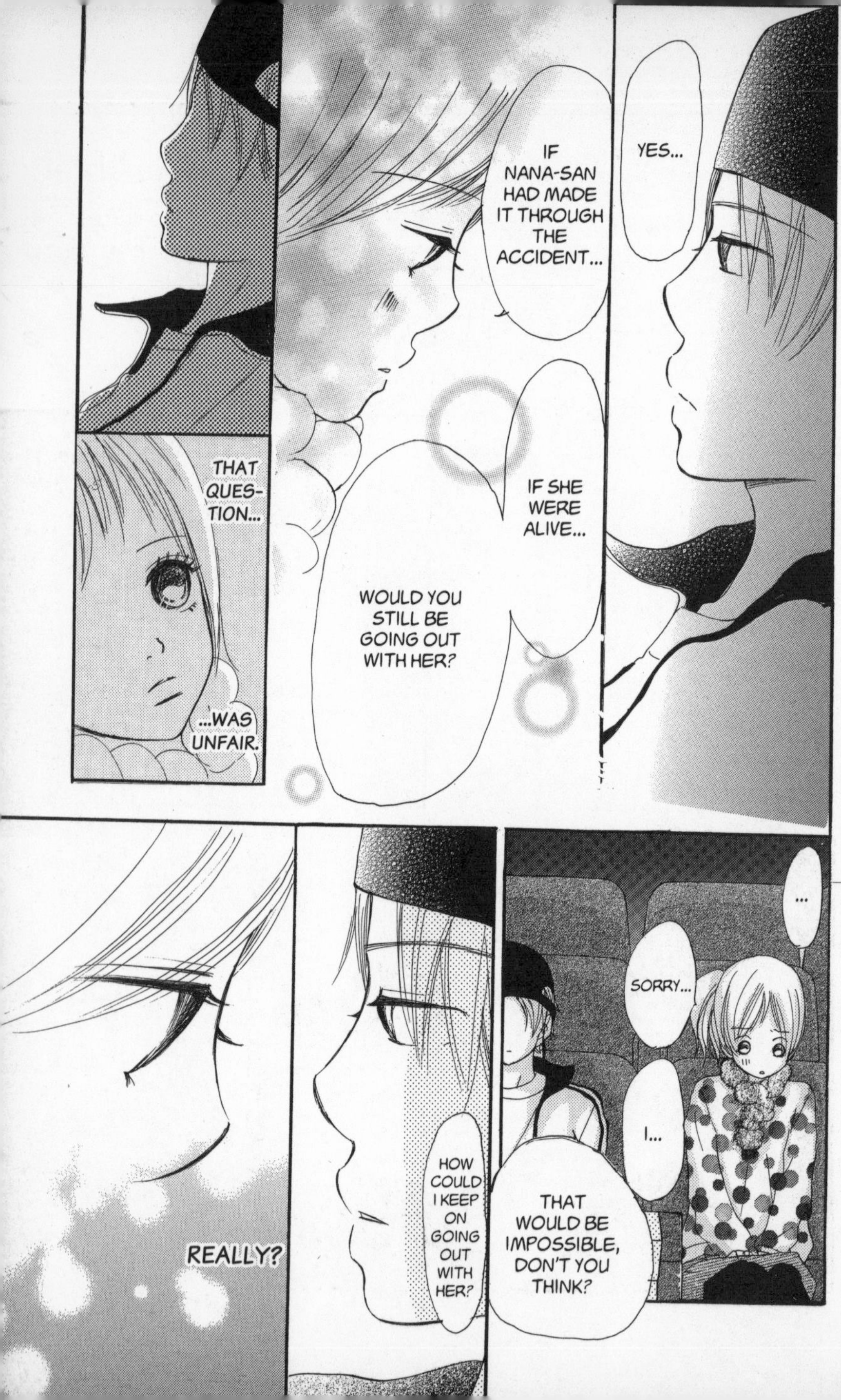
YES...
IF NANA-SAN HAD MADE IT THROUGH THE ACCIDENT...
IF SHE WERE ALIVE...
WOULD YOU STILL BE GOING OUT WITH HER?
THAT QUES-TION...
...WAS UNFAIR.
...
SORRY...
I...
THAT WOULD BE IMPOSSIBLE, DON'T YOU THINK?
HOW COULD I KEEP ON GOING OUT WITH HER?
REALLY?

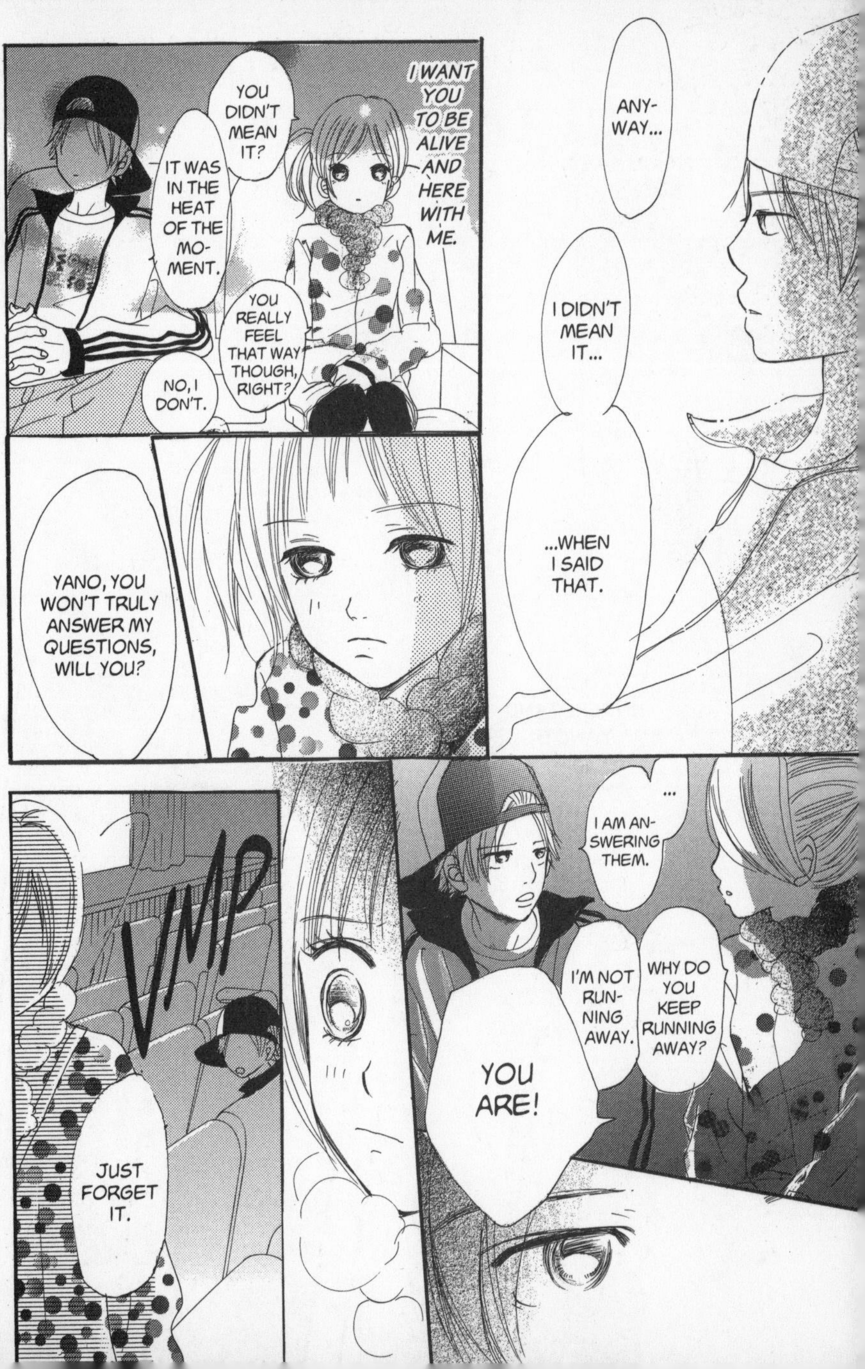
ANY-WAY...
I DIDN'T MEAN IT...
...WHEN I SAID THAT.
I WANT YOU TO BE ALIVE AND HERE WITH ME.
YOU DIDN'T MEAN IT?
IT WAS IN THE HEAT OF THE MO-MENT.
YOU REALLY FEEL THAT WAY THOUGH, RIGHT?
NO, I DON'T.
YANO, YOU WON'T TRULY ANSWER MY QUESTIONS, WILL YOU?
...
I AM AN-SWERING THEM.
WHY DO YOU KEEP RUNNING AWAY?
I'M NOT RUN-NING AWAY.
YOU ARE!
VMP
JUST FORGET IT.

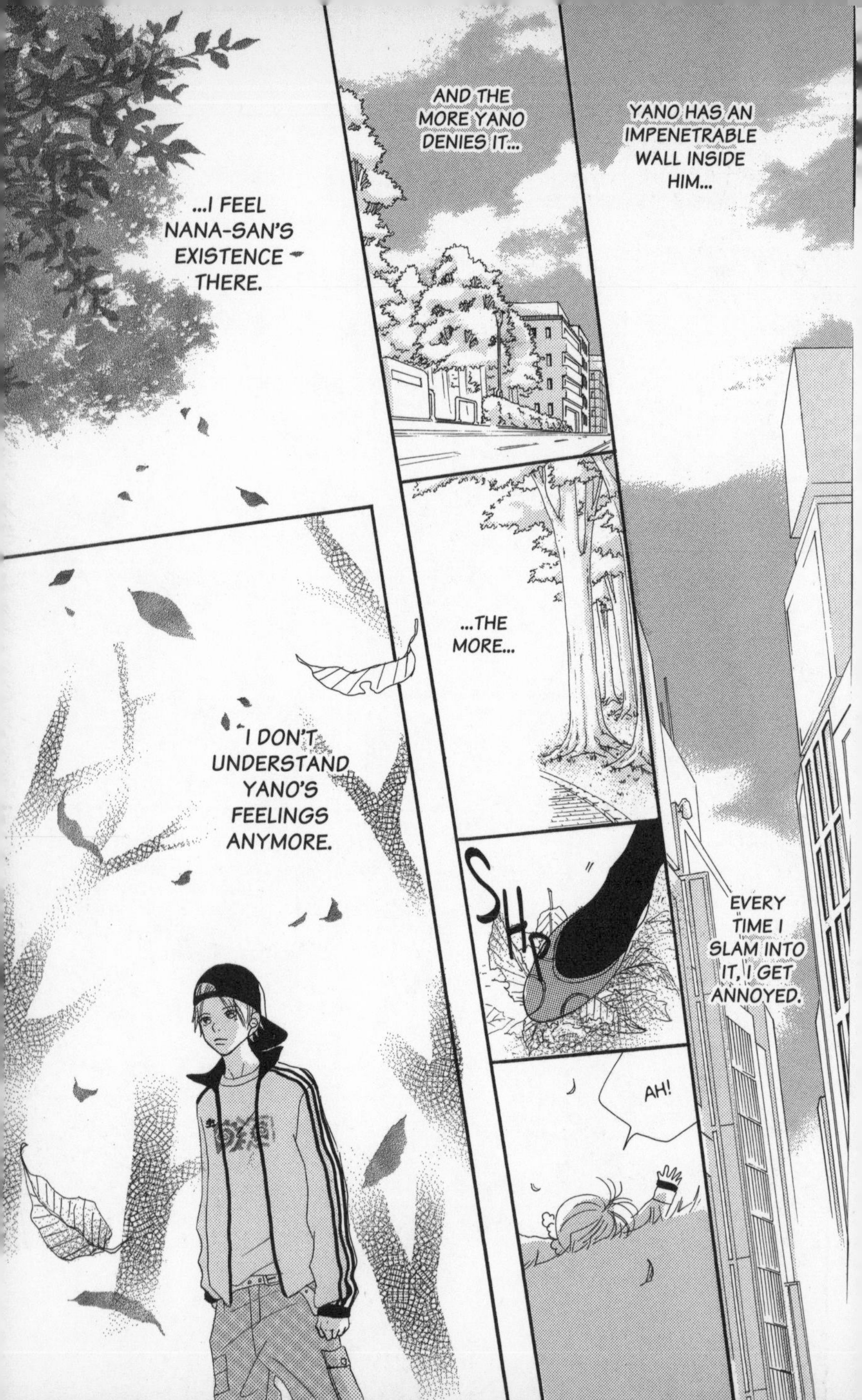
YANO HAS AN IMPENETRABLE WALL INSIDE HIM...
EVERY TIME I SLAM INTO IT, I GET ANNOYED.
AND THE MORE YANO DENIES IT...
...THE MORE...
SHP
AH!
...I FEEL NANA-SAN'S EXISTENCE THERE.
I DON'T UNDERSTAND YANO'S FEELINGS ANYMORE.

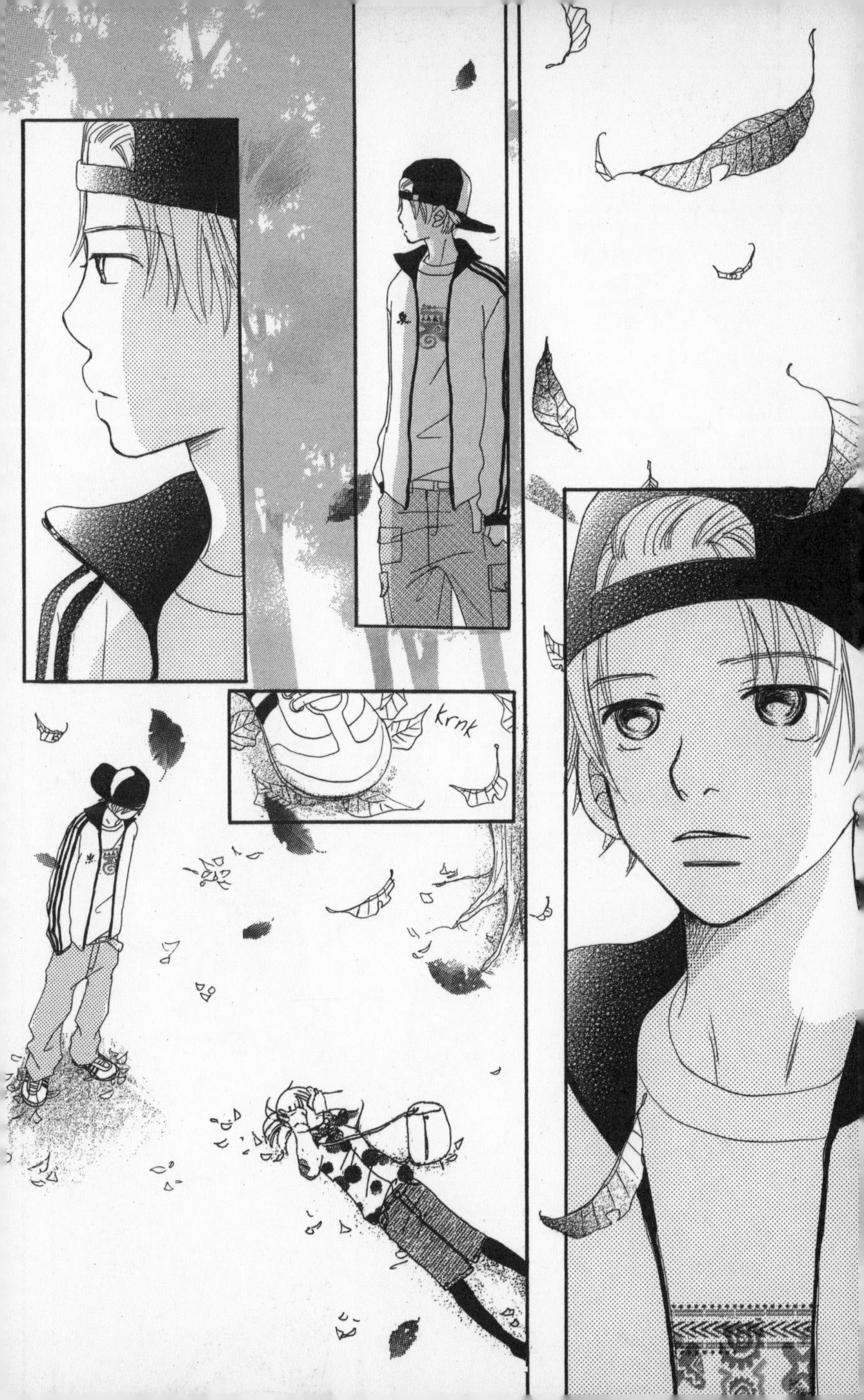
krnk

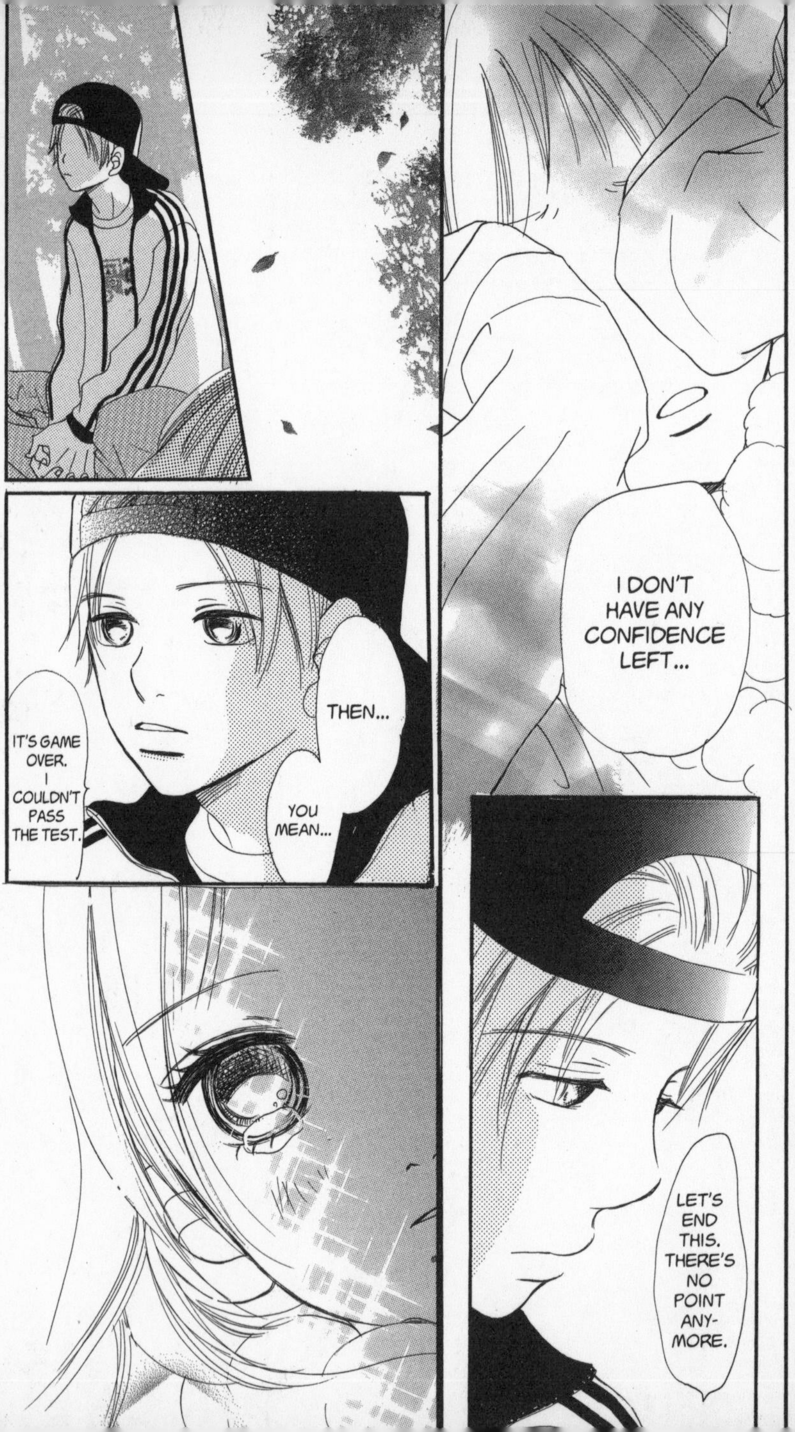
I DON'T HAVE ANY CONFIDENCE LEFT...
THEN...
YOU MEAN...
IT'S GAME OVER. I COULDN'T PASS THE TEST.
LET'S END THIS. THERE'S NO POINT ANY-MORE.

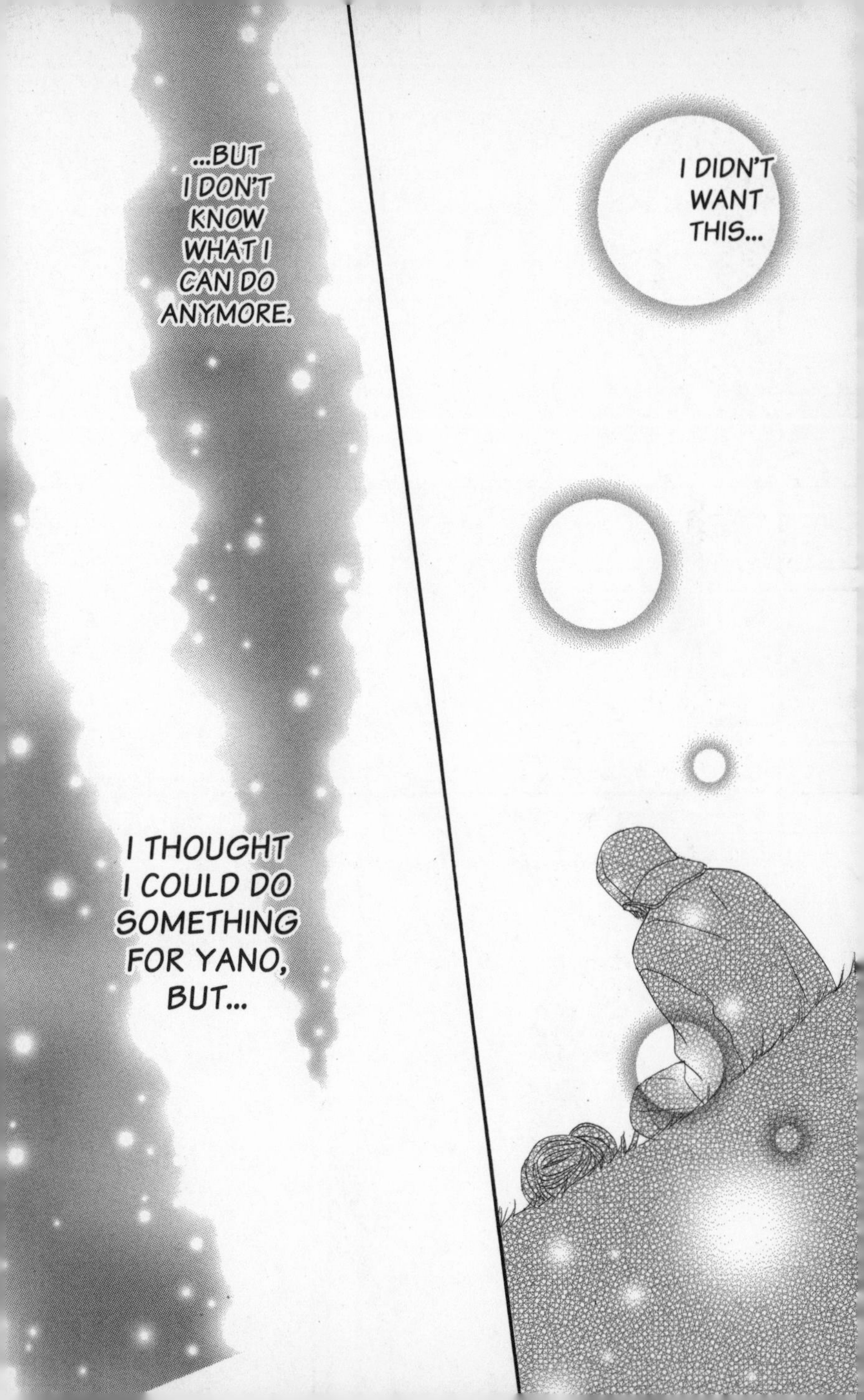
I DIDN'T WANT THIS...
...BUT I DON'T KNOW WHAT I CAN DO ANYMORE.
I THOUGHT I COULD DO SOMETHING FOR YANO, BUT...

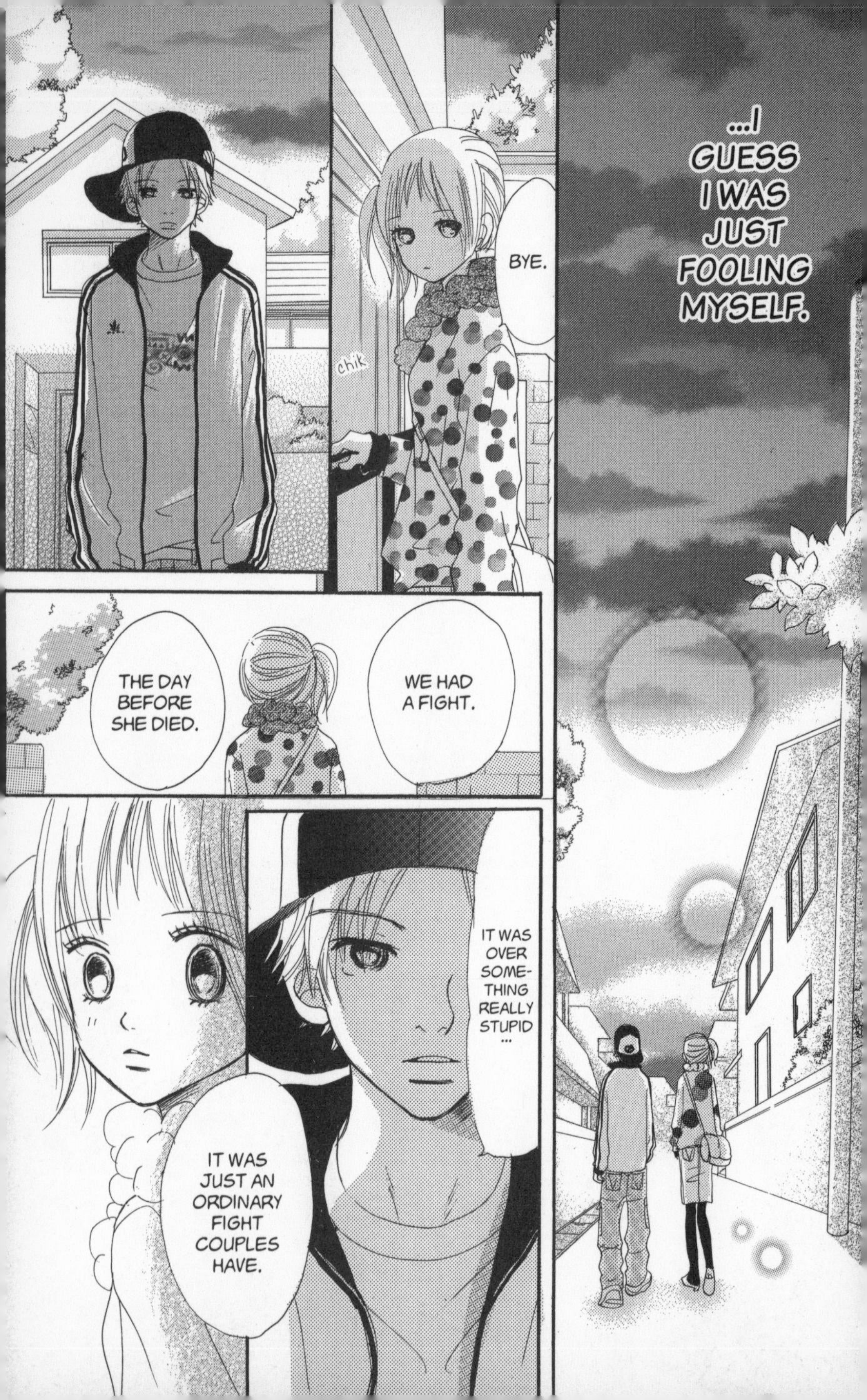
...I GUESS I WAS JUST FOOLING MYSELF.
BYE.
chik
WE HAD A FIGHT.
THE DAY BEFORE SHE DIED.
IT WAS OVER SOMETHING REALLY STUPID ...
IT WAS JUST AN ORDINARY FIGHT COUPLES HAVE.

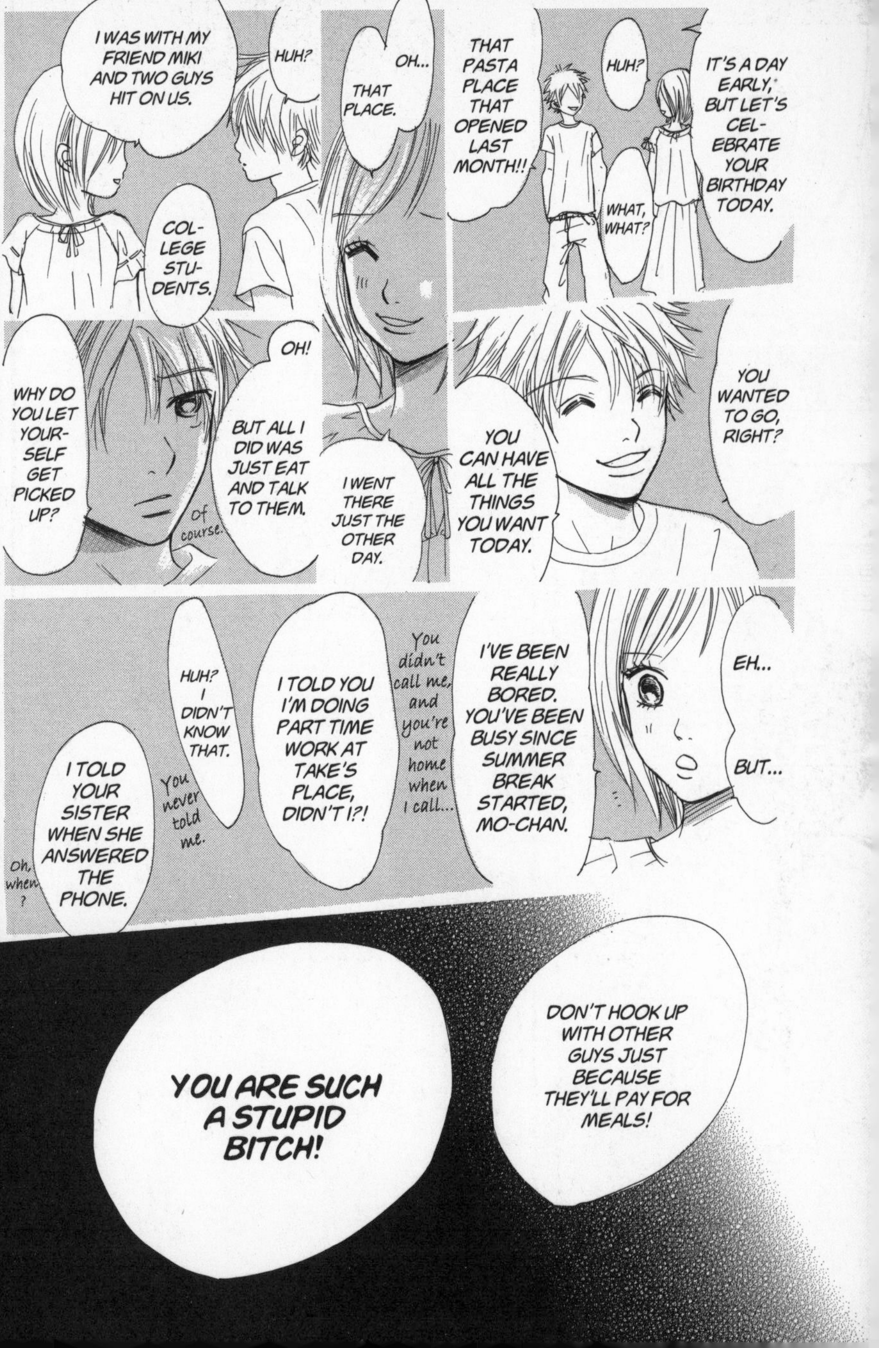
IT'S A DAY EARLY, BUT LET'S CELEBRATE YOUR BIRTHDAY TODAY.
HUH?
WHAT, WHAT?
THAT PASTA PLACE THAT OPENED LAST MONTH!!
YOU WANTED TO GO, RIGHT?
YOU CAN HAVE ALL THE THINGS YOU WANT TODAY.
OH... THAT PLACE.
I WENT THERE JUST THE OTHER DAY.
HUH?
I WAS WITH MY FRIEND MIKI AND TWO GUYS HIT ON US.
COLLEGE STUDENTS.
OH!
BUT ALL I DID WAS JUST EAT AND TALK TO THEM.
Of course.
WHY DO YOU LET YOURSELF GET PICKED UP?
EH...
BUT...
I'VE BEEN REALLY BORED. YOU'VE BEEN BUSY SINCE SUMMER BREAK STARTED, MO-CHAN.
You didn't call me, and you're not home when I call...
I TOLD YOU I'M DOING PART TIME WORK AT TAKE'S PLACE, DIDN'T I?!
HUH? I DIDN'T KNOW THAT.
You never told me.
I TOLD YOUR SISTER WHEN SHE ANSWERED THE PHONE.
Oh, when?
DON'T HOOK UP WITH OTHER GUYS JUST BECAUSE THEY'LL PAY FOR MEALS!
YOU ARE SUCH A STUPID BITCH!

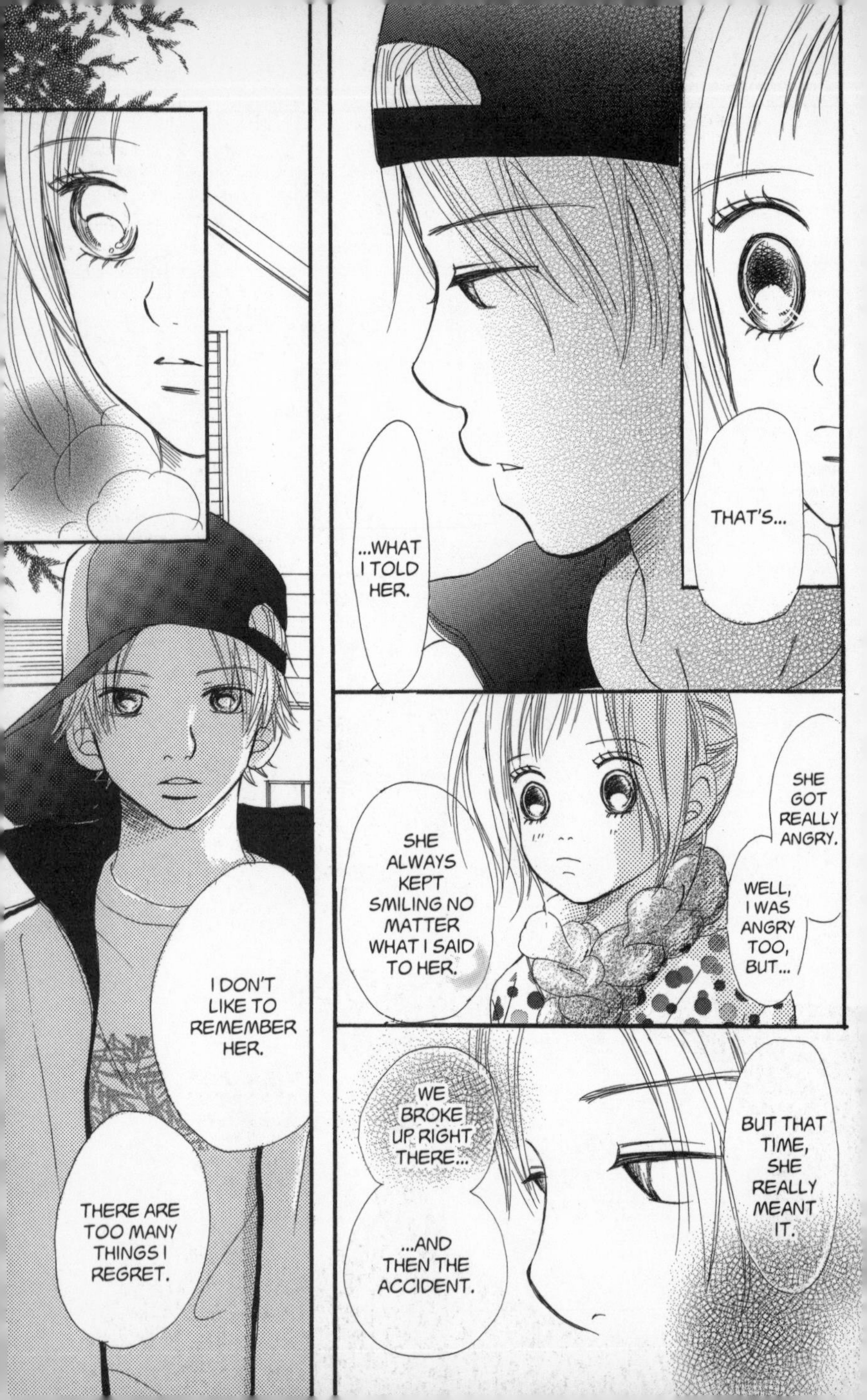
THAT'S...
...WHAT I TOLD HER.
SHE GOT REALLY ANGRY.
WELL, I WAS ANGRY TOO, BUT...
SHE ALWAYS KEPT SMILING NO MATTER WHAT I SAID TO HER.
BUT THAT TIME, SHE REALLY MEANT IT.
WE BROKE UP RIGHT THERE...
...AND THEN THE ACCIDENT.
I DON'T LIKE TO REMEMBER HER.
THERE ARE TOO MANY THINGS I REGRET.

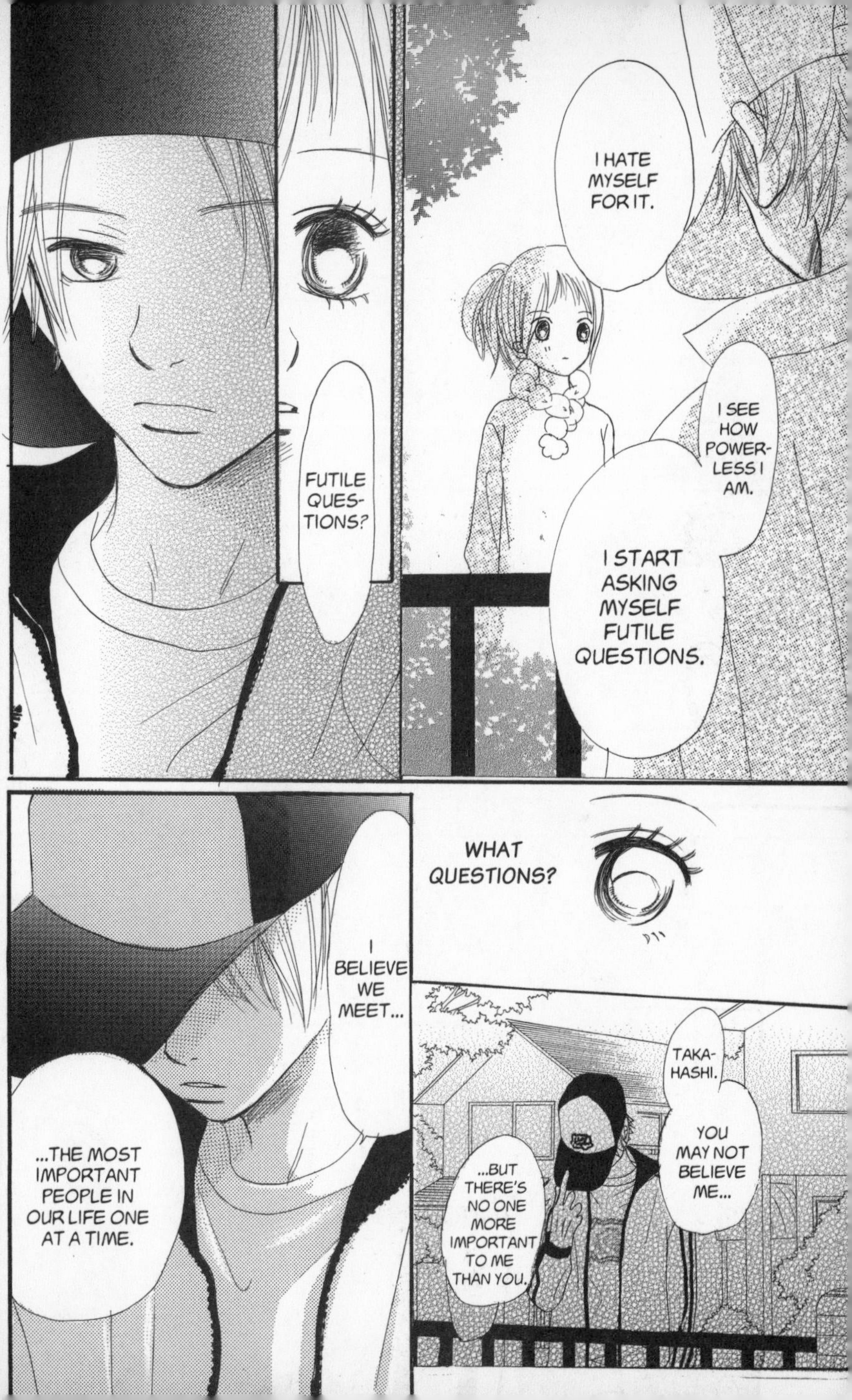
I HATE MYSELF FOR IT.
I SEE HOW POWER-LESS I AM.
I START ASKING MYSELF FUTILE QUESTIONS.
FUTILE QUES-TIONS?
WHAT QUESTIONS?
TAKA-HASHI.
YOU MAY NOT BELIEVE ME...
...BUT THERE'S NO ONE MORE IMPORTANT TO ME THAN YOU.
I BELIEVE WE MEET...
...THE MOST IMPORTANT PEOPLE IN OUR LIFE ONE AT A TIME.

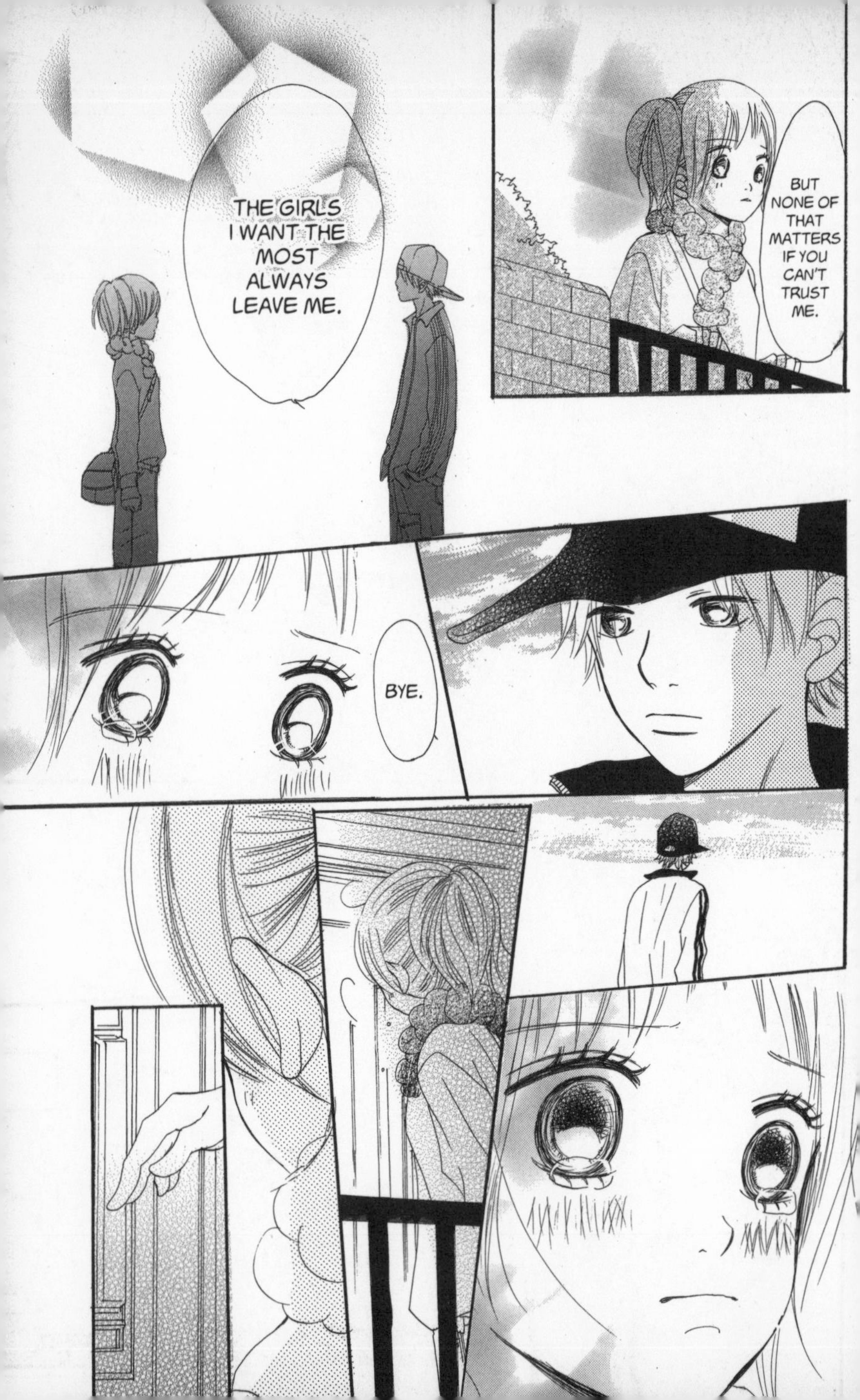
BUT NONE OF THAT MATTERS IF YOU CAN'T TRUST ME.
THE GIRLS I WANT THE MOST ALWAYS LEAVE ME.
BYE.

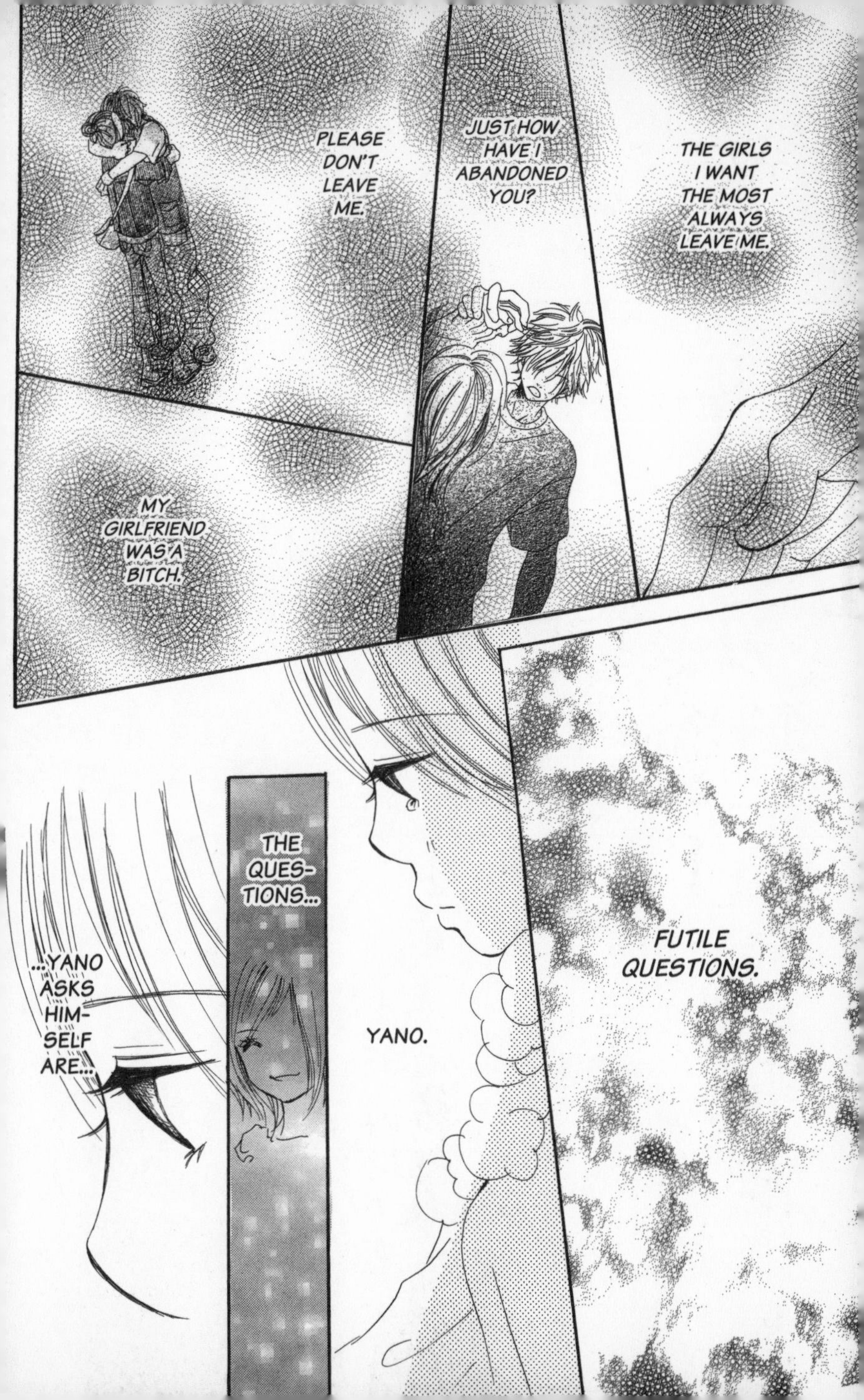
THE GIRLS I WANT THE MOST ALWAYS LEAVE ME.
JUST HOW HAVE I ABANDONED YOU?
PLEASE DON'T LEAVE ME.
MY GIRLFRIEND WAS A BITCH.
FUTILE QUESTIONS.
YANO.
THE QUES-TIONS...
...YANO ASKS HIM-SELF ARE...

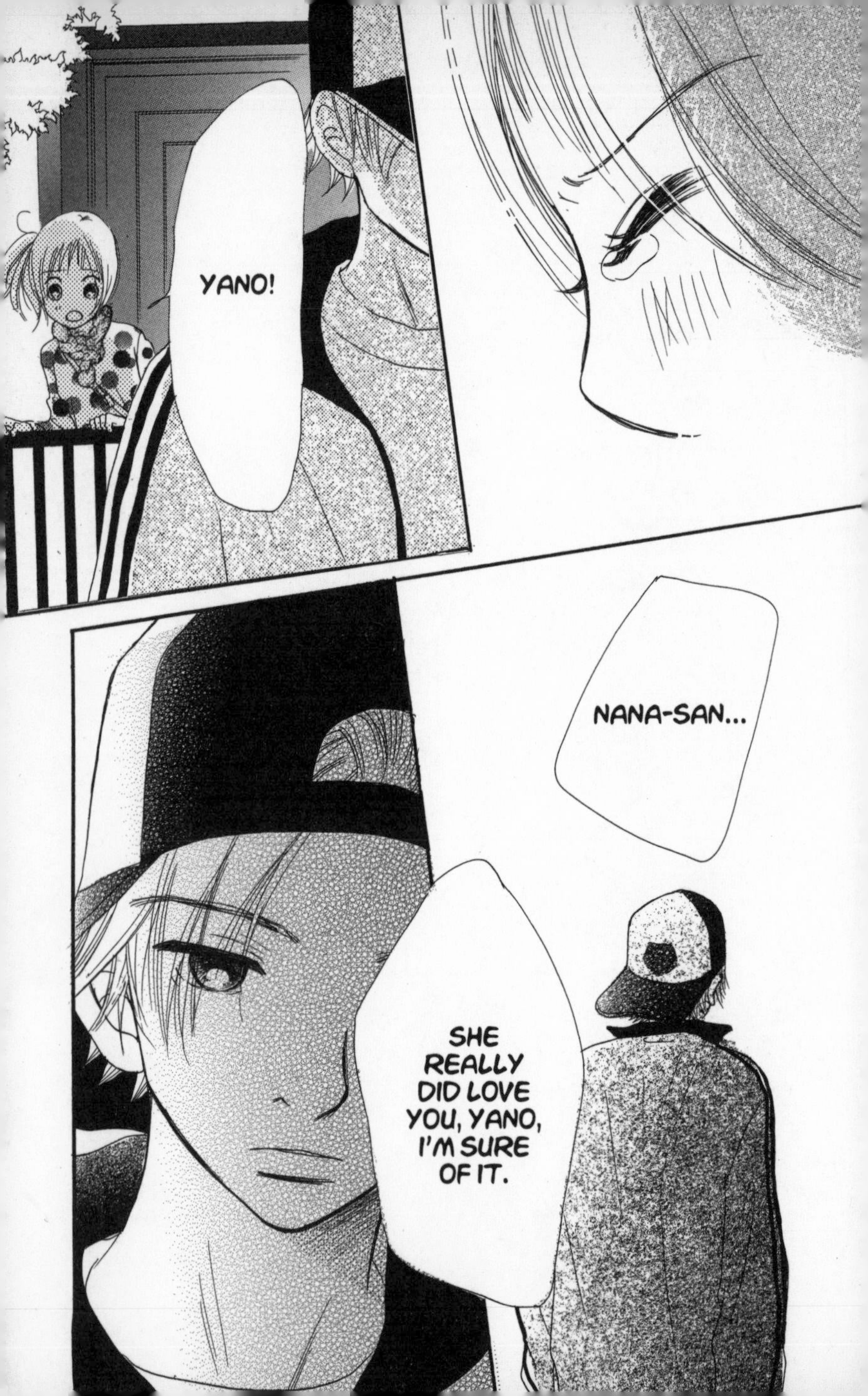
YANO!
NANA-SAN...
SHE REALLY DID LOVE YOU, YANO, I'M SURE OF IT.

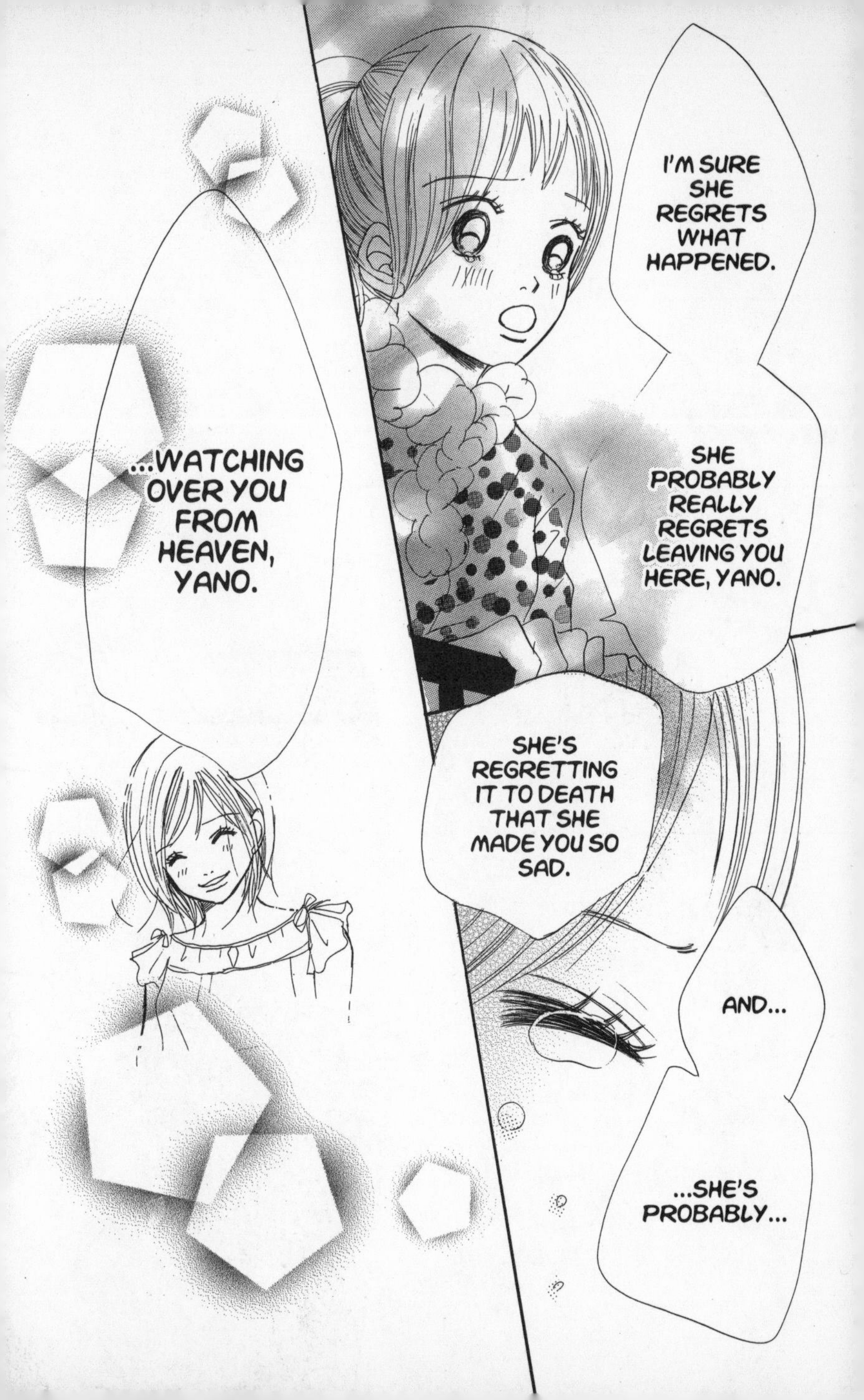
I'M SURE SHE REGRETS WHAT HAPPENED.
SHE PROBABLY REALLY REGRETS LEAVING YOU HERE, YANO.
SHE'S REGRETTING IT TO DEATH THAT SHE MADE YOU SO SAD.
AND...
...SHE'S PROBABLY...
...WATCHING OVER YOU FROM HEAVEN, YANO.

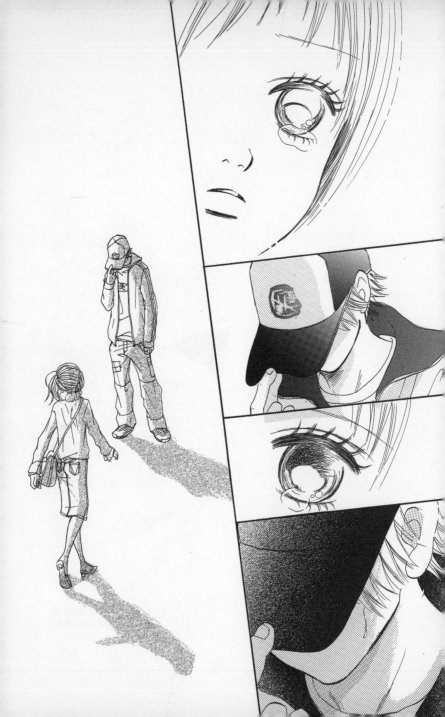

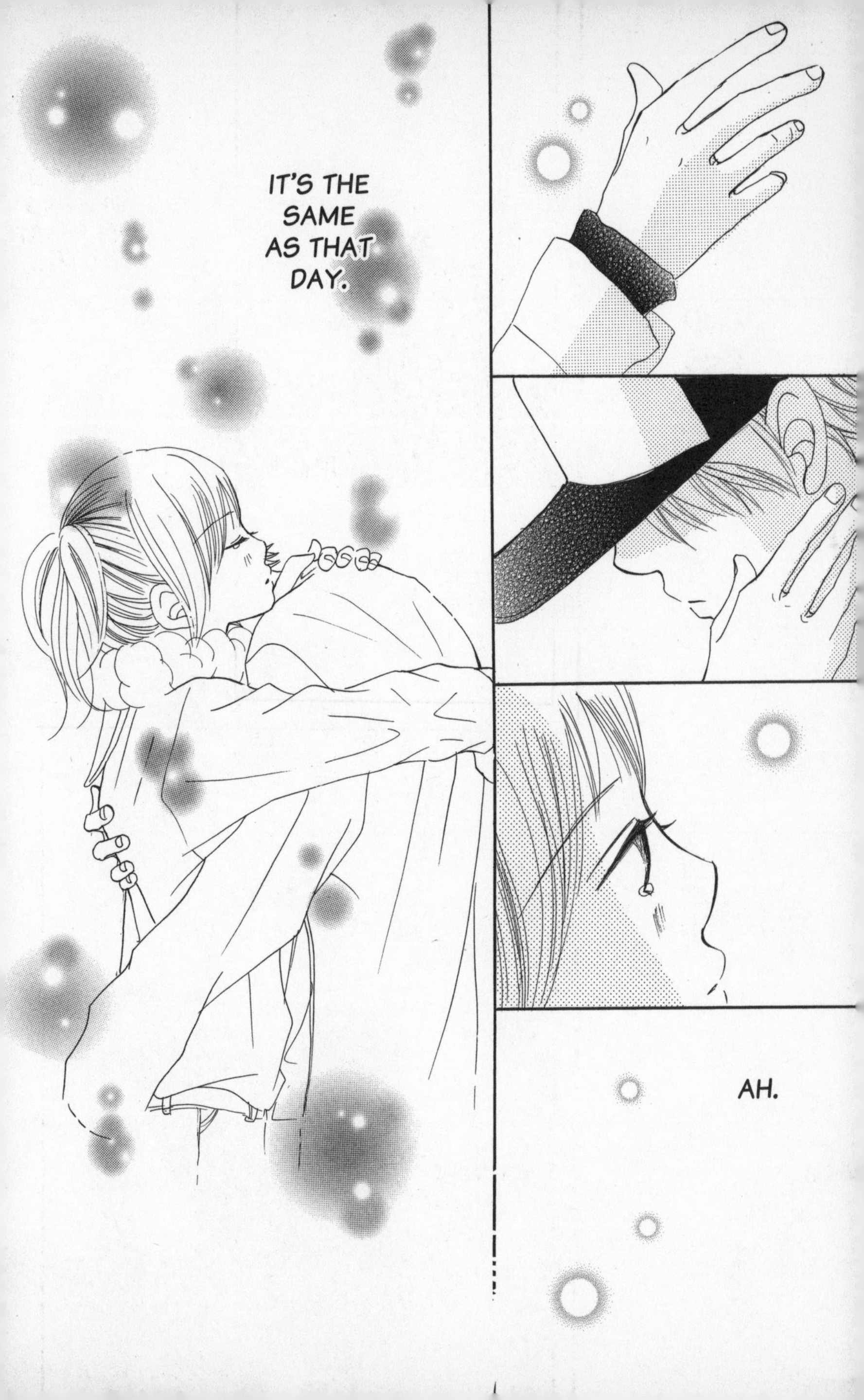
AH.
IT'S THE SAME AS THAT DAY.

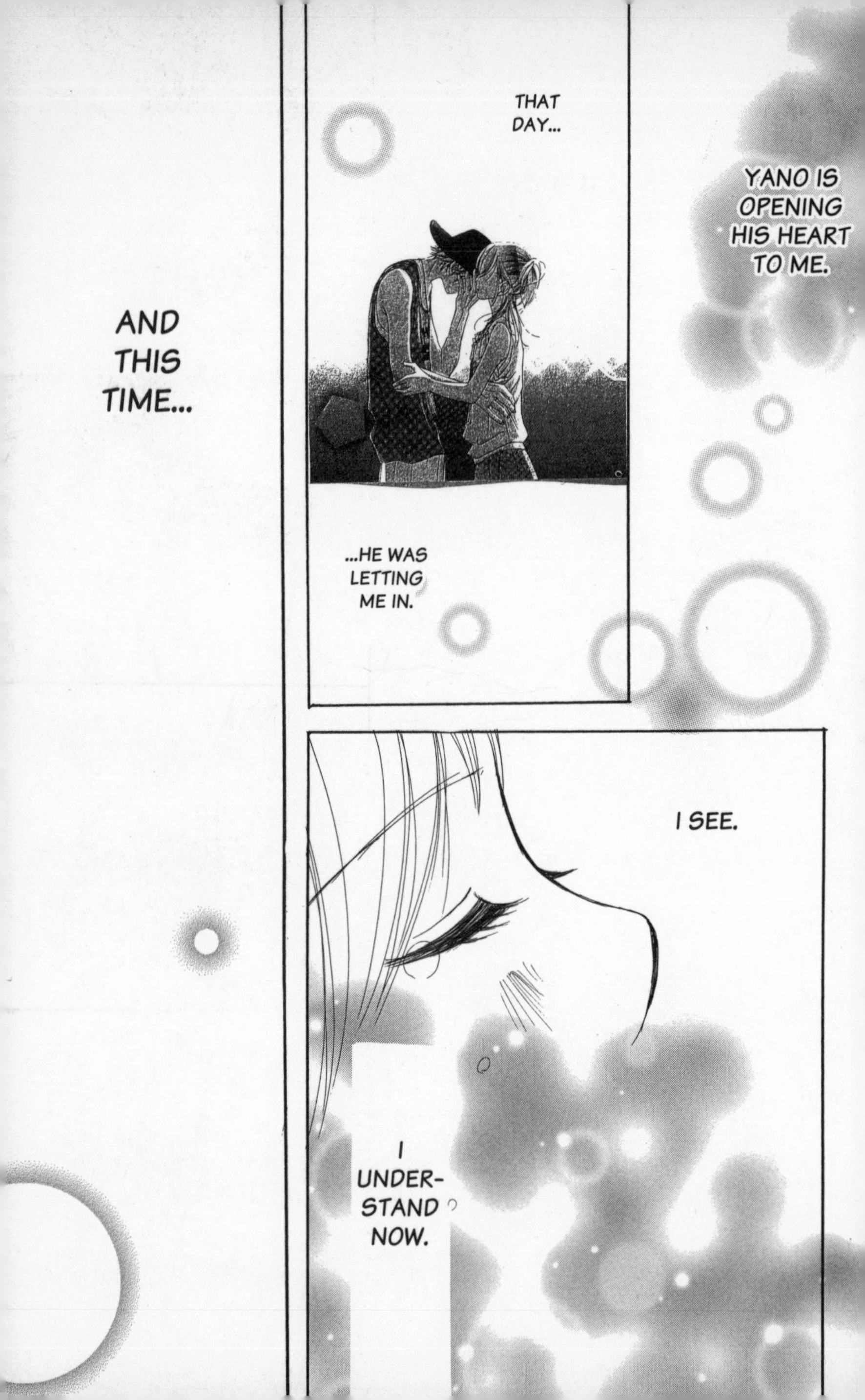
YANO IS OPENING HIS HEART TO ME.
THAT DAY...
...HE WAS LETTING ME IN.
I SEE.
I UNDER-STAND NOW.
AND THIS TIME...

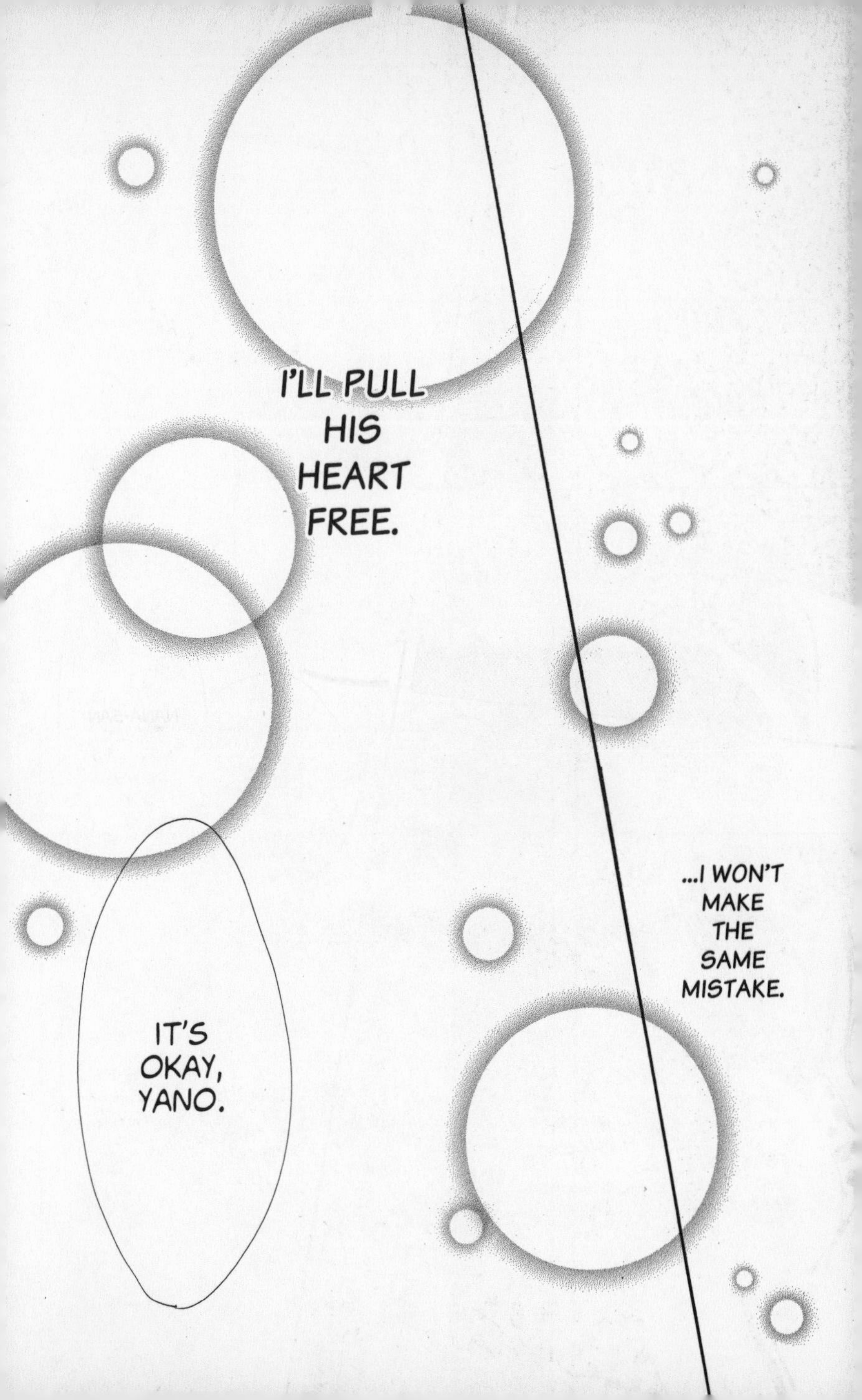
...I WON'T MAKE THE SAME MISTAKE.
I'LL PULL HIS HEART FREE.
IT'S OKAY, YANO.

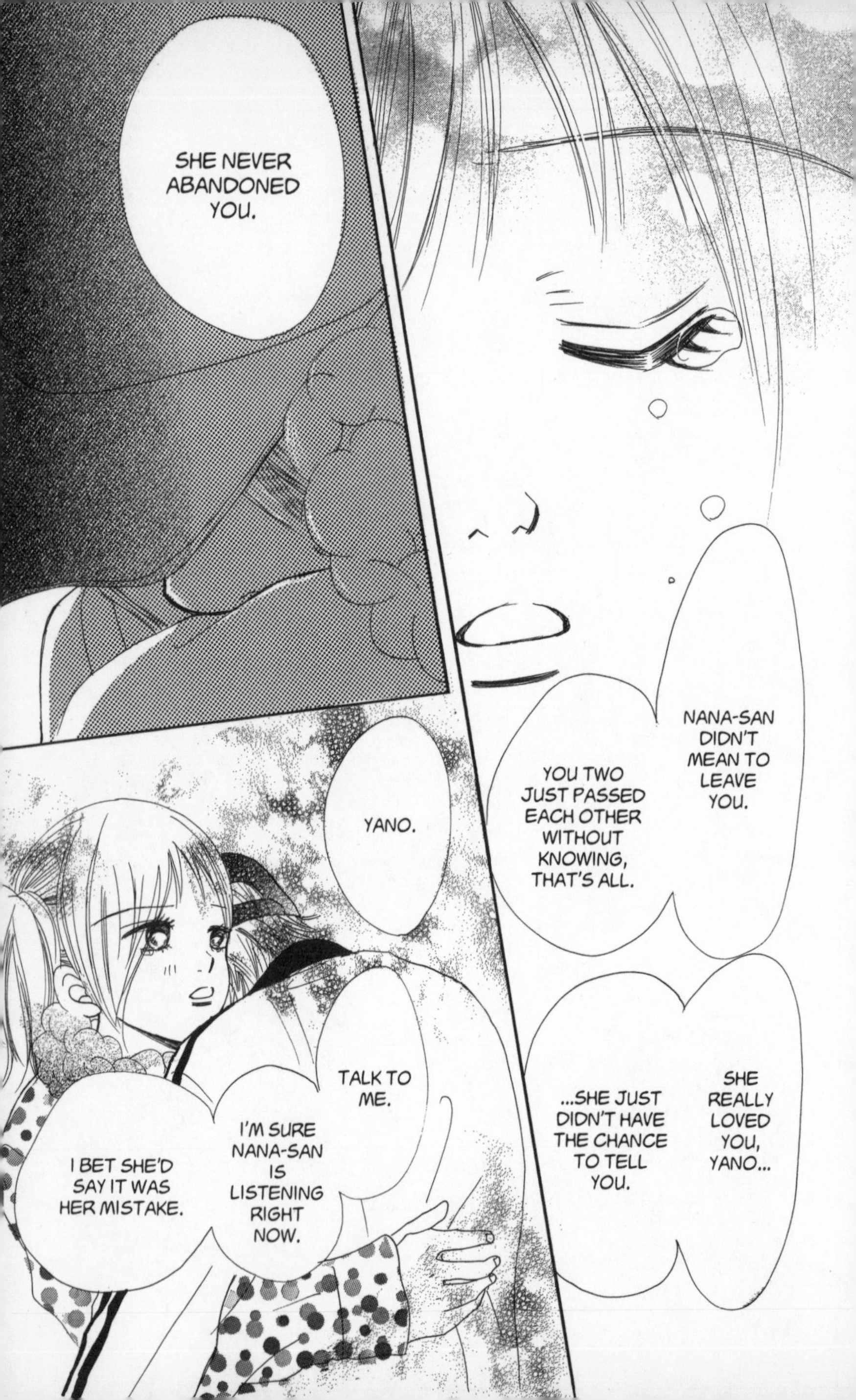
SHE NEVER ABANDONED YOU.
NANA-SAN DIDN'T MEAN TO LEAVE YOU.
YOU TWO JUST PASSED EACH OTHER WITHOUT KNOWING, THAT'S ALL.
SHE REALLY LOVED YOU, YANO...
...SHE JUST DIDN'T HAVE THE CHANCE TO TELL YOU.
YANO.
TALK TO ME.
I'M SURE NANA-SAN IS LISTENING RIGHT NOW.
I BET SHE'D SAY IT WAS HER MISTAKE.

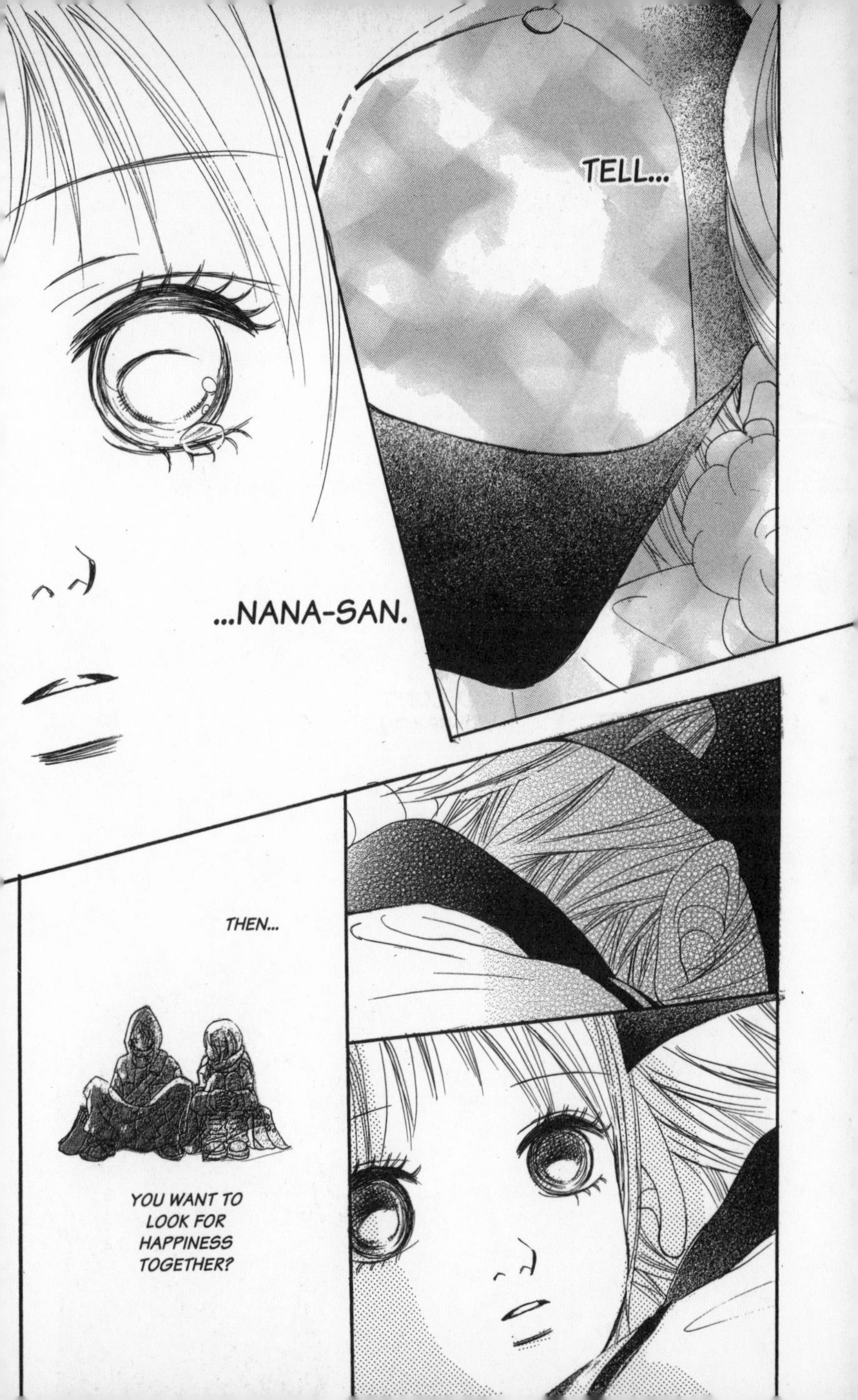
TELL...
...NANA-SAN.
THEN...
YOU WANT TO LOOK FOR HAPPINESS TOGETHER?

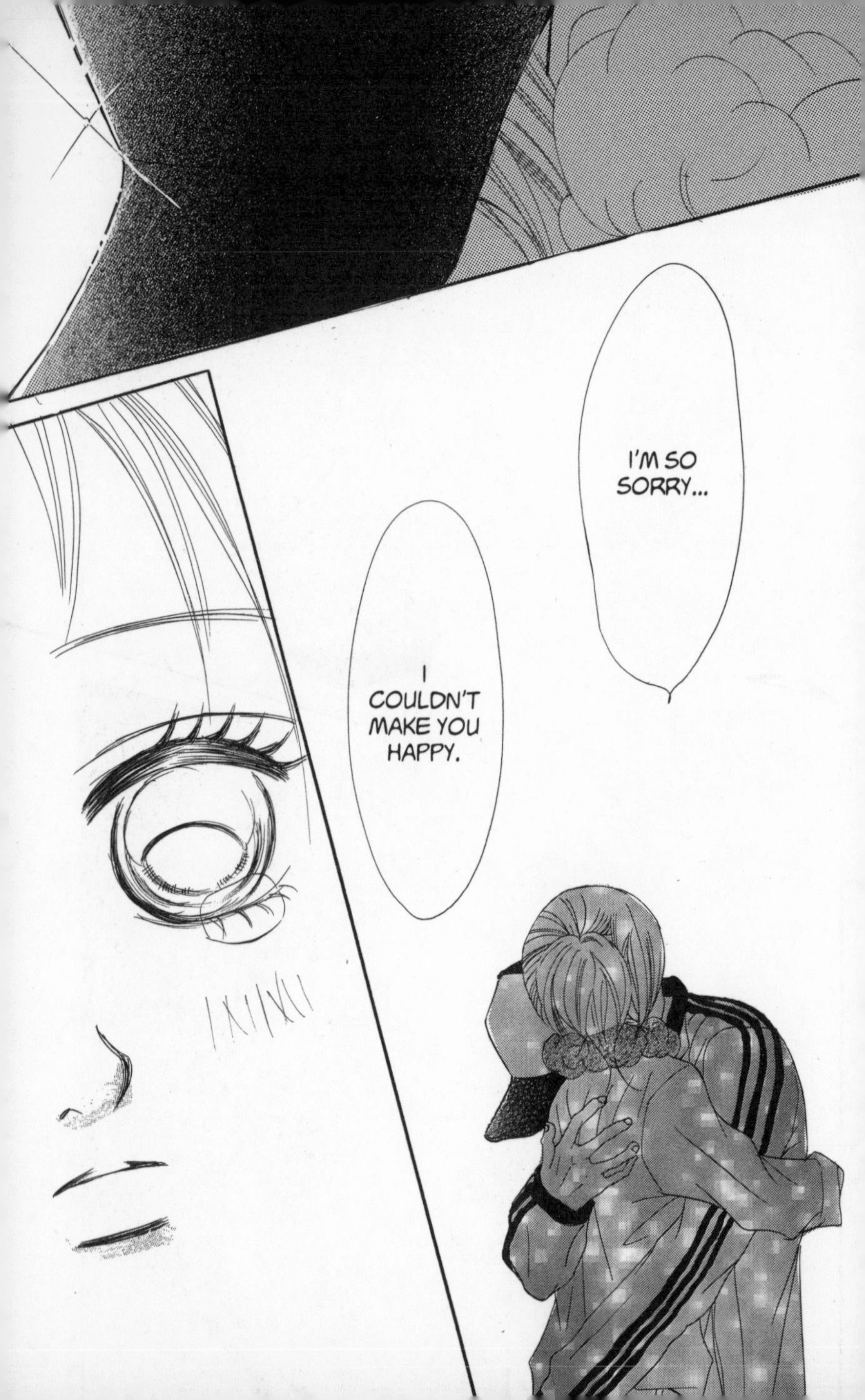
I'M SO SORRY...
I COULDN'T MAKE YOU HAPPY.

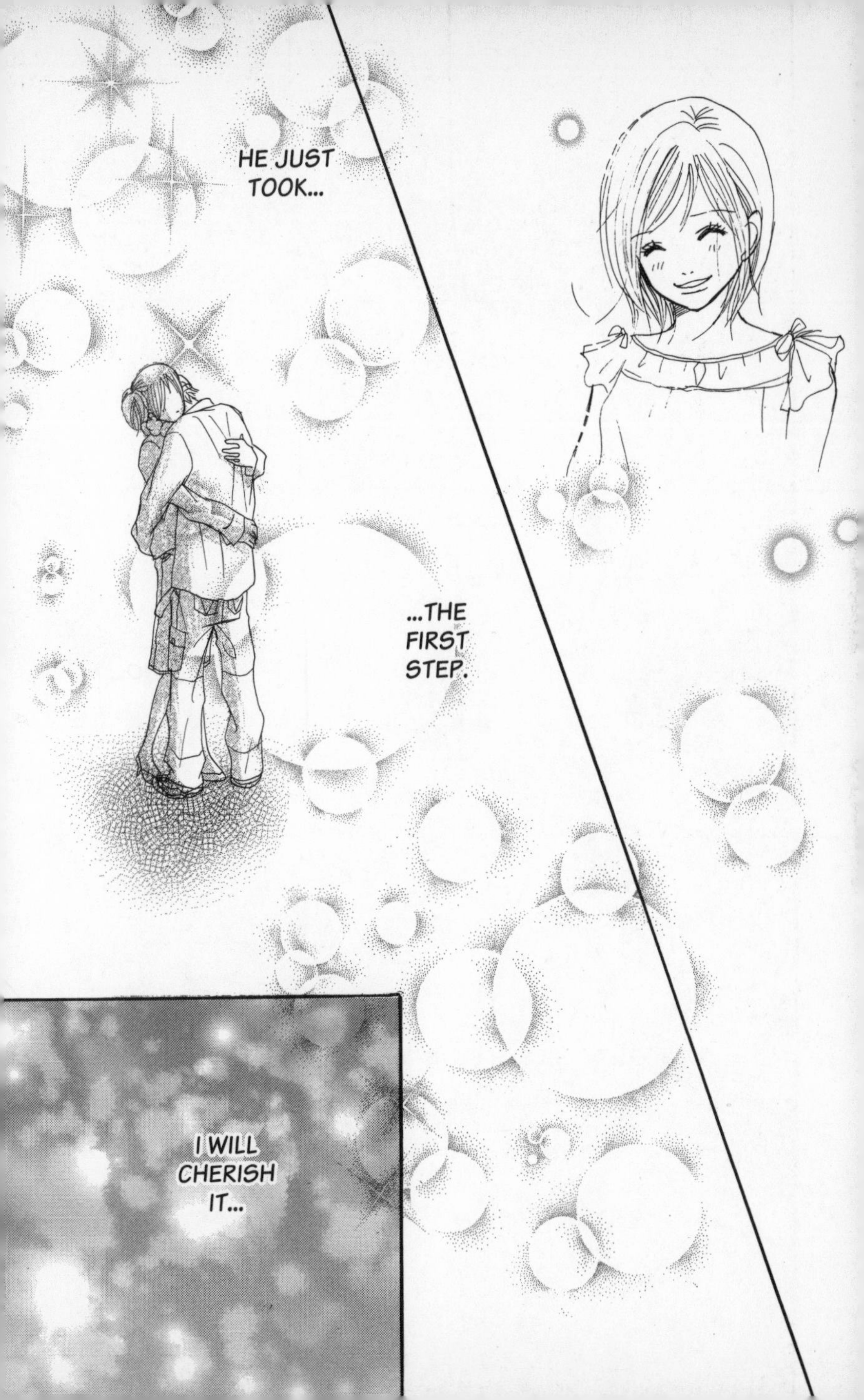
HE JUST TOOK...
...THE FIRST STEP.
I WILL CHERISH IT...

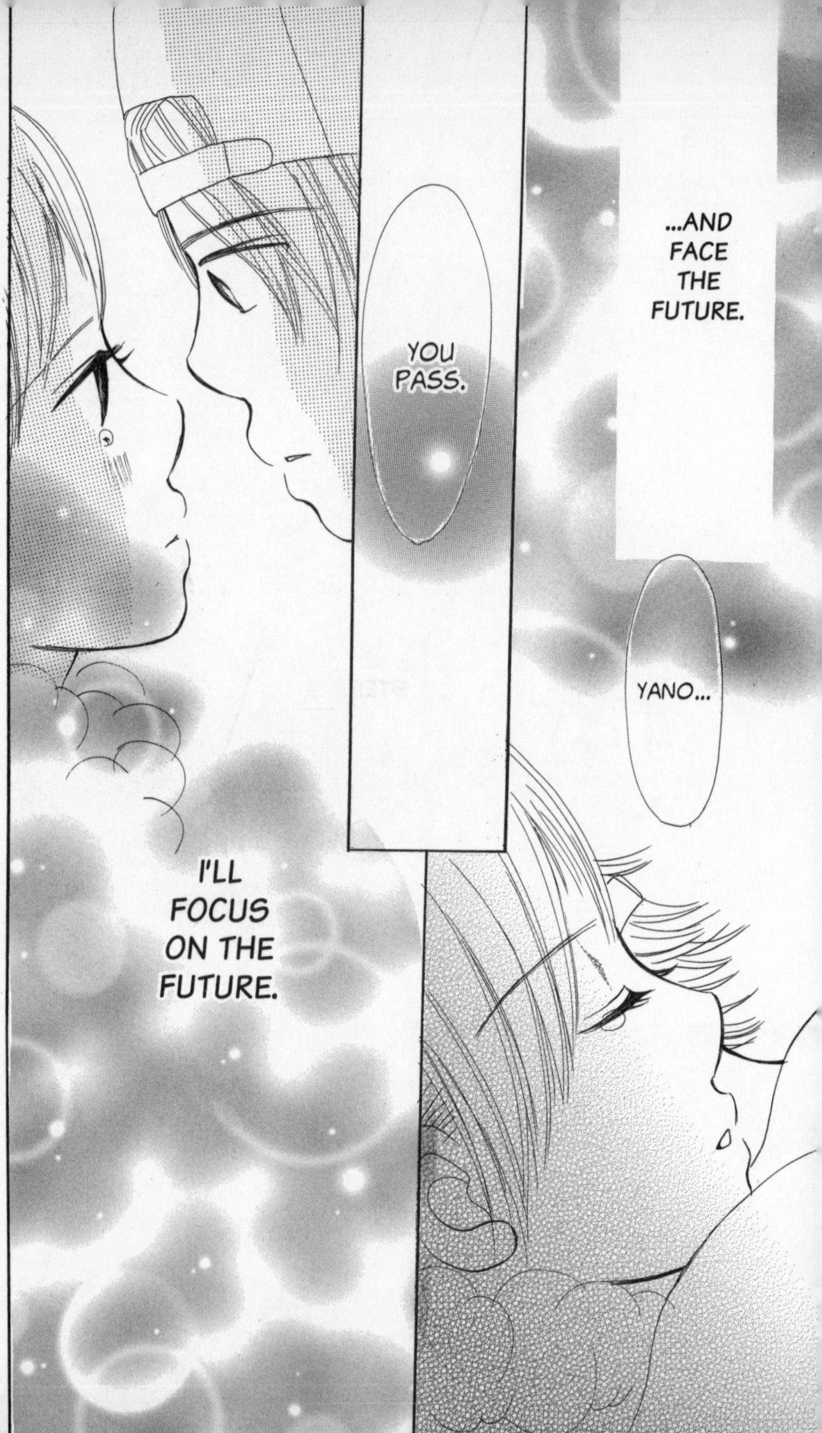
...AND FACE THE FUTURE.
YANO...
YOU PASS.
I'LL FOCUS ON THE FUTURE.

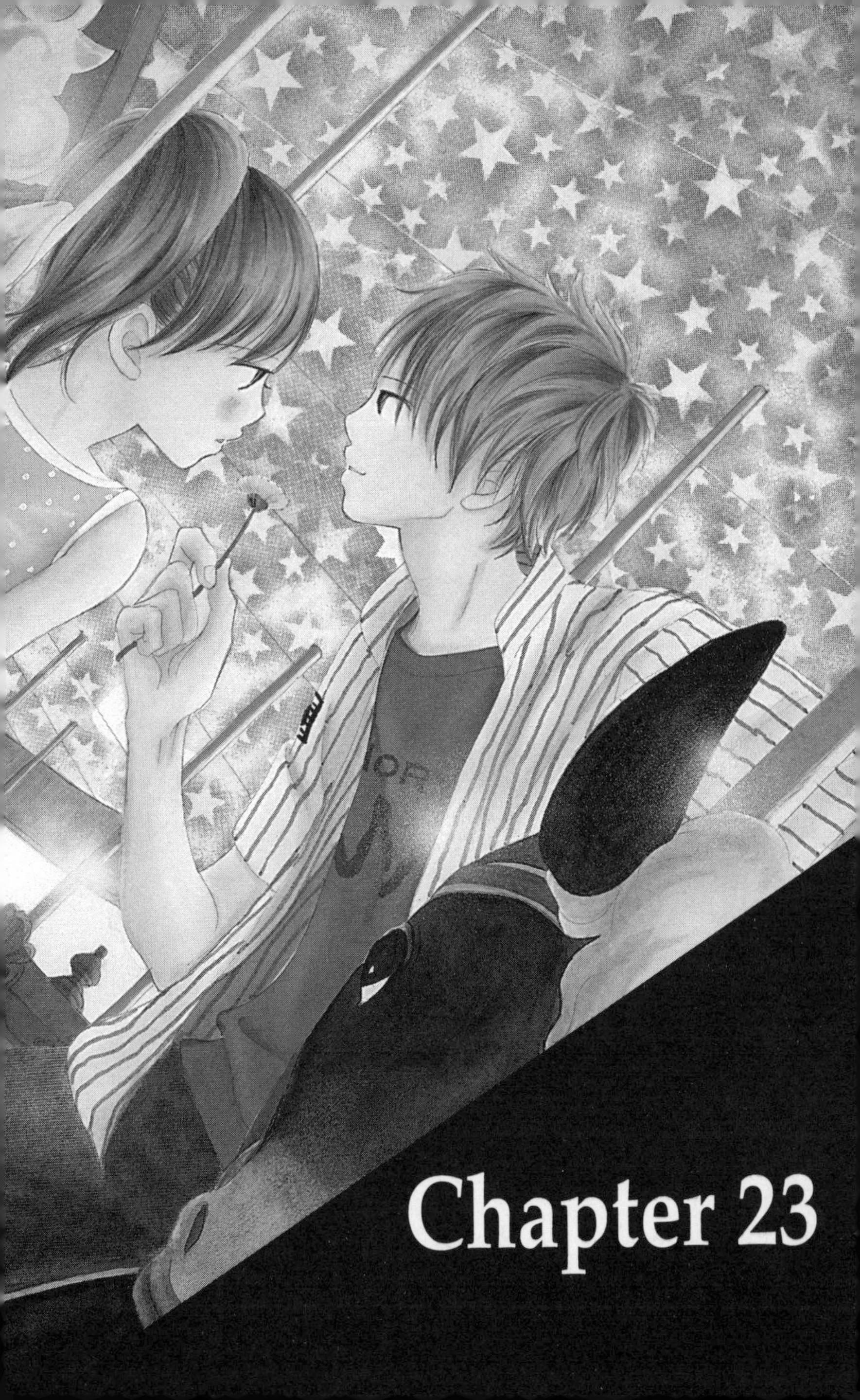

# Chapter 23

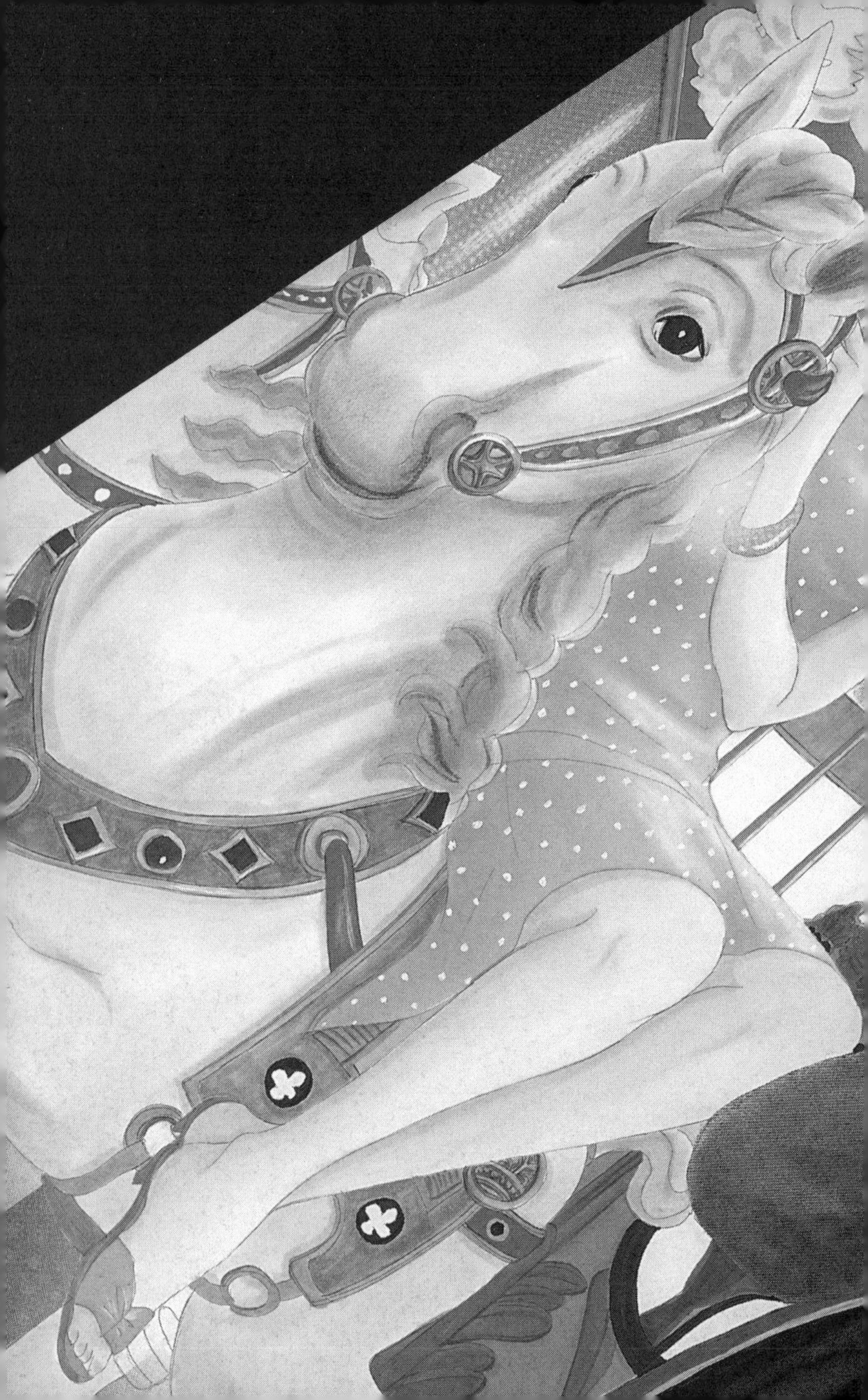

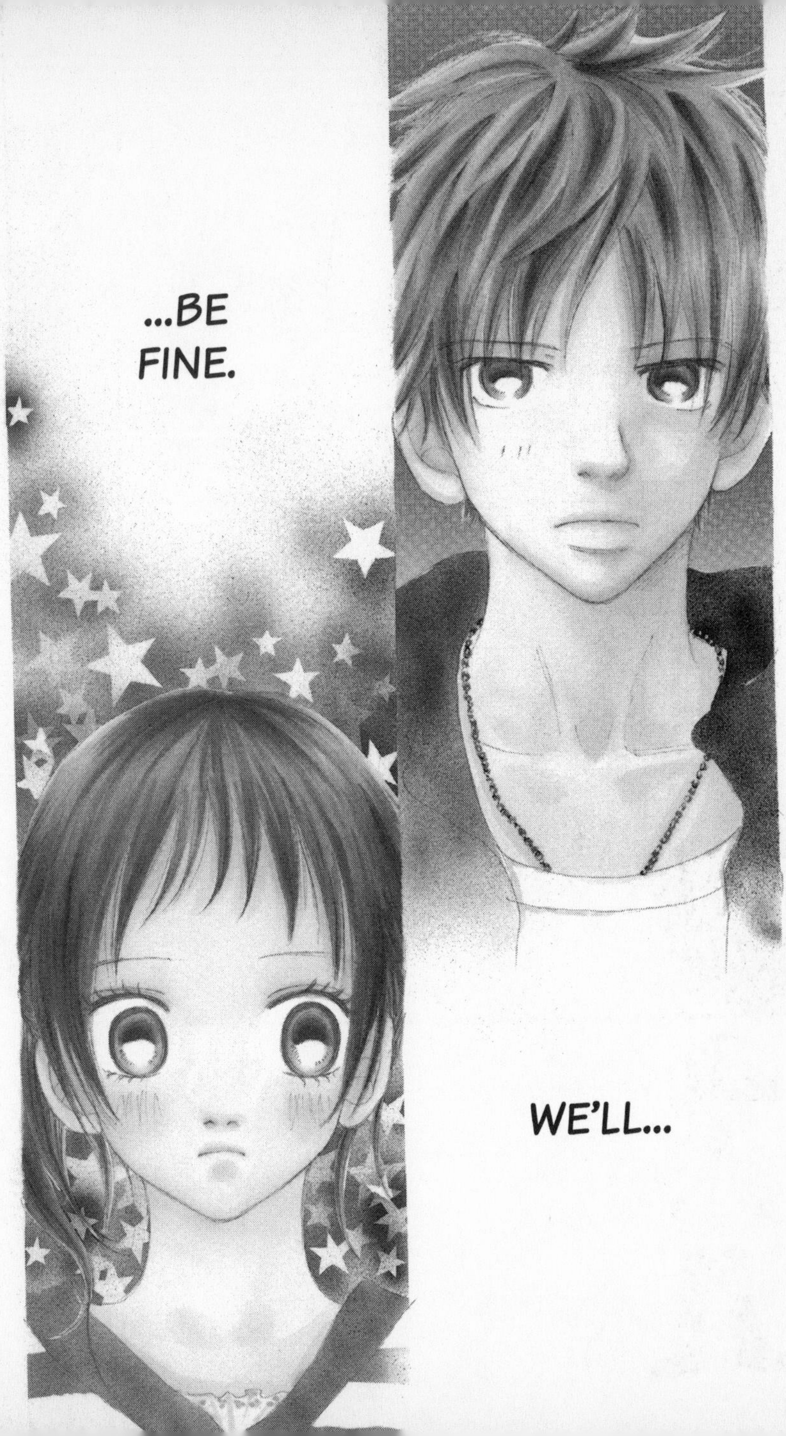
WE'LL...
...BE FINE.

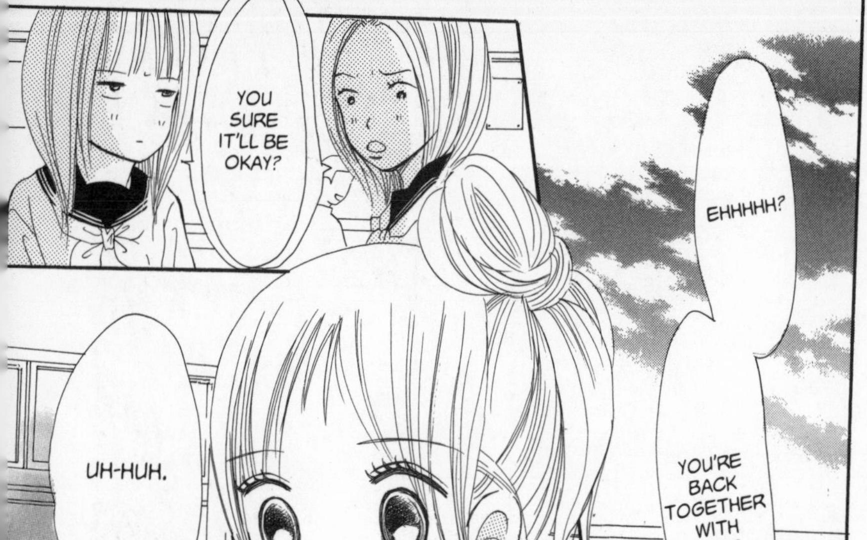
EHHHHH?
YOU'RE BACK TOGETHER WITH HIM?
YOU SURE IT'LL BE OKAY?
UH-HUH.
HA HA HA

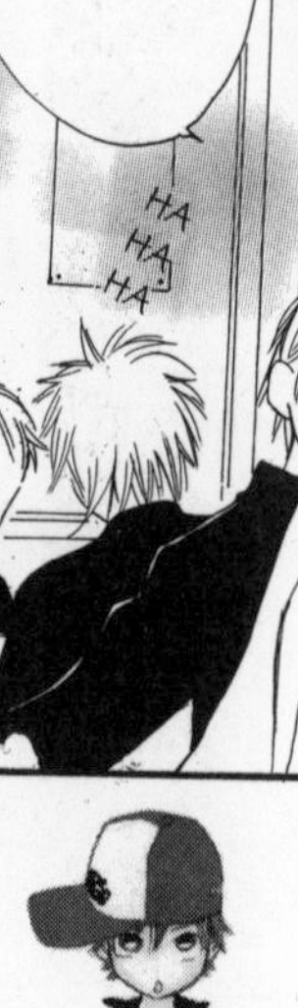

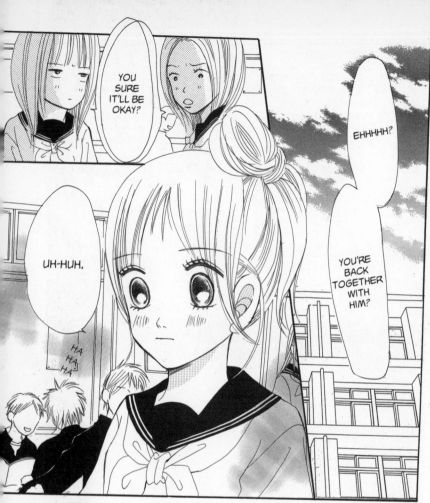

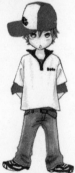

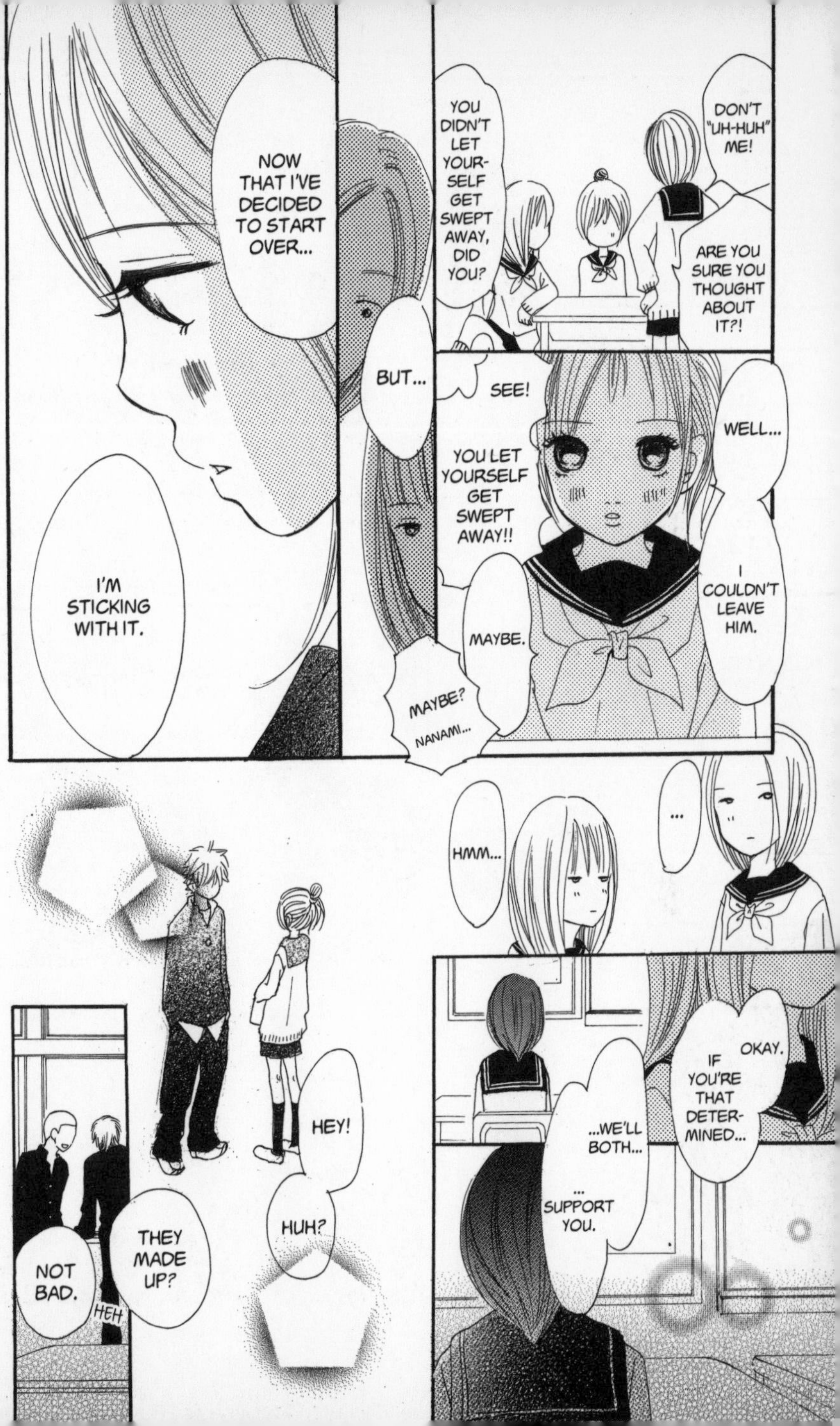
DON'T "UH-HUH" ME!
ARE YOU SURE YOU THOUGHT ABOUT IT?!
YOU DIDN'T LET YOURSELF GET SWEPT AWAY, DID YOU?
BUT...
WELL...
I COULDN'T LEAVE HIM.
SEE!
YOU LET YOURSELF GET SWEPT AWAY!!
MAYBE.
MAYBE?
NANAMI...
NOW THAT I'VE DECIDED TO START OVER...
I'M STICKING WITH IT.
...
HMM...
OKAY.
IF YOU'RE THAT DETERMINED...
...WE'LL BOTH...
... SUPPORT YOU.
HEY!
HUH?
THEY MADE UP?
NOT BAD.
HEH

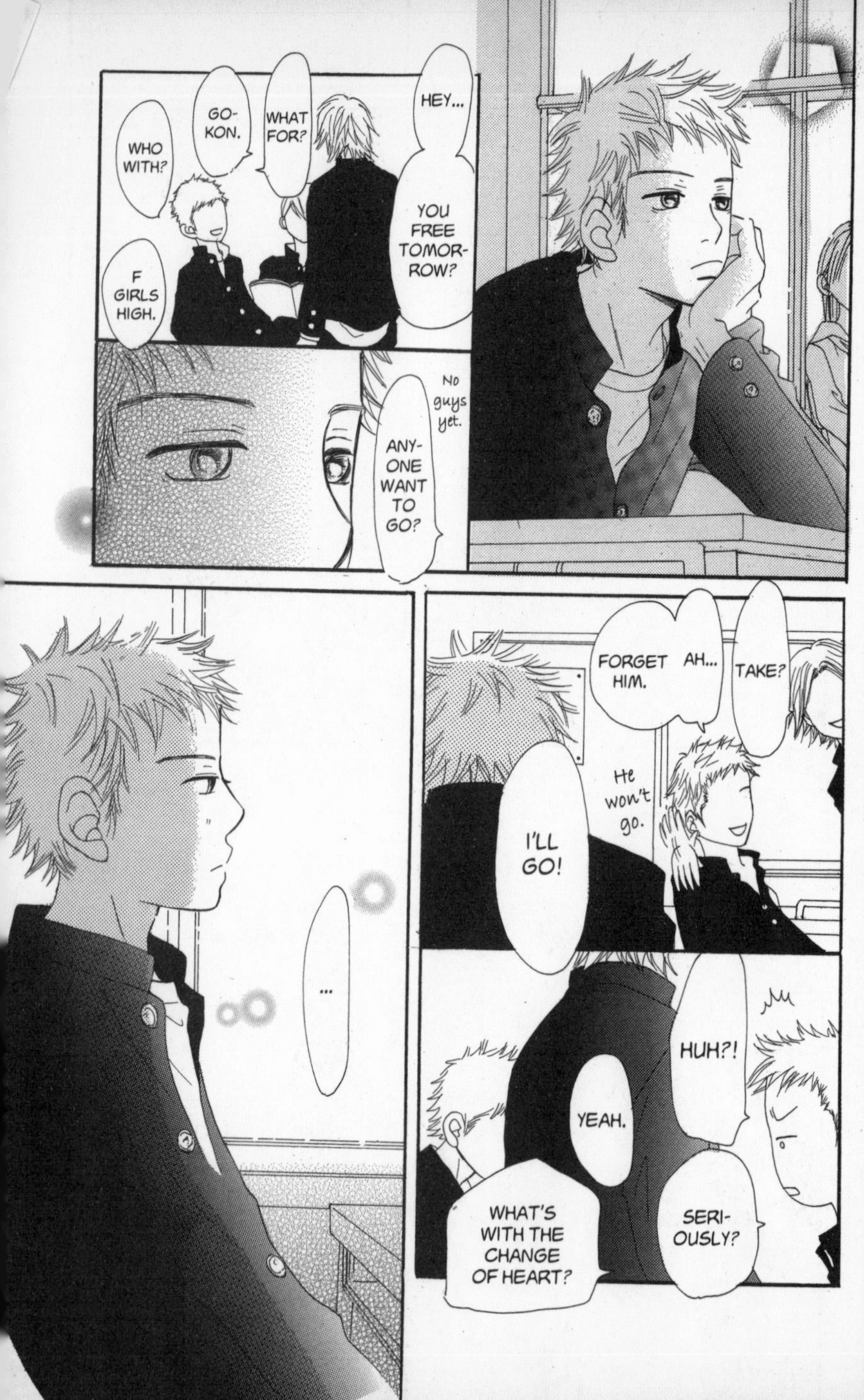
HEY... YOU FREE TOMORROW?
WHAT FOR?
GO-KON.
WHO WITH?
F GIRLS HIGH.
No guys yet.
ANYONE WANT TO GO?
TAKE?
AH...
FORGET HIM.
He won't go.
I'LL GO!
HUH?!
SERIOUSLY?
YEAH.
WHAT'S WITH THE CHANGE OF HEART?
...

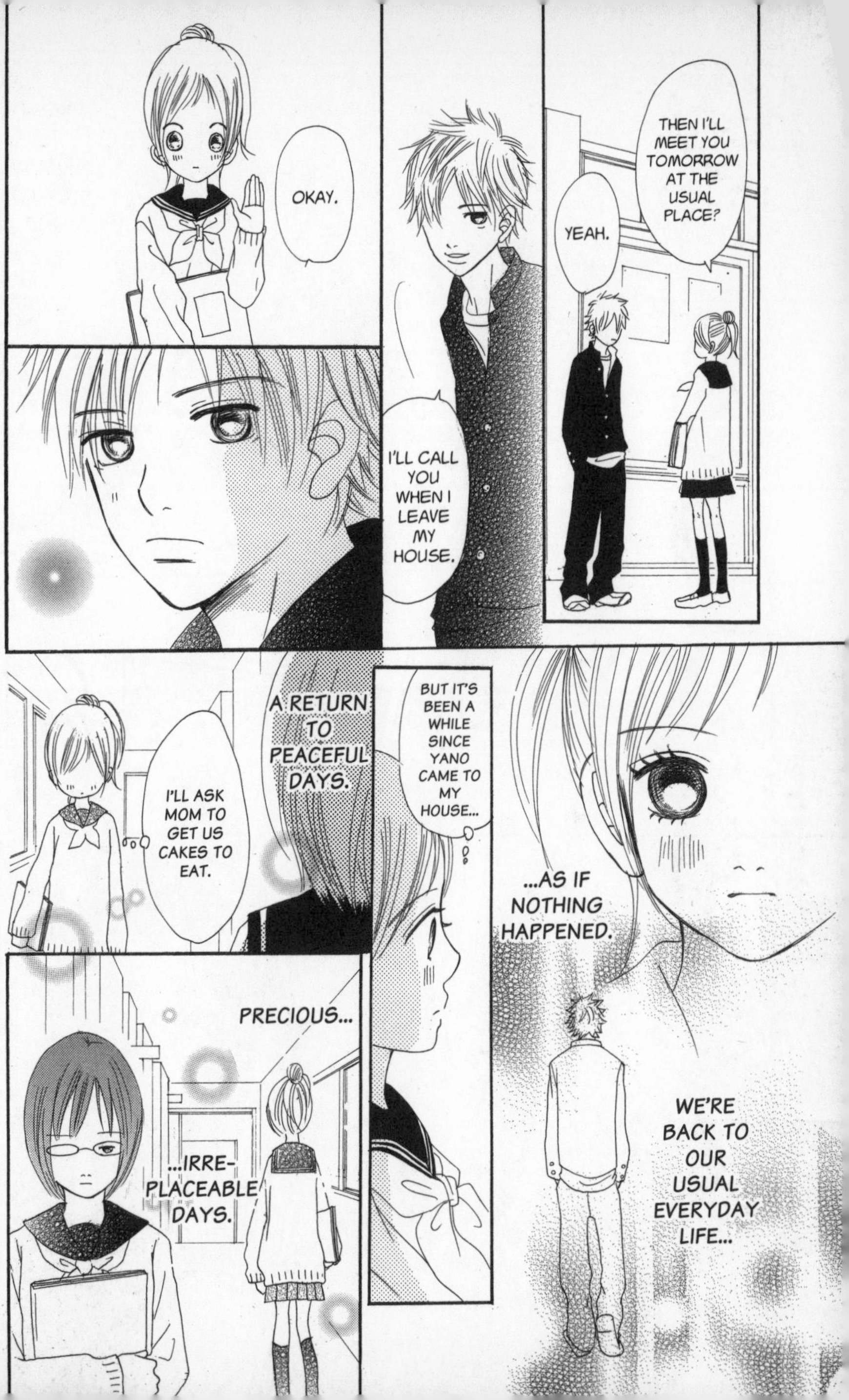
THEN I'LL MEET YOU TOMORROW AT THE USUAL PLACE?
YEAH.
I'LL CALL YOU WHEN I LEAVE MY HOUSE.
OKAY.
WE'RE BACK TO OUR USUAL EVERYDAY LIFE...
...AS IF NOTHING HAPPENED.
BUT IT'S BEEN A WHILE SINCE YANO CAME TO MY HOUSE...
A RETURN TO PEACEFUL DAYS.
I'LL ASK MOM TO GET US CAKES TO EAT.
PRECIOUS...
...IRRE-PLACEABLE DAYS.

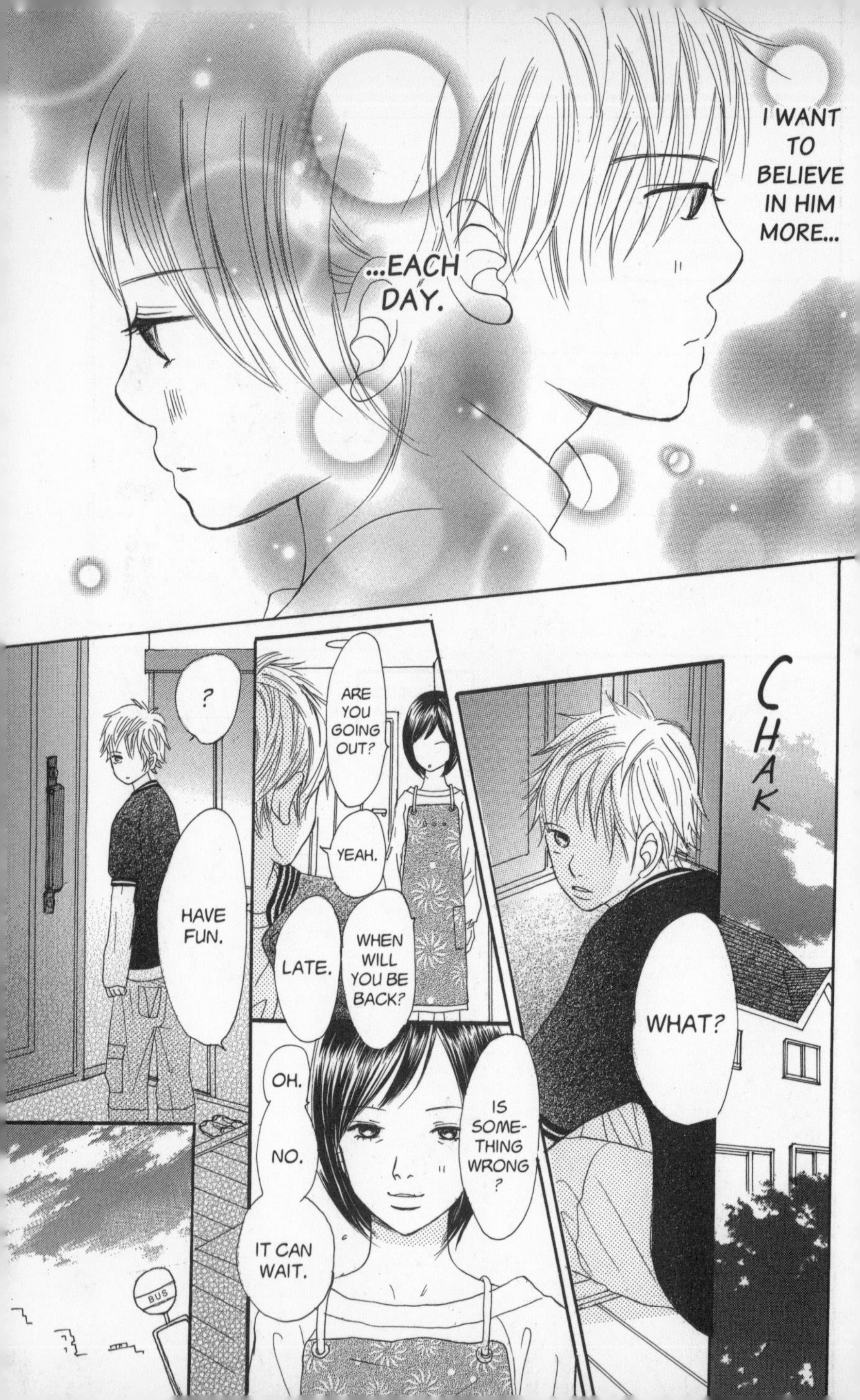
I WANT TO BELIEVE IN HIM MORE...
...EACH DAY.
CHAK
WHAT?
ARE YOU GOING OUT?
YEAH.
WHEN WILL YOU BE BACK?
LATE.
IS SOME-THING WRONG?
OH.
NO.
IT CAN WAIT.
?
HAVE FUN.

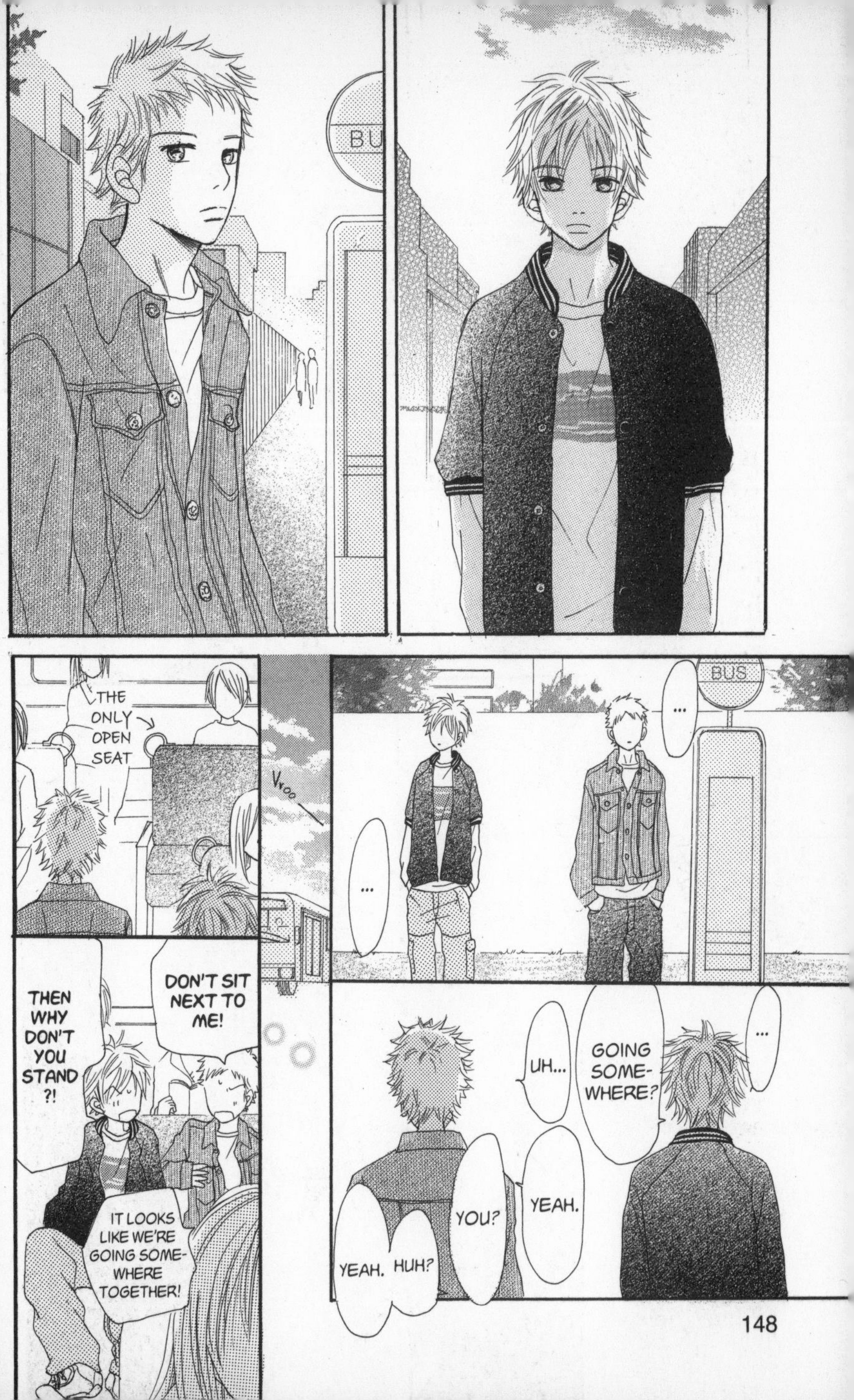
...
...
...
GOING SOME-WHERE?
UH...
YEAH.
YOU?
HUH?
YEAH.
THE ONLY OPEN SEAT
Vroo
DON'T SIT NEXT TO ME!
THEN WHY DON'T YOU STAND?!
IT LOOKS LIKE WE'RE GOING SOME-WHERE TOGETHER!

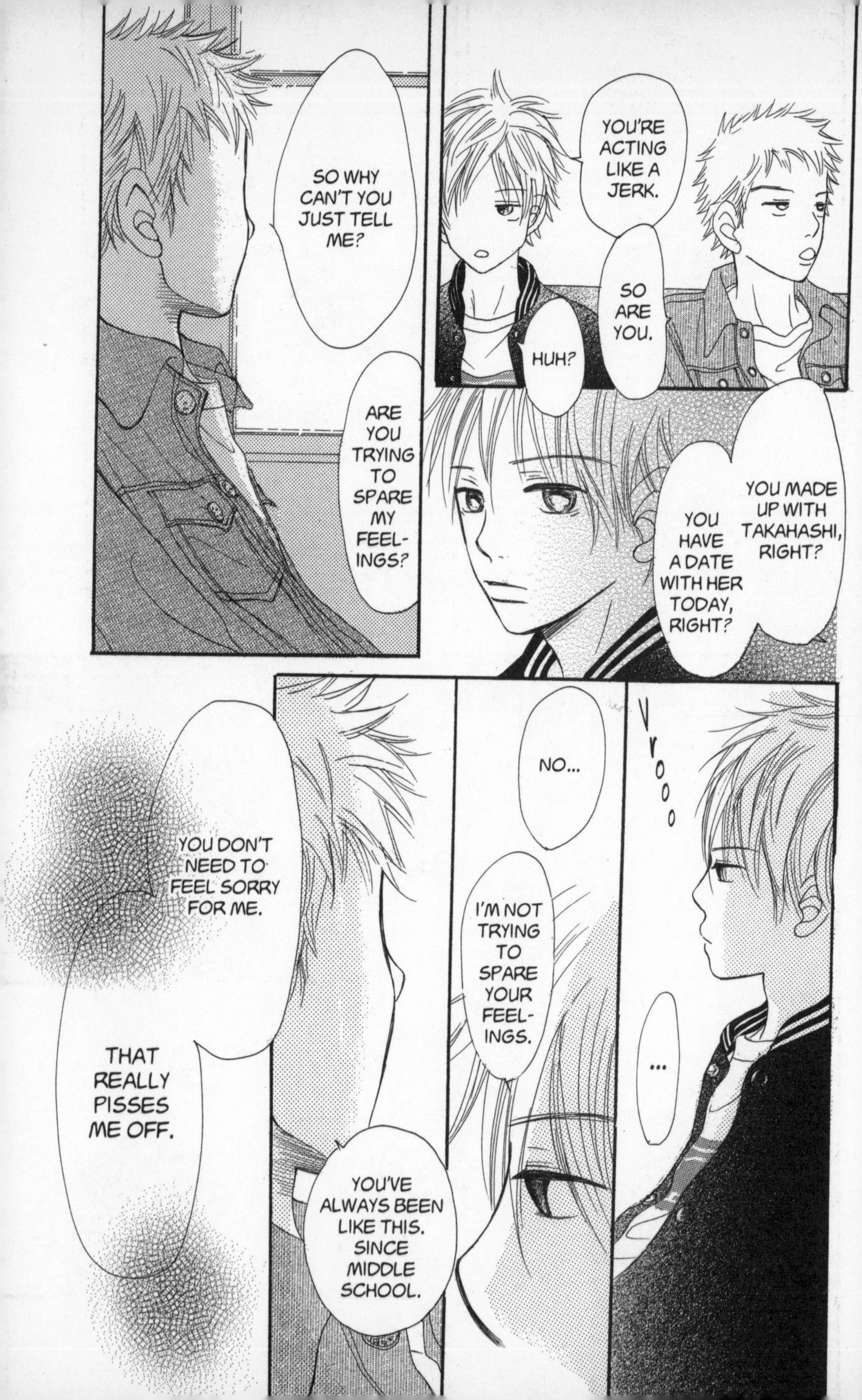
YOU'RE ACTING LIKE A JERK.
SO ARE YOU.
HUH?
YOU MADE UP WITH TAKAHASHI, RIGHT?
YOU HAVE A DATE WITH HER TODAY, RIGHT?
SO WHY CAN'T YOU JUST TELL ME?
ARE YOU TRYING TO SPARE MY FEEL-INGS?
Vrooo
...
NO...
I'M NOT TRYING TO SPARE YOUR FEEL-INGS.
YOU'VE ALWAYS BEEN LIKE THIS. SINCE MIDDLE SCHOOL.
YOU DON'T NEED TO FEEL SORRY FOR ME.
THAT REALLY PISSES ME OFF.

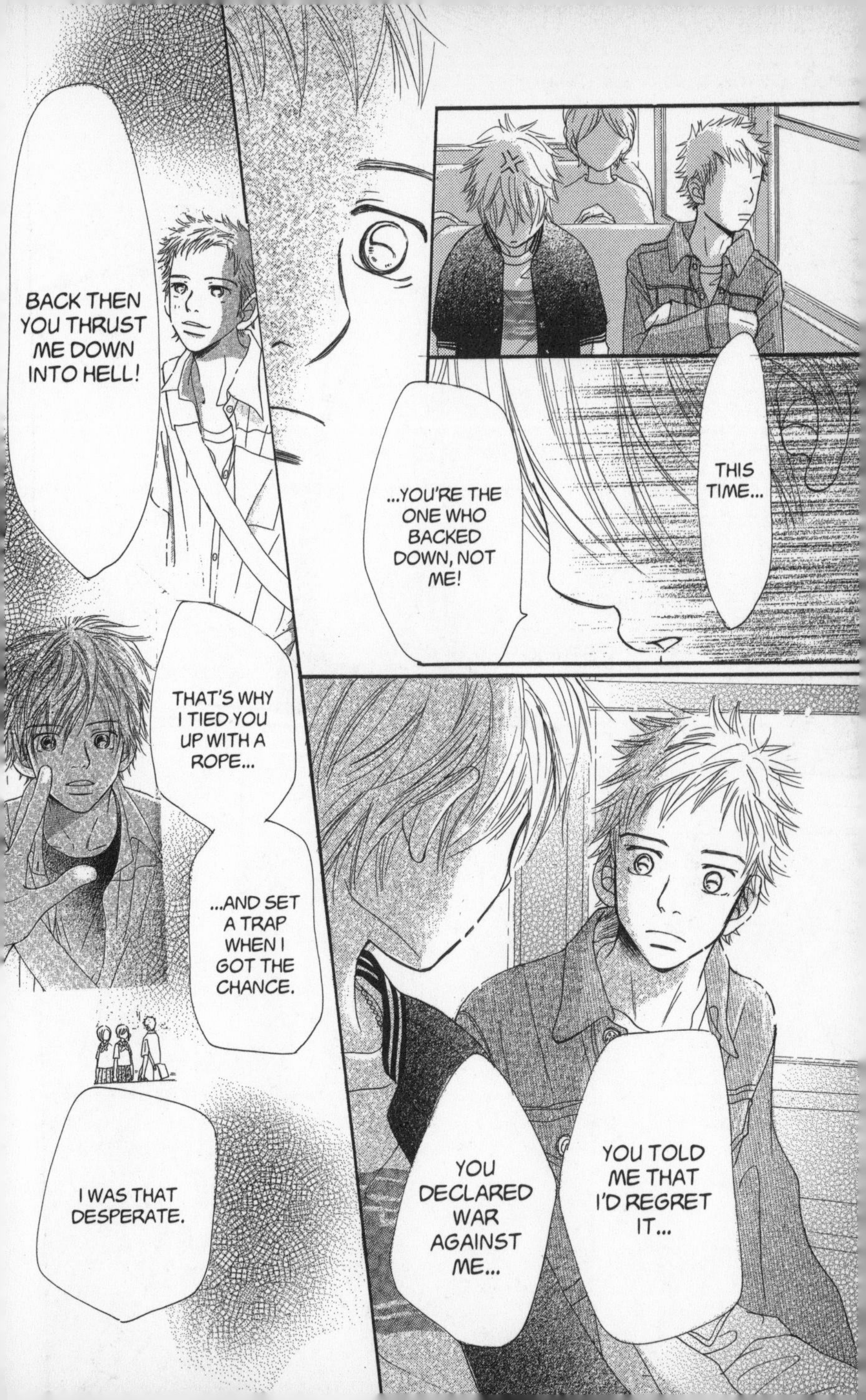
THIS TIME...
...YOU'RE THE ONE WHO BACKED DOWN, NOT ME!
YOU TOLD ME THAT I'D REGRET IT...
YOU DECLARED WAR AGAINST ME...
BACK THEN YOU THRUST ME DOWN INTO HELL!
THAT'S WHY I TIED YOU UP WITH A ROPE...
...AND SET A TRAP WHEN I GOT THE CHANCE.
I WAS THAT DESPERATE.

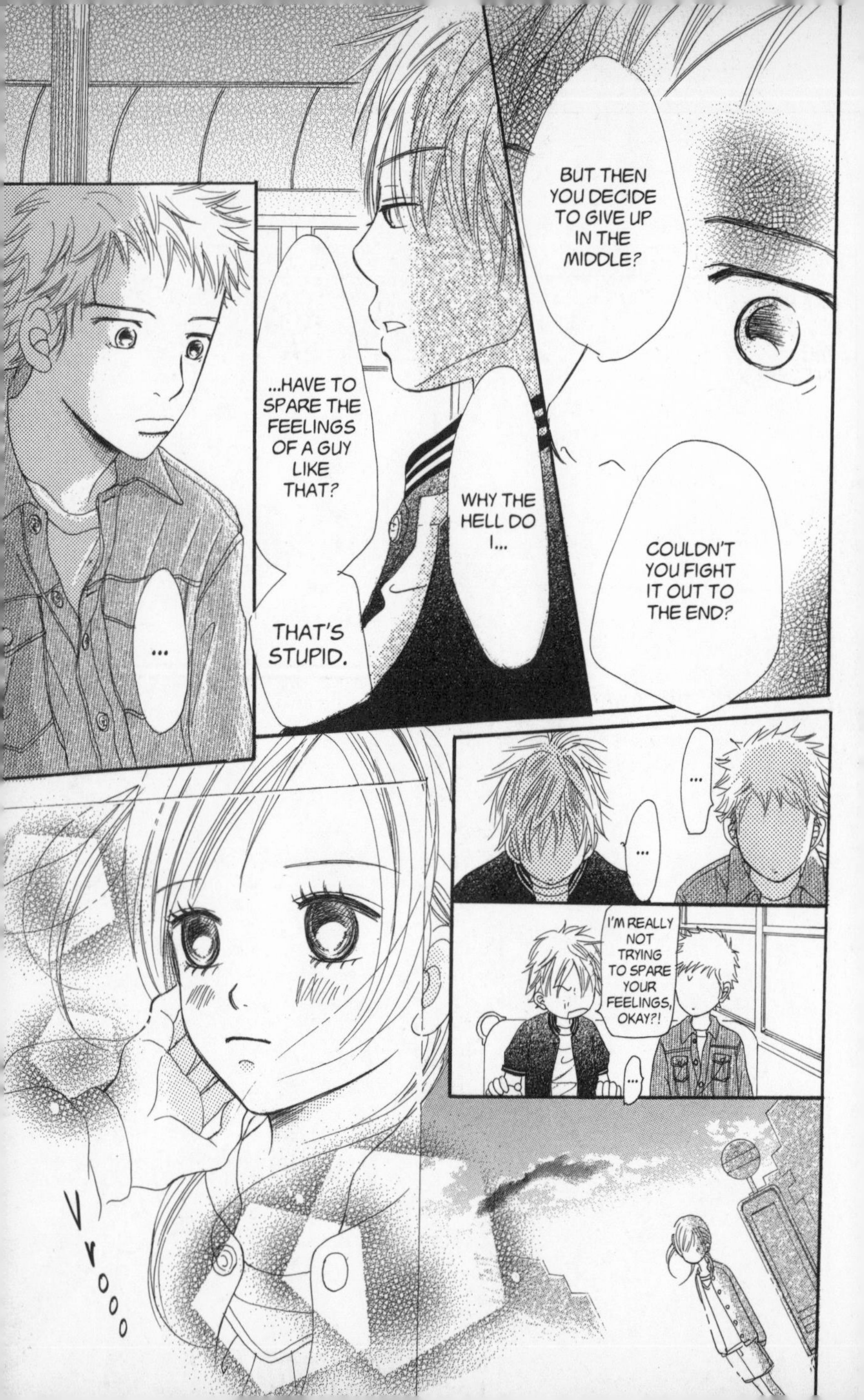
BUT THEN YOU DECIDE TO GIVE UP IN THE MIDDLE?
COULDN'T YOU FIGHT IT OUT TO THE END?
WHY THE HELL DO I...
...HAVE TO SPARE THE FEELINGS OF A GUY LIKE THAT?
THAT'S STUPID.
...
...
...
I'M REALLY NOT TRYING TO SPARE YOUR FEELINGS, OKAY?!
...
Vrooo

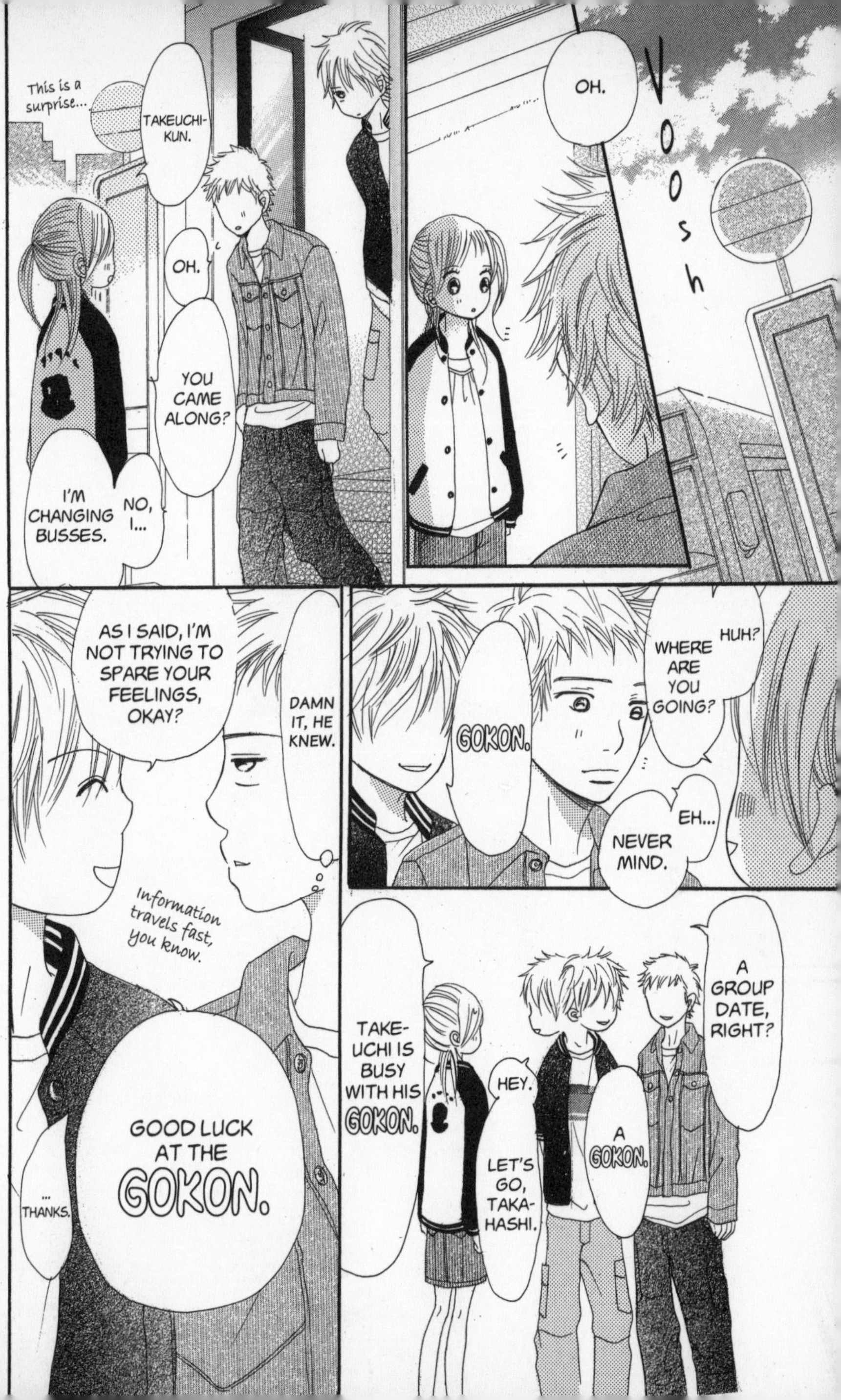
OH.
VOOSH
TAKEUCHI-KUN.
This is a surprise...
OH.
YOU CAME ALONG?
NO, I...
I'M CHANGING BUSSES.
HUH?
WHERE ARE YOU GOING?
GOKON.
EH... NEVER MIND.
A GROUP DATE, RIGHT?
A GOKON.
HEY.
LET'S GO, TAKAHASHI.
TAKEUCHI IS BUSY WITH HIS GOKON.
DAMN IT, HE KNEW.
AS I SAID, I'M NOT TRYING TO SPARE YOUR FEELINGS, OKAY?
Information travels fast, you know.
GOOD LUCK AT THE GOKON.
...THANKS.

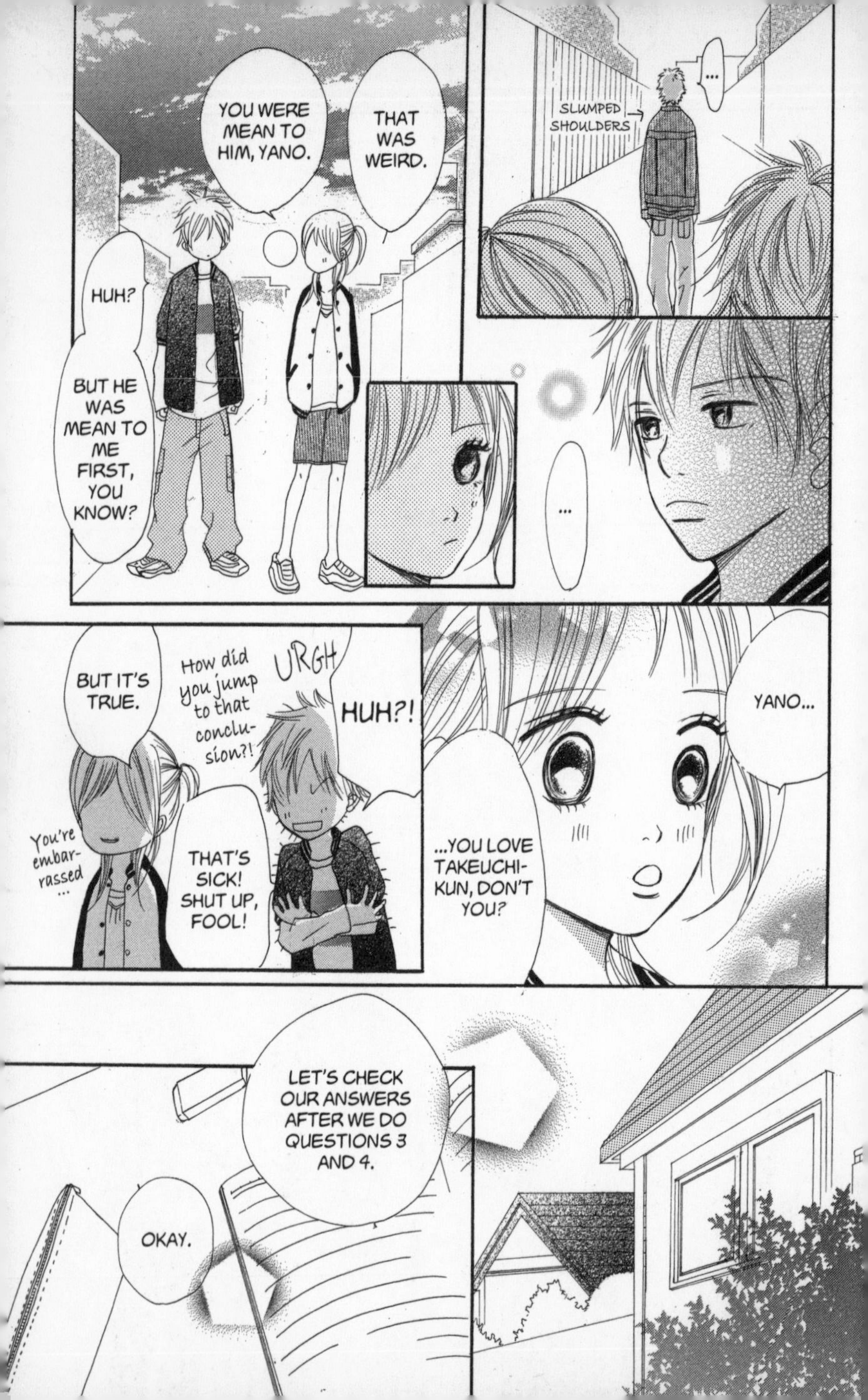
...
SLUMPED SHOULDERS
...
YOU WERE MEAN TO HIM, YANO.
THAT WAS WEIRD.
HUH?
BUT HE WAS MEAN TO ME FIRST, YOU KNOW?
YANO...
...YOU LOVE TAKEUCHI-KUN, DON'T YOU?
URGH
HUH?!
How did you jump to that conclusion?!
BUT IT'S TRUE.
THAT'S SICK! SHUT UP, FOOL!
You're embarrassed...
LET'S CHECK OUR ANSWERS AFTER WE DO QUESTIONS 3 AND 4.
OKAY.

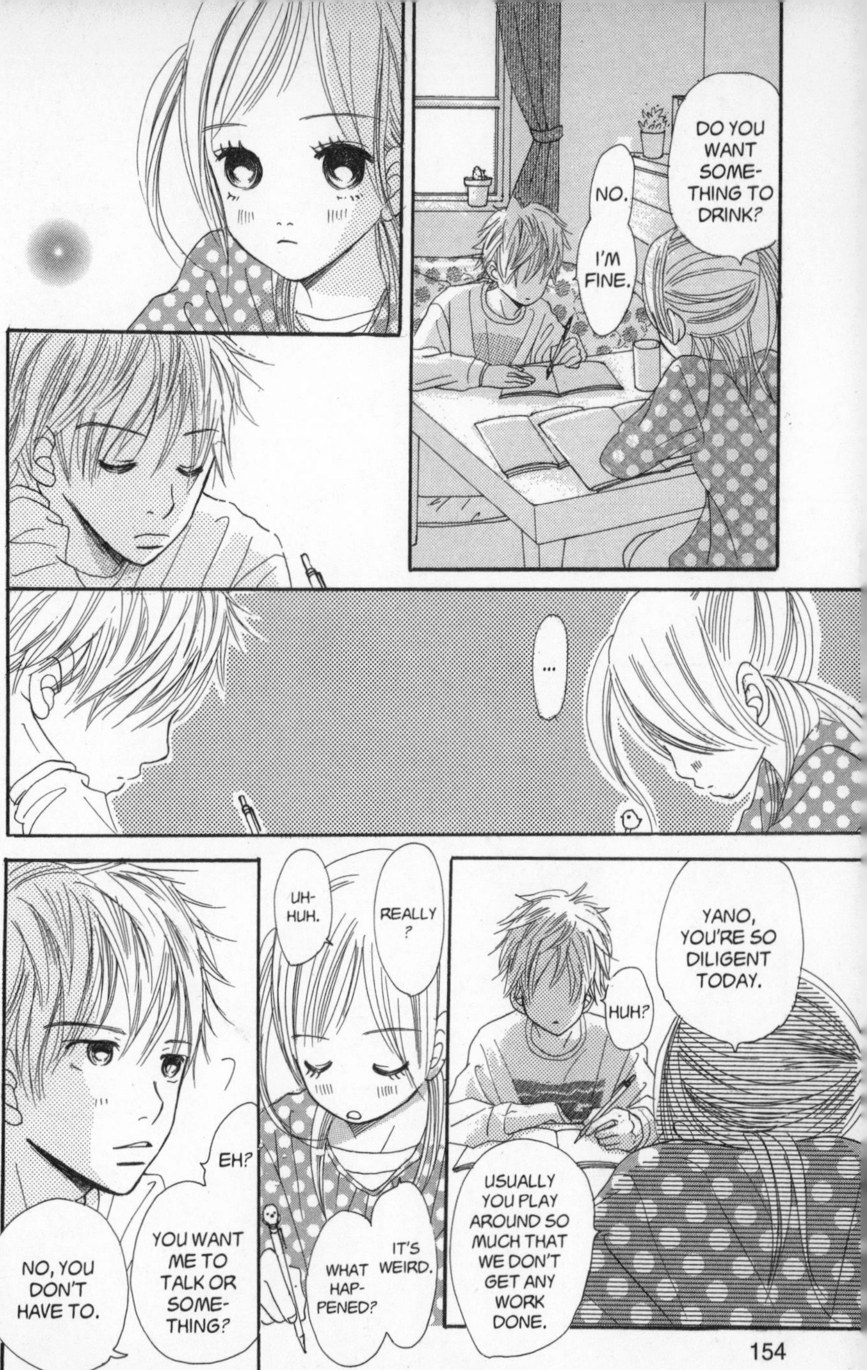
DO YOU WANT SOME-THING TO DRINK?
NO.
I'M FINE.
...
YANO, YOU'RE SO DILIGENT TODAY.
HUH?
USUALLY YOU PLAY AROUND SO MUCH THAT WE DON'T GET ANY WORK DONE.
REALLY?
UH-HUH.
IT'S WEIRD.
WHAT HAP-PENED?
EH?
YOU WANT ME TO TALK OR SOME-THING?
NO, YOU DON'T HAVE TO.

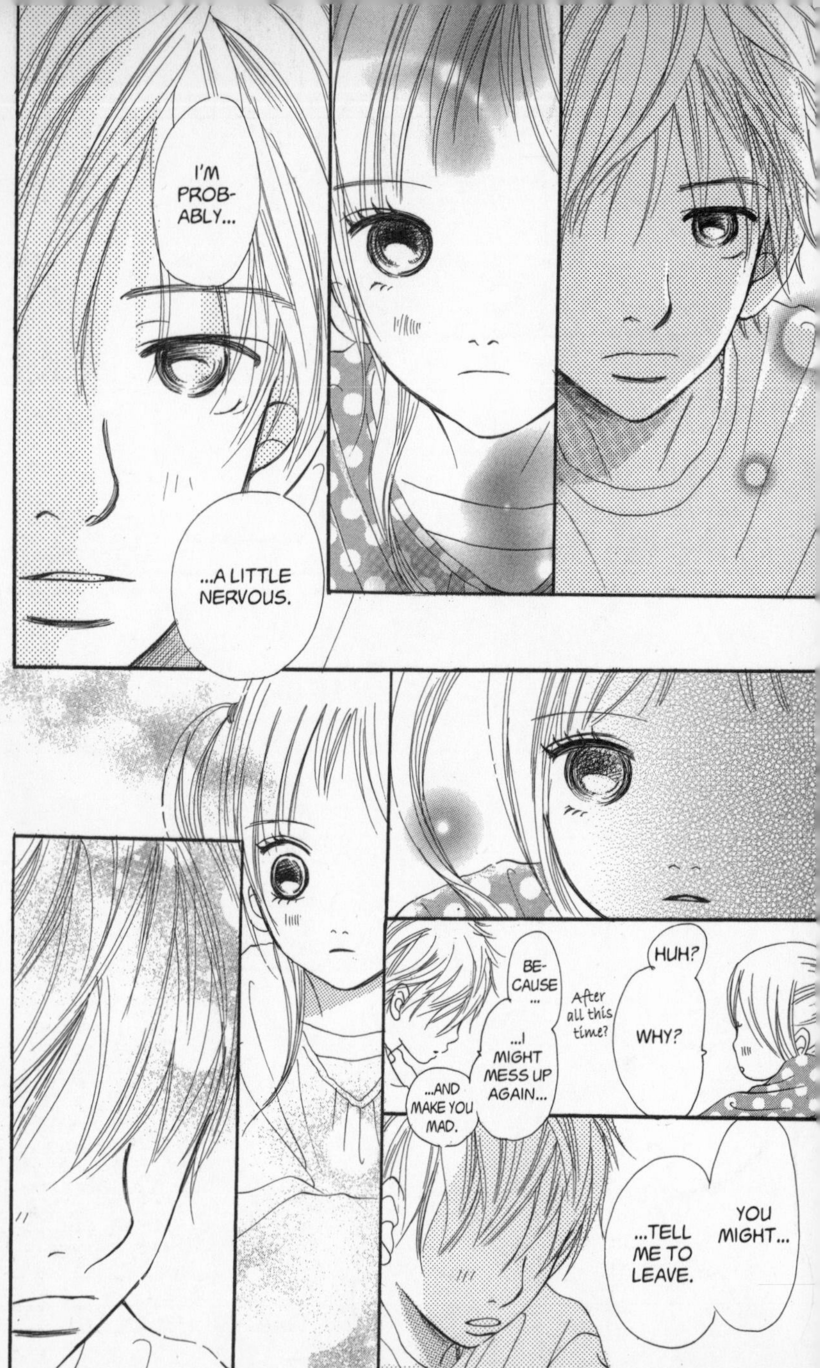
I'M PROBABLY...
...A LITTLE NERVOUS.
HUH?
WHY?
After all this time?
BE-CAUSE...
...I MIGHT MESS UP AGAIN...
...AND MAKE YOU MAD.
YOU MIGHT...
...TELL ME TO LEAVE.

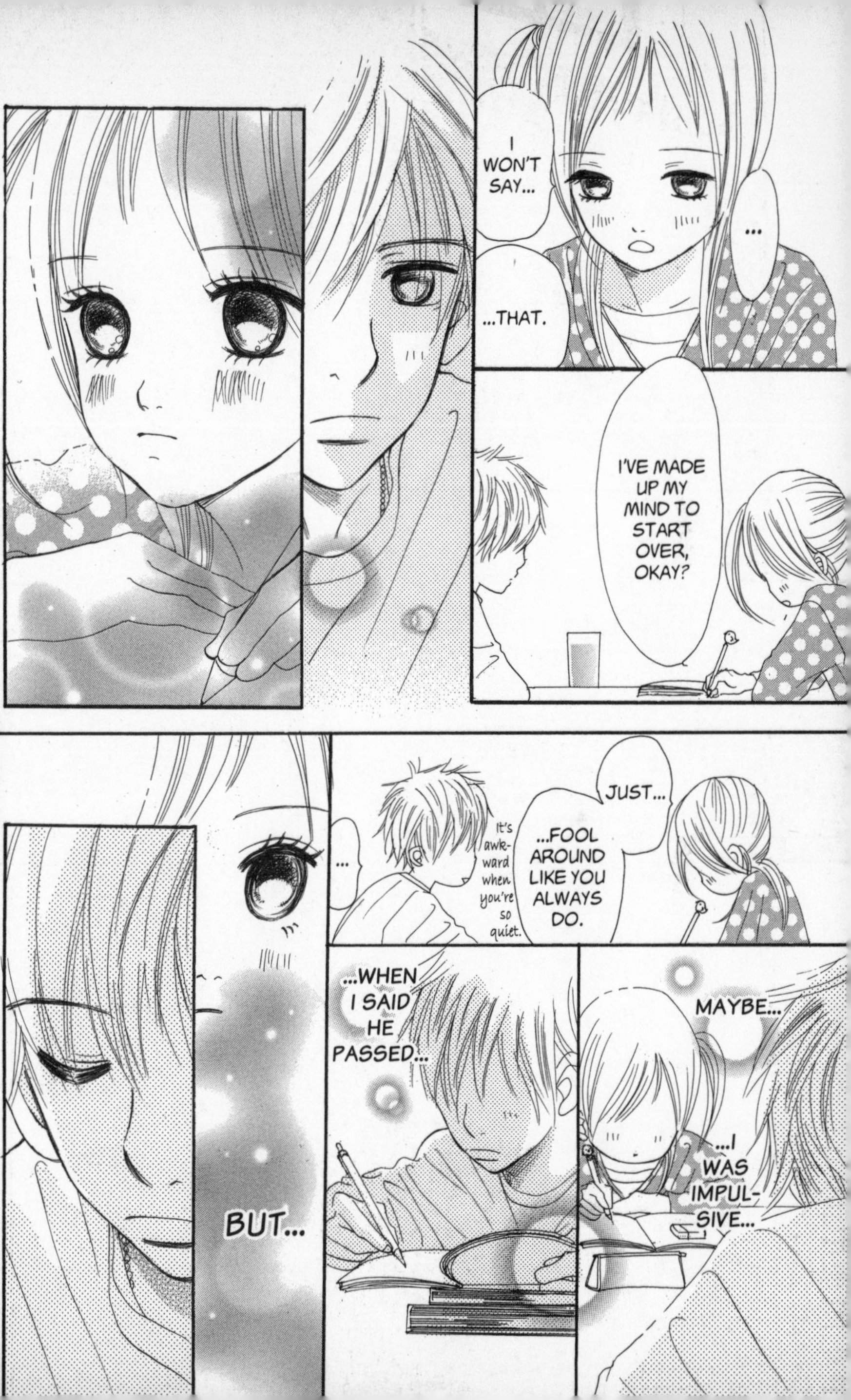
...
I WON'T SAY...
...THAT.
I'VE MADE UP MY MIND TO START OVER, OKAY?
JUST...
...FOOL AROUND LIKE YOU ALWAYS DO.
It's awkward when you're so quiet.
...
MAYBE...
...I WAS IMPULSIVE...
...WHEN I SAID HE PASSED...
BUT...

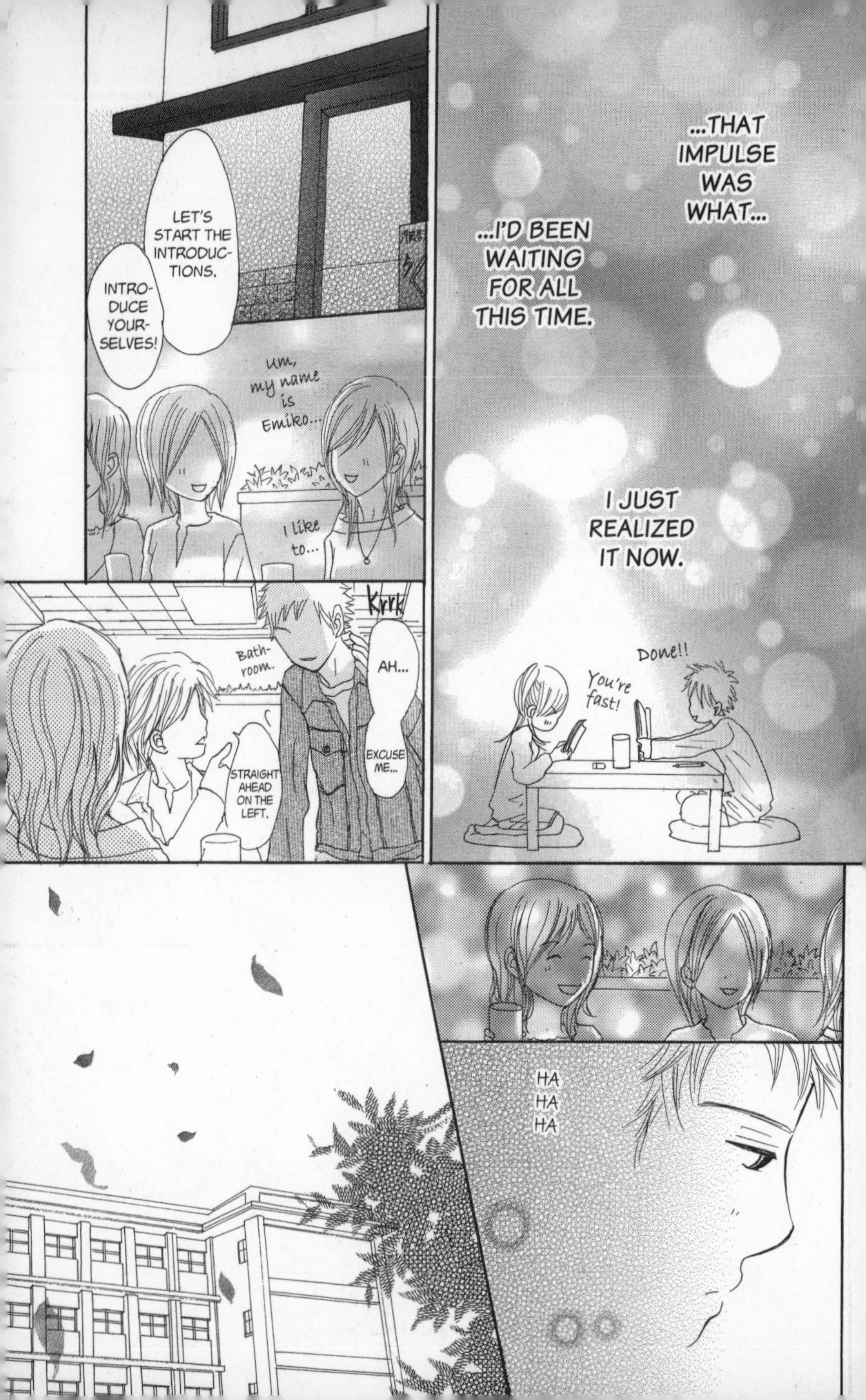
...THAT IMPULSE WAS WHAT...
...I'D BEEN WAITING FOR ALL THIS TIME.
I JUST REALIZED IT NOW.
Done!!
You're fast!
LET'S START THE INTRODUC-TIONS.
INTRO-DUCE YOUR-SELVES!
Um, my name is Emiko...
I like to...
Krrk
AH...
EXCUSE ME...
Bath-room.
STRAIGHT AHEAD ON THE LEFT.
HA HA HA

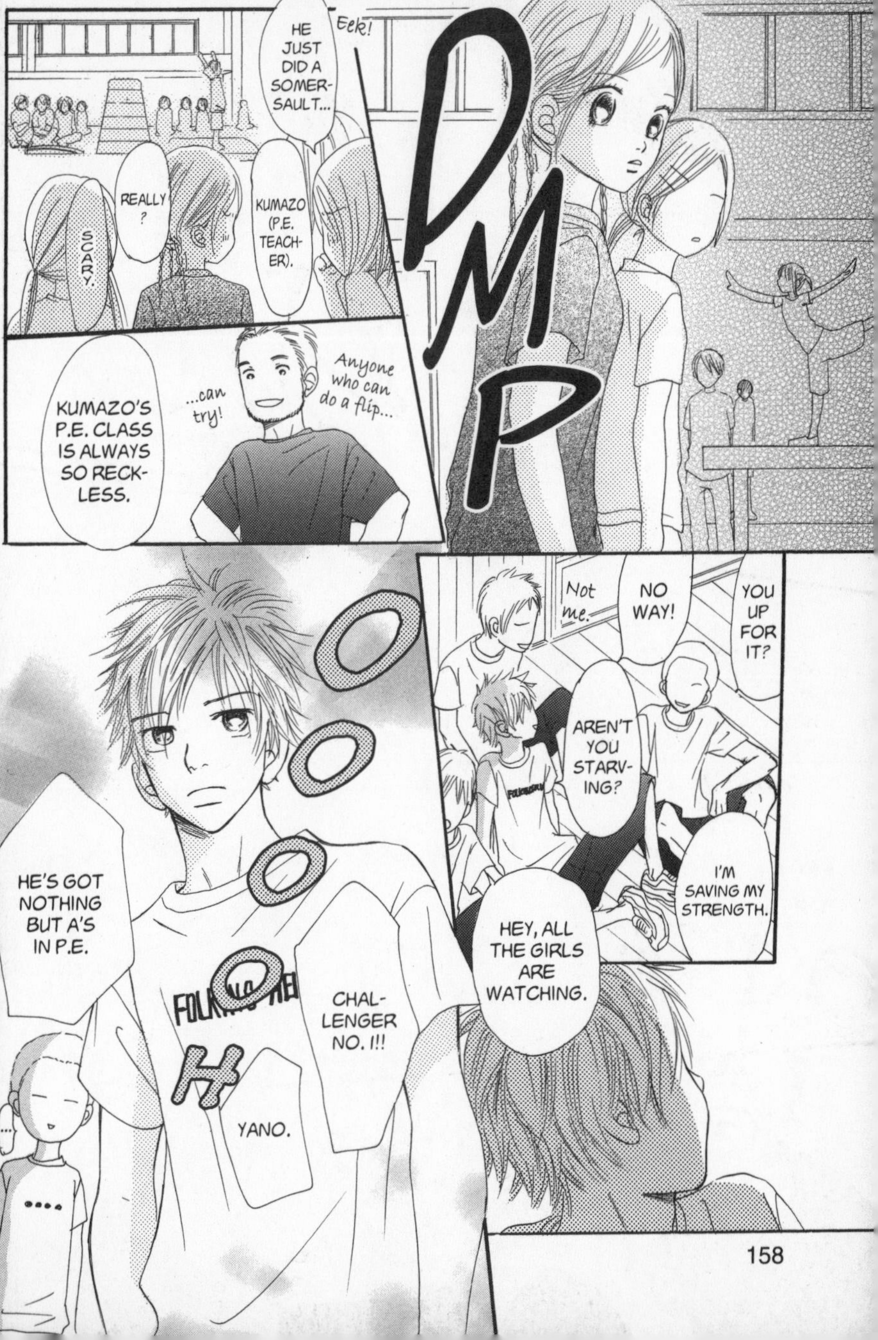
DMP
Eek!
HE JUST DID A SOMER-SAULT...
KUMAZO (P.E. TEACHER).
REALLY?
SCARY.
Anyone who can do a flip...
...can try!
KUMAZO'S P.E. CLASS IS ALWAYS SO RECK-LESS.
YOU UP FOR IT?
NO WAY!
Not me.
AREN'T YOU STARV-ING?
I'M SAVING MY STRENGTH.
HEY, ALL THE GIRLS ARE WATCHING.
OOOOH
CHAL-LENGER NO. 1!!
YANO.
HE'S GOT NOTHING BUT A'S IN P.E.
...
....

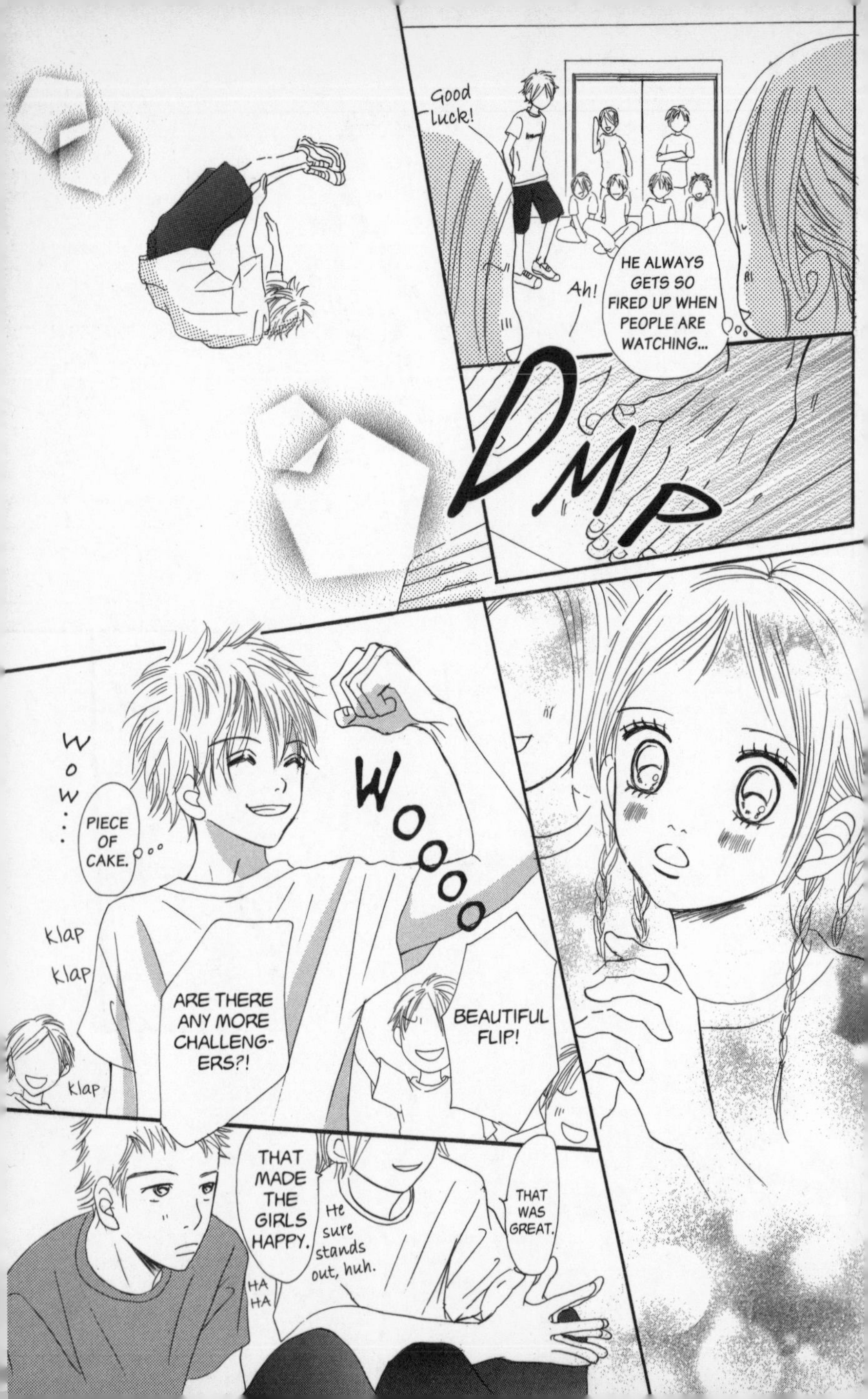
Good luck!
HE ALWAYS GETS SO FIRED UP WHEN PEOPLE ARE WATCHING...
Ah!
DMP
WOOOOO
WOW...
PIECE OF CAKE.
BEAUTIFUL FLIP!
ARE THERE ANY MORE CHALLENGERS?!
klap
klap
klap
THAT WAS GREAT.
He sure stands out, huh.
THAT MADE THE GIRLS HAPPY.
HA HA

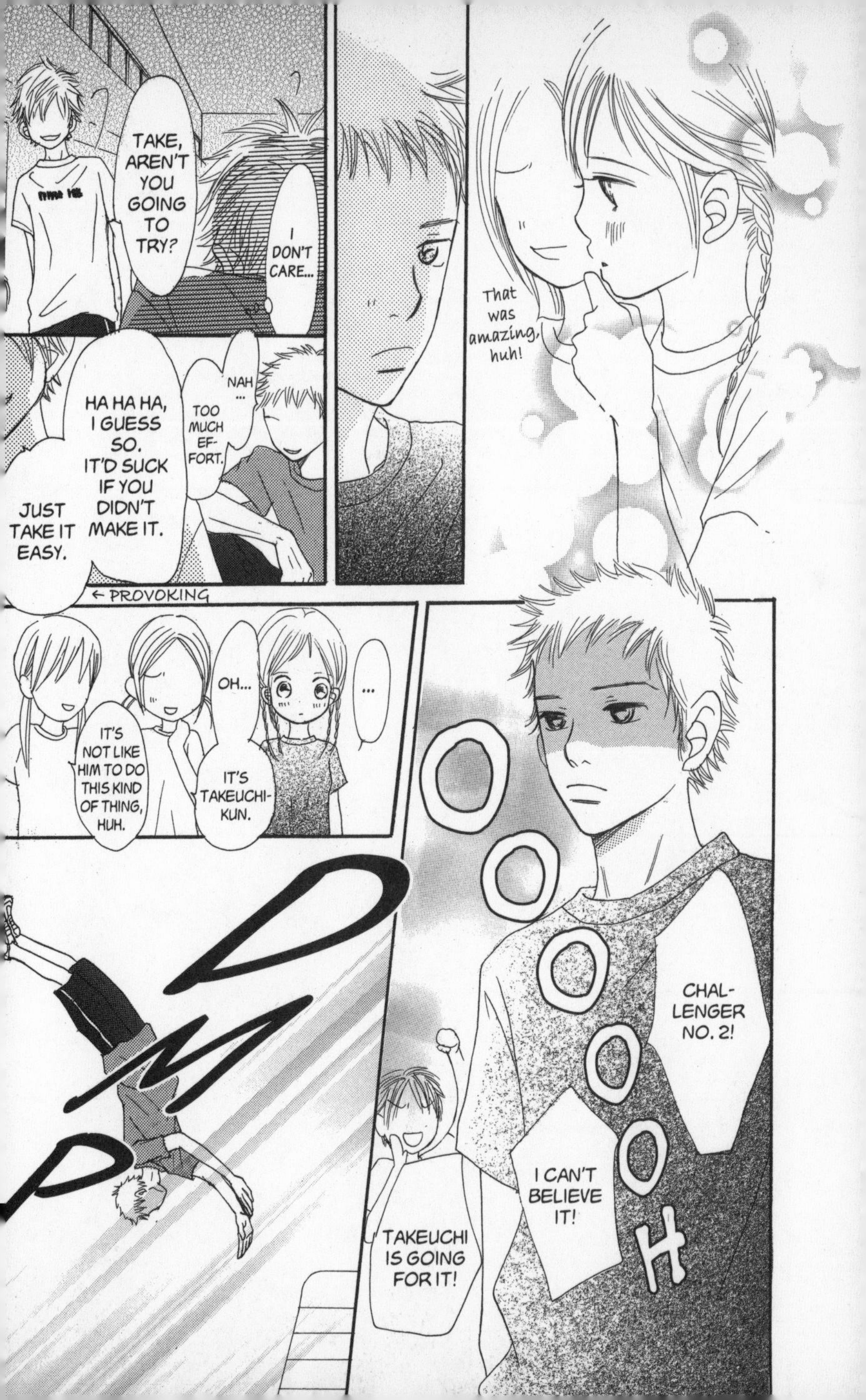
That was amazing, huh!
TAKE, AREN'T YOU GOING TO TRY?
I DON'T CARE...
NAH... TOO MUCH EFFORT.
HA HA HA, I GUESS SO. IT'D SUCK IF YOU DIDN'T MAKE IT.
JUST TAKE IT EASY.
← PROVOKING
OOOOOH
CHALLENGER NO. 2!
I CAN'T BELIEVE IT!
TAKEUCHI IS GOING FOR IT!
...
OH...
IT'S TAKEUCHI-KUN.
IT'S NOT LIKE HIM TO DO THIS KIND OF THING, HUH.
DMP

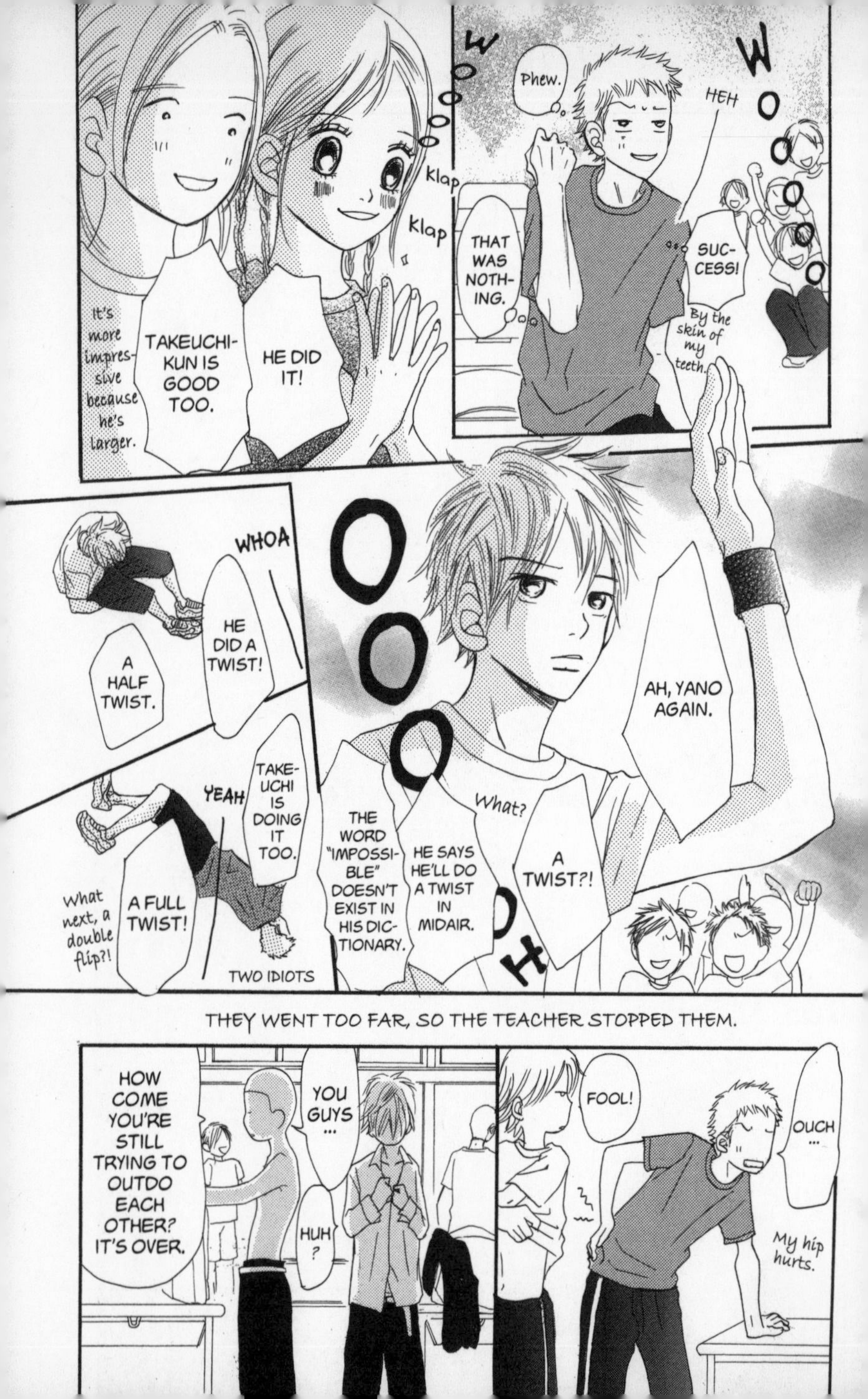
WOOOOO
Phew.
HEH
THAT WAS NOTHING.
SUCCESS!
By the skin of my teeth.
WOOOOO
Klap
Klap
HE DID IT!
TAKEUCHI-KUN IS GOOD TOO.
It's more impressive because he's larger.
OOOOH
AH, YANO AGAIN.
A TWIST?!
What?
HE SAYS HE'LL DO A TWIST IN MIDAIR.
THE WORD "IMPOSSIBLE" DOESN'T EXIST IN HIS DICTIONARY.
WHOA
HE DID A TWIST!
A HALF TWIST.
YEAH
TAKEUCHI IS DOING IT TOO.
A FULL TWIST!
What next, a double flip?!
TWO IDIOTS
THEY WENT TOO FAR, SO THE TEACHER STOPPED THEM.
OUCH...
My hip hurts.
FOOL!
YOU GUYS...
HUH?
HOW COME YOU'RE STILL TRYING TO OUTDO EACH OTHER? IT'S OVER.

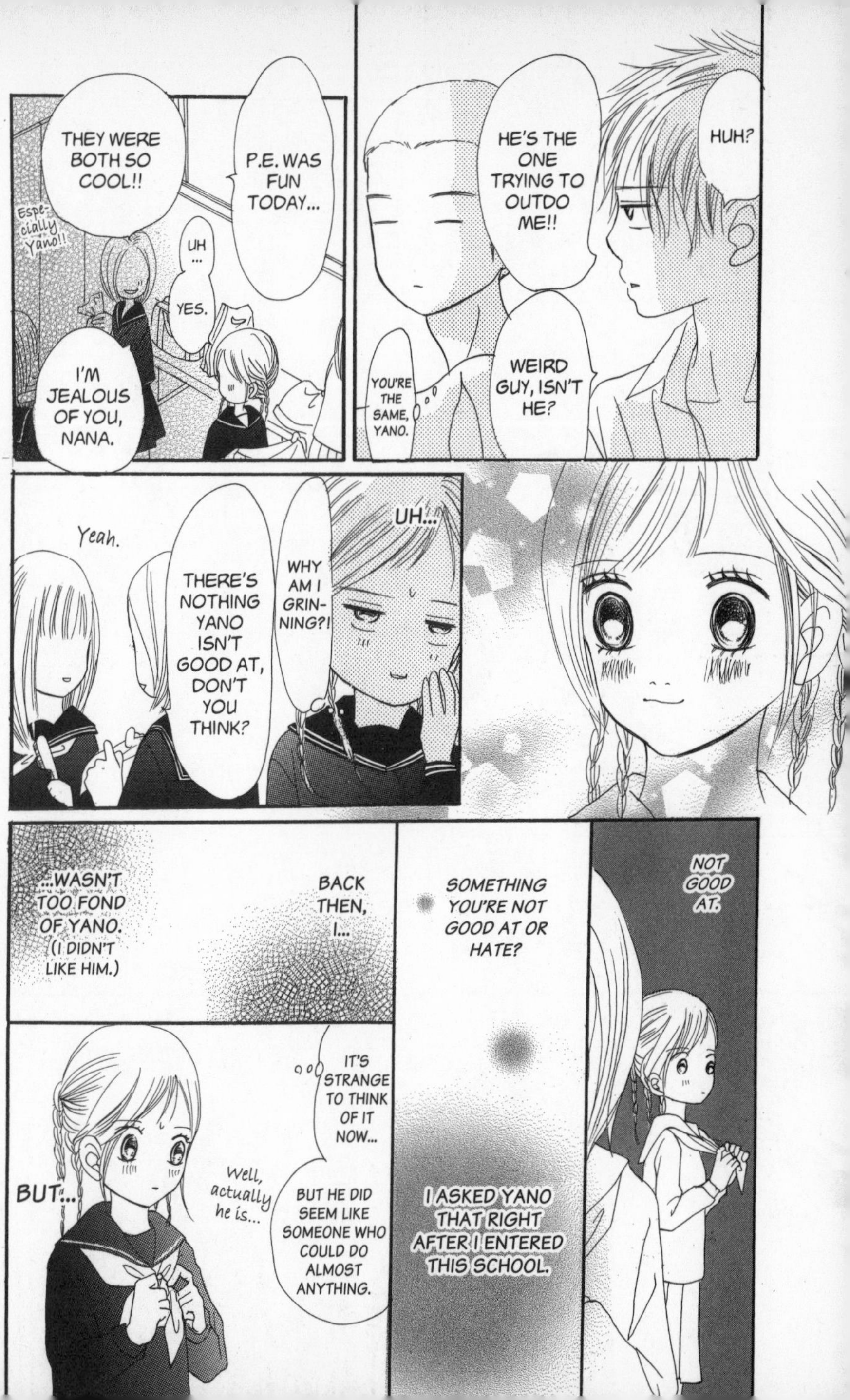
HUH?
HE'S THE ONE TRYING TO OUTDO ME!!
WEIRD GUY, ISN'T HE?
YOU'RE THE SAME, YANO.
P.E. WAS FUN TODAY...
THEY WERE BOTH SO COOL!!
Especially Yano!!
UH...
YES.
I'M JEALOUS OF YOU, NANA.
UH...
WHY AM I GRINNING?!
THERE'S NOTHING YANO ISN'T GOOD AT, DON'T YOU THINK?
Yeah.
NOT GOOD AT.
SOMETHING YOU'RE NOT GOOD AT OR HATE?
I ASKED YANO THAT RIGHT AFTER I ENTERED THIS SCHOOL.
BACK THEN, I...
...WASN'T TOO FOND OF YANO.
(I DIDN'T LIKE HIM.)
IT'S STRANGE TO THINK OF IT NOW...
BUT HE DID SEEM LIKE SOMEONE WHO COULD DO ALMOST ANYTHING.
Well, actually he is...
BUT...

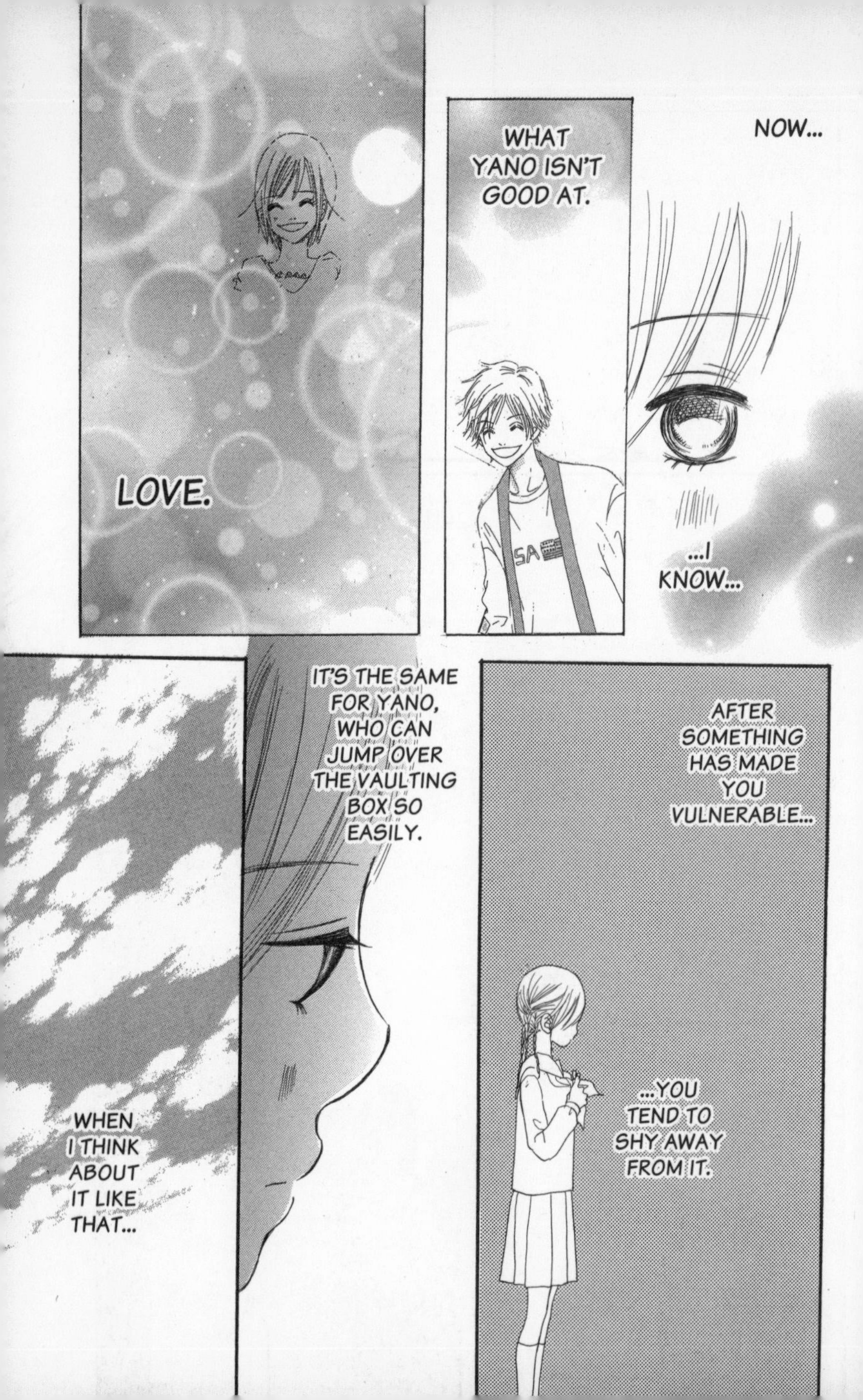
NOW...
...I KNOW...
WHAT YANO ISN'T GOOD AT.
LOVE.
AFTER SOMETHING HAS MADE YOU VULNERABLE...
...YOU TEND TO SHY AWAY FROM IT.
IT'S THE SAME FOR YANO, WHO CAN JUMP OVER THE VAULTING BOX SO EASILY.
WHEN I THINK ABOUT IT LIKE THAT...

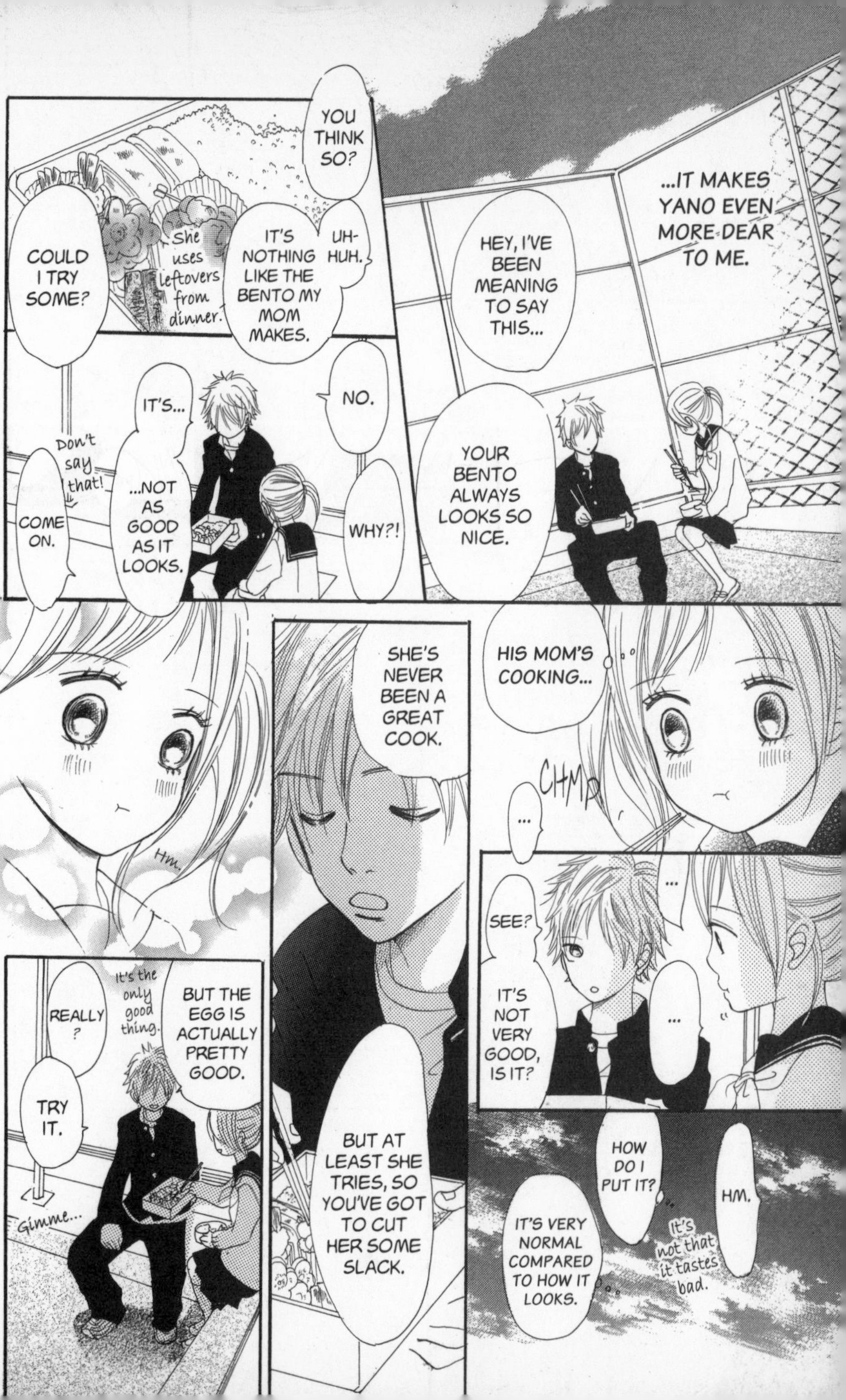

...IT MAKES YANO EVEN MORE DEAR TO ME.
HEY, I'VE BEEN MEANING TO SAY THIS...
YOUR BENTO ALWAYS LOOKS SO NICE.
YOU THINK SO?
UH-HUH.
IT'S NOTHING LIKE THE BENTO MY MOM MAKES.
She uses leftovers from dinner.
COULD I TRY SOME?
NO.
WHY?!
IT'S...
...NOT AS GOOD AS IT LOOKS.
Don't say that!
COME ON.
HIS MOM'S COOKING...
CHMP
...
...
SEE?
IT'S NOT VERY GOOD, IS IT?
...
HM.
HOW DO I PUT IT?
IT'S VERY NORMAL COMPARED TO HOW IT LOOKS.
It's not that it tastes bad.
SHE'S NEVER BEEN A GREAT COOK.
BUT AT LEAST SHE TRIES, SO YOU'VE GOT TO CUT HER SOME SLACK.
Hm.
REALLY?
It's the only good thing.
BUT THE EGG IS ACTUALLY PRETTY GOOD.
TRY IT.
Gimme...

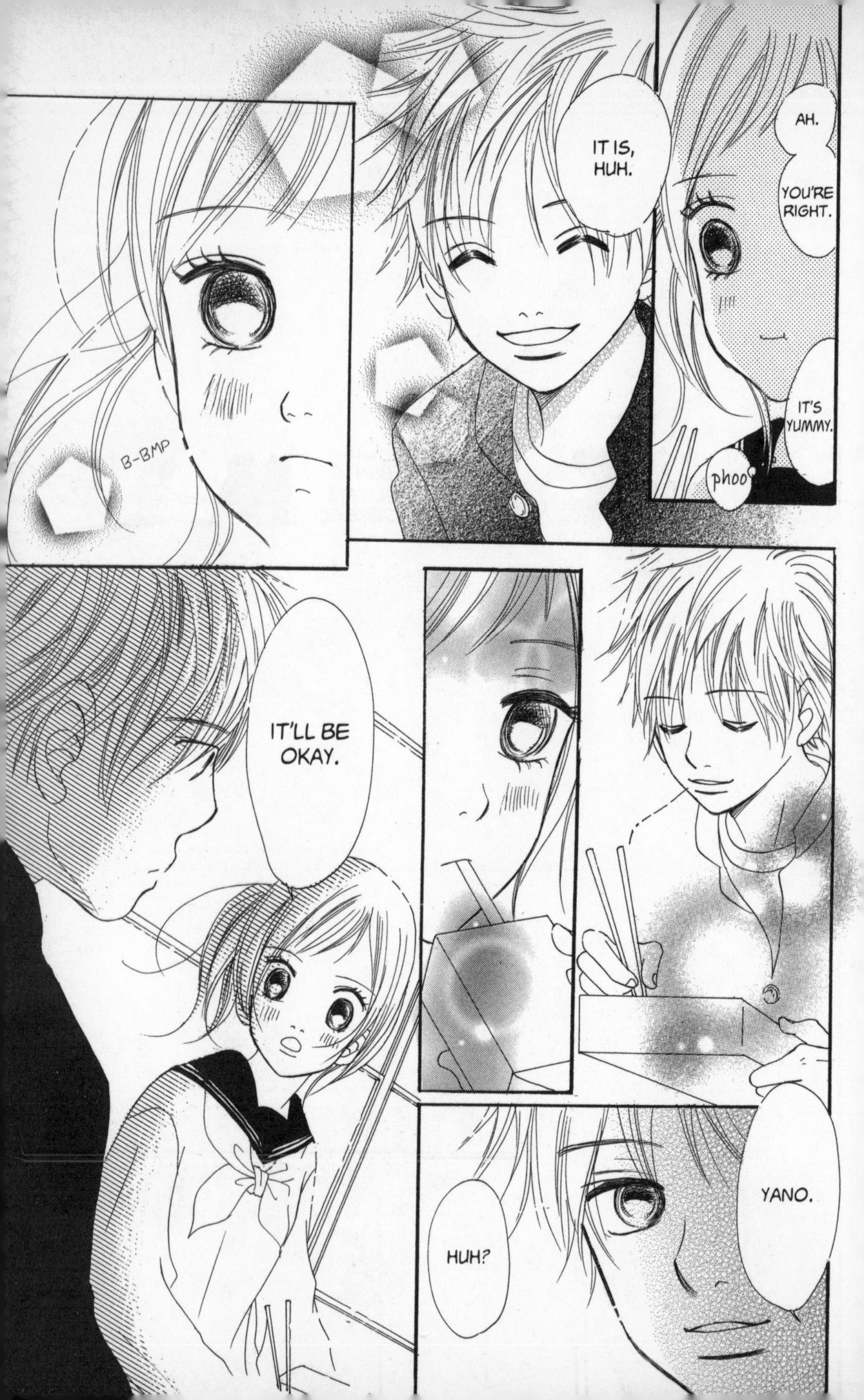
AH.
YOU'RE RIGHT.
IT'S YUMMY.
phoo
IT IS, HUH.
B-BMP
YANO.
HUH?
IT'LL BE OKAY.

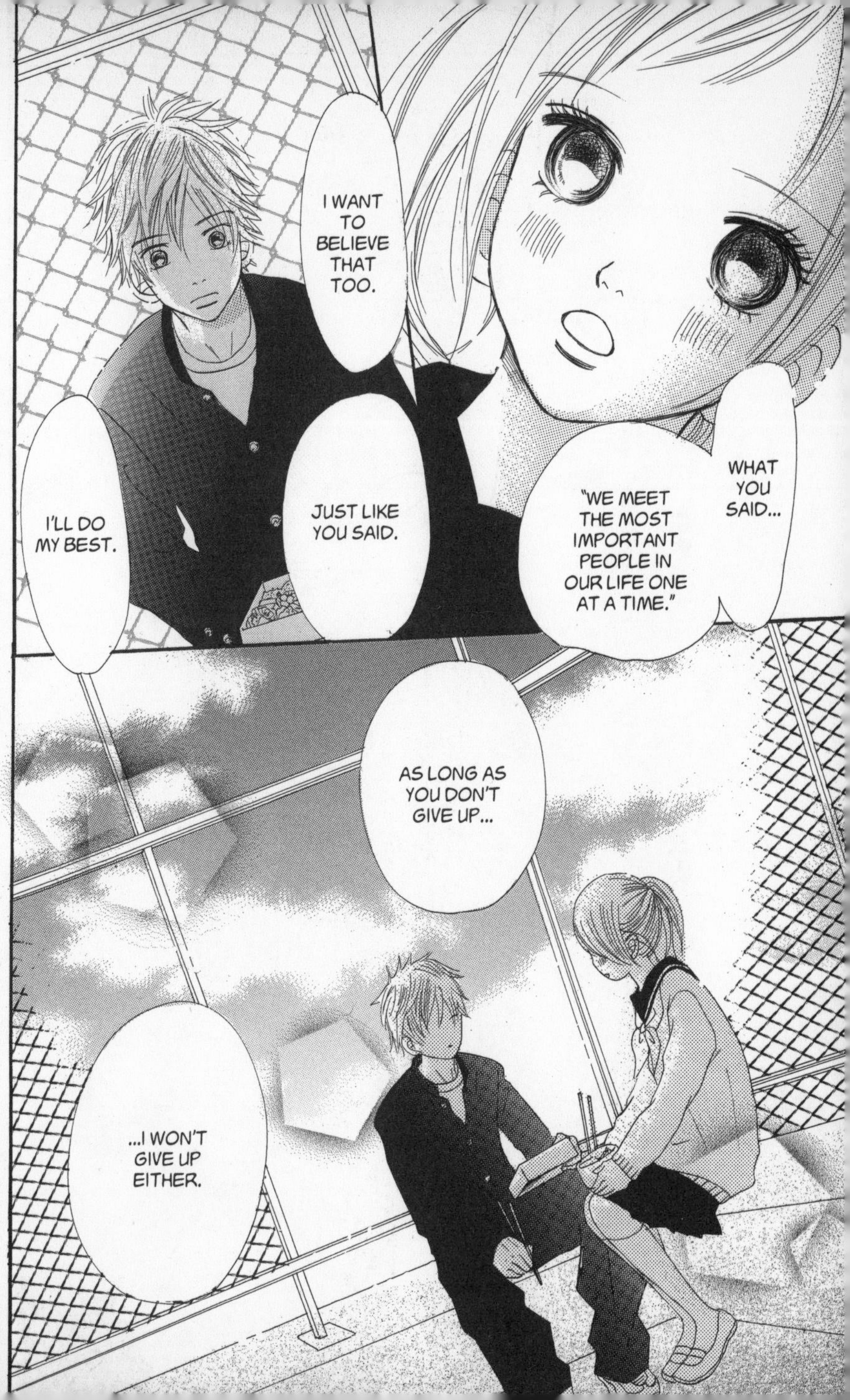

WHAT YOU SAID...
"WE MEET THE MOST IMPORTANT PEOPLE IN OUR LIFE ONE AT A TIME."
I WANT TO BELIEVE THAT TOO.
JUST LIKE YOU SAID.
I'LL DO MY BEST.
AS LONG AS YOU DON'T GIVE UP...
...I WON'T GIVE UP EITHER.

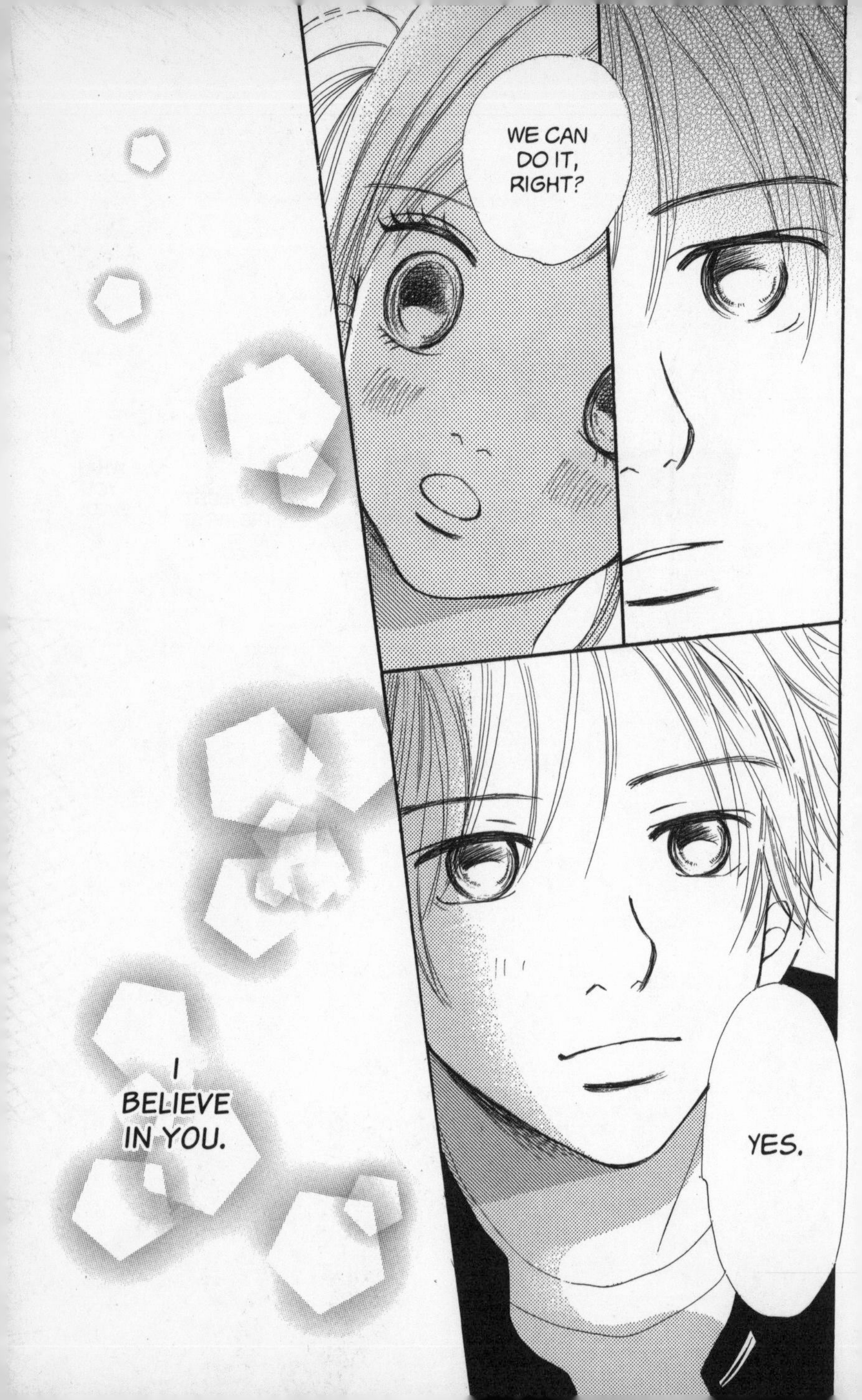
WE CAN DO IT, RIGHT?
YES.
I BELIEVE IN YOU.

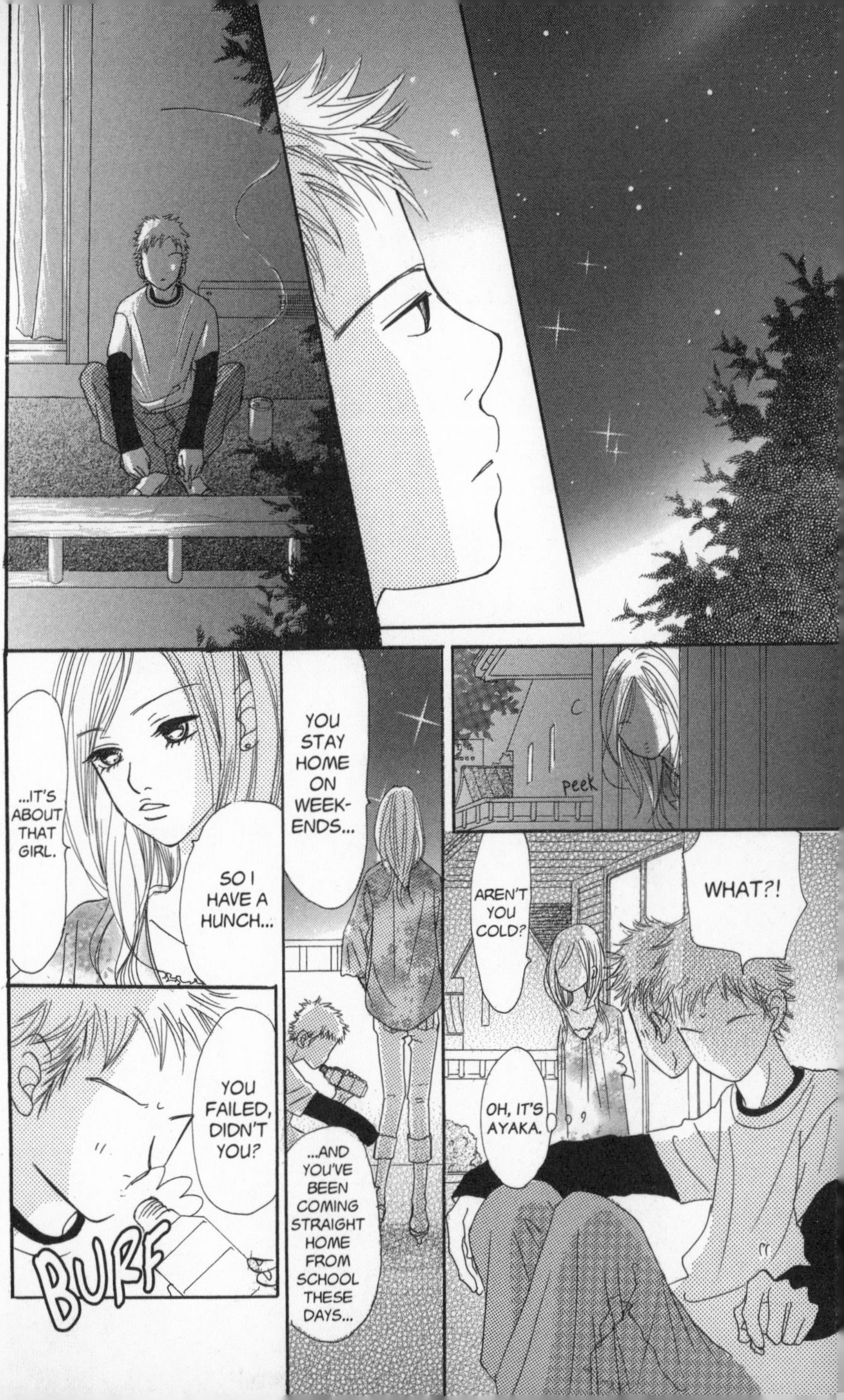
peek
WHAT?!
AREN'T YOU COLD?
OH, IT'S AYAKA.
YOU STAY HOME ON WEEK-ENDS...
...AND YOU'VE BEEN COMING STRAIGHT HOME FROM SCHOOL THESE DAYS...
SO I HAVE A HUNCH...
...IT'S ABOUT THAT GIRL.
YOU FAILED, DIDN'T YOU?
BURF

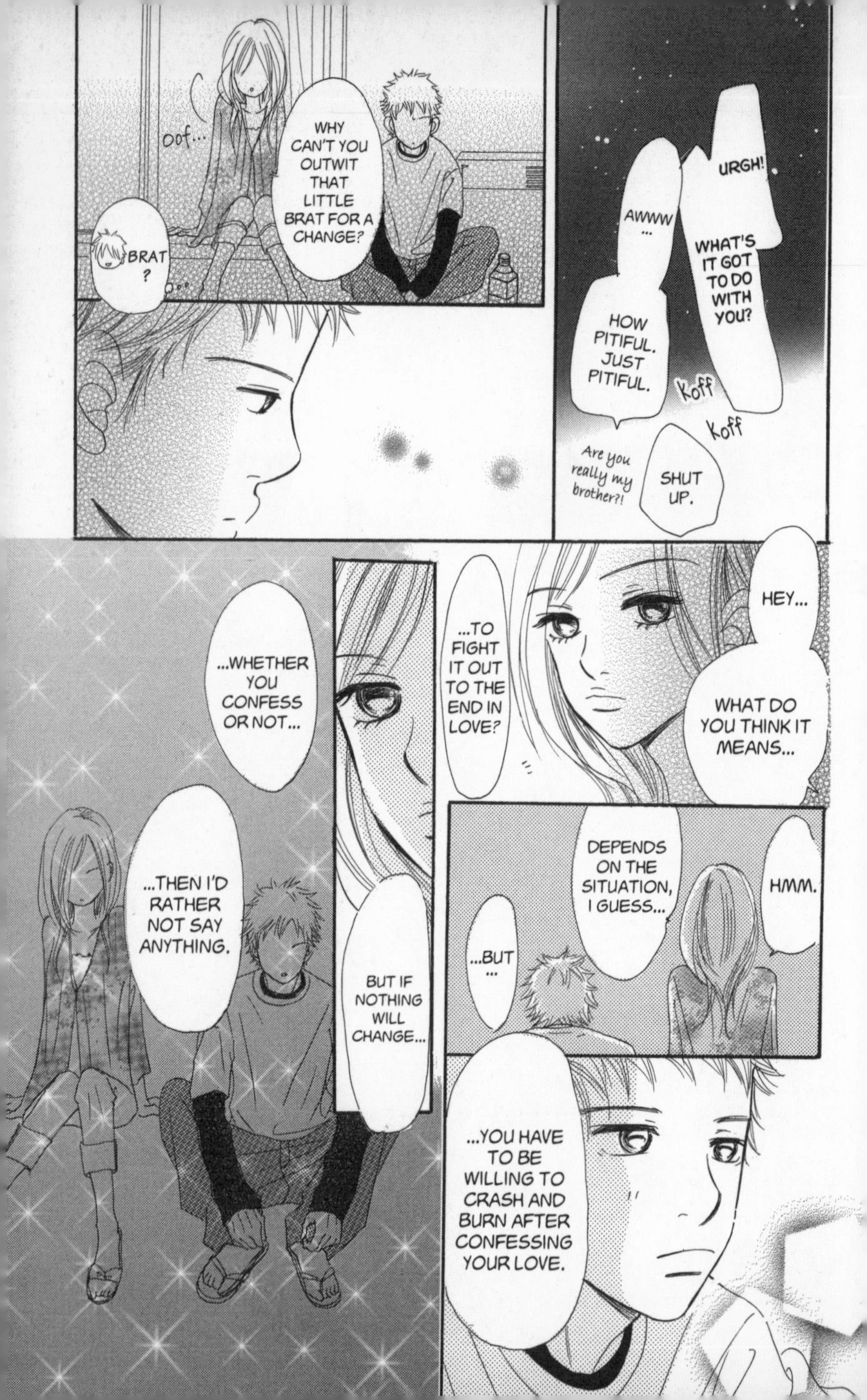
URGH!
WHAT'S IT GOT TO DO WITH YOU?
AWWW...
HOW PITIFUL. JUST PITIFUL.
Koff Koff
SHUT UP.
Are you really my brother?!
WHY CAN'T YOU OUTWIT THAT LITTLE BRAT FOR A CHANGE?
oof...
BRAT?
HEY...
WHAT DO YOU THINK IT MEANS...
...TO FIGHT IT OUT TO THE END IN LOVE?
HMM.
DEPENDS ON THE SITUATION, I GUESS...
...BUT...
...YOU HAVE TO BE WILLING TO CRASH AND BURN AFTER CONFESSING YOUR LOVE.
BUT IF NOTHING WILL CHANGE...
...WHETHER YOU CONFESS OR NOT...
...THEN I'D RATHER NOT SAY ANYTHING.

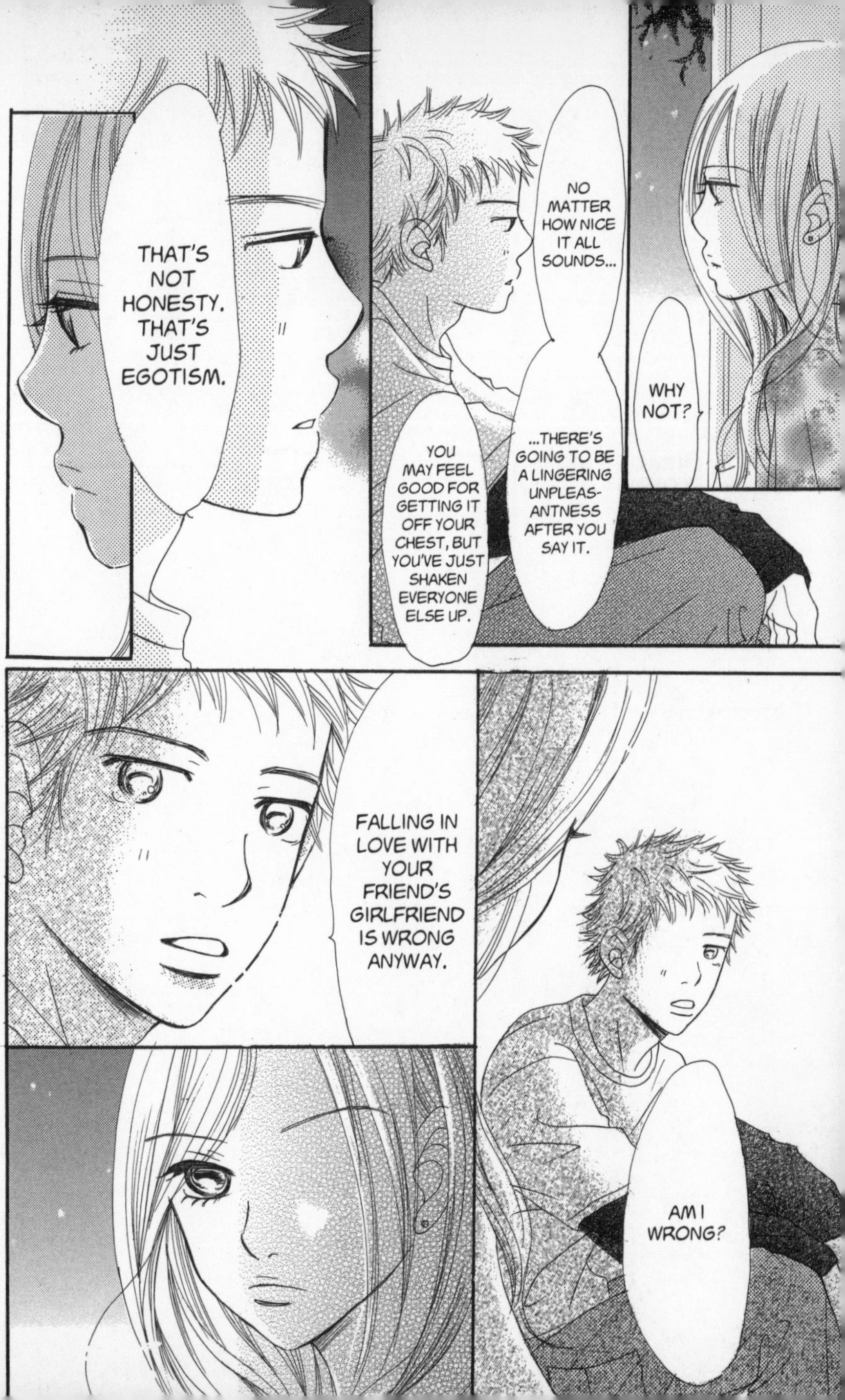
WHY NOT?
NO MATTER HOW NICE IT ALL SOUNDS...
...THERE'S GOING TO BE A LINGERING UNPLEAS-ANTNESS AFTER YOU SAY IT.
YOU MAY FEEL GOOD FOR GETTING IT OFF YOUR CHEST, BUT YOU'VE JUST SHAKEN EVERYONE ELSE UP.
THAT'S NOT HONESTY. THAT'S JUST EGOTISM.
AM I WRONG?
FALLING IN LOVE WITH YOUR FRIEND'S GIRLFRIEND IS WRONG ANYWAY.

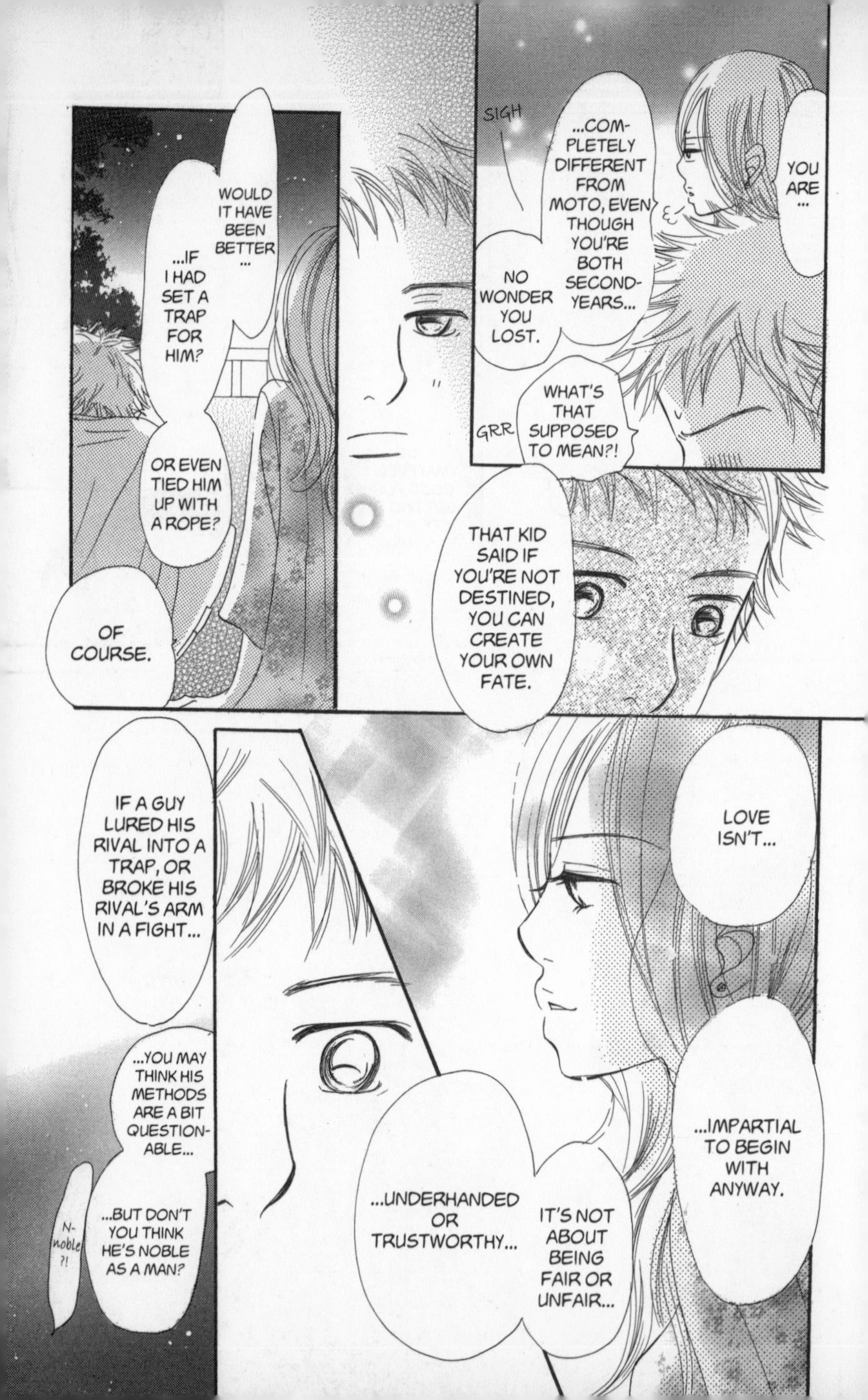
YOU ARE ...
...COMPLETELY DIFFERENT FROM MOTO, EVEN THOUGH YOU'RE BOTH SECOND-YEARS...
SIGH
NO WONDER YOU LOST.
GRR
WHAT'S THAT SUPPOSED TO MEAN?!
THAT KID SAID IF YOU'RE NOT DESTINED, YOU CAN CREATE YOUR OWN FATE.
WOULD IT HAVE BEEN BETTER ...
...IF I HAD SET A TRAP FOR HIM?
OR EVEN TIED HIM UP WITH A ROPE?
OF COURSE.
LOVE ISN'T...
...IMPARTIAL TO BEGIN WITH ANYWAY.
IT'S NOT ABOUT BEING FAIR OR UNFAIR...
...UNDERHANDED OR TRUSTWORTHY...
IF A GUY LURED HIS RIVAL INTO A TRAP, OR BROKE HIS RIVAL'S ARM IN A FIGHT...
...YOU MAY THINK HIS METHODS ARE A BIT QUESTIONABLE...
...BUT DON'T YOU THINK HE'S NOBLE AS A MAN?
N-noble?!

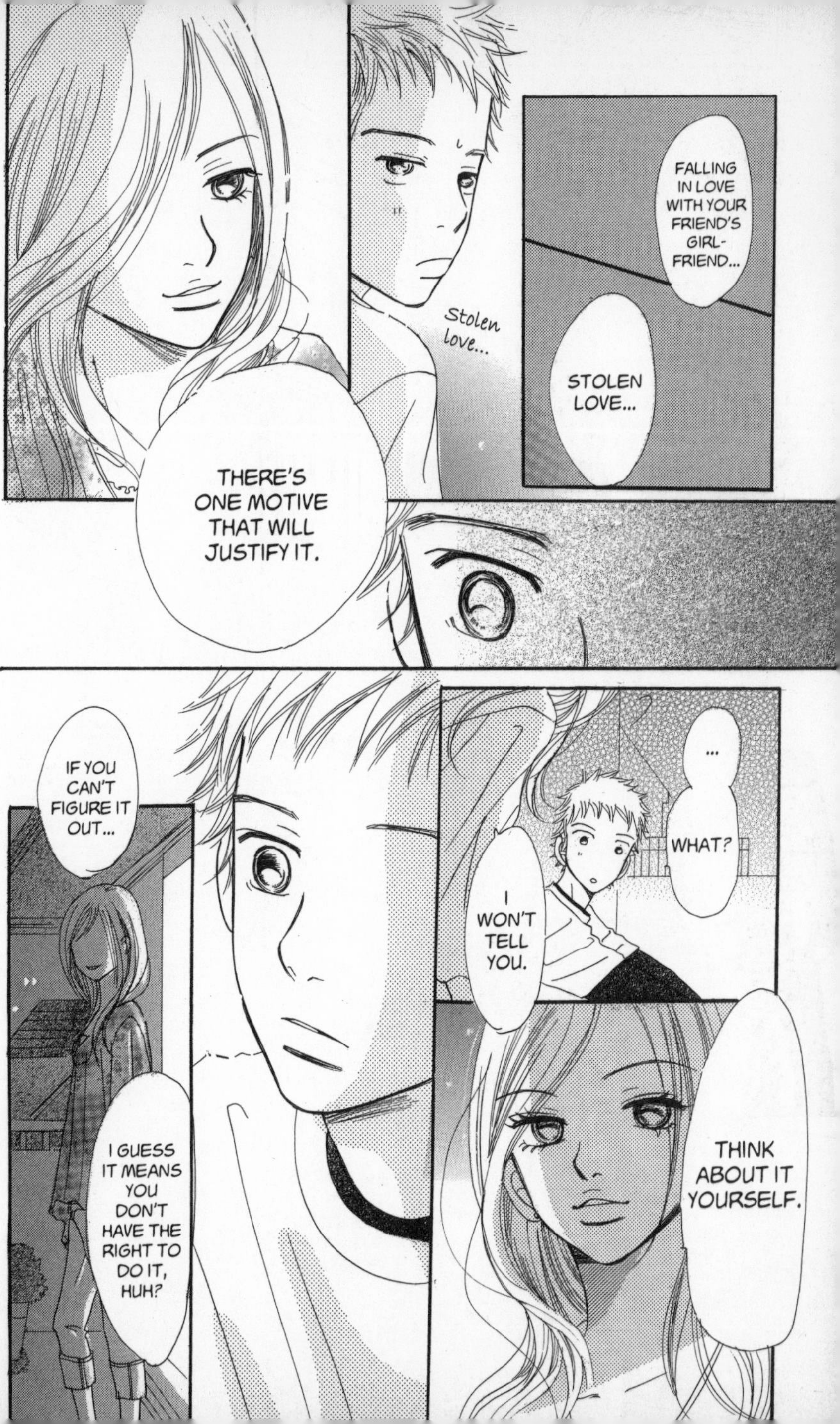
FALLING IN LOVE WITH YOUR FRIEND'S GIRL-FRIEND...
STOLEN LOVE...
Stolen love...
THERE'S ONE MOTIVE THAT WILL JUSTIFY IT.
...
WHAT?
I WON'T TELL YOU.
THINK ABOUT IT YOURSELF.
IF YOU CAN'T FIGURE IT OUT...
I GUESS IT MEANS YOU DON'T HAVE THE RIGHT TO DO IT, HUH?

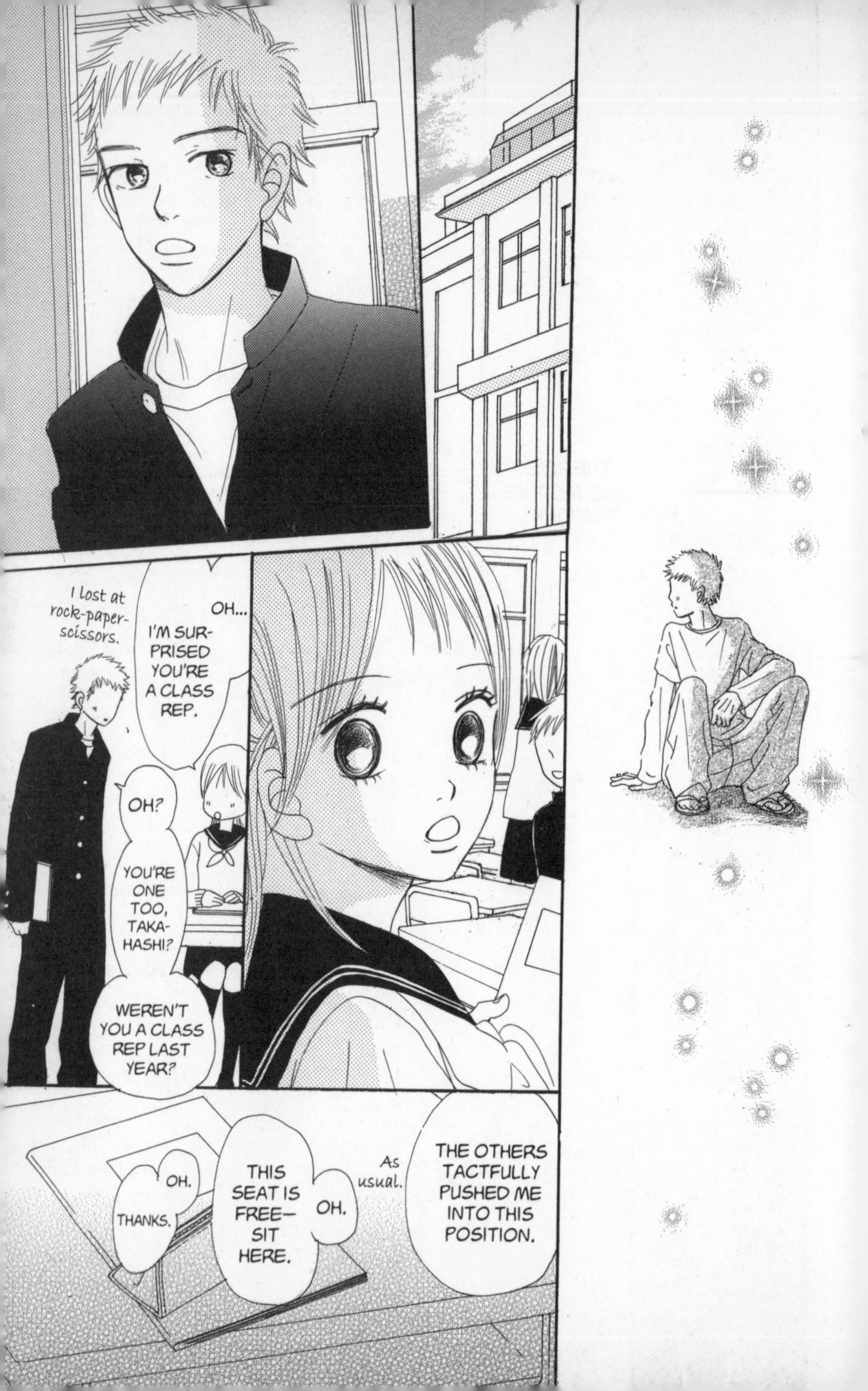
OH... I'M SURPRISED YOU'RE A CLASS REP.
I lost at rock-paper-scissors.
OH?
YOU'RE ONE TOO, TAKAHASHI?
WEREN'T YOU A CLASS REP LAST YEAR?
THE OTHERS TACTFULLY PUSHED ME INTO THIS POSITION.
As usual.
OH.
THIS SEAT IS FREE—SIT HERE.
OH.
THANKS.

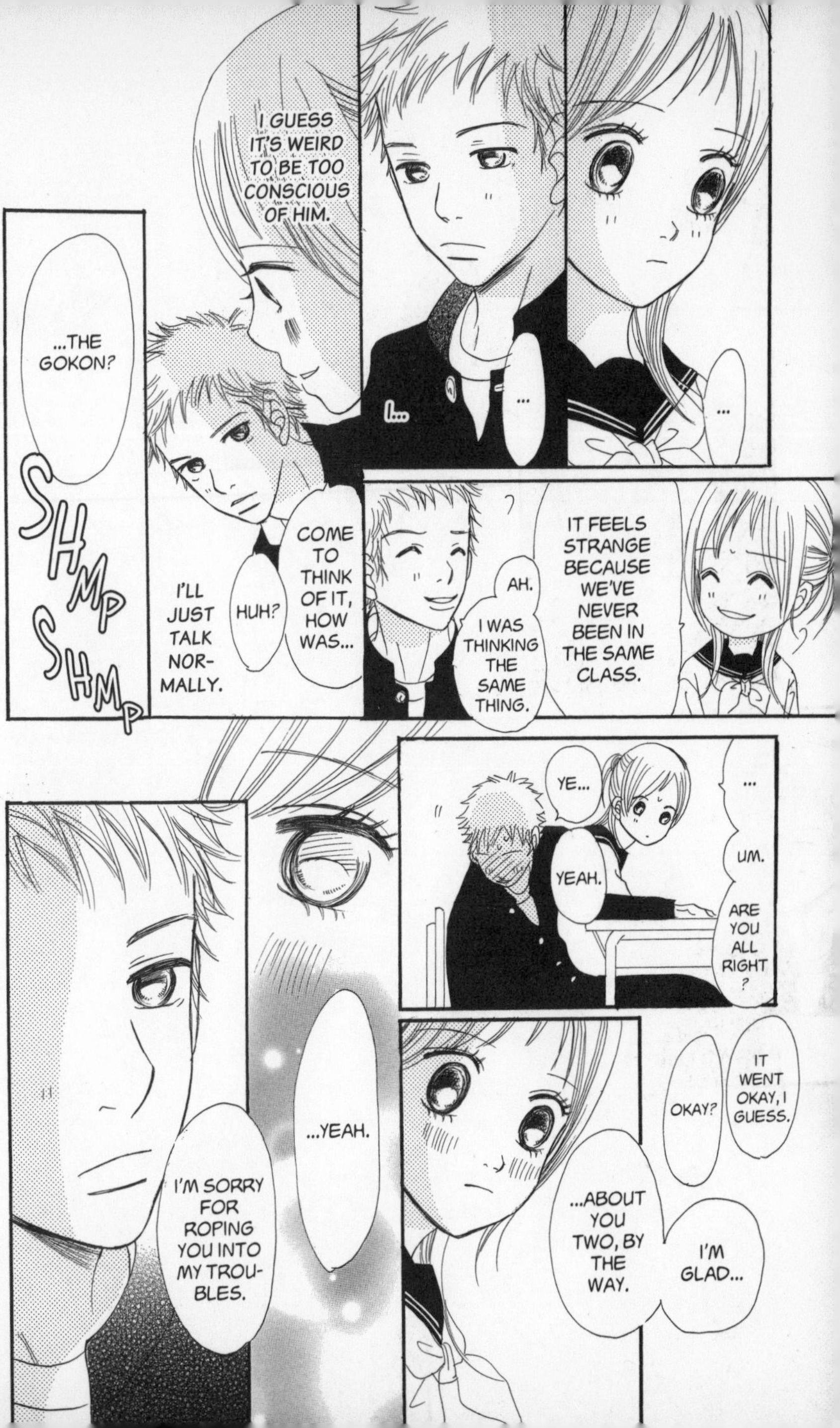
...
...
I...
I GUESS IT'S WEIRD TO BE TOO CONSCIOUS OF HIM.
IT FEELS STRANGE BECAUSE WE'VE NEVER BEEN IN THE SAME CLASS.
AH.
I WAS THINKING THE SAME THING.
COME TO THINK OF IT, HOW WAS...
HUH?
I'LL JUST TALK NOR-MALLY.
...THE GOKON?
SHMP SHMP
...
UM.
ARE YOU ALL RIGHT?
YE...
YEAH.
IT WENT OKAY, I GUESS.
OKAY?
I'M GLAD...
...ABOUT YOU TWO, BY THE WAY.
...YEAH.
I'M SORRY FOR ROPING YOU INTO MY TROU-BLES.

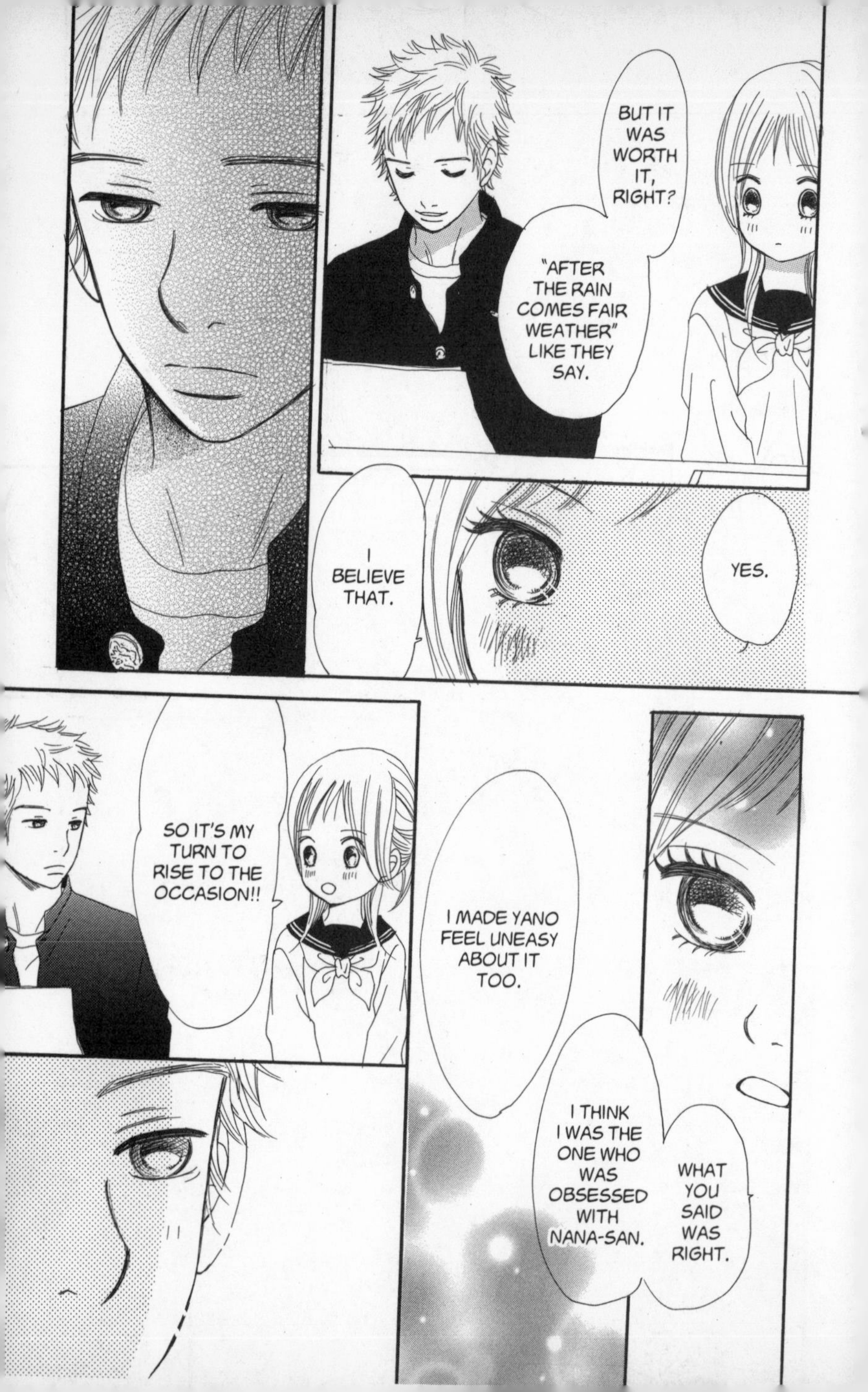
BUT IT WAS WORTH IT, RIGHT?
"AFTER THE RAIN COMES FAIR WEATHER" LIKE THEY SAY.
YES.
I BELIEVE THAT.
WHAT YOU SAID WAS RIGHT.
I THINK I WAS THE ONE WHO WAS OBSESSED WITH NANA-SAN.
I MADE YANO FEEL UNEASY ABOUT IT TOO.
SO IT'S MY TURN TO RISE TO THE OCCASION!!

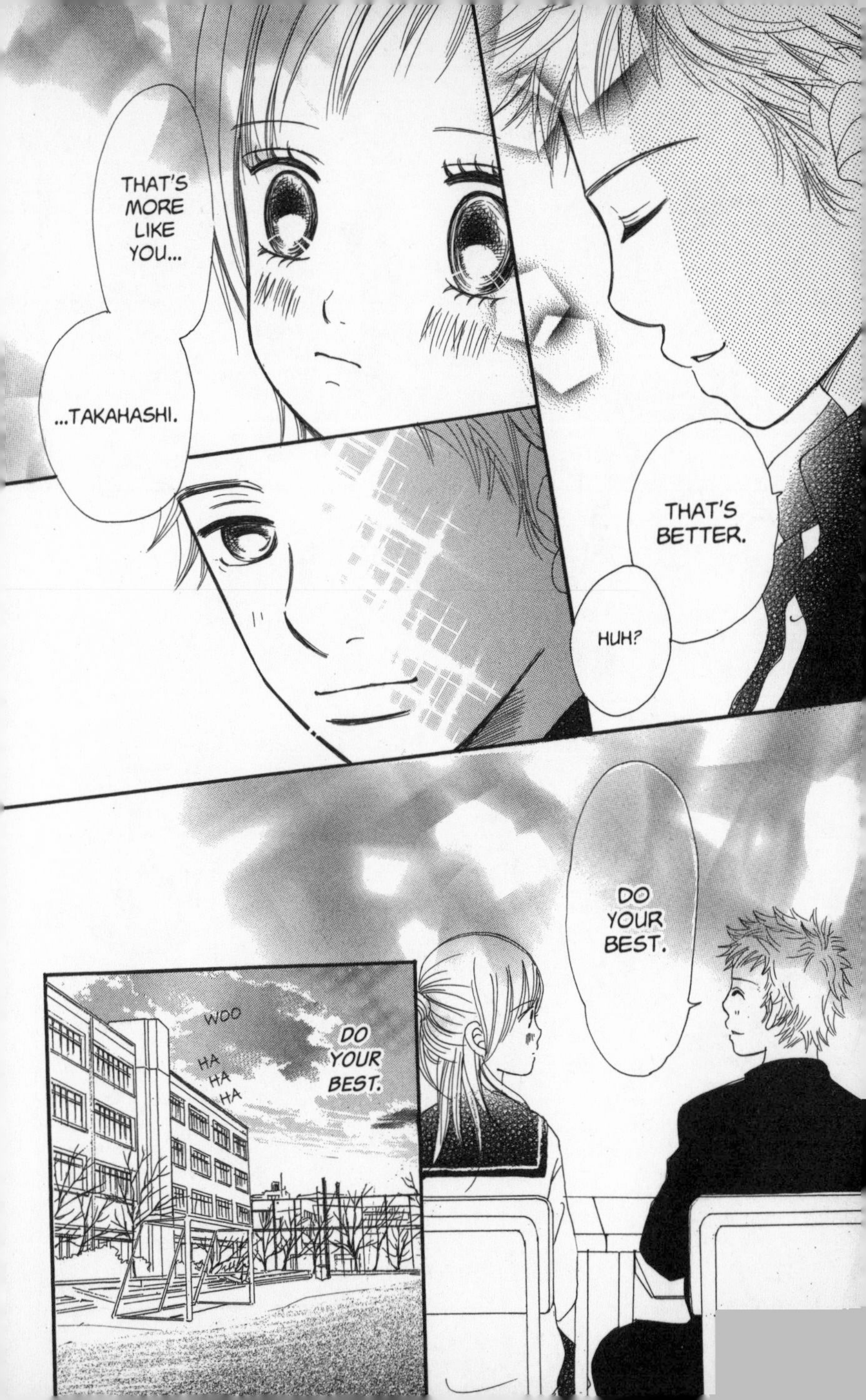
THAT'S BETTER.
HUH?
THAT'S MORE LIKE YOU...
...TAKAHASHI.
DO YOUR BEST.
DO YOUR BEST.
WOO
HA HA HA

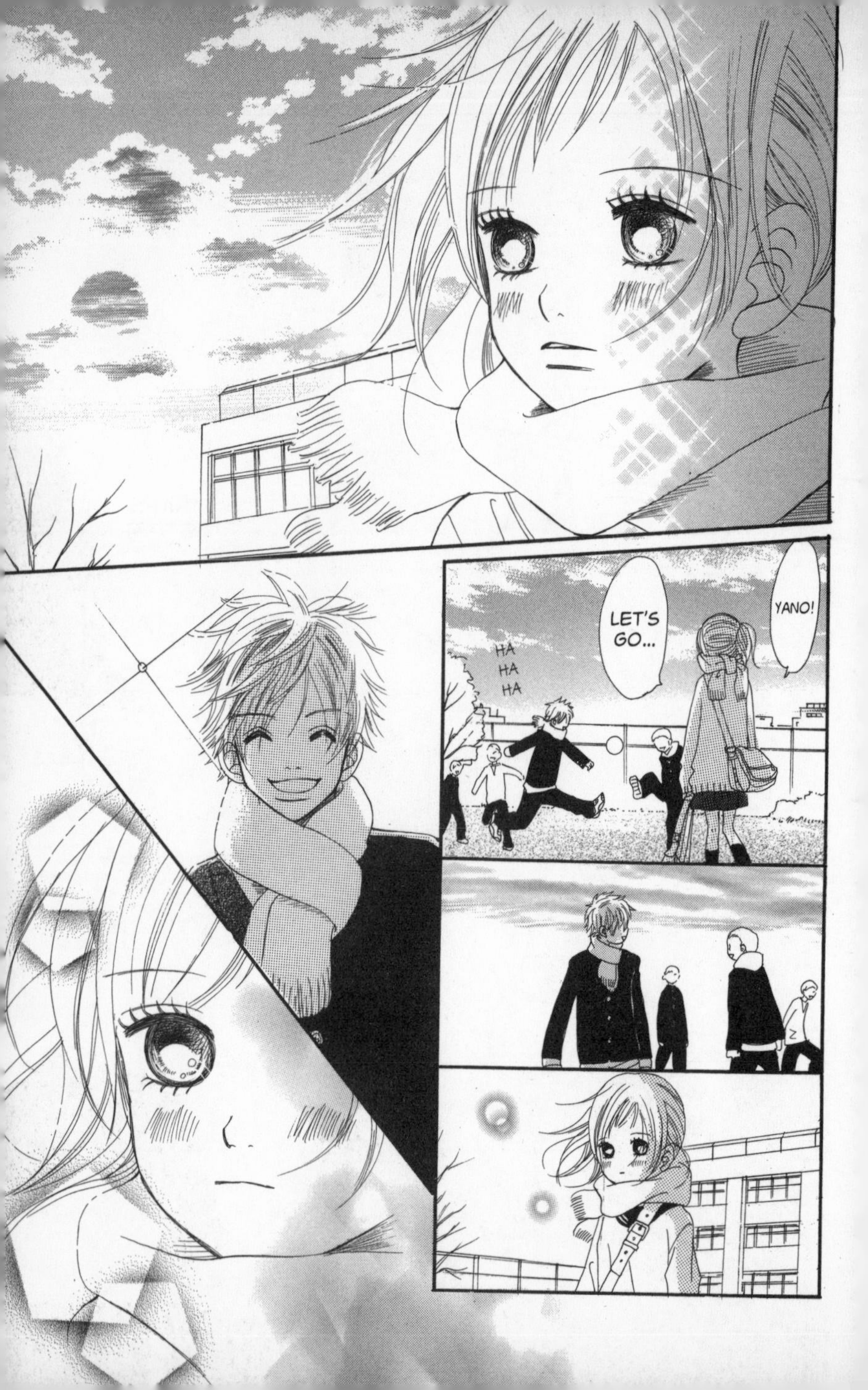
YANO!
LET'S GO...
HA HA HA

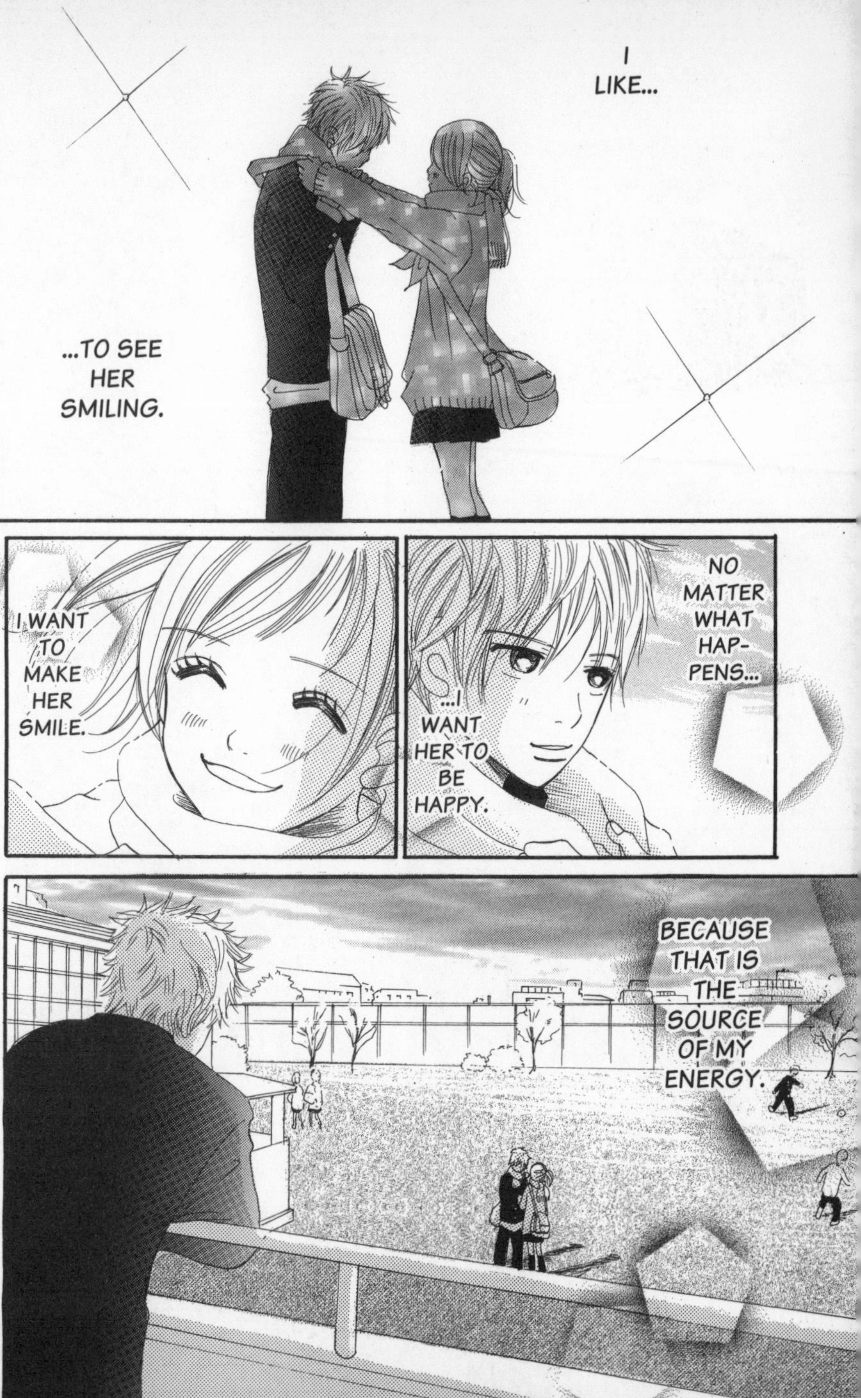
I LIKE...
...TO SEE HER SMILING.
NO MATTER WHAT HAP-PENS...
...I WANT HER TO BE HAPPY.
I WANT TO MAKE HER SMILE.
BECAUSE THAT IS THE SOURCE OF MY ENERGY.

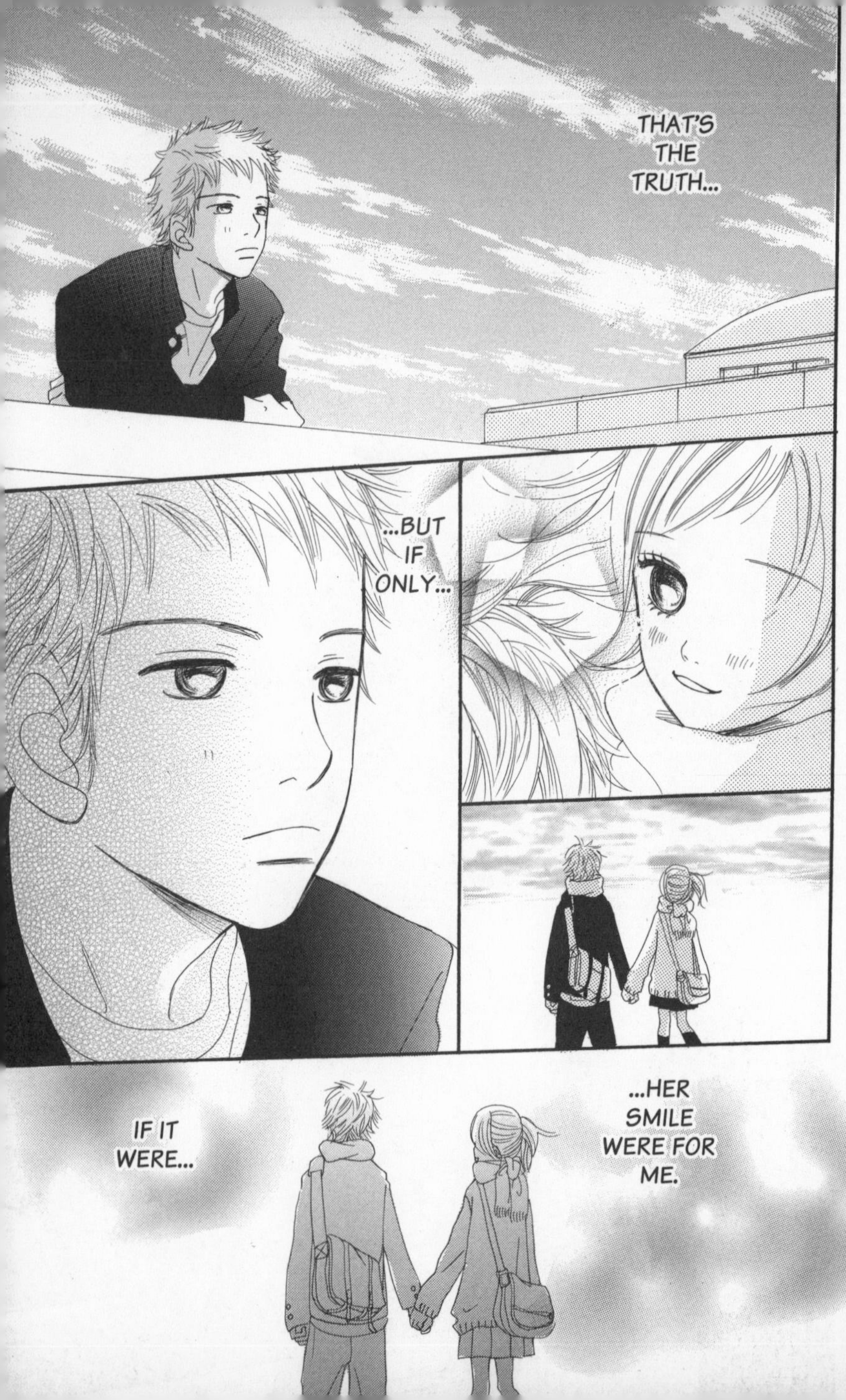
THAT'S THE TRUTH...
...BUT IF ONLY...
IF IT WERE...
...HER SMILE WERE FOR ME.

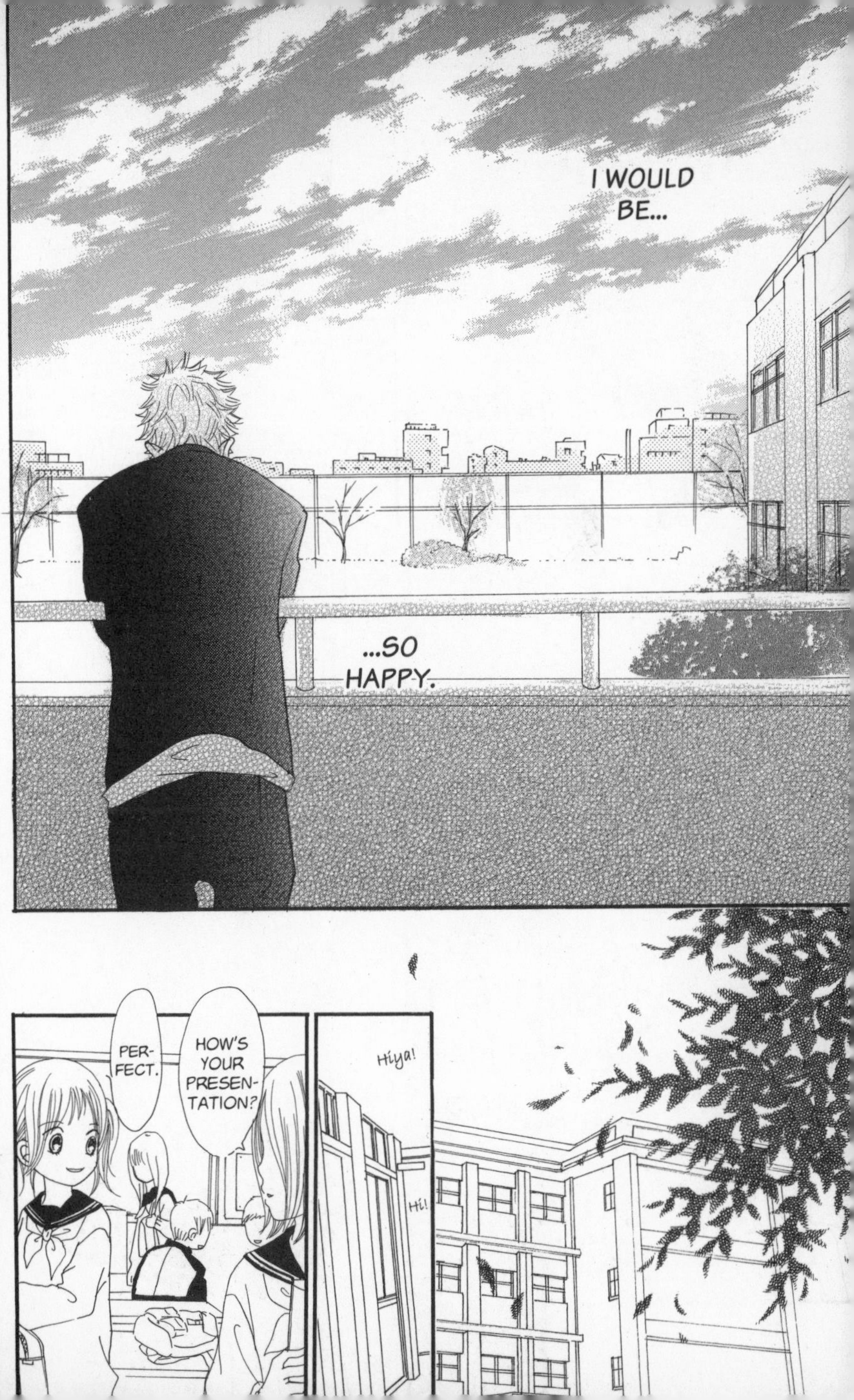
I WOULD BE...
...SO HAPPY.
Hiya!
Hi!
HOW'S YOUR PRESENTATION?
PER-FECT.

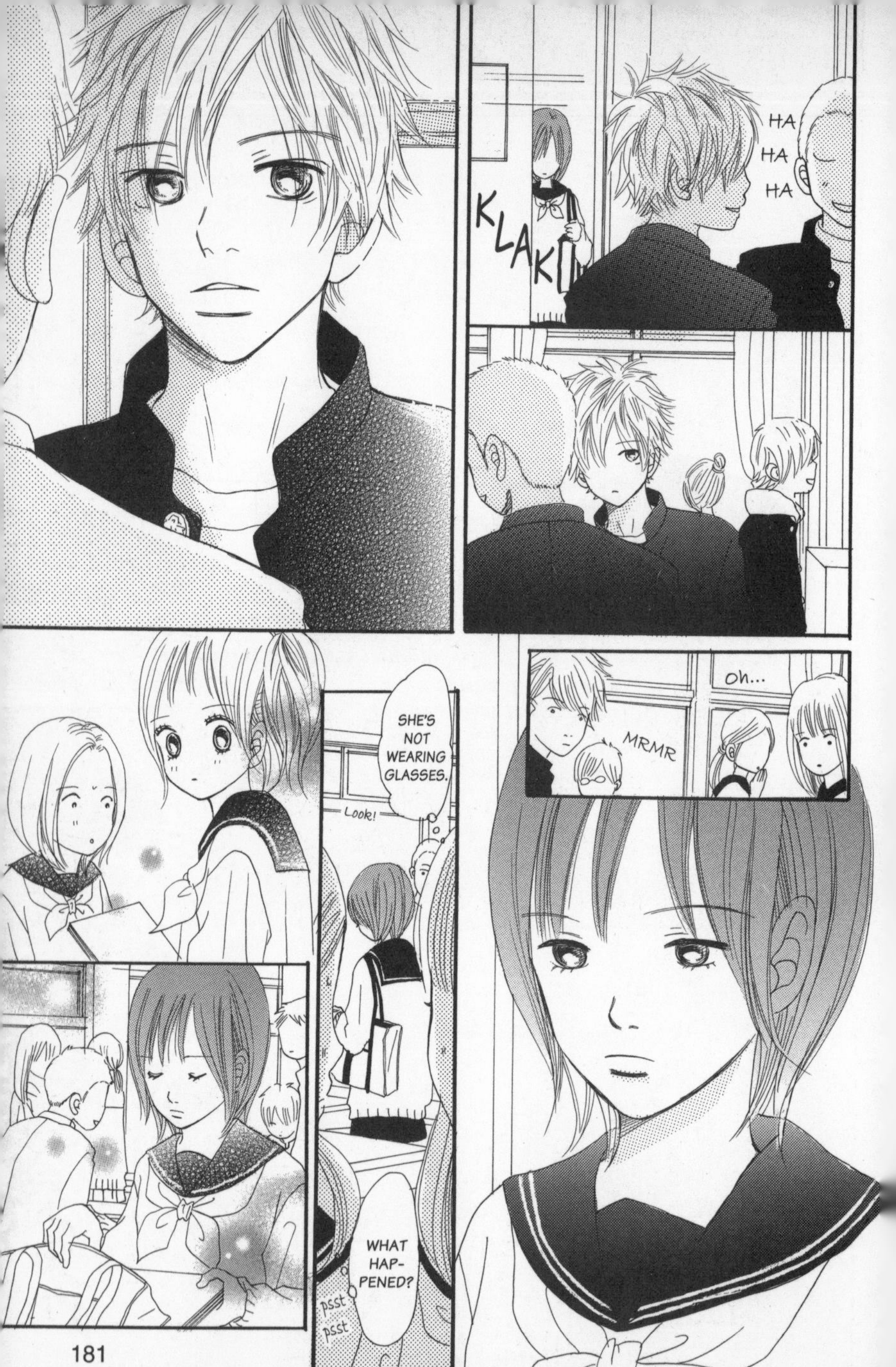
HA
HA
HA
KLAK
Oh...
MRMR
SHE'S NOT WEARING GLASSES.
Look!
WHAT HAP-PENED?
psst
psst

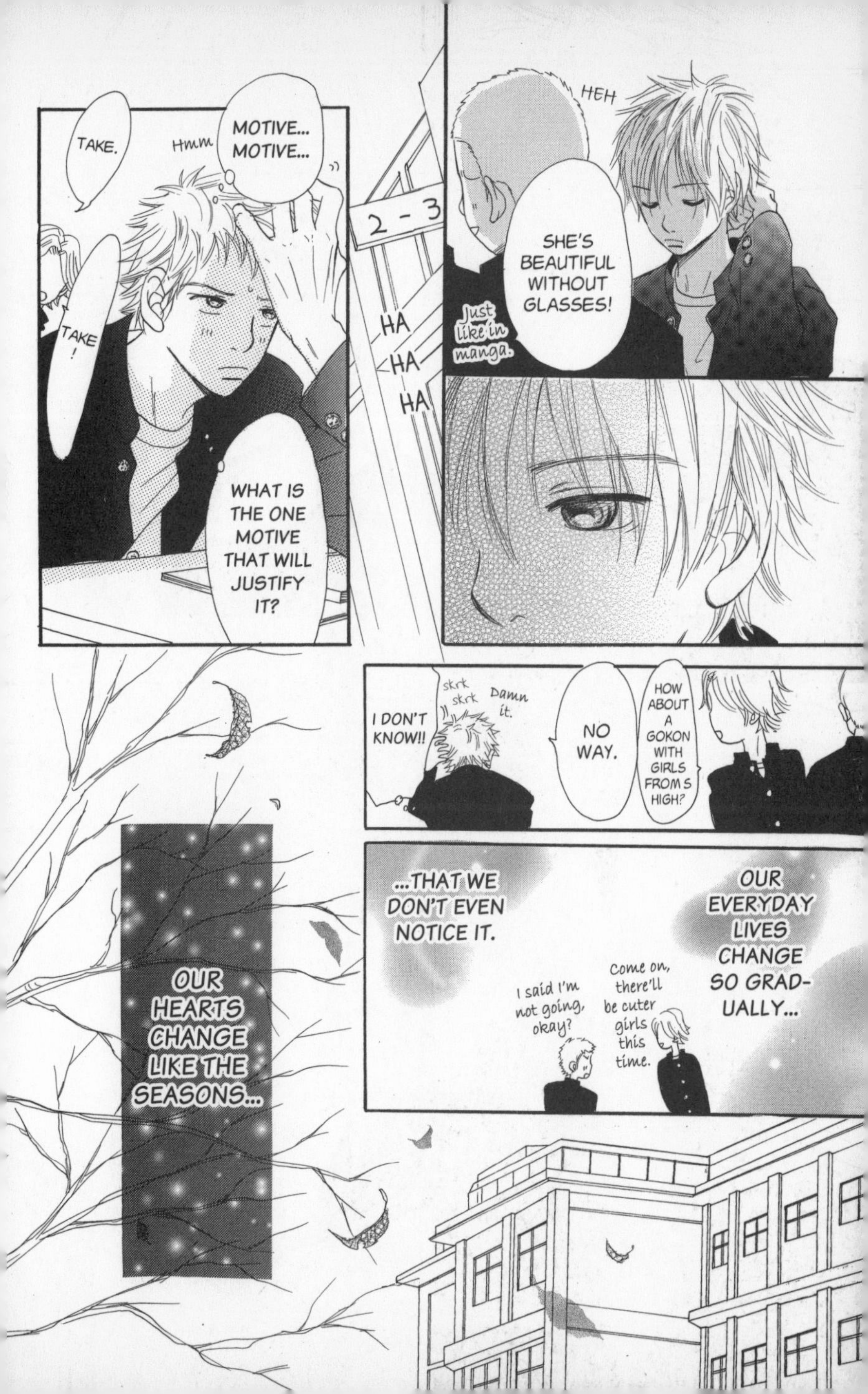
HEH
SHE'S BEAUTIFUL WITHOUT GLASSES!
Just like in manga.
HA HA HA
MOTIVE... MOTIVE...
Hmm
TAKE.
TAKE!
WHAT IS THE ONE MOTIVE THAT WILL JUSTIFY IT?
HOW ABOUT A GOKON WITH GIRLS FROM S HIGH?
NO WAY.
Damn it.
skrk skrk
I DON'T KNOW!!
OUR EVERYDAY LIVES CHANGE SO GRAD-UALLY...
Come on, there'll be cuter girls this time.
I said I'm not going, okay?
...THAT WE DON'T EVEN NOTICE IT.
OUR HEARTS CHANGE LIKE THE SEASONS...

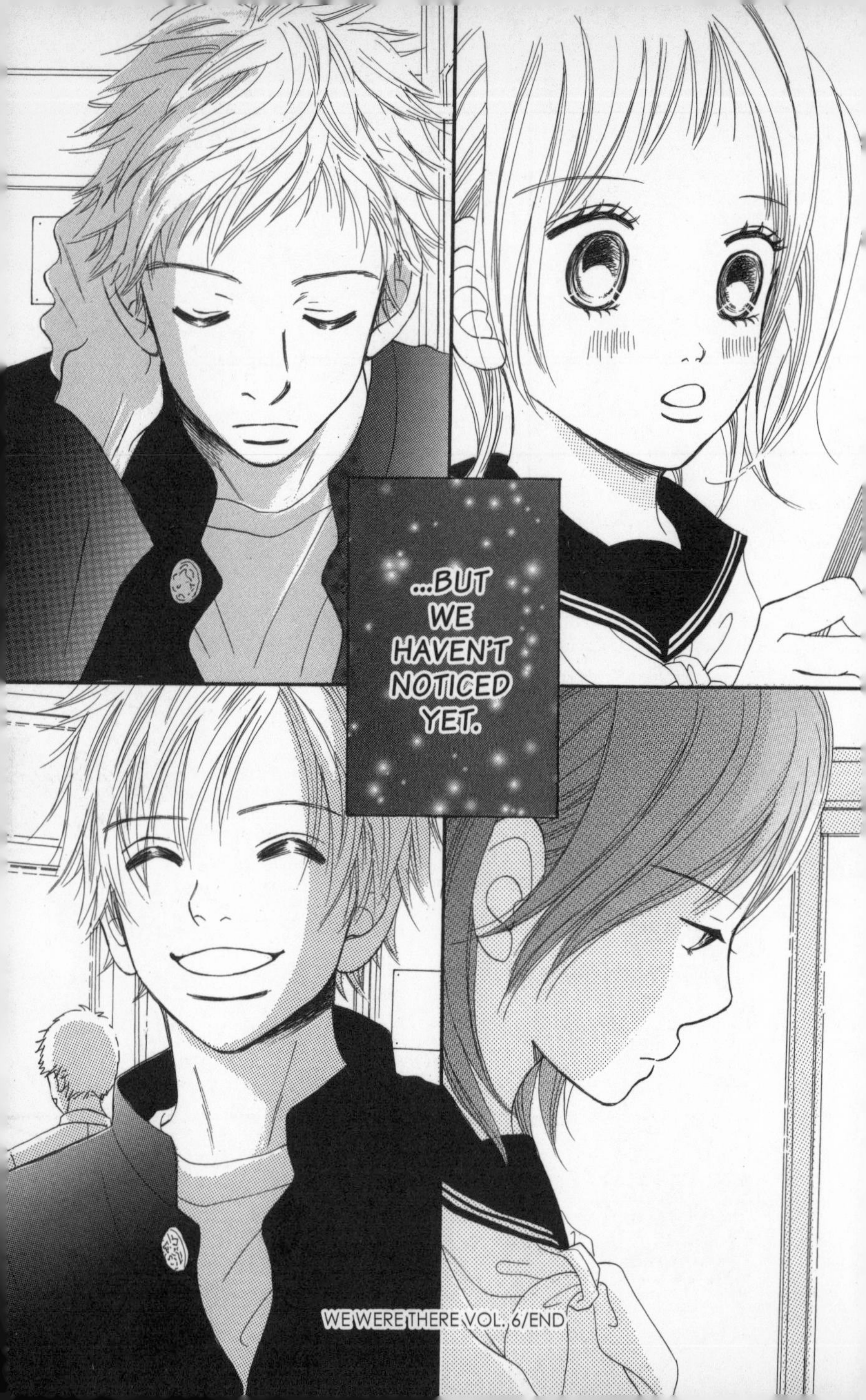
...BUT WE HAVEN'T NOTICED YET.
WE WERE THERE VOL. 6/END

## Notes

### Honorifics
In Japan, people are usually addressed by their name followed by a suffix.
The suffix shows familiarity or respect, depending on the relationship.
Male (familiar): first or last name + kun
Female (familiar): first or last name + chan
Adult (polite): last name + san
Upperclassman (polite): last name + senpai
Teacher or professional: last name + sensei
Close friends or lovers: first name only, no suffix

### Nana-chan vs. Nana-san
Nanami's nickname is "Nana-chan." Yano's ex-girlfriend
was a year older, so she was known as "Nana-san."

### Terms
Takeshi Goda is a character in the *Doraemon* manga.
*Love★Com* is a shojo manga.
Marumi and Chibimi are plays on Nanami's name. *Maru* means "round"
and *chibi* means "shorty."
Kumazo is probably a nickname. *Kuma* means "bear."